AMERICAS

AMERICAS

New Interpretive Essays

Edited by

Alfred Stepan

Americas is a coproduction of WGBH Boston
and Central Television Enterprises for Channel 4, U.K.,
in association with the School of International and
Public Affairs at Columbia University, the Latin American
and Caribbean Center at Florida International University,
and Tufts University.

Americas: New Interpretive Essays is part of a college credit course from

 The Annenberg/CPB Collection

New York   Oxford
OXFORD UNIVERSITY PRESS
1992

Oxford University Press

Oxford   New York   Toronto
Delhi   Bombay   Calcutta   Madras   Karachi
Kuala Lumpur   Singapore   Hong Kong   Tokyo
Nairobi   Dar es Salaam   Cape Town
Melbourne   Auckland   Madrid

and associated companies in
Berlin   Ibadan

Published by Oxford University Press, Inc.,
200 Madison Avenue, New York, New York 10016

Oxford is a registered trademark of Oxford University Press

Library of Congress Cataloging-in-Publication Data
Americas : new interpretive essays / edited by Alfred Stepan.
p.   cm.   This book was developed for the . . . Americas television course"—
Prelim. p. v.   Includes index.
Contents: The state of sovereignty and the sovereignty of states / Franklin W. Knight—The
state and development in historical perspective / Peter H. Smith—The state of economics in
Brazil and Latin America: is the past prologue to the future? / Albert Fishlow—The state of
revolution / Margaret E. Crahan and Peter H. Smith—Production, reproduction, and the
polity : women's strategic and practical gender issues / Helen I. Safa and Cornelia Butler
Flora—The construction of a Latin America feminist identity / Marysa Navarro-Aranguren—
Religion : reconstituting Church and pursuing change / Margaret E. Crahan—Remapping
culture / Jean Franco—Transforming memories and histories: / the meanings of ethnic resurgence for Mayan indians/ Kay B. Warren—Race, color, and class in the Caribbean / Anthony P. Maingot—Continent on the move : immigrants and refugees in the Americas / M.
Patricia Fernández Kelly and Alejandro Portes—The Americans : Latin American and Caribbean peoples in the United States / Rubén G. Rumbaut.

ISBN 0-19-507794-6   —ISBN 0-19-507795-4 (pbk.)
1. Latin America—Politics and government—1980–   2. Latin America—Social conditions.
3. Latin America—Economic conditions.   I. Stepan, Alfred.
F1414.2.A7155   1992   980.03'3—dc20   92-15716

Cover image: John Martinez
Cover Design: WGBH Design

9 8 7 6 5 4 3 2 1

Printed in the United States of America
on acid-free paper

This book was developed for the general reading public and for professors and students engaged in the *Americas* television course. This 13-unit television course consists of 10 one-hour public television programs, the textbook *Modern Latin America*, the reader *Americas: An Anthology*, a study guide, and a faculty guide. All of the publications are available from Oxford University Press.

Americas was produced for PBS by WGBH Boston and Central Television Enterprises for Channel 4, U.K., in association with the School of International and Public Affairs at Columbia University, the Latin American and Caribbean Center at Florida International University, and Tufts University.

Major funding for *Americas* was provided by the Annenberg/CPB Project, with additional funding from the Carnegie Corporation of New York,* the John D. and Catherine T. MacArthur Foundation, the Rockefeller Foundation, the Corporation for Public Broadcasting, and public television viewers.

Americas is closed captioned for the hearing impaired. [CC]

For more information about the print components of the *Americas* television course, contact:

Oxford University Press
200 Madison Avenue
New York, NY 10016
1-800-451-7556

For more information about television course licenses and off-air taping, contact:

Americas
PBS Adult Learning Service
1320 Braddock Place
Alexandria, VA 22314-1698
1-800-ALS-ALS8

For more information about *Americas* videocassettes and print materials, off-air taping and duplication licenses, and other video and audio series from the Annenberg/CPB Collection, contact:

Americas
The Annenberg/CPB Collection
P.O. Box 2345
South Burlington, VT 05407-2345
1-800-LEARNER

*The Carnegie Corporation of New York is not responsible for any statements or views expressed in the *Americas* programs or materials.

The *Americas* Project

WGBH Boston

Peter McGhee
*Vice President for National Program
    Productions*

Brigid Sullivan
*Vice President for Special
    Telecommunications Services*

Judith Vecchione
Executive Producer, Americas

Beth Kirsch
*Director of Educational Print and
    Outreach*

Patricia Crotty
*Project Director for Educational Print
    and Outreach*

Contents

AMERICAS

Introduction

ALFRED STEPAN

Since 1982, a group of scholars has been working together to create a public television series and course that would enable us to present to millions of viewers a vision of Latin America, the Caribbean, and the United States that would be informed by new realities, new questions, and new research. The 10–hour WGBH series *Americas* is the culmination of this project.

The project began when Mark Rosenberg of Florida International University started thinking about a television series on the Caribbean in late 1982. In 1984 the School of International and Public Affairs at Columbia University, and in 1985 Tufts University, joined the endeavor. I became Chairman of the Academic Advisory Board, Mark Rosenberg became Project Education Director, and Peter Winn of Tufts became Project Academic Director. In 1986 the three of us were fortunate in that we somehow convinced Peter McGhee, Vice President for National Program Productions of the public television station WGBH, Boston, to join us, and Judith Vecchione, who had won awards for her work on the *Vietnam: A Television History* and *Eyes on the Prize* series, became Executive Producer of the *Americas* project. The project came to fruition due to the support of the Annenberg/CPB Project, the Carnegie Corporation of New York, the John D. and Catherine T. MacArthur Foundation, the Rockefeller Foundation, and the Corporation for Public Broadcasting, as well as coproduction funding from Channel 4, U.K. This particular volume would not have been possible without the moral and financial support of the Carnegie Corporation of New York, and the constant encouragement and timely advice of their Program Officer and Director of Publications, Avery Russell.

This book is an outgrowth of the public television series, but it has its own special life history. In the process of working together for almost a decade, our group of scholars, drawn from the academic disciplines of history, comparative literature, anthropology, sociology, de-

3

mography, women's studies, economics, and political science, engaged in more interdisciplinary "trespassing" than we had ever done before. In the process, we came to the conclusion that the Americas we had begun talking about in 1982 had undergone such profound transformations by 1992 that most of us needed to recast fundamentally how we approached our topics. The television series and the essays in this book present new interpretations of the Americas, but they do so in radically independent, if complementary, ways.

A well-conceived and well-executed hour-long documentary can convey the sights and sounds of a region and the faces, voices, and emotions of human beings confronting new predicaments, in a way that even the best essay cannot. Likewise, an essay by a distinguished scholar, who has studied his or her subject for decades, can include a reflexive discussion of the evolution of the topic, an exploration of sources, and the persuasive presentation of a "new interpretation" in a form not suitable or indeed even possible in film. This volume represents our reflections on our experiences in developing this project. It is divided into three parts, concerning the role of the state, the role of new social and cultural movements, and the question of new social identities. Our goal is not to be comprehensive in scope but to provide insight into areas we feel are urgently in need of "re-vision."

Probably at no time since the independence period has the region of Latin America and the Caribbean witnessed such wide-ranging and significant controversy about the past, present, and future roles of the state. Thus the title of Part I, "Contested States." We begin the volume with an analysis of ideas of sovereignty, written by the Jamaican-born historian Franklin Knight. As the struggle for democracy and development takes on a new intensity, there is a growing debate about sovereignty. Sovereignty in Latin America did not originally reside with the colonial settlers, and certainly not with the indigenous peoples of the region, but with the Spanish and Portuguese monarchs who possessed the territories as their "patrimonial" domains. The independence wars and the events leading to the subsequent fragmentation of states in Spanish America gave rise to a very narrow definition of sovereignty, revolving around the defense of external borders rather than the defense of citizens' rights. This definition of sovereignty in turn has frequently played into the hands of the military, who again and again have usurped power with the claim that they, more than competing factions or political parties, uniquely stood for and defended national sovereignty against internal and external enemies. The United States' history of intervention in the region further exacerbated the tendency for groups on the right and on the left of the political spectrum to focus on nationalism, rather than on citizenship, as the essence of sovereignty.

As the twentieth century ends, the sovereignty issue has taken new turns. In the struggle against military regimes there has been a renaissance of civil society, and the emergence of an insistence that citizens and their elected representatives should be the sources of state sovereignty. But at the same time, in some countries, such as Peru and Colombia, the drug economy and internal strife have eroded the essence of what Max Weber, the great social scientist, considered a key characteristic of a modern state: a monopoly on the use of legitimate force in the territory. For these countries, where there is no state or only a weakened state, the conquest of sovereignty by their citizens is very problematic.

A related issue concerns suprasovereignties. Just as the European Community is redefining sovereignty for its member states, so the possibility of Mexico and the United States joining in a North American Free Trade Area (NAFTA) may prefigure a new meaning of sovereignty in the hemisphere. Should Mexico enter this free trade area, many others may well join—Chile has already said it is next in line. As a historian, Knight correctly leaves his essay at this point. As the editor, let me say why I believe NAFTA will grow as an issue. There have been many facile comparisons made between the European Economic Community (EEC) and NAFTA. However, the EEC and NAFTA differ in three critical ways that have been barely discussed. First, the European Community is self-consciously a political community of states open only to democracies. For advocates of democracy it seems unfortunate that the first prospective Latin American country to join NAFTA, namely Mexico, is the only major country in the hemisphere that is not now, and indeed never has been, a democracy. Second, in the European Community, there is an increasing acceptance of the ideas that the members' sovereignty should be pooled, and that community-wide elected institutions for making cooperative decisions are necessary. NAFTA, on the other hand, has no such representative decision-making organization. Third, the EEC, precisely because it is a political as well as an economic community, has numerous mechanisms for regional income transfer, as a way of diminishing inequalities among the member states. Other than the growth promises of the economic market itself, NAFTA has no redistribution mechanisms.

A second contested area concerns how the state resolves questions about its size and function. We are living in a new historical era in which cries for "state shrinking" are on the rise. In this context, Peter H. Smith, who began his career as a historian and is now a political scientist, conducts a valuable revisionist interpretation of the history of the Latin American states and their development projects. He argues that the Latin American states have historically had three major development "projects," all more successful than contemporary state-shrinking advocates admit, though all with flaws that need to be examined. In the colonial period, the mercantilist states had numerous achievements, but their achievements were measured fundamentally in terms of increases in revenue to the empires, not to the dependent territories. The liberal developmental state, of which Argentina in the early twentieth century is the prime example, was successful enough by the end of the 1920s to rank among the top eight economies in the world. However, this liberal model of development had no dimension of political liberalism, it further aggravated income inequalities, and it did not balance industrial development with agricultural exports. Economic liberalism and the veneer of political democracy collapsed with the world depression.

The most recent developmental model in Latin America has focused on state-led industrialization, which, unlike the Asian "tigers" of Korea, Taiwan, and Singapore, has concentrated on industrialization for the domestic market. Much of the industrialization in Latin America occurred behind high tariff walls, which produced goods that were not competitive in the world market. With this model, Argentina recovered from the world depression faster than the United States did with its New Deal. However, since the state-led industrialization had a high import component and neglected agriculture, Latin America was frequently vulnerable to balance-of-payments crises. This development model came to an end when the oil crisis led international banks to lend at very low interest rates to Latin America in the mid-1970s. But when real interest rates soared in the late 1970s, these debts doubled or tripled and became unpayable when the world economy slowed in the 1980s.

Latin America is now searching for a new model of development that for the first time will combine a strong dose of economic liberalism and its attendant pressures of global economic competition, with political liberalism and its attendant pressures of democratic political competition. Smith argues that this delicate balancing of economic restructuring and political democratization will be made almost impossible if indiscriminate "state bashing" continues.

In the third essay, the award-winning economist Albert Fishlow picks up and extends Smith's argument. Fishlow accepts that the Latin American and Caribbean economies need deep restructuring. Some of his proposals parallel those advocated by the neoliberal orthodoxy of most international financial institutions: inefficient public sector industries should be sold, high tariffs lowered, and state budgetary deficits reduced. However, his prescription for the Latin American states is fundamentally different from those of the neoliberals. He notes that the only two countries in Latin America to have restructured their economies to become increasingly more globally competitive and less inflationary are those that had the strongest and most consistently supported state macropolicies, namely Chile in the 1980s and Mexico from 1987 to 1992. Korea, Taiwan, and Singapore also featured macroeconomic policies bolstered by strong states. I may add that the postwar German and Japanese restructurings cannot be understood either without taking into consideration the important role played by state policy in creating these market miracles. When Fishlow examines Latin America's most troubled large economy, Brazil, he argues that the decisions concerning what and how to privatize will require strong and effective state planning, that shrinking of state budget deficits will require an enhanced state capacity to tax, and that management of Brazil's foreign debt crisis requires not state-shrinking rhetoric but the constitution of a new, democratically supported base, for consistent and strong state policy packages.

The final area in which the meaning of the state is being contested concerns revolution. When we began this project about a decade ago, the Nicaraguan Revolution was new, the Salvadoran guerrilla movement was growing, and the Cold War was intensifying. Today, the context of revolution has itself been revolutionized. What are the accomplishments and what is the future of revolution? The Cuban Revolution as it developed in the 1960s, the Nicaraguan Revolution as it came to power in the 1970s, and the Salvadoran guerrilla struggle as it mounted in the 1980s must be seen in relation to the Cold War. The causes of discontent in all three cases were domestic, and the primary leadership in all three cases was domestic, but these revolutionary movements evolved in an ideological and international context that gave them critical allies. The historians Margaret Crahan and Peter Smith draw up a new balance sheet of revolutionary achievements and accomplishments. Their essay shows that in a hemisphere marked by land inequality, the biggest land distributions were in Cuba and Mexico. In a hemisphere lacking in basic preventive-health medical plans, Cuba's achievements still stand as an unanswered challenge in the Americas. And while secondary school graduation is relatively low in the hemisphere, Cuba and even war-torn Sandinista Nicaragua made great educational strides. The Cold War has ended, and the external supports for revolution are gone, but the problems of land, health, and education remain for the majority of citizens in Latin America. The resurgence of civil society has contributed to new organizations through which Latin American citizens seek collective goods. The revolution in the international context could result in new democratic paths to collective goods. But as Crahan and Smith warn, if countries like Peru do not simultaneously carry out the arduous tasks of economic and political restructuring, the advance of the Sendero Luminoso and the erosion of the state may present the hemisphere with new, and deeply disturbing, faces of revolution.

In Part II of our volume we explore the "new voices/new visions" that have recently emerged in the Americas. Some of the most important and original of these have come from women's organizations and feminist movements. The essay by anthropologist Helen Safa and sociologist Cornelia Butler Flora is primarily interested in social movements of poor women, who, given the economic crisis of the 1980s and the retraction of the welfare role of the state, have increasingly played a role in organizing the community as a way to fulfill what Safa and Flora call "practical gender goals" in the area of family survival. Their efforts have involved the creation of collective kitchens in much of Latin America, an enhanced role for women in the design of basic facilities in the poor settlements that ring most of Latin America's cities, the increasing entrance of women into the productive sector, and, in the case of Argentina's Madres de la Plaza de Mayo, the fearless and persistent protest of military actions that have led to the "disappearance" of their children. Safa and Flora's thesis is that Latin American and Caribbean women's increased participation in the public sphere has led women's groups increasingly to formulate "strategic gender goals" as well. What began as movements of poor women, with little or no connection with feminist groups, have emerged in the last decade with extended agendas—against male violence, and for abortion rights and equality in the workplace—which lead them increasingly to join forces with feminist groups.

Cultural historian Marysa Navarro-Aranguren takes a different starting point for her essay. Her explicit concern is with Latin American and Caribbean feminist groups per se. Drawing on her personal participation in many of the most important Latin American feminist meetings in the past decade, virtually none of the documents or theoretical texts of which are yet available to non-Spanish or non-Portuguese readers, she deftly analyzes how middle-class women of the 1970s in universities, guerrilla groups, and especially in progressive political movements came to develop a perception of their needs that led to a "double militancy" in political groups and in feminist groups. Given feminists' close relationship to politics, she argues that many sought out alliances with the organizations created by poor and working-class women. The result, she believes, is not only a new feminist voice in Latin American politics, but, given its uniquely broad class base, complex social agenda, and emphatic political orientation, a new voice in the world feminist movement.

Another "reconstituted" voice in Latin America is that of the Catholic Church. The majority of Catholics in the world are Latin Americans, and two of the most innovative religious developments within the Catholic Church in the twentieth century—liberation theology and base Christian communities—are theologically and socially Latin American in origin. Latin America is also in the forefront of the debate concerning the future role of women in the Church. Margaret Crahan cites a survey that shows that more than 50 percent of the nuns in Chile favor the creation of women priests in their country, whereas only 7 percent of the Chilean bishops support such an innovation. The theological support by many bishops in Latin America for the "preferential option for the poor" has led to conflicts with the Polish-born Pope John Paul II. Some analysts even have spoken of an almost schismatic struggle of the "people's church" in Latin America against the "institutional church" of Pope John Paul II. With a knowledge based on 25 years of study of the Church in such countries as Cuba, Chile, Nicaragua, and Brazil, and a fine understanding of the doctrinal and political issues at stake, Margaret Crahan gives a nuanced evaluation of the prospects for the Latin American Church as it confronts these new external and internal pressures.

The "magical realist" novels of García Márquez and others have made most of the world aware of Latin America's pioneering contributions to modern literary culture. However, Jean Franco, who teaches comparative literature, argues that we need to "remap" our understanding of the new cultural terrain in the Americas. Franco is a pioneer in the new field of "cultural studies." In her original and provocative essay, she explores, via an analysis of themes ranging from bilingual "performance art" in New York, to "colonial discourse" in the Andean region, the double revolution that she sees occurring in "cultural production" and "cultural criticism," which together are producing new voices and visions in the Americas.

We conclude this volume by analyzing "American identities in formation." One of the most interesting processes of identity formation concerns the indigenous peoples of the Americas. In the last few years, indigenous groups have created their own research centers and convened hemisphere-wide meetings to explore, redefine, and reassert their identities. Yet, virtually nothing has been written about this new phenomenon. In a richly reflexive essay, interpretive anthropologist and ethnographer Kay B. Warren returns to Mayan communities she first studied 20 years ago. Local ethnic politics, of course, had changed significantly, but even more so had national society, with the activism of Mayan academic and political organizations in the late 1980s. With an all too rare discussion of the "cultural processes through which observers produce their knowledge of other cultures," Warren admits her discomfort when her invited lectures to Mayan audiences, which implicitly rejected "essentialism" (the concept of a constant core of identities) and espoused "constructionism" (the concept of continuously socially constructed identities), were enthusiastically challenged by one group of anthropologists and met with angry silence from another group of applied linguists. Warren dialectically unravels the meanings of these different reactions and in so doing reveals how contemporary Mayan communities and ethnic nationalists transform memories and histories for themselves and for local communities, in a way that is vastly more complex and creative than that envisioned in what Warren calls the four dominant fallacies of "Indianness" in North American formulations.

Anthony P. Maingot, a sociologist born in Trinidad, has a concern different from that of Warren. His objective is to understand how the numerous permutations of race, color, and class play out in the Caribbean, with its overlay of British, French, Dutch, and Spanish colonial heritages, and its peoples of African, Asian-Indian, and European origins. He documents and explains the extraordinarily different combinations of race, class, and color in Haiti, the Dominican Republic, Martinique, Curaçao, and Trinidad. In an era when the racial and cultural heterogeneity of the Americas is causing some people concern, it is significant that Maingot ends his essay with a quote from that staunch critic of Caribbean racism, the Welsh social scientist Gordon Lewis: "If racial democracy is to survive anywhere in the twentieth century, then, it probably stands its best chance in the Caribbean."

M. Patricia Fernández Kelly, the Mexican-born cultural anthropologist, and Alejandro Portes, the Cuban-born demographic sociologist, combine their skills and sensitivities to examine the causes and consequences of the massive hemispheric migration in which more than 5 million people per year cross national borders in the Americas. The migration that has been most studied and stereotyped is migration into the United States. Fernández Kelly and Portes insist, however, that less than 10 percent of the hemisphere's migrants settle in the United States, and that to understand the situations, purposes, and identities of migrants, we first need to study migration within Latin America itself. What emerges from their essay is an extremely rich canvas of flows of professional and technical specialists, of rural contract laborers, and of political refugees, each group with its own sending and receiving patterns and social consequences.

Our final essay in this volume is an analysis of Latin American and Caribbean peoples in the United States. Rubén G. Rumbaut, a Cuban-born sociologist who has studied Vietnamese and Central European as well as Hispanic migration, presents one of the first critical assessments of the implications of the 1990 census. He clearly shows that present patterns ensure that the 1990s will be the decade with the largest migration in U.S. history, but that the total number of immigrants will still be lower than its proportion at the turn of the century. He also definitively demonstrates how U.S. foreign policy actions account for the "chain migrations" from Cuba, the Philippines, Mexico, Puerto Rico, and Vietnam.

Rumbaut's essay offers a much needed perspective on some increasingly controversial issues. For example, Asians are often held up as "model migrants" in implicit contrast to Hispanic Americans. The achievements of Asian migrants are partially accounted for by the fact that 40 percent are college graduates *before* they come to the United States, whereas college graduates in the total U.S. population are only 16 percent. He also dispels any fear of Quebec-like linguistic separatism within the Hispanic population. A recent study of Mexican-origin couples in Los Angeles found that among first-generation women, 84 percent spoke only Spanish in the home. By the third generation, 84 percent used only English in the home.

Rumbaut does not hide the problems. Clearly, the socioeconomic data he presents about Puerto Ricans (who have been citizens since 1917) is disturbing. But the overall picture of Hispanic identity in the United States that emerges from Rumbaut's analysis is similar to that mentioned by Warren and Franco: "It is no longer a process of assimilation or of lost identity but rather the fashioning of a new and plural personality."

Columbia University
February 1992

PART I

Contested States

1

The State of Sovereignty and the Sovereignty of States

FRANKLIN W. KNIGHT

Political cultures are the products of social realities and particular histories.[1] The apparent differences between the United States and the rest of the Americas can largely be explained by their separate histories and contrasting realities. The problem of sovereignty represents a case in point. Both the United States and the Latin American and Caribbean states regard sovereignty as an important aspect of their nationality. Both concepts of sovereignty, however, derive from slightly different traditions.

In Latin America and the Caribbean sovereignty reflects more closely an early sixteenth-century notion of the independent, self-sufficient, geographically defined state as a prerequisite for sovereignty. It also clearly reflects the authoritarian political position of the Castilian monarchy in the New World during the sixteenth century.[2] By contrast, the idea of sovereignty in the United States reflects the universal concerns of an expansive industrial capitalism and the geopolitical imperatives of a world superstate.[3] Latin American and Caribbean states are only now coming to grips with the complex ramifications of the capitalist, industrial state and with the exception of Fidel Castro's Cuba, and possibly Brazil, do not contemplate the possibility of superpower status.

The idea of the sovereign state should not be confused with the general concept of sovereignty.[4] The sovereign state is one whose government exercises supreme and independent authority. The concept of sovereignty—ideally associated with a ruler or monarch—seeks to establish the ultimate source of legitimate authority within a political constituency and is often expressed in terms of "the general will."

Both the concept of the sovereign state and the concept of sovereignty, however, have had a fairly long and interrelated tradition. De-

11

fining sovereignty has been part and parcel of the contentious conflict among community, authority, political power, and group relations that developed, especially after the Middle Ages. In England, such political conflict resulted in the Magna Carta when, in 1215 on the plains of Runnymede, a group of English barons joined with members of the Church to force King John (1167?–1216) to sign a document outlining certain basic civil rights. It also contributed to the rise of the tradition of conciliar government in France.[5] Sovereignty, therefore, is not simply the mere exercise of independent political power. It is an attribute of political authority and the ultimate repository of political legitimacy.

As individual monarchies gave way to national states, sovereignty assumed more ambiguous characteristics, redefining and transforming itself consonant with the fluid changes of political authority and political association.[6] Different countries define sovereignty in different ways, and often the self-serving ways in which they have defined it—or the connotations they have attached to it—have undergone considerable change. The various problems of sovereignty are fully illustrated in the history of Latin America, as well as in the rest of the world.

The notion of sovereignty that pervaded the political language of the United States in the eighteenth century and afterward came mainly from the English tradition.[7] When Thomas Cranmer, Henry VIII's conveniently appointed archbishop, declared in 1533 that "this realm of England [was] an empire," he was forcefully articulating a novel concept of sovereignty for his time. But Cranmer's (and Henry's) definition of sovereignty had a narrowly limited aim of clarifying the fuzzy lines of political authority as feudalism faded. The resultant Act of Supremacy sought not only to elevate the English monarchy but also to equate the political power of religious and secular authorities within a defined territory. Cranmer (and his monarch) had the immediate aim of undermining the absolute authority of the pope in England, of making the English monarch supreme in England. They did not argue for an absolute monarchy immune from any restraint whatsoever. The Act of Supremacy was not, in itself, an Act of Sovereignty—merely an attempt to assert the autonomy of the English monarch versus all others.

The rise of a new type of political state—the so-called new monarchies between the end of the fifteenth century and the beginning of the seventeenth century—created the conditions for a new definition of the concept of sovereignty.[8] This clearly resulted from the internal conflicts over political authority that plagued Spain during the time of Ferdinand and Isabella; Italy during the time of Niccolò Machiavelli; France during the time of Catherine de' Medici; or England during the years of Charles Stuart and Oliver Cromwell.[9] In states confronting political chaos, ideas surfaced designed to diagnose the circumstances and prescribe permanent solutions to the problems created by conflicting loyalties.

Since the seventeenth century the concept of sovereignty, much like the nature of political authority itself, has moved from the prerogatives of divinely appointed monarchs to the concerns of democratically constituted states.[10] The contestants have been the government, nominal heads of state, and civil society. Political stability required a formulation of the basis of governmental authority as well as civilian loyalty.

The earliest formulations of what may be called formal theories of sovereignty appear in the sixteenth century. A work by the French Catholic thinker Jean Bodin (1530–96), *Les Six Livres de la République (The Six Bookes of a Commonweale)*, first published in 1576, contains the basis for what may be seen as just such a theory. Bodin's book was a vivid reflection of the political reality of his fledgling state. Concerned about the prolonged religious and civil strife in France, Bodin saw a strong monarchy as the most efficacious solution for social chaos. Unlike Machiavelli, he did not support an unfettered absolutism in which the monarch—in Machiavelli's case, the prince—had no religious or moral restraint. The monarchy's sovereignty was the repository of the harmonious reconciliation of community customs and traditions with *raison d'état*. In a way this was a challenge to the divine right of monarchy, but a long way from the establishment of the source of the general will.

Bodin's idea found later developments and refinements in the works of the English thinker Thomas Hobbes (1588–79), especially in *Leviathan*, published in 1651. Hobbes too was the product of a severely contested and constitutionally contentious era of English politics, in which the protagonists were king and Parliament—with unfortunately fatal consequences for Charles I. Hobbes's major contribution was the articulation of a type of sovereignty vested in the people but exercised through the monarch.

F. H. Hinsley has captured the essence of the argument presented by Hobbes:

> It was a misuse of language to call the multitude or the subjects the People; they were not a People without the will of the rulership. On the other hand, the People as opposed to the multitude ruled in every true political society because the authority, will and action of the Ruler was the authority, will and action of every individual. As well as extinguishing the People's separate personality Hobbes transformed the right of the Ruler by substituting for the Prince the abstract notion of the state.[11]

Both Bodin and Hobbes (and, later, Rousseau) sought a constitutional way of establishing political order and eliminating chaos, and in their separate ways advocated a strong but limited monarchy. Together they saw sovereignty as the exercise of a unitary political will, and a sovereign entity as one capable of expressing its will in an unfettered way. For Hobbes this will came from the monarch. For Rousseau, the basic repository of sovereignty rested in the general will of society, a sort of majority, democratic rule.[12]

The notion of the general will as a community of competing interests and groups gained further explication in the ideas of John Locke (1632– 1704)—especially in *An Essay Concerning Human Understanding* and *Two Treatises on Government,* both published in 1690—and Charles-Louis de Secondat, Baron de Montesquieu (1689–1755)—especially in *The Spirit of Laws,* published in 1748. Locke in essence postulated two separate repositories of sovereignty—the monarch and Parliament—that together constituted the political state.[13] This constitution accepted the supremacy of the monarch as long as he did not become a tyrant. In its own ambiguous way, the argument supported a monarch who could do no wrong, a parliament that could not overthrow the monarch, and a people who reserved an intrinsic right (defined by the American colonists in 1776 as an inalienable right) to resist tyranny.

During the nineteenth century liberals sought to use the theories of Locke and Montesquieu as the basis of the principles of government, while conservatives—and later socialists and radicals—tended to resort to the formulation of unitary wills found in Hobbes and Rousseau. It is quite clear that attitudes toward sovereignty, consonant with attitudes toward the state, derived from personal, local, and regional considerations.

In 1649 members of the English Parliament executed the king because had they lost their argument and their war, they would have lost their own heads. Better the king's head than theirs! But Charles's theoretical supremacy constituted the same immediate threats as Oliver Cromwell's exalted supremacy of the Commonwealth. If sovereign monarchs did not, and increasingly could not, wield absolute authority, sovereign states have encountered similar problems. Sovereignty gradually became an issue that transcended the geographical domain of the politically constituted state. Sovereignty eventually came to assume complex international dimensions of power, authority, security, and law.[14] This partly explains the English (and to some degree, Dutch) suspicion of and resistance to the Family Compact between the Bourbon monarchies of France and Spain during the eighteenth century.[15] Security at home became inextricably intertwined with security abroad in the form of changing political alliances.

Nowhere is this merging of the national and the international dimensions of sovereignty clearer than in the case of the relations between the United States and Latin America since the late eighteenth century.

Both North American and Latin American movements for independence were by-products of the general Age of Enlightenment, with its pronounced advocacy of rational political structures. Both movements reflected, to some degree, the contractual notions of Jean-Jacques Rousseau (1712–78) as outlined in *Du contrat social,* published in 1762. Rousseau's contractual theory initiated the constitutional tradition in both the United States and, to some degree, the emerging Caribbean and Latin American states during the early years of the nineteenth century. In 1797 Toussaint Louverture gave the French colony of Saint Domingue a new constitution, modeled after the 1791 French constitution. This constitution created not only a new society but also a new polity. In 1797 Francisco de Miranda (1750–1816), the Venezuelan revolutionary who had served several years with the French forces in their revolution, remarked, "We have before our eyes two great examples, the American and the French Revolutions. Let us prudently imitate the first and carefully shun the second."[16] The French colonial revolution taking place in what later became Haiti was too radical, too horrible, and too chaotic to find much appeal among the new Latin American political leaders. Elite empowering, not political restructuring, represented the early nineteenth-century goals of the Latin American revolutions.

Ironically, although the United States and Latin America both started with a common intellectual, philosophical, and constitutional basis for the state and sovereignty, their understanding and applications of sovereign conduct have diverged sharply in succeeding years. In the United States the pursuit of constitutional sovereignty involved a parallel pursuit of democracy. In Latin America constitutional sovereignty was grafted on the tradition of monarchical absolutism associated with Castile and the empire. This is the point that Nicholas Canny and Anthony Pagden make in *Colonial Identity in the Atlantic World*:

> In the writings of the American revolutionaries, Magna Carta, Coke, Locke, and Montesquieu are all used to substantiate the same argument, that it was the British government that, in its thirst for power, had violated the natural rights of the English in America and had undermined the natural rights of the kingdom. A similar set of claims grounded upon an appeal to ancient traditions of the citizen may be found in the declarations of the Spanish American insurgents; only here it is Suárez instead of Locke and the *Siete Partidas* in place of Magna Carta.[17]

The divergent ways in which North Americans and Latin Americans viewed the state, liberty, and sovereignty derived in part from the genesis of their political formation, as well as their social composition. In the late eighteenth century the British empire was a national entity in which the colonists retained rights their ancestors had won in the prolonged struggle between king and Parliament during the seventeenth century (and some would even date it back to the Magna Carta in 1215). In British North America the colonists had a shared notion of sovereignty that reflected the generally ambiguous idea of the king in Parliament as the basis of authority. Since these colonists considered their representative assemblies to be the proxy of the English Parliament, they felt that the English monarch could not act contrary to their collective colonial wishes, even though he had the support of his Parliament in England. "No taxation without representation," therefore, was an effective, though hardly legitimate, appeal. Both in England and in the British North American colonies, however, political representation remained the province of a selected male bourgeois group. And that was where they invested sovereignty. But even then the newly created state divided sovereignty between the separate states and the federal government.

Latin Americans at the beginning of the nineteenth century, by contrast, composed parts of an extensive patrimonial state that had briefly and unsuccessfully tried to convert itself into a national state during the period of the reforms of Charles III (1716–88).[18] Spanish Americans had been vassals of the absolutist Castilian monarchy based on a series of secular agreements and papal pronouncements dating back to the era of Christopher Columbus. The notion of an explicit, layered, political contract—or what in the United States evolved into the thorny issue of "states' rights"—was a recent recognition when the Spanish empire began to self-destruct after the invasion of Napoleon and the decapitation of legitimate sovereignty in 1808. But instead of clearly demarcated territories, the Spanish Americans found themselves with unwieldy, overlapping administrative jurisdictions of viceroyalties, *audiencias* (regional high court jurisdictions), and municipalities.[19] With the exception of Brazil, the attempt to form great empires in Latin America failed.

The United States revolted in 1776 against what they perceived as an unjust monarch who had violated natural laws and trampled on the sovereignty of the colonial entities' rights. Their Declaration of Independence did not immediately establish a single sovereign nation but a unified collection of co-equal, sovereign states that contractually vested certain determined powers in the federal government, as we noted before.[20]

Spanish Americans (along with their metropolitan counterparts) revolted at first against the usurpation of their sovereignty—vested in the persons of Charles IV (1748–1819) and his absolutist-inclined son, Ferdinand VII (1784–1833)—by Napoleon Bonaparte. Initially the Spanish Americans and Spanish formed juntas in Aranjuez, and later, Seville, that declared their loyalty to their exiled monarch. For them sovereignty still essentially resided in the person of the monarch. The alliance between Spain and the colonies did not hold for long, but it lasted long enough for the general junta of Cádiz to declare Spain and Spanish America one nation in 1812. Neither in Spain nor in Spanish America could Spaniards and Creoles agree on the nature of sovereignty and the administrative structure of the state. So by 1812 elements in the colonies sought not an integrated Spanish state but separate and equal states. Precisely because of the presence of a monarchy on Brazilian soil, the transition from colony to independence became relatively fluid in 1822.[21] When the Spanish monarch refused to accept the new liberal constitution of Cádiz, Spanish Americans realized that their political independence would be incompatible with monarchy and an empire of co-equal parts. As David Bushnell put it, "With the Spanish government of national resistance against the French, the Creole juntas of 1810 shared not only many of the arguments that served to justify their existence but a common profession of loyalty to Ferdinand VII. Whether sincere or not in that profession of loyalty the juntas could expect no co-operation either from the authorities in Spain or from loyalist officials still holding command in America."[22]

In the United States the sovereignty of the state was qualified by a wider conviction of the universal good, as represented in constitutional, liberal democracy. In Latin America, on the other hand, in most cases the internal security of the geographical entity of the state took precedence over any notions of liberal democratic rule. In the United States the Declaration of Independence constituted a prerequisite for the establishment of an autonomous, democratic state (if not a democratic society). This was, after all, not difficult where the elites establishing the new political system were relatively homogeneous, both intellectually and socially. Internal challenges to the structure did not reach critical proportions until the Civil War, nearly 75 years after the establishment of the state.

By contrast, Latin Americans—with the notable exception of Brazilians—spent nearly their entire first century after independence trying to establish a secure state. For in overthrowing the Castilian monarchy, a considerable proportion of the politically competitive groups still ardently believed that only the monarchical form of government could resolve the profound conflicts among classes, races, regions, and religious organizations. Mexico declared itself an independent empire under Agustín de Iturbide (1783–1824) in 1821, but the uneasy alliance of army, Church and conservative Creole elites broke down within two years, plunging the country into a civil war that lasted sporadically until 1867. This division forced the exasperated Mexican conservatives to support the French-sponsored invasion of 1864–67 by the Archduke Maximilian Hapsburg (1832–67). In Mexico, as elsewhere in Spanish America, the sovereignty issue became subsumed in the quest for a secure state and a legitimate government to succeed the Castilian monarchy. Political order took precedence over political rights.

Not surprisingly, considerable skepticism existed in official and private circles in the United States that the recent ex-Spanish colonies would ever constitute free and sovereign states. Nevertheless, Latin Americans thought that was exactly the purpose of their agonizing struggle. This emerged quite clearly from the painful observations of two representative thinkers of the different states: John Adams (1735–1826) of the United States, and Juan Bautista Alberdi (1810–84) of Argentina. In the 1820s John Adams found the notion of a democratic Latin America as absurd as it was "to establish democracies among the birds, beasts and fishes."[23] Late in the twentieth century many people in the

United States still consider democracy an unfamiliar foreign concept to most Latin Americans.[24]

In 1853 Juan Bautista Alberdi would disappointedly complain that the Spanish American republics had experienced too many "democratic revolutions."[25] But the almost spontaneous revolutions throughout Latin America between 1810 and 1827 were not truly democratic. Indeed, with the exception of the Haitian revolution between 1792 and 1804, the turmoil of the Spanish American states resulted in anything but democratic societies by 1853. In Haiti, social democracy—the total independence of the slave majority, and their control of the government and social structure—was not accompanied by political democracy. Throughout Latin America the Creoles expelled their European superiors but showed scant willingness to broaden the political system to include meaningful representation for the numerical majority of Indians, *mestizos, mulattos,* and various other nonwhites.[26]

When the Latin American states won their independence in the first few decades of the nineteenth century, they manifested some characteristics that would inhibit the facile reconciliation of political authority and the ready development of a general consensus regarding sovereignty's place in the new states. Indeed, valid questions were raised in many states about the very nature of this sovereignty. The political and social organization by cities, ethnicities, and classes—not to mention the peculiar organization and cohesiveness of the Roman Catholic Church—laid the basis for a continuing struggle among regions, groups, and personalities over the exercise of political power. These divisions made the first attempts at independence rather complex civil wars, as the cases of New Spain and Gran Colombia illustrate. Both these entities fragmented into a number of smaller states: New Spain lost substantial portions of its territory to the United States and to the Central American republics; New Granada split into Venezuela, Ecuador, and Colombia, from which Panama itself later split. Sovereignty could not be decided before there was agreement on the nature of the state, and this proved elusive as well as illusory.

With the exception of Brazil and Chile, powerful supporters of both centralist and federalist governments prolonged the military phase of the independence movements and virtually guaranteed that chaos would be an inescapable legacy of the newly formed states. To resolve the dilemma of diffuse political authority—itself an open invitation to political instability—Simón Bolívar had proposed at the constitutional convention of Ocaña in 1828 a strengthening of the presidency in order to forestall the probable tyranny of Congress. But tyranny remained a prominent feature in the governments of Latin America, either at the local level of *caciques* or at the regional and national level of *caudillos.*[27] Political power inevitably came to be associated with strong rulers who imposed their notion of sovereignty on the state. Power, however, did not necessarily mean legitimacy.

Those states such as Brazil and Chile that managed to avoid or significantly mitigate the political chaos of the immediate postindependence years manifested some peculiar local characteristics.

Brazil, as we mentioned before, had a fortuitous transitional monarchy. Pedro II, especially after 1840, successfully mediated between factions in a way that forestalled major military revolts. While not democratic (even in the restricted and restrictive sense applicable to the United States at that time), the Brazilian system operated in such a way that Brazilians accepted their government's legitimacy until 1889.[28] The overthrow of the monarchy in 1889 did not represent a major political change or a substantial reconstitution of the social basis of political power.

Like Brazil, Chile also emerged from its war of independence fairly rapidly and with minimal internal conflict, thanks to its geographical isolation, and to the numerical superiority and organizational cohesiveness of the landed, commercial, and administrative elites of the Santiago intendancy.[29] The Conservative alliance under Diego Portales (1793–1837) that won the short civil war in 1830 managed to impose a durable system that combined a strong executive, pragmatic co-optation, and regular (though highly controlled) elections. This worked satisfactorily until 1891, when Congress reduced the inordinate power of the presidency. By then the economy and the society had changed to such a degree that the old elites of conservatives and liberals were no longer able to maintain their unchallenged control of political office.[30] Of course, the successful pursuit of the border wars against Peru and Bolivia between 1836 and 1839, and again between 1879 and 1883, also helped consolidate the state while strengthening the government. Nevertheless, by the end of the century the political organization proved incapable of accommodating the strains of a greatly altered economic and social situation. The Chilean state, like others throughout Latin America, had to confront the challenges of nationhood from increasingly politicized urban laborers and peasant groups within the state.

By the beginning of the twentieth century, however, most Latin American states had resolved their geographical boundaries and began to expand the representative nature of their governments—although it would be much later before women were given the vote. Nationalism compounded the sovereignty issue, since the plural nature of the societies made it difficult to integrate the various conflicting classes and groups within an effective political system. Resolving the plural constituencies proved much more difficult than the intra-elite disputes of the first half of the nineteenth century over how sovereignty ought to be manifested. Those early disputes were settled in a variety of ways, including exhaustion through civil wars (Mexico, Chile, Bolivia); the convenience of novel elite-congealing philosophies, such as Comtian positivism or Spencerian utilitarianism (Mexico, Colombia, Brazil); constitutional accommodation (Chile, Uruguay, Argentina, Venezuela); and expanding local economies.[31] The newer disputes involved class as well as race and ethnicity and continue to be divisive aspects of the present Latin American and Caribbean political conflict.[32]

But by the time of the Mexican Revolution in 1910, Latin Americans found the autonomy of their states threatened again from without as well as within. The most visible external threat emerged from the increasing perception that the United States and its midnineteenth century promulgation of Manifest Destiny would gradually and surreptitiously incorporate the entire hemisphere, if not in a formal way then certainly informally. Mexico, having lost much northern territory to its neighbor, was, of course, the most sensitive about U.S. military expansionism. And there was good reason for the other Latin American and Caribbean states to be greatly concerned.

In 1895 U.S. Secretary of State Richard Olney had written to the government of Great Britain that "the United States is practically sovereign" in South America "and its fiat is law upon the subjects to which it confirms its interposition." This was the threat that brought a resolution of the Venezuela–British Guiana boundary dispute, but it demonstrated that the United States had become more actively jingoistic than previously and that the way it regarded sovereignty was also changing.

The result of the Spanish-American War in 1898 demonstrated that the physical threat was not restricted to Mexico and Central America. The Treaty of Paris, ending the war, handed control of the former Spanish colonies of Cuba, the Philippines, and Puerto Rico to the United States. Beside annexing Hawaii, the United States increased its machinations in Panama, which became independent from Colombia in 1903. Even more threatening to the states of Latin America and the Caribbean was the enunciation of the Roosevelt Corollary to the Monroe Doctrine, contained in the president's annual message to Congress in 1904. It added a new regional policing authority to U.S. military power. "Chronic wrongdoing," the president declared, "or an impotence which results in a general loosening of the ties of civilized society, may in America, as elsewhere, ultimately require intervention by some civilized nation."

Military occupations of Cuba (1899–1902 and 1906–9), Nicaragua (1909–33), Haiti (1915–1934), and the Dominican Republic (1916–24) under the "Big Stick policy," accompanied by an energetic economic and cultural expansion throughout the hemisphere, did much to erode the admiration and respect for the United States prevailing a century earlier.[33] By the end of World War I the United States seemed to have a double standard for sovereignty, one applied to the European states and another to neighboring states in the hemisphere. The Latin American response to the North American attitude was an insistence on state sovereignty as an absolute right, repeated in national constitutions as well as in ineffective regional organizations, such as the Pan American Union (the forerunner of the Organization of American States).[34]

The "Big Stick policy" of overt military intervention gave way in the 1930s during the Franklin D. Roosevelt administration to a "Good Neighbor policy" emphasizing more subtle means of arriving at the same goal—U.S. hegemony in the hemisphere. This policy had less to do with changing concepts of sovereignty than with realpolitik in international affairs. In 1948 the loosely structured Pan American Union became the Organization of American States, designed to foster closer military, economic, and cultural ties among the majority of independent states in the hemisphere. It never became a really effective instrument of asserting Latin American and Caribbean sovereignty. Subsequent military interventions in Guatemala (1954), Cuba (1961), the Dominican Republic (1965), Grenada (1983), and Panama (1989) indicated that the unilateral military option still remained an important aspect of U.S. foreign policy.[35] At the same time, nonmilitary interventions in British Guiana (1953), Chile (1973), and probably Jamaica in the late 1970s reinforced the precarious nature of political independence throughout the hemisphere.

Overt external military aggression remains the most visible but not the only threat to sovereignty and political independence. Most Latin American and Caribbean states during the post-World War II era have had to consider internal threats as well. These have originated from their military officers, from disgruntled civilian groups, sometimes with ideological motivations, and from international agencies and corporations.

The military role in Latin American government began with the wars of independence. The tradition continued with the age of the *caudillos*. Military individuals, such as Antonio López de Santa Anna (1794–1876) in Mexico, Antonio Guzmán Blanco (1829–99) in Venezuela, and Juan Manuel de Rosas in Argentina (1793–1877), used their access to arms and the ability to eliminate their opposition to take over national governments. Their success, however, stemmed from personal attributes and did not represent the military as a political constituency.

Rather, the military as a political constituency is a distinctly twentieth century phenomenon. With the increase in urban populations, general disorder and specific economic discontent on the part of labor groups, civilian governments began to feel threatened. A number of governments began to rely increasingly on military services to maintain public order. By the 1940s the military had itself become an identifiable political pressure group, comparable to organized labor unions or chambers of commerce. The Second World War—and the series of bilateral military agreements signed with the United States during and immediately after the war—reinforced the distinctive position of the military. But it also did more. It made the military more politically sensitive and ideologically fastidious. To the military, the notion of sovereignty was subordinate to concern for public order.[36]

Domestic military intervention took two forms. The first was to take over the government and proscribe all forms of non-approved political activity. The second was to be an effective power within the civilian government, capable of subverting policy, and even occasionally overthrowing the government. The military domination of political structures that began in Peru (1962–1963 and 1968–1980), Brazil (1964–1985), Argentina (1966–1970 and 1976–1982), Ecuador (1972–1979), Uruguay (1973–1985), and Chile (1973–1990) represented serious, prolonged, but eventually unsuccessful attempts on the military's part to alter the social and institutional basis of political power. Even when civilians were employed in certain sectors—finance, industry, or agriculture, for example—they had to follow policies made or approved by the military as a whole. To these military governments we owe the practice of "bureaucratic authoritarianism."

In Colombia, El Salvador, Haiti, Honduras, Guatemala, and Panama, the military has operated in collaboration with influential conservative civilian sectors (and occasionally external supporters) to wage incessant war on guerrillas and peasants who either contested the legitimacy of the government or wished to remain neutral in the conflict.

Three cases in the region were unusual: Cuba, Grenada, and Nicaragua. In Cuba, Fidel Castro and a small armed band overthrew the government of Fulgencio Batista in 1959, severed relations with the United States, and established military and commercial relations with the Soviet Union that enabled Cuba to survive the hostility and economic isolation of its former North American partner. The success of the revolution did much for Cuba's self-esteem and sense of independence and sovereignty. By refusing to hold any elections until the late 1970s the Castro government failed to legitimize itself in the eyes of many foreign states, as well as among the nearly 10 percent of the population who left the island in the aftermath of the revolution.[37] With the collapse of the Soviet Union and a rapidly changing international world order, the Cuban government has found itself extremely isolated and vulnerable, both at home and abroad. It urgently needs to find a way to legitimize its presence locally and internationally.

Between its beginning in 1979 and its sudden and untidy demise in 1983, the Grenadian Revolution of Maurice Bishop and his confused socialist comrades played itself out, first as farce and then as tragedy.[38] The dilemma of sovereignty in a small state was clearly brought home when the government abruptly self-destructed. Bishop was arbitrarily removed and murdered by his ruling colleagues, and the island quickly found itself invaded by a foreign power. The United States, although having no formal diplomatic relations with Grenada, invaded the country and terminated the political chaos.

In Nicaragua the Sandinistas tried their best to assert their national political and economic independence for 10 difficult years against the implacable hostility of the United States. They then found themselves surprisingly voted out of office in a general election. Without considerable external material support the Nicaraguan government could not exercise the normal sovereignty expected of an independent state. Yet the threats to sovereignty were not always overtly military, as in Nicaragua.

The Cuban Revolution inspired a broad nationalist attack on foreign multinational corporations throughout the Caribbean in the 1960s and 1970s. Part of the aggressive attitude toward the multinational corporations stemmed from the euphoria of the revolution, with rising expectations accompanying the wave of independence that created more than a dozen ministates in the Caribbean between 1962 and 1983. The expectant populations felt that independence meant not only local control of their economies, but also the liberty to decide their international policies. The result was a series of nationalizations of foreign enterprises and an attempt to establish a "new international economic order." In Guyana the government nationalized foreign bauxite properties owned by Alcan and Reynolds and the sugar estates of Tate and Lyle and Bookers Limited. The Trinidad government bought out the oil companies operated by Texaco and Shell. The government of the Dominican Republic acquired the sugar operations of Gulf and Western. The Jamaican government of the first Michael Manley administration in the 1970s assumed control of the banks, tourism industry, and sugar companies. It also successfully imposed a 7.5 percent levy on the bauxite companies operated by Alcoa, Alcan, Kaiser, Reynolds, and Anaconda, which resulted in a sevenfold increase in royalties paid to the government.

But the bauxite struggle in Jamaica was a painfully instructive lesson in the limitations of sovereignty for small states. On the surface the issue seemed clear-cut. The Jamaican government felt that the simple, limited tax paid by the companies in 1972 had not been changed in the more than twenty years since it was negotiated with the previous colonial governments. The Manley government sought to cajole the companies into agreeing to a new basis for an increased levy that would provide more revenue for the newly independent state. When the companies refused, the government unilaterally imposed a levy and had its action upheld by local courts.

At stake, however, was much more than merely seeking adequate compensation for a national resource. "The bauxite levy," claimed Winston K. Davis, a prominent official of the government at the time, "established that Jamaica was a sovereign country, and sovereignty is important for a small Third World country that had all along been under the clutches of dependency. And if nothing else established that sovereignty during the entire period of the Manley government, that one act established that sovereignty."[39]

But if the Jamaican government won the battle against the bauxite companies, they lost the war against multinational corporations. Shortly after the new levies were imposed, the bauxite companies wound down their operations in Jamaica and shifted their purchases to nonmembers of the newly created International Bauxite Organization, such as Brazil and Australia; within a very short time the windfall income diminished.[40] In addition, foreign investment in Jamaica became dramatically scarce. The economy of Jamaica in the late 1970s—like that of Nicaragua in the late 1980s—came close to complete collapse. In 1980 the Manley government was overwhelmingly defeated at the polls, and Manley's successor, Edward Seaga, renegotiated lower levies in return for increased international bauxite purchases. Seaga proved to be no miracle worker, and within a few years the Jamaican economy was again in a precarious situation.

A chastened, more pragmatic Michael Manley returned to power in 1989:

> Well, the truth is, you know, that it is an illusion to think that any country enjoys sovereignty in a sort of pure theoretical sense—the freedom to do whatever it likes. Nobody has the freedom to do whatever you like. But small countries are much more constrained by economic dependence. They are fragile. They are smaller. They have less capacity to influence the movement of economic trends in the world. And so people have to learn very early that there are severe limits in practice on this thing called sovereignty.[41]

Colombia represents an example of a different sort of internal threat to sovereignty. Here, internal divisions have become so great that they represent a domestic threat to the sovereignty and autonomy of the state. Although its size and economic status make it an unlikely candidate for external military invasion, the country has been wracked by a recurring, ferociously destructive civil discontent that flared in 1948. Called *La Violencia,* it continued until 1958, when the two major political parties called a truce and agreed to an orderly rotation of the presidency. By then the war had destroyed nearly 2 percent of the population, approximately 200,000 lives. Many groups felt excluded from the political arrangement that ended the conflict and took up arms against the government. By the early 1980s several guerrilla groups controlled vast stretches of national territory, mainly in the rural interior, and operated in open contempt of the national government.

Along with the guerrilla bands, and sometimes in alliance with them, were drug traffickers grown rich through their enormously lucrative export trade to North America and Europe. Like the guerrillas, the drug traffickers created their own armies and carved out zones they controlled with ruthless efficiency, especially the cities of Calí and Medellín, and the region of Magdalena del Medio. In 1989 the drug traffickers assassinated the leading presidential candidate, Luis Carlos Galan, near Bogotá, and brutally exposed the military weakness of the Colombian government. President Virgilio Barco appealed to the outside world for help against the drug dealers, and even agreed to the extradition of Colombian citizens to the United States in return for military aid. Barco's desperate measure raised serious questions about the threats to Colombian sovereignty and whether or not U.S. assistance mitigated or exacerbated the domestic situation. Civil war raged throughout the country.

Finally, in September 1990, the newly elected president, Cesar Gaviria, decided to make a deal with the guerrillas and drug traffickers. In return for their participation in a new constitutional assembly designed to reconstitute Colombian sovereignty, he would withdraw official military action against guerrilla and drug traffickers and suspend extradition of nationals. The new constitution brought a number of previously excluded groups into the government and redefined the nature of state sovereignty. The Colombian response is not only to a deteriorating domestic condition but also to a changing international situation involving relations between groups of states.

The concept of sovereignty continues to be fundamentally redefined and transformed at the end of the twentieth century. The catalyst for this change derives from two principal sources. One is a notable increase in ethnic nationalism. Although most pronounced in the territories of the former Soviet Union and Yugoslavia, ethnic nationalism is especially rife among African, Asian, and some American states. Ethnic nationalists seek autonomous political expression within the framework of existing states, or they seek to create separate states of their own by a process of irredentism. The degree of ethnic political identification in Latin America varies considerably. The most pronounced political activity is found among the East Indians of Trinidad and Guyana, Garifuna and Miskito of Nicaragua, San Blas of Panama, and the recently active Confederation of Indigenous Nationalities of Ecuador (CONAIE).[42]

Along with this fractious tendency runs an opposite process—to submerge national autonomy within greater units, or to delegate aspects of sovereignty to subunits.[43] Usually the supporters of these confederalist structures promise improved economic benefits for all participants. This was the motivation for the European Economic Community, established in 1957 by Belgium, France, Italy, Luxembourg, the Netherlands, and what was then West Germany, and designed to abolish all restraints on trade, capital flows, and transportation among the member states. Since then the organization has expanded to include Great Britain, Ireland, Denmark, Spain, Portugal, and Greece. The Community promised to integrate social and political structures by 1992.

Similar attempts at expanding economic units with a goal of future political cooperation are also being actively discussed throughout the Americas. These include the Organization of Eastern Caribbean States, the Caribbean Community, and proposed cooperation among the South American states and the North American states of Mexico, the United

States, and Canada. The degree of probable success of these larger units will depend on a shifting combination of local, regional, and international factors.

Since the fifteenth century, sovereignty has invariably been a dynamic concept, responding to both local and international conditions. It has also been intimately connected with a variety of unpredictable forces. In Latin America it has reflected both the absolutist and constitutional traditions of the Spanish American empire as well as the well-founded fear of foreign intervention, especially from the United States of America. At the end of the twentieth century notions of sovereignty reflect internal political threats, and in addition the economic force of multinational corporations and variations in the patterns of world commerce. The rapidly changing international context, especially the coalition of nation states as consolidated economic entities, makes the notion of sovereignty increasingly a question of international law and divided authority rather than the sole prerogative of autonomous entities.

Notes

1. See, for example, Bernard Guernée, *States and Rulers in Later Medieval Europe,* trans. Juliet Vale (New York: Blackwell, 1985), especially, 4–18, where he traces the etymology of both *state* and *sovereignty.* This is a far more sophisticated explanation of the rise of governments and the state than that found in Louis Hartz, *The Founding of New Societies. Studies in the History of the United States, Latin America, South Africa, Canada and Australia* (New York: Harcourt Brace, 1964). My discussion in this essay gratefully reflects the opinions of Gary Kates, John Martin, Teresita Martínez Vergne, Alida Metcalf, Linda K. Salvucci, Richard Salvucci, and Alfred Stepan's Arden House group on an earlier version.

2. This arises from the proprietary role of the monarchy of Castile over the lands encountered by Christopher Columbus. See John Parry, *The Spanish Theory of Empire in the Sixteenth Century* (Cambridge: Cambridge Univ. Press, 1940), 71: "The New Laws of 1542, the various *Ordenanzas sobre Descubrimiento,* and above all the great Colonial Code—the *Recopilación de Leyes de las Indias*—form the most impressive of all monuments to an absolute imperial sovereignty based upon the formal assumption that the Indies were the private estate of the rulers of Castile." See also Silvio Zavala, *New Viewpoints on the Spanish Colonization of America* (Philadelphia: Univ. of Pennsylvania Press, 1943), 5–37. By far the best treatment of the theme is Colin M. MacLachlan, *Spain's Empire in the New World. The Role of Ideas in Institutional and Social Change* (Berkeley: Univ. of California Press, 1988).

3. Anthony Pagden and Nicholas Canny see another difference between Latin America/the Caribbean and the United States in the role that race plays in the developing concept of nationalism and the nation-state after the nineteenth century. See *Colonial Identity in the Atlantic World, 1500–1800,* Nicholas Canny and Anthony Pagden (eds.), (Princeton: Princeton Univ. Press, 1987), 272–74.

4. This point is made very well in Keith Michael Baker *Inventing the French*

Revolution. Essays on French Culture in the Eighteenth Century (New York: Cambridge Univ. Press, 1990). My appreciation to Gary Kates for this reference.

5. See Guernée, *States and Rulers*, 167–70.

6. See Andrew Vincent, *Theories of the State* (London: Blackwell, 1987); Julian H. Franklin, *John Locke and the Theory of Sovereignty* (Cambridge: Cambridge Univ. Press, 1978); F. H. Hinsley, *Sovereignty*, 2d ed. (Cambridge: Cambridge Univ. Press, 1986); Harold Laski, *Studies in the Problem of Sovereignty* (1917; reprint, New York: Fertig, 1968); Charles Merriam, Jr., *History of the Theory of Sovereignty Since Rousseau* (1900; reprint, New York: Garland, 1972).

7. Joseph R. Strayer, *On the Medieval Origins of the Modern State* (Princeton: Princeton Univ. Press, 1970).

8. G. R. Elton, *The Tudor Revolution in Government* (Cambridge: Cambridge Univ. Press, 1962). At the same time that the Spanish were establishing monarchical sovereignty at home they were also resolving theories about empire that differed significantly from the way Thomas Cranmer used the term. See J. H. Parry, *The Spanish Theory of Empire in the Sixteenth Century* (Cambridge: Cambridge Univ. Press, 1940: Folcroft, Pa: Folcroft Press, 1969).

9. Strayer, *Medieval Origins*, 35. For a comparison between Spain and Italy, see Adriano Prosperi, "La religione, il potere, le elites, incontri Italo-Spagnoli nell'eta della controriforma," *Annuario dell'Instituto Storico Italiano per l'eta moderna e contemporanea* 29–30 (1977–78), 499–529. I am grateful to John Martin for bringing this article to my attention.

10. For the important development of the idea of authority in the eighteenth and nineteenth centuries see Leonard Krieger, "The Idea of Authority in the West," *American Historical Review* 82:2 (April, 1977); 249–70, esp. 263–65.

11. Hinsley, *Sovereignty*, 142.

12. This point is further developed in Keith Michael Baker, *Inventing the French Revolution. Essays on French Political Culture in the Eighteenth Century* (Cambridge: Cambridge Univ. Press, 1990), 224–51.

13. Franklin, *Locke and Sovereignty*, 94–126.

14. The question of sovereignty was further complicated by the changing forms of empire in the nineteenth century. For a good study, see W. Ross Johnston, *Sovereignty and Protection: A Study of British Jurisdictional Imperialism in the Late Nineteenth Century* (Durham, N.C.: Duke Univ. Press, 1973), esp. 214–25.

15. Charles II (1661–1700), the last Hapsburg monarch, after a series of debilitating wars named as his successor Philip of Anjou (1683–1746), a Bourbon, who became Philip V of Spain in 1700. This succession embroiled Spain in a prolonged series of wars, beginning with the Wars of the Spanish Succession (1701–14), the Wars of the Quadruple Alliance (1718–20), the War of Polish Succession (1733–38), and the War of Austrian Succession (1740–48). The Family Compact involved three separate treaties between Spain and France: in 1733 and 1743, designed to counter English naval supremacy and Austrian aggression in Italy, and in 1761, to bring Spain into the Anglo-French conflict. During this last conflict the English captured Havana.

16. Quoted in Leslie Bethell (ed.), *The Independence of Latin America* (Cambridge: Cambridge Univ. Press, 1987), 44.

17. Canny and Pagden, *Colonial Identity*, 276.

18. MacLachlan, *Spain's Empire*, 123–35.

19. John Lynch, *The Spanish-American Revolutions, 1808–1826* (New York: Norton, 1973).

20. See Merriam, *Theory of Sovereignty,* 158–82.

21. On the Brazilian situation, see Lydia Magalhaes Garner, "In Pursuit of Order: A Study in Brazilian Centralization—The Section of Empire of the Council of State, 1842–1889" (Ph.D. diss., Johns Hopkins University, 1987).

22. David Bushnell, "The Independence of Spanish South America," in Leslie Bethell (ed.), *The Independence of Latin America* (Cambridge: Cambridge Univ. Press, 1987), 105.

23. Quoted in Bushnell, "Independence of Spanish South America," 106.

24. Lawrence E. Harrison, *Underdevelopment Is a State of Mind* (Cambridge: Harvard Univ. Press, 1985). The perceptual differences between the Americas are indeed long-standing. See the marvelous selections from the literature in John J. TePaske (ed.), *Three American Empires* (New York: Harper & Row, 1967).

25. Torcuato S. Di Tella, *Latin American Politics. A Theoretical Framework* (Austin: Univ. of Texas Press, 1990), 1.

26. A useful summary of conditions may be found in the extract from the *Cambridge History of Latin America* published as Leslie Bethell (ed.) *Spanish America after Independence c.1820–c.1870* (Cambridge: Cambridge Univ. Press, 1987).

27. For an excellent explanation of the phenomenon of *caciques* and *caudillos,* see Frank Safford, "Politics, Ideology and Society," in Bethell, *Spanish America after Independence,* 48–122.

28. See Garner, "In Pursuit of Order."

29. Simon Collier, *Ideas and Politics of Chilean Independence, 1808–1833* (Cambridge: Cambridge Univ. Press, 1967).

30. Simon Collier, Harold Blakemore, and Thomas Skidmore (eds.), *The Cambridge Encyclopedia of Latin America and the Caribbean* (Cambridge: Cambridge Univ. Press, 1985); 246–48; Di Tella, *Latin American Politics,* 54–60. See also the collection of essays in Leslie Bethell (ed.), *Latin America. Economy and Society, 1870–1930* (Cambridge: Cambridge Univ. Press, 1989).

31. Charles Hale, *Mexican Liberalism in the Age of Mora 1821–1853* (New Haven: Yale Univ. Press, 1968), and *The Transformation of Liberalism in Late Nineteenth Century Mexico* (Princeton: Princeton Univ. Press, 1990); Claudio Véliz, *The Centralist Tradition in Latin America* (Princeton: Princeton Univ. Press, 1980).

32. Some recent publications on the subject include Winthrop R. Wright, *Café con Leche. Race, Class, and National Image in Venezuela* (Austin: Univ. of Texas Press, 1990); Richard Graham (ed.), *The Idea of Race in Latin America, 1870–1940* (Austin: Univ. of Texas Press, 1990); George Reid Andrews, *Blacks and Whites in São Paulo, Brazil, 1888–1988* (Madison: Univ. of Wisconsin Press, 1991); and Pierre-Michel Fontaine (ed.), *Race, Class and Power in Brazil* (Los Angeles: Univ. of California Press, 1985).

33. Emily S. Rosenberg, *Spreading the American Dream. American Economic and Cultural Expansion, 1890–1945* (New York: Hill & Wang, 1982); Mira Wilkins, *The Maturing of Multinational Enterprise, 1914–1970* (Cambridge: Harvard Univ. Press, 1974).

34. F. V. Garcia-Amador, "Latin American Law," in Arthur Larson and C. Wilfred Jenks (eds.), *Sovereignty Within the Law* (New York: Oceana, 1965), 123–40.

35. The invasion of the Dominican Republic in 1965, while carried out pri-

marily by troops from the United States, did have the official approval of the Organization of American States.

36. Perhaps the best studies on the military and politics are by Robert Potash, *The Army and Politics in Argentina, 1928–1945* (Stanford: Stanford Univ. Press, 1969) and *The Army and Politics in Argentina, 1945–1962* (Stanford: Stanford Univ. Press, 1980) and by Alfred Stepan, *The Military in Politics: Changing Patterns in Brazil* (Princeton: Princeton Univ. Press, 1971).

37. Jorge I. Dominguez, *Cuba: Order and Revolution* (Cambridge: Harvard Univ. Press, 1978).

38. The best book on the short-lived Grenada revolution is Gordon K. Lewis, *Grenada: The Jewel Despoiled* (Baltimore: Johns Hopkins Univ. Press, 1987).

39. Winston K. Davis was ambassador to the Organization of American States as well as ambassador to Cuba during the first Manley administration, 1972–80. He made the statement in an interview with WGBH in May 1991 for the *Americas* program, "Get Up! Stand Up!"

40. Raymond Vernon, *Sovereignty at Bay: The Multinational Spread of U.S. Enterprises* (New York: Basic Books, 1971), while generally correct in its descriptions was premature in its assessment of the Jamaican bauxite case (41–45).

41. Michael Manley interview with WGBH, May 1991, in "Get Up! Stand Up!"

42. In 1990, CONAIE virtually crippled the country for three days with a series of strikes, as well as kidnappings of military personnel and *hacendados*. For background to the increasing ethnic consciousness in Ecuador, see Norman E. Whitten, *Cultural Transformations and Ethnicity in Modern Ecuador* (Urbana: Univ. of Illinois Press, 1981).

43. See for example, Ivo D. Duchacek, Daniel Latouche, and Garth Stevenson (eds.), *Perforated Sovereignties and International Relations. Trans-Sovereign Contacts of Subnational Governments* (Westport, Conn.: Greenwood Press, 1988).

2

The State and Development in Historical Perspective

PETER H. SMITH

State intervention is often held responsible for Latin America's economic problems. It is commonly alleged that the region's failures—poverty, backwardness, and inequality—are the direct result of excessive government intervention in the marketplace. In a variety of ways, according to this view, the Latin American state has interfered consistently and counterproductively in economic matters: it has imposed subsidies, regulations, and monopolies. It has distributed rewards on the basis of allegiance, not efficiency, creating cadres of bureaucrats and parasites. The consequences have been rigidities, distortions, disincentives—and, of course, corruption—which have hindered the free market's "invisible hand." In short, underdevelopment is a result of state interventionism.

The basic purpose of this essay is to re-evaluate the historical role of the state in the political economy of Latin America by examining three distinct strategies: the *mercantilism* of the colonial era; the *liberalism* of the nineteenth century; and the turn toward (for lack of a better phrase) the *industrial developmentalism* of the twentieth century. As we shall see, each of these approaches had its own logic and rationale; each had some measure of success; and, for diverse reasons, each gave way to a subsequent experiment.

I explore the practical application of these strategies to one of the region's major nations: Argentina. Although Argentina played a relatively brief and minor role within the Spanish American empire, it would come to represent the quintessential success story of the liberal formula from the 1880s to the 1930s. And in its complex way, it would illustrate both the potentials and the pitfalls of the quest for industrialization from the 1930s to the 1950s. Since the midnineteenth century, in fact,

Argentina has been an intellectual and cultural leader in Latin America; as such, it has exemplified and epitomized the region's contemporary search for formulas and policies.

Through the course of this analysis I propose to offer a broad reassessment of the economic role of the Latin American state. I intend to show not only that the state has always been active in economic matters, as its critics would agree, but also that it has often been effective. Latin America's developmental problems arise not so much from the state or state intervention per se, but from other causes. Principal among them have been both the region's disadvantageous location in the world economy, and internal contradictions within long-run economic strategies. By implication, I further suggest that the answer to Latin America's modern-day problems lies not in dismantling the state, but in redefining its role within a plausible strategy for long-term economic growth.

Experiments in Political Economy

The Spanish Crown wanted to establish a monopoly over its holdings in the New World. Soon after Columbus "discovered" the Americas in 1492, just as Ferdinand and Isabella were completing the expulsion of the Moors, the monarchy began intensive efforts to bring the area directly under royal control. The ultimate decision was to create a Council of the Indies in Spain and a series of royally appointed officers, the most important being viceroys ("vice-kings") in Lima and Mexico City. Under a complex arrangement, the Church also came to accept substantial royal direction in the New World. Underpinning the political structure of colonial Spanish America was a set of values and assumptions that legitimized state power through monarchical, elitist rule.

(For the colonial period I focus largely on the Spanish empire in America. The experience of Portuguese America was different for at least three major reasons: Portugal had more extensive interests in the Far East; the indigenous civilization in Brazil was not comparable to that of the Aztecs or the Incas; and Brazil did not offer much silver or gold. And because the Portuguese monarchy fled to Rio de Janeiro in 1808, the Brazilian path to independence would be unlike that of Spanish America.)

Economic policy reflected the prescriptions of then prevailing mercantilist theory. According to this approach, the goal of all economic activity was to enhance the power and prestige of the nation and the state. The point bears emphasis: the purpose of economics was to strengthen the state—in this instance, the Spanish Crown—both in its control over domestic society and especially in its relationship to other sovereign states. The accumulation of power was to be measured through the possession of precious bullion—that is, gold or silver. Mercantilist policymakers thus sought to run a favorable balance of trade, with exports exceeding imports, since this would increase the store of coinage or bullion. (This emphasis on trade gave the doctrine its name.) Mercantilist theory entailed two central premises: a de-emphasis on the individual pursuit of prosperity, and a presumption that the state should take an active role in the regulation of commerce and finance.

Following this logic, Spain attempted to establish a monopoly over wealth discovered in the New World. The initial target was mining, first of gold and then of silver, since this could increase the royal supply of bullion. The second goal was to maintain complete control over commerce, thus assuring a favorable balance of trade for the metropolis (and a negative balance for the colonies). As a result, Spanish authorities gave low priority to economic development within the colonies. They paid little attention to agriculture, for example, and actively discouraged manufacturing, since that could reduce the market for Spanish goods in the Americas.

A central pillar for the colonial economy, especially on the Spanish American mainland, was labor provided by culturally diverse indigenous peoples whom the conquerors called "Indians." Stripped of their cultural and political achievements, the Aztecs of Mexico and the Incas of Peru were put to work in mines and fields. Natives supplied labor through a variety of legal mechanisms—as conquered vassals, slaves, indebted peons, and, ultimately, as wards of the Crown under systems known as *encomienda* and *repartimiento*. It was their work that extracted precious metals from the mines. Their tribute filled the coffers of the Crown and its appointed emissaries. And it was the decline in the Indian population, as a result of conquest and disease, that would lead to the weakening of the mercantilist economy.

Brutal as it was, mercantilism enjoyed substantial success. Spain acquired considerable wealth from the New World. It maintained effective control of its far-flung holdings for nearly 300 years, and in so doing created a powerful and capable bureaucracy.[1] Ironically enough, it was the success of the mercantilist enterprise—especially the extraction of bullion from the Americas—that contributed to the ultimate debilitation of the Spanish economy in the seventeenth and eighteenth centuries. The mercantilist formulation contained the seeds of its own destruction; to achieve its goal (and its demise), however, required the construction of a strong and efficacious state.

Eventually, Spain proved unable to maintain its hold. The influx of bullion from the New World provided economic stimulation for rival European powers (Britain, France, Holland)—which began making territorial inroads within the Western Hemisphere. The growth of contraband trade, itself a response to rigid mercantilist policies, created a thriving illicit economy. Over time new social forces appeared within the colonies, most conspicuously a native-born "creole" elite. Spain at-

tempted to reassert its authority with a series of eighteenth-century reforms, but the result was only to hasten its demise. Cries for local autonomy led to demands for sovereign independence. Armed conflict
engulfed the region for more than a decade. By the 1820s almost all
of Spanish America (except Cuba and Puerto Rico) had attained independence.[2]

Throughout the early nineteenth century most of Latin America reduced its links with the world economy. Creole landowners converted
their holdings into autonomous, self-sufficient entities, rather than producing goods for domestic or foreign markets. Mining came to a standstill, partly as a result of the physical destruction of the Wars of Independence. Manufacturing was modest, done mostly by artisans in small
establishments. Politics became a crude power struggle among rival *caudillos,* swashbuckling leaders of paramilitary bands that assaulted the
national treasury for private gain; in some countries rival camps described themselves as "liberals" and "conservatives," though the ideological difference between them was often obscure. The state started to
wither away.

The Industrial Revolution in Europe precipitated the next major
transformation in the political economy of Latin America. By the midnineteenth century, industrialization in England and elsewhere was
producing strong demand for agricultural commodities and raw materials. Factory workers needed food, and industrialists were seeking raw
materials, particularly minerals. Both incentives led European governments and investors to begin looking abroad—to Africa, Asia, and, of
course, Latin America.

Economic policy in Latin America would take the form of liberalism,
an emphasis on exporting raw-material goods and importing manufactured products from abroad. Instead of attempting to close the region
off from outside influence, as in the case of mercantilism, economic
liberalism would seek to exploit the "comparative advantage" of Latin
America's resource endowments through intensive interaction with the
industrializing centers of the world economy. At least rhetorically, the
emphasis would be on freedom of trade and laissez-faire.

But this did not mean a minor role for the state. On the contrary,
the liberal state in Latin America took decisive steps to facilitate and
sustain the region's new insertion into the evolving world economy. Especially in former centers of the Spanish empire, the state set out to
destroy neofeudal remnants of colonial society—the structures of patronage and privilege that threatened to inhibit the development of
capitalism. One key achievement of the liberal state was to reduce the
economic power of the Church, particularly its hold over land, a step
that opened up financial markets and made possible the emergence of
a new, profit-oriented agricultural elite.[3] In Mexico and other countries
the granting of individual land titles within traditional Indian commu-

nities had a dual effect: it made high-quality land available for purchase and incorporation into commercial *haciendas*, and it created a landless laboring class available for employment as peons.[4]

The nineteenth-century liberal state assumed considerable responsibility for the labor force. Wherever workers were scarce, elites sought to import them from abroad (as the Argentine Juan Bautista Alberdi once put it, "To govern is to populate"). In the 1880s Argentina and Brazil began aggressive campaigns to encourage immigration from Europe; Chile received a smaller but substantial flow of workers. Proactive recruitment of labor was less apparent in countries with large Indian populations, or with enslaved Africans, but it occurred throughout the region.

In addition, the liberal state undertook to discipline the work force. In Guatemala, for example, the government supervised and enforced the seasonal migration of workers from traditional villages to coffee plantations; in El Salvador, it monitored labor relations between displaced peasants who had come to be employed by capitalist landlords. On banana plantations and in other settings, the nineteenth-century state consistently opposed labor organization, broke strikes, and championed the interests of the capitalist class.

The liberal state actively courted foreign investment, especially for the creation of infrastructure. Railroads were a conspicuous favorite. In Argentina the government actually guaranteed a minimum profit margin to a British railroad concession; in Mexico the government eventually purchased a majority share in railways, not so much for the purpose of creating a state enterprise as to rescue the indebted companies.[5]

In short, the liberal state played an active role in promoting Latin America's export economies. But the ultimate goal of this activism contrasted sharply with mercantilism. Instead of seeking to enhance of the power of the state, liberalism sought to facilitate the performance of the economy. Turning mercantilist logic on end, the liberal state placed its efforts and resources at the service of the economy—and of dominant economic forces in society.

Partly for this reason, the liberal state was inconsistent in performance. No clear prescription existed for state roles. Its very activity posed a contradiction: according to liberal ideology, the state should have only a minimal role in matters economic. Almost by definition, there could be no long-term developmental "plan," and, not surprisingly, the nature and extent of governmental involvement in economic matters varied from country to country.[6] Policymakers tended to follow market signals and, more decisively, to carry out the wishes of economic elites, rather than pursue an overall design.

Adherence to economic liberalism often went hand in hand with social and political elitism—thus contradicting patterns in Europe and

North America, where economic and political liberalism appeared to go hand in hand. Latin America's ruling groups, mostly of European descent themselves, frequently explained their relative lack of national development through the alleged racial inferiority of their native populations. Backwardness resulted from the Indians (or, in post-slave societies, from the blacks). Adding to this racist doctrine were theories of environmental determinism that argued that high civilization could never be sustained in the tropics. Contact with Europe and the United States would accordingly help offset the natural disadvantages of Latin America and elevate the level of society.

Contemporary science lent additional conviction, if not enlightenment, to regnant liberal doctrine. Applied to Latin America, the positivist teachings of Auguste Comte emphasized the state's obligation to sustain the welfare of the working class but, more important, stressed the desirability of economic development without social mobilization: the positivist slogan "Order and Progress" was officially adopted by the government of Brazil, and it found countless adaptations elsewhere. A second source of pseudoscientific inspiration came from Social Darwinism, which offered the reassuring hypothesis that material progress was a necessary precondition for political liberty; in the long run, economic development would establish foundations for political democracy. (As a further attraction, Social Darwinism did not purport to encumber the state with social responsibilities.) Eagerly seizing on these arguments, the dictatorial Rafael Núñez proclaimed the commitment of his administration in Colombia to "scientific peace." Similarly, Porfirio Díaz and his *científico* associates in Mexico announced their intent to govern through *poca política y mucha administración*.

In practice, this quest for political authority took two basic forms. In one version, as in Argentina and Chile, landowners and other economic elites took direct control of the government. They sought to build strong, exclusive regimes, usually with military support, often proclaiming legitimacy through adherence to constitutions superficially resembling U.S. and European models. In both countries mild competition prevailed among political parties that, at least in this early phase, tended to represent different factions of the aristocracy. There was more agreement than disagreement about basic policy issues, however, and little serious opposition to the idea of export-oriented economic growth. Competition was restricted, voting was often a sham, and public debate was generally mild and genteel. One might think of such regimes as a kind of "oligarchic democracy."

A second pattern involved the imposition of dictatorial strongmen, often military officers, to assert law and order—again, for the ultimate benefit of the landed elite. Porfirio Díaz of Mexico, who took power in 1876, is perhaps the most conspicuous example, but the pattern also appeared in Venezuela, Peru, and much of Central America. In contrast to oligarchic democracy, in which elites exercised direct political power, here it was the indirect application of elite rule through dictators who did not themselves come from society's upper ranks.

In either case, the emphasis was on stability and social control. Dissident groups were suppressed and the struggle for power was contained within restricted circles. Indeed, one of the basic goals of these regimes was to centralize power and consolidate authority. This yielded a paradox: as applied in nineteenth-century Latin America, economic liberalism offered a justification for political authoritarianism. This found eloquent illustration in one of the oxymorons so common to the region: the concept of "republican dictatorship."

Despite internal contradictions, liberal economic policies achieved their fundamental goals. The major Latin American countries underwent startling transitions from the 1880s onward. Argentina, with its vast and fertile pampas, became a leading exporter of agricultural and pastoral goods—wool, wheat, and beef. Chile resuscitated copper production, an industry that had fallen into decay after the independence years. Cuba produced coffee as well as sugar and tobacco. Mexico came to export a variety of raw material goods, from henequen to sugar to industrial minerals, particularly copper and zinc.

As development progressed, investment flowed into Latin America from the industrial nations, particularly England. Between 1870 and 1913 the value of Britain's investments in Latin America went from £85 million to £757 million—an increase of nearly ninefold. By 1913 British investors owned approximately two-thirds of the total foreign investment in Latin America. One of the most common British investments was railroad construction in Argentina, Mexico, Peru, and Brazil. Investors from Britain, France, and the United States also put capital into mining ventures, particularly in Mexico, Chile, and Peru.

These developments were accompanied by the importation of manufactured goods, especially from Europe. Latin Americans purchased textiles, machines, luxury items, and other finished products in steadily growing quantities. In practice, liberal policy thus led to the promotion of export-import development. Efficient integration of commercial agriculture into the modern world economy required, almost everywhere, economies of scale that relied on highly concentrated patterns of land tenure. This either created or exacerbated inequality in land distribution. As a result, the liberal program for export-import development reinforced and codified profound inequalities within Latin American society.

Predictably enough, the viability of these systems would become "dependent" on decisions and trends in the center of the world economy. As subsequent critics would later assert, nineteenth-century Latin America entered the global economy in a position of dependency—what analysts in the 1960s and 1970s would label *dependencia*.

Consolidation of the export-import model of growth prompted fundamental changes in the region's social structure. First in sequence, if not in importance, was the modernization of the upper-class elite. Landowners and property owners were no longer content to run subsistence operations on their *haciendas*; instead, they sought commercial opportunities and the maximization of profits. Cattle raisers in Argentina, coffee growers in Brazil, sugar barons in Cuba and Mexico—all were seeking efficiency and gain. This led to an entrepreneurial spirit that marked a significant change in the outlook and behavior of elite groups. It also led to incipient forms of industrialization by the early twentieth century.

A second transformation was the appearance and growth of middle social strata. Occupationally, these consisted of professionals, merchants, shopkeepers, and small businessmen who profited from the export-import economy but who did not hold upper-rank positions of ownership or leadership. Most often found in cities, middle-sector spokesmen were usually seeking a clearly recognized place in their society. Within oligarchic democracies their demands sometimes resulted in political reforms that led to modest openings and opportunities; the resulting regimes might be thought of as "co-optative democracies."

A third major change concerned the working class. Near the turn of the century workers began to organize themselves, first in mutual-aid societies and later in unions. Their role in vital sectors of the export-import economies—especially in railways and docks—gave them critical leverage. And their contact with comrades and movements outside Latin America (such as the International Workers of the World, or "Wobblies") offered examples and prescriptions for activism.[7] The years between 1914 and 1927 saw a remarkable surge of labor mobilization. This was the high point of anarchist, anarcho-syndicalist, and syndicalist influence, when the capital cities of Latin America were rocked by general strikes and demonstrations. Latin America suddenly seemed to be joining the class confrontations then shaking Germany, Russia, and the United States.

The Great Depression had initially catastrophic effects on the export-import economies of Latin America. International demand for coffee, sugar, metals, and meat underwent sharp reduction—and Latin American leaders could find no alternative outlet for their products. Both the unit price and the quantity of Latin American exports declined, resulting in a 48 percent drop in total value between 1925–29 and 1930–34. Once again, events at the industrialized center of the world-system had decisive (and limiting) effects on the peripheral economies of Latin America and the Third World.

The ensuing depression exerted great pressure on Latin American political systems, many of which suffered military coups (or attempted coups). Within a year or so of the October 1929 stock market crash, army officers had sought or taken power in Brazil, Chile, Peru, Guatemala, El Salvador, and Honduras. (This occurred in Argentina too but for somewhat different reasons.)[8] It would be an exaggeration to say that the economic effects of the Depression alone caused these political outcomes; but they cast into doubt the viability of the export-import model of growth, helped discredit ruling political elites, and made the citizenry more prepared to accept military regimes. From the early 1930s onward, the military reasserted its role as a principal force in Latin American politics.

Given the global economic crisis, Latin American rulers could pursue two major options. One was to forge even closer commercial linkages to the industrialized nations to secure a steady share of the market, whatever its size and dislocations. As we shall see, Argentina took this approach in 1933. The idea was to salvage the workability of the export-import model, despite the reduction in consumer demand.

An alternative tack, not necessarily inconsistent with the first, was to embark on an industrialization program—what I call industrial developmentalism. One of the goals of this policy, often supported by the military, was to strengthen economic independence. The idea was that by building its own industry, Latin America would become less dependent on Europe and the United States for manufactured goods. The Latin American economies would become more integrated and self-sufficient, in other words, and consequently less vulnerable to the kind of shocks brought on by worldwide depression.

A second goal was job creation. Concentrated almost entirely in cities, the Latin American proletariat was growing in size but still struggling to organize and sustain union movements. In contrast to the previous generation, however, it was now trying to exert power as a social force. In some countries, such as Chile, union movements were relatively free of arbitrary government involvement. Elsewhere, as in Mexico and Brazil, politicians recognized labor as a potential political resource and took a direct hand in stimulating and controlling labor organizations. Whether perceived as ally or threat, the urban working class was seeking secure employment, and Latin American leaders saw industrialization as one way to respond.

But the most plausible *form* of industrial development was not simply to copy the paths traced by nineteenth-century Europe. Instead, Latin America's economies started producing manufactured goods they had formerly imported from Europe and the United States. Hence the name for this approach: "import-substitution industrialization," also known as ISI.

In the 1920s and 1930s industrialization was generally seen as a supplement to agricultural development, not as a replacement for it. To some extent this early turn toward industry had a "defensive" quality, as a fortuitous and not entirely desirable response to a downturn in external conditions; for many policymakers it was a second-best option, and they consistently stressed their belief in the compatibility of industry and agriculture. Indeed, considerable skepticism existed about the feasibility of long-term industrial development. Policymakers approvingly cited the Ricardian distinction between "artificial" and "natural" industries, based on national factor endowments, and firmly withheld support for artificial—largely manufacturing—activities throughout most of the 1930s. In Brazil, government loans to artificial industries were prohibited as late as 1937, and the Bank of Brazil did not begin making significant loans to manufacturers until 1941. In Mexico, too, Nacional Financiera was established in 1934 but did not extend serious support to industry until the early 1940s. Much the same applied to Chile's famous CORFO.[9]

Ideological and theoretical support for industrial developmentalism would not emerge forcefully until the 1940s, and it would come from two principal sources. One was nationalism, the long-held desire for autonomy and self-determination. As intellectuals and policymakers surveyed the results of the nineteenth-century liberal experiment, many concluded that the nations of Latin America could achieve true political independence only on the basis of economic independence. For them this meant industrialization.

A second inspiration came from an initially unlikely source: a technocratic body of the United Nations known as the Economic Commission on Latin America (ECLA). Created in the late 1940s and led by the remarkably able Raúl Prebisch, an Argentine economist, ECLA began publishing throughout the 1950s a series of technical reports demonstrating that, over time, commercial relationships worked to the systematic disadvantage of primary-producing countries. The price of manufactured goods went up faster than the price of agricultural and mineral commodities, so the developing countries of Latin America obtained less and less real value for their export products. Though ECLA refrained from explicit policy recommendations, there were two logical solutions to this dilemma: to establish international commodity agreements, and, for the larger countries, to undertake industrialization.[10]

From the late 1930s to the 1960s, ISI policies met with relative success, at least in major countries. The Depression and World War II afforded tacit protection and explicit opportunity for infant industries at home. States would play major roles in taking advantage of this situation. Governments restricted foreign competition through tariffs and quotas, encouraged local investment through credits and loans, stimulated domestic demand through public-sector expenditures, and, perhaps most important, took direct part in the process by forming state-owned companies. Argentina, Brazil, and Mexico developed significant industrial plants that helped generate economic growth. For Mexico, indeed, this was the era of the much vaunted "economic miracle."

The social consequences of ISI were complex. One was the formation of an entrepreneurial capitalist class—an industrial bourgeoisie. In Chile, members of this group came principally from the families of the landed elite. In Mexico and Argentina, they came from more modest social origins and therefore presented a potential challenge to the hegemony of the traditional ruling classes. But the basic point remains: industrialization, even of the ISI type, created a new power group in Latin American society. Its role would be much debated as the century continued.

The political expression of industrial developmentalism took two distinct forms. Key among them was the continuation and extension of co-optative democracy, through which industrialists and workers gained (usually limited) access to power by electoral or other competition. An example was Chile, where political parties were reorganized to represent the interests of new groups and strata in society, especially labor and business. Under this system, they were co-opted into the governing structure, and as long as this arrangement lasted their participation lent support to the regime.

A more common response involved the creation of multiclass "populist" alliances. The emergence of an industrial elite and the invigoration of the labor movement made possible a new, proindustrial alliance merging the interests of entrepreneurs and workers—in some cases directly challenging the long-standing predominance of agricultural and landed interests. Each of these alliances was created by a national leader who exploited and relied upon state power. Thus did Getúlio Vargas build a multiclass, urban-based populist coalition in Brazil in the 1930s, as would Juan Perón in Argentina in the 1940s.

Most populist regimes shared four central characteristics. They tended to be authoritarian: they usually represented coalitions of one set of interests against another (such as landed interests) that were by definition prevented from participation. This involved some degree of both exclusion and repression. Second, as time would tell, populist regimes represented interests of classes—workers and industrialists—that were bound to conflict among themselves. Third, the maintenance of such regimes therefore depended in large part on the personal influence of individual leaders (such as the charismatic Perón or the manipulative Vargas). And finally, the reconciliation of differing interests led to the frequent use of unifying rhetoric and symbols—particularly, and most conveniently, nationalism. The internal contradictions within populist coalitions also meant that, with or without magnetic rhetoric or leadership, they would be hard to sustain during economic adversity. They often fell apart when times got hard.

The transitions from mercantilism to liberalism to industrial developmentalism took different forms in different countries. Let us explore the case of Argentina.

Argentina: The Triumph of Liberalism

Colonial Argentina's development served as eloquent testimony to the demise of Spanish mercantilist policies. Initially the area around the

Río de la Plata was virtually ignored by the conquering Spaniards: despite its hopeful name, the region had neither precious metals nor an exploitable Indian civilization, so it was placed under the administrative jurisdiction of distant Peru. It was only in the late eighteenth century, when European smugglers and rivals threatened to take over the region, that Spain established a viceroyalty in Buenos Aires. But this was too little too late: indeed, the creole elite of Buenos Aires played a leading role in the quest for independence in the 1810s and 1820s.

Consequently, nineteenth-century Argentina emerged largely as a "frontier society." Especially in the humid pampas and the littoral, in and around Buenos Aires, hardly any neofeudal remnants characteristic of colonial rule existed. In contrast to Mexico, for instance, there were no powerful church, no traditional Indian communities, no independent peasantry, no would-be nobility. There would be no need for a *reforma* to destroy these institutions. In these senses, as Tulio Halperín Donghi has pointed out, Argentina was "born liberal."[11] And as in the contemporaneous United States, the state's primary task would be to carry on a series of Indian wars to gain control of valuable land.

As occurred elsewhere in Latin America, newly independent Argentina plunged into a bitter struggle over the direction of the national political economy. One faction consisted of "unitarians," mainly from the province of Buenos Aires, who wanted to nationalize the city of Buenos Aires (then part of the province), extend political control over the rest of the country, break down internal barriers, and open doors to international trade. Another group was composed of "federalists" from the interior, who agreed on the desirability of nationalizing the city of Buenos Aires but who staunchly supported provincial sovereignty and wanted tariffs to protect their local industries. There were also "federalists" from the province of Buenos Aires who vigorously opposed the city's nationalization—that would take away the province's monopoly on customs revenues—and advocated free trade in economics.

The conflict took many years to resolve. In 1829 Juan Manuel de Rosas—a tough and energetic cattle rancher who could outride, outfight, and outcurse his rugged gaucho followers—became the governor of Buenos Aires province and began spreading autocratic rule over the whole of Argentina. Assisted by efficient spies and an ambitious wife, he appealed to popular masses with his charisma and he favored *estancieros* with his economic policies, thus furthering the formation of a landed aristocracy. Himself an ardent Buenos Aires federalist, Rosas laid the groundwork for the eventual imposition of a unitarian solution.

This conflict, and its resolution, created the basis for a liberal consensus within the Argentine elite. The adoption of liberal tenets did not come about simply because of their theoretical elegance or doctrinal superiority. As in other countries, it occurred as the result of struggle.

The groups that had the most to gain from liberalism emerged victorious, and their triumph established the basis for liberal hegemony.

Even so, Argentine liberalism was not without internal tensions. Considerable ambivalence prevailed about the significance of the frontier itself: in contrast to Frederick Jackson Turner, the great U.S. historian who interpreted the American frontier as the cradle of democracy, intellectuals such as Domingo Sarmiento regarded the Argentine countryside as a primitive source of political "barbarity." There was even more profound discomfiture over the question of equality. While Argentine liberals extolled the virtues of rural pursuits, which would enable the country to find a profitable niche in the emerging world economy, they paid only lip service to the ideal of an agrarian society of independent farmers. For the most part they regarded the rural sector as a homogeneous bloc under the leadership of the landed elite. Ultimately, the liberal formulation of "free trade" in the international economy legitimized and sustained the unequal distribution of land and wealth within the domestic economy.[12]

Leaders who came to power after Rosas's defeat in 1852, especially Bartolom Mitre and Domingo Sarmiento, applied their liberal programs with vigor. Continuing to employ authoritarian methods of political control, they drew up plans for representative government. With some modifications, the Argentine constitutions of 1853 and 1860 bore strong, if ultimately superficial, resemblance to their model in the United States. In economics Argentine thinkers accepted the liberal principles of comparative advantage and laissez-faire—with two major modifications. Unlike Adam Smith, whose view of the wealth of nations was more or less static, they stressed the dynamic characteristics of economic growth and regarded reliance on exports and imports as a prelude to the ultimate and desirable goal of economic transformation and development (often under the generic label of *industrialización*). They also assigned an activist role to the state. The government's most pressing task was to increase manpower by encouraging European immigration: hence Alberdi's famous aphorism, "To govern is to populate." Furthermore, the state should provide concessions for foreign capital that was badly needed for infrastructural development—transportation, ports, some local industry.

By the 1870s national leadership had passed from the post-Rosas reformers to the landed aristocracy. Through the stabilizing policies of Mitre and Sarmiento, government by chaos had turned into government by upper-class elite. This was the era of the well-bred and vastly talented "Generation of 1880," a small group of men who held the keys to power and influence. Led by Julio A. Roca, hero of the Conquest of the Desert from the Indians, they and their followers placed the state at the service of economic forces, and devised a strategy of export-import development that guided the country for the next half century or more. Their success would lead to the eclipse of the traditional gaucho, the fiercely self-reliant figure who would be celebrated and mourned in the great epic poem of the 1870s, *Martín Fierro*. (Once again, this classic demonstrated ambiguities within the ruralist ethos: revered by Argentine liberals, Fierro was himself a victim of liberal policies.)[13]

Argentine aristocrats employed a stark brand of liberalism to justify their policies and power. They drew on the pseudoscience of Herbert Spencer as well as the theories of Adam Smith, stoutly maintaining that competition was the guiding principle of life: if an aristocracy governed Argentina, it was due to natural law. Along with laissez-faire, the survival of the fittest was the watchword of the day. Partly conditioned by the widespread vogue of positivism, Argentina's leaders ardently pursued material progress.

Meanwhile, the steady growth and increasing accessibility of consumer markets in Europe during the late nineteenth century created strong demand for agricultural goods. The Generation of 1880 was anxious to exploit this opportunity. As Alberdi had recommended, the state actively encouraged immigration from Europe. Farmers and workers flocked to Argentina in great numbers. Some were discouraged by the practical difficulties of acquiring land, or by economic crises, as in 1890, and made their way back home. Others came merely as migrant workers, like the Italian *golondrinas* (or "swallows"), who would harvest one crop in Argentina and another at home. But net immigration was immense. Coming to a country with only 1.7 million residents in 1869, foreigners added more than 2.6 million residents in the following 40 years. By 1914, approximately 30 percent of Argentina's population was foreign-born; around this time in the United States, another haven for European emigrants, only 13 percent was foreign-born.

Another plank in the liberal platform was the attraction of foreign capital, particularly for railroad construction. A series of extravagant concessions by Argentine governments eventually bore fruit. In 1880 there were only 2,300 kilometers of track in the country; by 1910 there were nearly 25,000. Significantly enough, the lines all radiated from the city of Buenos Aires—the country's leading port—and most of them ran through agricultural production zones in the provinces of Buenos Aires, Santa Fe, Entre Ríos, and Córdoba.

With rising demand abroad, increasing manpower at home, and transportation facilities in place, a thriving economy developed: Argentina exported raw materials to Europe, mainly Great Britain, and imported manufactured goods from abroad. The value of exports increased at an average annual rate of 7 percent between 1880 and 1920. Total output increased by roughly 4.5 percent a year from 1900 to 1930, while per capita income, despite the immigration, grew at an annual average of 1.2 percent. During the 1920s and 1930s Argentina was consistently regarded as one of the half dozen most prosperous countries in the world.[14]

Despite its evident success, the reliance on export-import develop-ment entailed fundamental weaknesses. Argentina was extremely vul-nerable to economic influence from abroad. Stimulated by official pol-icy, foreign capital came to control a high proportion of the country's total fixed investments—by the 1920s, between 30 and 40 percent. Per-haps more important, the concentration on exports and imports left Argentina at the mercy of the international market. Up to the 1930s, exports—mostly foodstuffs and agricultural commodities such as beef and wheat—contributed about one-quarter of the GNP. If overseas de-mand for these goods dried up, it was not easy for Argentina to turn to new products or markets. Imports of manufactured items and capi-tal goods were equally significant. As time would tell, sudden reduc-tions in overseas trade would threaten disaster for the national econ-omy.

This pattern of development produced startling inequities. One di-mension of imbalance was regional. While economic expansion pro-ceeded on the pampas, and the city of Buenos Aires became a fashion-able cultural center, the old interior fell into a state of stagnation. Mendoza and Tucumán escaped this sorry fate, largely because of their wine and sugar production, but other central and northwestern prov-inces—notably Jujuy, La Rioja, Santiago del Estero, Salta—experienced severe economic and social decay. The interior had lost the battle of the nineteenth century, and the price of defeat was impoverishment.

A second dimension followed horizontal lines. Within the booming coastal economy, wealth was highly skewed. In the rural zones, cattle-rich *estancieros* built elegant chalets, while foreign-born tenant farmers and displaced native migrants eked out harsh existences amid igno-rance and isolation. In the cities, aristocrats lounged in elite clubs while workers struggled to keep up with the cost of living. Economic expan-sion provided considerable opportunity for upward mobility—more so than elsewhere in Latin America—but discrepancies still remained.

Initially the political corollary of export-import development in Ar-gentina was oligarchic democracy, a system of limited representative-ness and elite cohesion. The Generation of 1880 itself acquired political strength from several sources. They controlled the army, elections (through fraud if necessary), and the only real political party. They made most significant decisions among themselves, by a process of *acuerdo*—informal "agreement" with members of the executive branch—not by public contestation and debate.

In time, socioeconomic pressures forced aristocrats to broaden the base of the political system and relinquish part of their monopoly. In spite, and because, of its success, the export-import strategy provoked discontent among three major factions: (1) newly prosperous landown-ers of the coastal region; (2) descendants of old aristocratic families, often from the distant interior, who were unable to profit from the export-import pattern of growth; and (3) middle-class people who took part in the economic expansion but were excluded from the strong-holds of power. In the 1890s these three social elements combined to form the Radical party. Led first by Leandro Alem and then by Hipól-ito Yrigoyen, the Radicals boycotted elections against fraud and at-tempted a series of abortive political coups. Undeterred by failure, the Unión Cívica Radical (UCR, or Radical Civic Union) and its supporters continued their steadfast pursuit of political power. Intimately con-nected to the country's export-import development, they did not want to alter the existing political and economic structure as much as to con-trol it.

While the Radicals persisted in their opposition, President Roque Saenz Peña promoted an electoral reform in 1911–12 that called for univer-sal male suffrage, the secret ballot, and compulsory voting. Despite its apparently democratic implications, the plan was clearly meant to strengthen and perpetuate the prevailing oligarchic system. Alarmed by labor agitation and concurrent threats of violence, Saenz Peña and his colleagues wanted to assure stability through co-optation of the Radicals. In a way, the Saenz Peña reform was a tacit *acuerdo*; as such, it enabled a smooth transition from oligarchic to co-optative democ-racy.

With the application of the voting law in 1912, the Argentine politi-cal system underwent fundamental transformations. First, the popular base expanded. As under previous law, all Argentine males more than eighteen years of age were allowed to vote; nearly 1 million could claim this right in 1912, a number that would climb to 3.6 million by the mid-1940s. Because of the mandatory voting clause and the reduction in fraud, electoral turnout was high. But the Saenz Peña reform opened the political system in a limited, restrictive way. By excluding the large number of unnaturalized working-class immigrants, the law actually of-fered voting rights to less than half the adult male population around the date of its first application. In effect, suffrage was effectively ex-tended from the upper class to selected segments of the middle class but not to the urban working class.

A second, and immediate, result of these changes was to ensconce the Radical party in power. Yrigoyen won the presidential election of 1916. In keeping with the performance of the liberal state elsewhere in Latin America, he crushed a labor movement in 1918–19. The violence of this episode would be remembered as the "tragic week" of Argen-tina's history, and its frightful legacy (plus continuing repression) would help keep labor quiescent for another generation. Institutionally, how-ever, the political system came to represent a potential threat to the socioeconomic system, even in the absence of major disagreements over policy, through both the rise of professional politicians and the state's incipient autonomy.

Subsequent tension in the political sphere was exacerbated by the world economic crash of 1929, though Argentina was not hit as early or as hard as some countries. The prices and values of beef exports held firm until 1931. The wheat market was suffering badly, but mainly because of a drought; besides, grain farmers exerted scant political influence, partly because so many were still unnaturalized immigrants. In 1930 real wages underwent a brief decline and unemployment was starting to spread, but labor agitation was still at a modest level.

As a crisis swelled over the continuing legitimacy of the semidemocratic system, the opposition responded with force. In September 1930 a coalition of officers and aristocrats ousted Yrigoyen and set up a provisional government. The new leadership was divided in many ways but agreed on one basic point: the state should be restored to its traditional position in the service of dominant socioeconomic forces. One group, led by General Agustín P. Justo, sought a return to pre-1916 (or pre-1912) politics. This faction believed that Yrigoyen had grossly abused electoral and parliamentary procedures. With him and his followers out of the way, conflict would be restrained, the threat of class struggle would disappear, the *gente bien* would rule once again. Semidemocracy would resume its proper functions, and Argentina could salvage and strengthen its export-import pattern of growth.

Another group, led by General José F. Uriburu, had a more drastic solution: the creation of a semifascist corporate state. The problem was not Yrigoyen or his partisans but the system itself, they maintained. Combining some versions of Catholic precepts with admiration of Mussolini's Italy, Uriburu sought to establish a hierarchical order based on social function. He thought the vote should be "qualified" so the most cultivated members of society would have predominant influence on elections; he wanted to reorganize congress to take power away from political professionals—"agents of political committees," as he disdainfully called them. In his "functional democracy," legislators would represent not parties but corporate interests—such as ranchers, farmers, workers, merchants, industrialists, and so on. This kind of vertical structure would create a basis for rule by consensus, eliminate class conflict, and, perhaps most important—in Argentina—reintegrate the political system and economic systems.

Although Uriburu directed the provisional government, the Justo group eventually won out. Elections took place but only within strict limits: apologists described the rigging of results as "patriotic fraud," while opponents came to lament the 1930s as a "tragic decade." Justo and his collaborators stressed the need for harmony, for *Concordancia*. Politics was as it used to be.

Seeking to rescue the export-import pattern of growth, the Justo administration negotiated the Roca-Runciman Pact of 1933. Under this agreement Britain promised to uphold its import quotas for Argentine beef and allow for state participation in the meat-packing business in return for firm commitments on the peso-pound exchange rate and preferential tariffs for British-made goods. Controversial from the moment it was signed, the Roca-Runciman treaty represented the consummate effort by a Latin American nation to resurrect the benefits of the liberal *economía agroimportadora.*

At the same time, Argentina's policymakers began to turn toward import-substitution industrialization. As foreign goods and capital were growing scarce, economic architects of the *Concordancia* began to promote domestic investment. None other than Luis Duhau, the minister of agriculture, described the rationale for the government program in late 1933:

> The historic stage of our prodigious growth under the direct stimulus of the European economy has finished. . . . After writing off the external stimulus, due to the confused and disturbing state of the world economy and policy, the country should look into itself, with its own resources, for the relief of its present difficulties. The plan proposes to stimulate efficiently industrial output using two different means: the construction of reproductive public works and by adjusting imports to the country's real capacity to pay.

To dispel any possible ambiguity, Federico Pinedo, the minister of the treasury, made clear that tariff protection was intended to promote domestic industry:

> The execution of a vast program of public works will result in an immediate increase in the demand for a great quantity and variety of goods which Argentina produces, or could produce. And here we reach a point which must be noted: the preventive control of imports will enable us to avoid such a demand stimulating imports, so that it will be used to promote domestic economic activities.[15]

In keeping with these goals, Argentine leaders implemented a complex package of interventionist measures. They increased import duties and, as noted, expanded public works, especially through a massive road-building campaign. They used multiple exchange rates in order to encourage exports and discourage imports. To sustain aggregate demand, the government in 1933 devalued the peso, a step that not only favored exports over imports, but also reversed the falling trend in the domestic price level, which had transferred income away from entrepreneurs with net debtor positions. While maintaining balanced budgets, authorities expanded real federal expenditures, which by 1937 were 27 percent above the 1932 level. Moreover, the Justo economic team founded the Central Bank (in 1935) and established a series of regulatory agencies to monitor rural products.

In general, these interventionist policies achieved remarkable success. After dropping by 14 percent between 1929 and 1932, GDP expanded every year until 1940. During this entire period the growth in manufacturing decisively outpaced the rural sector. No serious open urban unemployment existed in Argentina after 1934. By 1939 the real Argentine GDP was nearly 15 percent above the level of 1929 and 33 percent above that of 1932—indicating that, all in all, Argentina's performance was much stronger than that of the United States under the New Deal.[16]

Curiously, then, it was a government explicitly devoted to the interests of the landowning class that articulated and espoused a program of import-substitution industrialization in Argentina. Messrs. Duhau and Pinedo saw no inherent contradiction in this fact. They regarded industrial and agricultural development as entirely compatible with one another and, indeed, probably surmised that much of the industrial investment would come from the landed elite. Like contemporaries elsewhere, they also made sharp distinctions between natural and artificial industries.

Policymakers of the *Concordancia* promoted industrial development as an essentially defensive maneuver, as a means of coping with unfavorable circumstances. As Carlos Díaz-Alejandro observes, "Economic authorities were not committed to industrialization per se, as the Perón regime would claim to be in later years, and lacked a clearly articulated industrialization plan (which few countries had at that time)."[17] And as Díaz-Alejandro implies, the political die was thus cast. Initially an achievement of a neoaristocratic coalition, ISI would eventually become the rallying cry of a surging populist movement.

Political confrontations and indecision during World War II led to another military coup in 1943. Concurrent with this development was a continuing growth in the size and consciousness of the urban working class, many of whose members had migrated from the countryside to the city—only to find that real wages were falling below their 1929 levels. Literate, mobile, and articulate, if not always well organized, the urban proletariat was emerging as a major social force.

Enter an ambitious colonel named Juan Perón. Using his position as secretary of labor, and later minister of war as well as vice president, Perón employed a carrot-and-stick method to win the support of industrial workers: old laboring groups and new, lifelong urban residents, as well as recent migrants from the pampas. A hero to the *descamisados* (or "shirtless ones," somewhat like the *sansculottes* of revolutionary France), Perón won the presidential election of 1946 with a solid 54 percent majority—over the indiscreet resistance of the U.S. State Department and the combined opposition of all the traditional political parties.

Once in office, Perón turned toward what I have called industrial developmentalism—or, more explicitly, import-substitution industrialization. The idea was to promote industrial development through activist state policies. This would enhance the nation's economic independence, create a new social cadre of businessmen beholden to Perón, and, in this way, build and consolidate a populist coalition.

To pursue this goal Perón constructed an informal corporate state. Argentine society was thenceforth to be organized according to functional groups: industrialists, farmers, laborers, and so on, with a powerful state at the top. Conflicts between the various sectors would be resolved by governmental fiat, presumably to maintain social harmony. In general, the overall scheme bore striking resemblance to the corporate utopia envisioned by Uriburu in the early 1930s. This fact alone is not surprising, since both Perón (who took part in the 1930 overthrow of Yrigoyen) and Uriburu found ideological inspiration in Mussolini's Italy. Yet the difference was as profound as it was simple: Perón established urban workers as one of the central pillars in his political edifice, along with the armed forces, whereas Uriburu would have relegated labor to a minor position.

The state intensified its interventionist role in economic affairs. A host of statutes came forth to regulate the organization of functional groups. Institutions sprang up to govern the economy. Most notable among them was the Instituto Argentino de Promoción del Intercambio (IAPI), which set up a state-run monopoly on exports and used its earnings to promote industrial development. The result was a massive transfer of resources from the rural sector through the state to the nascent manufacturing sector. In declaring its purposes, the administration even launched a Five-Year Economic Plan.

Notwithstanding these appearances, the Peronist state did not have a truly coherent economic strategy. It had, above all, a political agenda—the nurturing of the populist, multiclass coalition. Accordingly, the role of the state was not to take over direct command of economic matters; it was to organize, administer, and coordinate disparate economic forces. (State-run enterprises under Perón did not usually usurp the role of the domestic private sector; on the contrary, they tended to concentrate on services and infrastructure. Only IAPI came to pose an intrusive challenge to established interests.) In the final analysis, economic policy sought to achieve and maintain equilibrium among social and political forces. Despite its authoritarian features, the Peronist state did not enjoy much genuine autonomy: it relied more on regulation than leadership, more on political adjustments than coherent planning.[18]

ISI appeared to work at first. Argentina's gross domestic product grew by 8.6 percent in 1946 and at the startling rate of 12.6 percent in 1947. That same year Perón paid off the country's entire foreign debt, marking the occasion with a ceremonial "declaration of economic independence." In 1948 Argentina nationalized the British-owned railways, and later took over foreign interests in telephone and port facilities. The manufacturing sector flourished, especially in the consumer goods sector, and workers fared well at the start. Using a variety of means, including the encouragement and forced settlement of strikes, Perón brought about a significant reallocation of economic benefits. The wage and salary share of national income, which by one measure fluctuated around 45 percent in the decade prior to 1946, reached an unprecedented height of 60 percent in the years from 1949 through 1954.

Around 1949, however, economic difficulties began to appear. The exhaustion of foreign reserves—due more to the importing needs of consumer-oriented industry and the cost of welfare programs than to carelessness or corruption (often alleged to explain overpayment for British-owned railroads in 1948)—started a cycle of inflation. Drought curtailed the production of primary goods for export and consumption. World market prices for key exports fell off, and international demand for Argentine beef began to decline. The rising cost of importables slowed industrial production. As a result, real wages sagged. Per capita GNP declined sharply after 1948 and reached a nadir in 1952; by 1955 per capita output was still below the 1947–48 levels. The political implications were extremely grave; Argentina was entering a zero-sum game.

Perón reacted to this situation in two ways. On the one hand, he loosened state control of the economy. IAPI relaxed its grip on the export sector, the government slowed down its drive to industrialization, and doors were reopened to foreign investment—as in the celebrated Standard Oil contract of 1954. A series of orthodox stabilization measures cut back the inflation rate. Eventually the state stopped fixing wages and prices and allowed real wages to decline. On the other hand, the regime tightened its political control. The year 1949 saw not only the explicit formulation of *Justicialista* ideology but also the creation of the highly organized Peronist party (Partido Peronista). And Perón began to accelerate the cycle of conflict. Unwisely, at least in retrospect, he attempted to meddle in internal military affairs. After Evita's death in 1952, he turned his attention from the army to the labor unions, led now by faithful loyalists. A Peronist crowd pillaged the aristocratic Jockey Club in 1953. He quarreled with the Church in 1954. As tension mounted, Perón had only the starkest of alternatives: arming the workers for civil war, or leaving office. Faced by this dilemma, Perón quit the country in 1955.

In retrospect, the Peronist experiment aptly illustrates the weaknesses of ISI development. Typically, import-substitution industrialization produces a spurt of growth in the short run but encounters limits in the medium and longer term. National markets, especially in countries with modest populations, are subject to saturation; production processes continue to require substantial imports of capital goods; higher production costs are passed on to consumers in protected markets; near monopoly discourages investment in technology. Once established under state protectionism and sheltered by tariff walls, highly subsidized and inefficient local firms are unable to compete in the international market. Moreover, concentrating resources in industrial development tends to weaken the agricultural sector. After Perón's departure, ISI would produce a series of "stop-go" cycles in Argentina, each one

punctuated by more and more drastic political solutions. Fragile democracies would give way to increasingly institutionalized and repressive military dictatorships. Ultimately, Argentina and major Latin
American countries would turn away from industrial developmentalism
in search of yet new strategies.

Reflections on the Role of the State

Over the course of history, the state has performed an activist role in
the economic development of Latin America. Such a pattern is by no
means unique to the region. Even in allegedly laissez-faire capitalist
societies, such as the late nineteenth-century United States, the state
has performed vital economic functions. Indeed, the whole concept of
a laissez-faire state exists only as theoretical construct, not as empirical
reality, and even then it is tautological: the state would adopt a mini-
malist posture toward economic matters on the basis of political decisions, rather than in deference to some abstract higher truth. A state
choosing to refrain from economic activism is nonetheless making a
choice.

Nor does the Latin American state's economic role in itself provide a
convincing explanation for the persistence of poverty, underdevelopment, or backwardness throughout the region. It must be noted, first,
that periods of substantial growth and transformation have prevailed
throughout Latin American history. In its own terms, the mercantilist
strategy of the colonial period achieved a considerable measure of success for Spain; so did the liberal approach of the nineteenth century
and the import-substitution model of the twentieth century for Latin
America. Second, the inherent limitations within these strategies derived not from the state's performance. The central difficulty came not
from incapacity within the state—ignorance, corruption, inefficiency—
or from the extent of state participation in the economy.

The principal shortcoming derived, rather, from the internal logic of
the development strategies themselves. In Latin America none of the
major alternatives—mercantilism, liberalism, or industrial developmentalism—could provide a long-term path toward self-sustaining economic growth with social equity. Within its historical context, each
strategy enjoyed a good deal of ideological support and had political
backing. But each one also contained internal contradictions that proved
ultimately fatal. And it is revealing that these successive experiments
took place within ever shortening time frames: mercantilism lasted for
centuries, liberalism thrived for perhaps half a century, and import-
substitution industrialization endured for a matter of decades. Time
has been growing short in Latin America.

Whatever the reason, repeated cycles of innovation and experimen-
tation have not bequeathed to Latin America the developmental capa-

bilities that have recently become so evident in postwar Asia. Why has Latin America not been able to emulate the experience of postwar Japan? Or of the "four tigers"—Singapore, South Korea, Taiwan, and Hong Kong? Why has Latin America not erected the kind of "developmental state" so essential to Asian success?

As described in the Pacific/Asian region, the developmental state not only establishes rules and regulations for economic activity, it also establishes priorities and preferences for the structure and content of economic development. According to Chalmers Johnson, it has several key characteristics:

> A developmental elite creates political stability over the long term, maintains sufficient equality in distribution to prevent class or sectoral exploitation (land reform is critical), sets national goals and standards that are internationally oriented and based on nonideological external referents, creates (or at least recognizes) a bureaucratic elite capable of administering the system, and insulates its bureaucrats from direct political influence so that they can function technocratically. It does not monopolize economic management or decision making, permit the development of political pluralism that might challenge its goals, or waste valuable resources by suppressing noncritical sectors (it discriminates against them with disincentives and then ignores them).[19]

Policy choices by the development state must be "market-conforming" to work, and must be based on economic and not political agendas.

The developmental state, as Johnson suggests, is "normally authoritarian."[20] (It does not necessarily follow, however, that a democratic regime would be inherently incapable of performing developmental functions.)[21] Regrettably enough, Latin America has no trouble meeting this political criterion. Authoritarianism has been the prevailing type of regime throughout the region's history, and even the trend toward democratization during the 1980s contains and/or disguises persisting authoritarian features.[22]

Indeed, some governmental episodes in Latin America bear close resemblance to the profile of the developmental state. For better or worse, the colonial period's mercantilist state more or less met the definitional criteria. (Revealingly enough, Johnson from time to time describes the developmental state as "neomercantilist.")[23] Some of the liberal states in Latin America, particularly under Porfirio Díaz in Mexico (1876–1910) and perhaps the Generation of 1880 in Argentina (1880–1930), shared some features of the developmental model. In more recent times, Brazil under military rule (especially 1964–74) and Chile under Augusto Pinochet (1973–88) would be candidates for inclusion in this general category. So might Mexico under the PRI.[24] Yet even these resemblances are partial, imperfect, and infrequent.

Why not the developmental state? Let us begin by dispensing with "national character" explanations and with simple-minded culturalist arguments about the "Confucian ethic" and "Hispanic legacy." They are circular (Asians act like Asians because they are Asian; Mexicans act like Mexicans because they are Mexican). They are ahistorical, since they cannot account for change over time. They are atheoretical, because they cite culture as a cause but do not explain the cause of the culture itself. They tend to discourage, rather than encourage, social inquiry. And for the most part, they are superficial and deterministic.

Nor is it a matter of bureaucratic competence. As in Japan, the colonial Spanish American bureaucracy recruited its membership from the most capable and well-trained segments of society. Likewise, the liberal state in Argentina and elsewhere staffed its ranks with skilled and highly educated elements. Industrial developmentalism drew its inspiration from the work of such celebrated international economists as Raúl Prebisch, and, as their nickname suggests, the "Chicago boys" who served the Pinochet regime in Chile had received advanced training at a prestigious U.S. university. To be sure, Latin American public bureaucracies may not possess the intellectual depth of their Asian counterparts—that is, they probably have not had equivalent levels of training and skill at lower and middle ranks—and this would no doubt have an impact on policy implementation. In and of itself, however, governmental capacity cannot account for discrepancies in regional economic performance.

A plausible explanation might focus on three factors. One concerns the international environment. Japan and the gang of four flourished most dramatically during the period of the now defunct Cold War. This brought considerable benefits, in terms of both aid and trade. Latin America, on the other hand, entered the world economy at a much earlier stage, and in the postwar period it never counted as a "frontline state" in the struggle against international Communism.[25] It was always a backyard of the United States, physically and figuratively; the Alliance for Progress was nothing like the Marshall Plan. In other words, Latin America always had to confront the harsh realities resulting from its marginal importance to the global economy and from U.S. hegemony throughout the region. It has been genuinely "dependent" in numerous and significant ways. Notwithstanding the current eclipse of *dependencia* analysis, the issues and consequences associated with dependency continue to demand serious attention.[26]

Another factor is the relative weakness of Latin America's capitalist class. The developmental state in Asia has typically relied on a collaboration with a vital and vigorous private sector. The prototypical case entails massive industrial conglomerates: *zaibatsu* or *keiretsu* in Japan, *chaebol* in Korea. These private firms have provided capital, accepted risk, and reaped rewards from economic change. Nothing comparable has existed in Latin America. Suggestively enough, episodes bearing some resemblance to the developmental state—Argentina under the landed oligarchy, Brazil under the generals—have occurred in times and places where the private sector has been relatively strong. For the most part, however, the private-public partnership characteristic of the developmental state has not flourished for a simple reason: one of the key partners has been missing.

Third, and last, is the issue of state autonomy. Theoretically and empirically, the developmental state enjoys a large degree of autonomy: it can define goals on the basis of economic rather than political criteria; it can impose its decisions on unwilling segments of the private sector and society; and it can implement policy over sustained periods of time. Stability and continuity enable the developmental state to persist in "plan-rational" behavior in the medium-to-long term.

Ever since the achievement of independence, Latin American states have had modest degrees of autonomy, at least by Asian standards. They have been subject to constant pressure from within and without; their decisions have been susceptible to veto by power groups at home, such as the landed oligarchy or organized labor, or abroad, such as the United States. At times dominant interests have often sought to *exploit* the state, especially during the liberal phase, rather than build up its autonomy. There have been instances of harmony between the public and private sectors—when, in its crudest form, the state has functioned as an "executive secretariat" for domestic and/or foreign capital—but these have been transitory episodes that have relied on enormous amounts of authoritarian repression. With the possible exception of postrevolutionary Mexico, even the populist authoritarian states that often initiated ISI policies proved unable to insulate themselves from political and societal pressures.

To some extent the level of social mobilization in Latin America has deprived the state of long-lasting autonomy. The peoples of Latin America have for centuries struggled to promote their interests through group solidarity, collective organization, and demands on public agencies. They have attempted, in one way or another, to use state power to challenge and curtail the power of oligarchs and vested interests. The general strike, with street demonstrations and volatile rhetoric, conveys a stereotypical image of contemporary Latin America: chaotic, verbose, inefficient. But in a deeper sense, it reflects the vigor and dynamism of Latin American society. Resolute insistence on the right to self-expression may have hindered the path of economic development; it also offers compelling witness to the power and durability of popular aspirations.

Notes

1. Strong in the sixteenth century, the colonial bureaucracy declined in quality and influence during the seventeenth century and recuperated during the eighteenth.

2. For a majestic treatise on the evolution of creole patriotism, see D. A. Brading, *The First America: The Spanish Monarchy, Creole Patriots, and the Liberal State, 1492–1867* (Cambridge: Cambridge Univ. Press, 1991).

3. Arnold Bauer, "Rural Spanish America, 1870–1930," in Leslie Bethell (ed.), *Cambridge History of Latin America,* vol. 4 (Cambridge: Cambridge Univ. Press, 1986), 177.

4. See Charles A. Hale, *Mexican Liberalism in the Age of Mora, 1821–1853* (New Haven: Yale Univ. Press, 1968), Hale, *The Transformation of Mexican Liberalism in Late Nineteenth-Century Mexico* (Princeton: Princeton University Press, 1989); and Brading, *First America,* chap. 29.

5. Steven Topik, "The Economic Role of the State in Liberal Regimes: Brazil and Mexico Compared, 1888–1910," in Joseph L. Love and Nils Jacobsen (eds.), *Guiding the Invisible Hand: Economic Liberalism and the State in Latin American History* (New York: Praeger, 1988), 136.

6. *Ibid.,* 117–44.

7. See Charles Bergquist, *Labor in Latin America: Comparative Essays on Chile, Argentina, Venezuela, and Colombia* (Stanford: Stanford Univ. Press, 1986).

8. Peter H. Smith, "The Failure of Democracy in Argentina, 1916–1930," in Juan Linz and Alfred Stepan (eds.), *The Breakdown of Democratic Regimes* (Baltimore: Johns Hopkins Univ. Press, 1978), part 3, 3–27.

9. Joseph L. Love, "Structural Change and Conceptual Response in Latin America and Romania, 1860–1950," in Love and Jacobsen (eds.), *Invisible Hand,* 1–33, esp. 23–25.

10. Joseph L. Love, "Raúl Prebisch and the Origins of the Doctrine of Unequal Exchange," *Latin American Research Review* 15: 3 (1980); 45–72. During the 1950s ECLA also published reports warning that ISI could work only in countries with large-scale domestic markets.

11. Tulio Halperín Donghi, "Argentina: Liberalism in a Country Born Liberal," in Love and Jacobsen (eds.), *Invisible Hand,* 99–116. The observation is reminiscent of the argument in Louis Hartz (ed.), *The Founding of New Societies* (New York: Harcourt, Brace, & World, 1964).

12. Halperín, "Liberalism," 100; Brading, *First America,* 621–28; and Nicolas Shumway, *The Invention of Argentina* (Berkeley: Univ. of California Press, 1991).

13. See Shumway, *Invention,* esp. 67–80.

14. See Carlos H. Waisman, *Reversal of Development in Argentina: Postwar Counterrevolutionary Policies and Their Structural Consequences* (Princeton: Princeton Univ. Press, 1987), 5–7.

15. As quoted in Carlos F. Díaz-Alejandro, *Essays on the Economic History of the Argentine Republic* (New Haven: Yale Univ. Press, 1970), 104–5.

16. *Ibid.,* 94–95.

17. *Ibid.,* 105.

18. See Waisman, *Reversal,* esp. chaps. 5–6.

19. Chalmers Johnson, "Political Institutions and Economic Performance: The Government-Business Relationship in Japan, South Korea, and Taiwan," in Frederic C. Deyo (ed.), *The Political Economy of the New Asian Industrialism* (Ithaca: Cornell Univ. Press, 1987), 136–64, with quote from 142–43. See also Chalmers Johnson, *MITI and the Japanese Miracle: The Growth of Industrial Policy, 1925–1975* (Stanford: Stanford Univ. Press, 1982), esp. chap. 1, "The Japanese Miracle."

20. Johnson, "Political Institutions," 143–45.

21. One difficulty with the idea of the "developmental state" is that it combines issues of both structure and function.

22. See Peter H. Smith, "Crisis and Democracy in Latin America," *World Politics* 43: 4 (July 1991), 608–34.

23. Johnson, *MITI*, 17.

24. A socialist "command economy," as in Cuba under Fidel Castro, does not qualify as a developmental state.

25. See Peter Evans, "Class, State, and Dependence in East Asia: Lessons for Latin Americanists," in Deyo (ed.), *Political Economy*; and Laurence Whitehead, "Tigers in Latin America?" *Annals of the American Academy of Political and Social Sciences* 505 (Sept. 1989), 142–51.

26. Papers presented at the conference on "Conceptual Approaches Toward the Third World in the Post–Cold War Era," sponsored by the Center for Iberian and Latin American Studies at the University of California, San Diego, May 1991, repeatedly stressed this idea. The point is particularly well captured by the title of a paper by Richard Fagen: "Dependency Is Dead! Long Live Backwardness, Inequality, Underdevelopment, Etc.!"

3

The State of Economics in Brazil and Latin America: Is the Past Prologue to the Future?

ALBERT FISHLOW

Introduction

Brazilian development in the post–World War II period presents Latin American success and failure in dramatic contrast. Initially, the Brazilian story was one of exception. Together with Mexico, Brazil was able to implement with relative success the import-substitution model of industrialization in the1950s, at a time when the early leaders in development, Argentina and Chile, failed. When that model faltered in the early 1960s, Brazil, under military dictatorship, was able to pursue a more open strategy that led to the "Brazilian Miracle" of 1968–73: extraordinarily rapid economic expansion averaging more than 10 percent a year. This gave way to the oil crisis, lesser expansion, and the accumulation of foreign debt. With the second oil shock of 1979 came a new effort at growth, but it had to be curtailed in 1981 as the country contracted under external pressure.

The story of the 1980s was unique. With the exception of significant but soon-to-fail economic recovery under the new civilian leadership in 1985 and 1986, the decade had been one of an aggregate decline in gross domestic product. Much of the explanation resides in the significant accumulation of debt, and the difficulty of servicing it during this period. A second civilian president, Fernando Collor de Mello, proved no more able to sustain his plans of economic recovery upon taking office early in 1990. Brazil now lags behind the continent's other major countries—Argentina, Chile, and Mexico—in achieving lower inflation rates and a return to regular increases in output.

This essay consists of four parts.[1] Part 1 briefly chronicles Brazil's economic evolution during the postwar period. Part 2 analyzes the specific blend of Brazilian politics and economics after 1973, focusing on three issues: First is the decision to follow a model of debt accumulation in the 1970s and to continue to expand, even if at a lower rate than during the miracle period. Second is an emphasis on the stabilization efforts of the early 1980s, including the first dependence on an IMF program since the 1964 military takeover. Third is a focus upon the Cruzado Plan in early 1986, an effort at stabilization that seemed to succeed initially but failed in the end. That failure, followed by the lack of success of subsequent ventures, including the Collor efforts in 1990 and 1991, defines the current crucial question: Can Brazil recover?

Part 3 casts the role of Brazil more broadly by focusing on the position of the state in Latin American economic development. Reduced government intervention seems to be the winning strategy. Earlier presumptions about the clear benefits of public guidance no longer orient development strategy in most countries of the region. Instead, claims about the advantages of market liberalization and privatization of state enterprise have gained new vitality. The decline of central planning in the former socialist countries provides added force. The new commitment to reduced state participation comes less from newfound ideological conviction about the virtues of the market than from ineffective macroeconomic policy in the 1980s. The principal problem confronted by the countries of the region is a fiscal shortfall, not massive inefficiency resulting from misallocation of resources.

Part 4 provides a short conclusion to this essay by focusing on two alternative directions of future change in the design of the developmental state in Latin America.

1. Evolution of the Brazilian Economy

Brazil entered the period following World War II with a virtually clean slate after reaching a debt reduction agreement in 1946. It was not long before new entry of capital became necessary to finance an ambitious industrialization drive. Disappointed by the absence of expected lending from the United States in the aftermath of close wartime collaboration, Brazil had to turn to private sources. Total capital inflows from direct investment and loans increased sharply after 1955, especially in the form of medium-term suppliers' credits. Inflation and external debt rose again as budget deficits increased and balance of payments problems became more severe. President Juscelino Kubitschek broke with the IMF rather than jeopardize rapid growth and his industrialization target program, and found finance elsewhere through reductions in reserves, short-term swap loans, and other compensatory measures. At the end of 1960, the external debt was double its 1955 level, and the new president, Jânio Quadros, faced serious debt and accelerating inflation.

In an effort to resolve these financial difficulties, ties with the IMF were restored and more orthodox policies followed. But that effort at stabilization was ended prematurely with Quadros's resignation in August 1961. Intense political agitation was added to economic disequilibrium. Quadros's successor, João Goulart, was viewed by conservative forces with suspicion, as a populist at best, and perhaps more radically inclined. After the stabilization program had been irreparably weakened by the concession of large public sector wage increases, the withdrawal of the IMF mission in 1962 complicated access to needed new external resources. Despite the new funds potentially available under the aegis of the Alliance for Progress, the United States was increasingly reluctant to support Goulart's reform efforts. Finally, as the economic situation deteriorated, a loan program was negotiated with the United States in 1963, but the conditions for its disbursement were never fulfilled. During this turbulent period capital inflow virtually ceased. The World Bank, previously an important source of official resources for Brazil, did not authorize a single loan to the country between 1960 and 1964.

When the military seized power in April 1964, inflation had mounted to almost 100 percent annually and housewives were protesting in the streets. The middle class welcomed the demise of a Goulart government that was both leftist and ineffectual. The new government predictably found a more favorable international reception. Debt rescheduling was facilitated, and new loans from the Agency for International Development as well as new IMF credits were made available.

However, debt rescheduling and new credits did not prevent a stabilization-induced recession, the result of contractionary monetary and fiscal policies. Import demand fell because of the reduction in aggregate demand. Combined with a recovery of exports, this produced trade surpluses from 1964 to 1966 and eliminated arrears and other short-term debts. The supportive international environment, however, helped prevent an even steeper decline in income and allowed the resumption of import growth in the early stages of recovery in 1967.

As Brazilian growth accelerated after 1967, the government embarked on a policy of tapping private capital to underwrite rapid expansion. Brazil was one of the first countries to respond in the late 1960s, when the Eurodollar market first welcomed and then actively sought developing countries as borrowers. Brazil relied more extensively on this external capital market than did any other developing country. It implemented a debt-led model of development to help finance the mushrooming capital and the intermediate goods imports associated with "miracle" rates of growth, which averaged close to 10 percent between 1968 and 1973. Another component of the growth strategy was explicit adaptation to inflation through indexation, not only of wages, rents, and financial assets (as introduced in 1964) but also of the exchange rate in 1968.

When the oil shock struck in late 1973, Brazil was the largest oil importer among the developing countries. Already faced with the prospect of weakening growth as the boom matured, the government was not inclined to risk a significant decline in real income from the sudden adverse terms of trade. Increased external debt was an attractive alternative. Borrowing could postpone the contractionary effects of the petroleum "tax" and permit domestic expansion to proceed. After a surge of imports and an increased current account deficit, Brazil opted to make adjustments through an ambitious program of generalized import substitution rather than export promotion or domestic recession.

An elastic supply of debt and brief episodes of slowed domestic activity were adequate to keep the balance of payments under control after 1973. Higher coffee and other commodity prices also contributed by reversing the terms of trade decline. Brazilian economic performance after the oil price shock remained above its growth level of 7 percent per year, and the results evoked widespread admiration for the success of the growth-led debt model. Now growth requirements determined the need for debt, rather than available capital permitting higher growth rates. Petrodollar recycling apparently had worked to transfer considerable resources to worthy developing countries, sustaining high rates of investment and economic growth. What had been only expedient to offset a disequilibrium in the world balance of payments turned into a significant development finance policy.

On the eve of the second oil shock, the Brazilian debt was the largest in the world. As such, it was especially vulnerable to the reversal in interest rates that was in the offing. Indeed, the debt had become so great that already in the late 1970s, before the sudden surge in interest rates, the reverse flow of service payments was beginning to cancel new inflows. Whereas the first stage of debt accumulation saw a large transfer of real resources, in later stages more and more borrowing was used simply to cover interest obligations on earlier loans. The dynamics of debt-led debt had become part of the Brazilian story, a process that rising interest rates would magnify with a vengeance.

Not surprisingly, in 1980—after oil prices had risen and interest rates were increasing—Brazil was one of the first countries to test the response of the private capital market to a large debtor facing a balance of payments crisis. Limited additional finance was available and only on more expensive terms as spreads widened. The favored borrowers were oil producers, not oil importers. Well before the generalized debt crisis in 1982, Brazil was forced to introduce a more austere set of policies and domestic adjustment in 1981. For the first time in the postwar period income declined. Brazilian discipline was rewarded with new capital flows. Markets seemed able to respond to debt problems with the right dosage of conditional liquidity, and countries seemed able to implement the right amount of belt-tightening.

When Mexico declared its virtual default in August 1982, Brazil—itself subject to sharply higher interest rates—replayed its earlier approach to private creditors. The Brazilian government insisted that its situation was distinct from that of Mexico and was capable of simple remedy. Government officials claimed that Brazil's domestic policies made it creditworthy and that the country needed only minimal new resources. With a congressional election in November threatening the government's control, politics precluded any official appeal to the IMF until after the votes had been counted. Then the inevitable acceptance of IMF supervision occurred, and Brazil joined the rapidly lengthening queue of problem cases. But Brazil did so with the disadvantage of having had its own, inadequate stabilization program on the table beforehand, which only served to reduce the amount of finance made available.

Brazil was therefore impelled to a stronger adjustment of its external accounts. What differentiated Brazil from other large Latin American debtors was a greater export recovery in 1984. Between 1982 and 1984, export receipts rose by 35 percent; with an almost 30 percent decline in imports, the current account was quickly balanced, and the foreign exchange constraint became less pressing. Led by industrial exports, output in 1984 was already on the way up. While the results for Brazil were worse than the Great Depression, the intervening decline in per capita income was smaller than for other problem debtors. Brazil's more diversified industrial base allowed for both export increases and import substitution.

In this sense, Brazilian adjustment was more successful than that elsewhere. In another sense it was less successful—progress in the external account was not matched internally. No sooner had successive letters of intent under IMF programs been dispatched than they became obsolete through accelerating inflation, which did violence to the monetary targets. This experience led to the development of new deficit concepts, adjusted for the widespread indexation of government debt, which are now widely applied to other countries. The Brazilian experience also led many, but not all, economists to the understanding that improving the balance of payments was not tightly linked to domestic equilibrium. Indeed, trade surpluses might themselves create new problems for macroeconomic policy.

A new civilian government took office in March 1985, and the rules of the stabilization game profoundly changed. In the hands of these leaders Brazil's large export surplus, only recently established, became a potent instrument of independence. Relations with the IMF deteriorated, and previous plans for a multiyear rescheduling agreement were scrapped. Although interest was fully paid, no inflows of new capital ensued. Recovery was now based on internal demand, with limited increase in imports. Inflation began to accelerate from already record levels of more than 200 percent. Despite strong output growth, additional worrying signs appeared: high real interest rates and increasing government internal debt service, low investment rates, and stagnant exports. Bold measures were necessary.

One such measure—the Plano Cruzado—was implemented in February 1986 as a substitute for a conventional recession-based strategy of stabilization. The similar Argentine Austral Plan had been put into place seven months earlier. Both were based on the premise that high inflation rates were driven by the inertial, self-replicating force of indexation. Accordingly, the Cruzado Plan forced a sophisticated, short-term standstill that maintained real income and abolished future indexation. Henceforth, inflation would be zero. In the words of then finance minister Dilson Funaro, Brazil would be a country of "Swiss inflation and Japanese growth." For a few months it seemed true, and generalized euphoria prevailed. But signs of disequilibrium from excess demand mounted without inducing an adequate compensatory response. Another election loomed, and in the best Brazilian political tradition, corrective actions were placed on hold.

Indirect tax increases, announced immediately after the election, proved much too late and much too little. Since their immediate impact was to raise prices, they were ineffective. The dam of controls had broken, and there was no restoring an orderly process of price and wage readjustment. Events rapidly moved out of control as inflation rates mounted. The government seemed powerless to implement policies. The deteriorating balance of payments was as significant as the mounting internal problem. Exports declined sharply as imports continued their modest rise in the last quarter of 1986, and the trade surplus rapidly eroded. Brazil's comfortable cushion of reserves had suddenly disappeared.

In February 1987 Brazil declared a moratorium on the largest part of its commercial bank debt. In part it was a strategy intended to appeal to internal nationalist sentiments and to strengthen support for a beleaguered president. In part it was a misguided effort to obtain broad international support and creditor-government intervention on behalf of a new political solution to the debt problem. And in part it was a final and unavoidable act reflecting errors in macroeconomic policy that contributed to a new liquidity crisis.

Brazil had thus been transformed from the epitome of the successful, well-behaved debtor to the challenger of the entire debt regime, unwilling to accept the burden of external adjustment at the expense of continuing economic growth. In the end, and not long after the event, Brazil was forced to yield and devise an alternative strategy incorporating negotiations with the banks. Industrialized countries appear to have little sympathy for public intervention or broader solutions. The closest resemblance to bold innovation was Citibank's dramatic upward revision of loan-loss reserves, now regularly maintained by all major banks. This accounting change created new possibilities for recording debts on bank books. The Brazilian renegotiation in 1988 once again moved the Brazilian debt to center stage but with disappointing results. Not until the spring of 1989 would official policy move to the side of debt reduction. When it did, Mexico, not Brazil, was the first beneficiary. Indeed, Argentina preceded Brazil in reaching agreement in 1992.

2. The Issues Raised

One theme highlighted by the Brazilian debt experience is the importance of political economy to the domestic response. Borrowing was frequently used as a conscious policy to achieve immediate gains. This is the sometime fatal attraction of debt: it holds out the prospect of something for nothing, at least for the time being. But the piper must eventually be paid. After 1973, Brazilian policymakers incorporated reliance on external finance into their adjustment strategy. When the country unexpectedly benefited from a more adverse international economy, successive administrations were faced with the consequences. Brazil's vaunted technocratic capacity more than met its match in the demands placed on policy by the oil and interest rate shocks. Ministers did not hesitate to improvise. Authoritarian though the government was, it still could not risk the consequences of an orthodox response to external disequilibrium.

Debt management policies were not always optimal. Sometimes they were flawed by inappropriate assumptions and incomplete models. Almost always they bowed to broader political objectives and considerations. For the most part, a controlled transition toward greater civilian participation was an important goal during this period.

Another side to the blend of politics and economics was adjusting to the changed international environment. Three essential elements emerge when considering Brazilian policy between 1979 and early 1986. First is the error of heterodox initiatives adopted in 1980 in a vain effort to sustain rapid economic growth in the face of the deteriorating international economy. Second is the inadequacy of the initial financing of the Fund stabilization program, its nominal monetary and fiscal targets, which were inappropriate for a highly inflation-indexed economy, and the striking divergence between the successful achievement of trade surpluses and increasing domestic disequilibrium. Third is the commitment of the new civilian government to designing its own policies and seeking its own solutions to the problem of sustained economic growth, of which the Cruzado Plan was the eventual outcome.

The key to the Cruzado Plan was recognizing the central role of indexing in projecting price increases into the future. To stop inflation effectively under such conditions requires a coordinated standstill of wages and prices. In order to work, the plan required eliminating other sources of inflationary pressure, especially fiscal deficits. However, fiscal policy was not neutral, and wage policy encouraged rather than restrained real wage increases that had already been in motion as a result of the 1985 expansion.

Comparing the failure of the Cruzado Plan with the 1964–67 success in decelerating inflation suggests three lessons. One is that it is easier to gain control over the fiscal deficit when public debt is small and foreign aid is available. The second is the Cruzado Plan's excessive boldness in aiming for zero inflation and abolishing indexation. While indexation contributes to inflation, it also protects against the kind of volatile inflation that occurred at the end of 1986 and the beginning of 1987. The third is the difficulty of managing neutral disinflation. In 1964 wage compression permitted continued progress in reducing the inflation rate. In 1986 real wages were increasing at the expense of profit margins, helping to provoke shortages, disorderly growth, and the creation of black markets.

The central question of the relation among budget deficits, external finance, and inflation gives rise to two important conclusions. The first is the virtue of clarifying and measuring these deficits in an indexed setting. Simple estimates mislead, compared with more thorough analyses. With a comprehensive analysis, it is possible to design a simple, two-equation model that incorporates debt finance in an open economy and specifies inflation dynamics in response to excess demand and indexing. This illuminates the link between accelerating inflation and the growing inability to finance the public sector deficit externally after 1979. The debt problem here is much deeper than its balance of payments consequences. The domestic macroeconomic structure is profoundly influenced by suddenly limiting access to external finance.

The responsiveness of imports and exports to devaluation is key to the relative weights of expenditure reduction and expenditure switching in adjustment. While Brazilian trade policy has long been protectionist and oriented to import substitution, compensating export subsidies, dating from the late 1960s, have contributed to the rising trend of industrial and nontraditional agricultural exports. Exchange rate indexation from 1968 on largely prevented the extremes of overvaluation seen in earlier periods. The year 1980 was a prominent and costly exception, when Brazil dabbled in "global monetarism." Unfortunately the experiment occurred just when the second oil shock hit; a less propitious moment for overvaluation could hardly have been picked.

Brazil, like other indebted countries, was forced to reduce imports massively after 1981. However, Brazil achieved a large rise in exports in 1984 and surpluses of more than $10 billion annually. This is what made continuing interest payments feasible and also led some to the conclusion that foreign exchange constraints to growth were no longer a central concern.

Closer analysis of Brazilian import demand and export supply casts doubt on this interpretation. Import elasticities in the 1980s show no decisive structural break with the 1970s. Higher growth rates thus imply more than proportional increases in imports, especially of capital goods. Relative price elasticities remain low, limiting the impact of real devaluation. For exports, such limited response is also the rule for primary commodities, which still made up one-third of total export receipts and are also less favorably influenced by expansion in industrial country income. A key point is the influence of capacity utilization, both on import demand and export supply. Prosperity threatens to diminish large trade surpluses rapidly and make increased external financing necessary.

The ultimate concern with the debt problem is its effect on growth and development. A direct measure of the problem's gravity is the continuing low ratio of capital formation to total income. Brazilian investment is inadequate to support high rates of sustained growth, let alone a competitive capability to ensure continued performance in exporting manufactured products. The position of the public sector is badly compromised by the need to extract resources from the private sector for debt service. Uncertainty and inflation encourage speculation in real assets and the black market, and detract from productive capital accumulation. Highly variable real wages provoke strong defensive reactions from organized labor, which is eager to protect labor's real income and is thus unwilling to stop pressing nominal wage demands.

Domestic adjustment can only go so far. Real resource transfers of 4–5 percent of the product cannot continue indefinitely. This is the lesson of the February 1987 moratorium. Analyses that focus on projecting the balance of payments miss this point. Massive trade surpluses are incompatible with high and sustainable rates of Brazilian growth. There are two ways out: more lending or reduced debt service.

Brazil has the capacity to absorb more debt productively. One problem, however, is the unreliable supply of additional flows. The Baker Plan formulated in 1985 has failed to meet its minimal and inadequate targets. The newer Brady Plan, to which increasing numbers of Latin American countries have subscribed, offers more hope. But its debt reduction has not been associated with a new wave of lending. Rather, the wave of the future is to rely on direct foreign investment, as was the case in the 1950s. And here Brazil stands behind Mexico and Chile.

The other difficulty is the great uncertainty of the international environment. Starting from a debt/export ratio that was close to 5 in 1987, no margin for error exists. Brazil is vulnerable to any and all adverse changes in interest rates, terms of trade, and industrialized country growth, not to mention domestic policy errors.

The basic lesson of this survey of Brazilian external debt is how quickly debt can turn from being part of the solution to becoming a central part of the problem. We may be approaching the point where it is again possible to unleash the productive forces in Brazil and other developing countries and to make up for a lost decade of development. But this will depend on understanding the lesson of the 1980s.

3. The Problem of the State

At least through the early 1970s, development economics largely defined itself as a subcategory by its emphasis on market imperfections and the potential for Pareto-improving government intervention. Attention was especially directed to how government could seek out dynamic externalities and exploit large divergences between private and public rates of return on investment. The belief was that private markets would lead to inferior solutions if left to themselves. After all, historical reliance on markets had not closed the development gap.

The World Bank has labeled such a perspective the "public interest" view.[2] One can determine several components. First, there is a problem of providing public goods and infrastructure when market response leads to inadequate supply or natural monopoly. Second, other market failures exist owing to externalities, imperfect information, and so forth. Third, state policy should determine appropriate levels of capital accumulation: future generations are unrepresented in private preferences of the present one. Finally, and not least, the concentration of private power and wealth is a reason for state intervention in the name of social justice and equality. This adds up to an active and positive role for the state by directly producing goods and services, managing revenues and expenditures, and regulating private activity.

In the specific context of Latin America, the theory of industrialization through import substitution enshrined almost all these principles. A pillar of the approach was the belief that static market signals overestimated the returns to primary exports due to the potential deterioration of the terms of trade. Prebisch's emphasis in the late 1940s on an inevitably negative trend rang true scant years after the decline in commodity prices during the Great Depression.[3] On the market's domestic side, private rates of return underestimated the advantages of investment in industry by neglecting three things: the savings gained by avoiding costly imports, the benefits of technological and labor skill externalities, and the consequences of coordinated production decisions. Individual consumption decisions did not add up to an appropriate savings rate, especially given the large disparities in income distribution. The government had not only to offer appropriate shadow prices through trade restrictions and credit and tax subsidies, but to undertake complementary investment in infrastructure and strategic sectors and increase overall capital accumulation.

For some larger Latin American countries, principally Brazil and Mexico, import-substitution policies were compatible with accelerated industrialization and high rates of aggregate growth. From 1953 to 1973, Brazil and Mexico increased their share of regional income from 43 to 54 percent, reflecting their relatively higher growth rates. For other countries the results were deficient. The share of regional income going to Argentina and Chile declined from 27 to 19 percent.[4]

But even where a strategy of import substitution worked, it succeeded at the expense of growing disequilibrium in three critical dimensions. First, policy-induced exchange rate overvaluation discriminated against exports, especially nontraditional ones, making the balance of payments and access to essential imports more precarious. Second, increased government expenditures were not matched by increased tax revenues, which thus gave rise to larger deficits financed primarily by accelerating inflation. Third, emphasizing industrialization frequently occurred at the expense of inadequate agricultural development, leaving significant pockets of rural poverty and hampering development of an ample internal market.

The import-substitution strategy was deliberately unbalanced, and thus not permanently viable even where initially favorable. Successful implementation required a timely adaptive response to stimulate exports, enhance revenues, and sustain increases in agricultural productivity. Few countries were so adroit. The region's first post-1945 development crisis dates to the early 1960s, as evidenced by an aggravating balance of payments problem and rising inflationary pressures afflicting many countries.

External constraints and fiscal deficits motivated new efforts to increase inflows of public resources. Through the creation of the Inter-American Development Bank and the Alliance for Progress, structural reforms were financed. These were still oriented to the domestic economy and in the spirit of public intervention. Indeed, planning was enshrined as a national requirement, and because of its political origins, the Alliance emphasized land reform and greater income equality.

By the mid-1960s, under continuing strains and sometimes under military aegis, the importance of market signals and opportunities for greater export expansion began to be more widely accepted. Import substitution thus was not a monolithic or unchanging doctrine. By the time a professional literature critical of the Latin American import-substitution style began to appear in the late 1960s and 1970s,[5] reality (and local criticism) had already made itself felt.

For Latin America as a whole, economic growth accelerated from 5.2 percent per year in the decade 1953–63 to 6.4 percent in 1963–73. The proportional increase in per capita performance was a much more dramatic 50 percent. The more successful countries were able to sustain a large public presence while also giving greater scope to market signals and the opportunities afforded by continuing expansion of international markets. Export performance and access to imports emerged as the most significant determinants of country growth rates during this period.[6]

Then came the oil shock. After 1973 regional growth slowed but was still higher than the results in other areas. Increased reliance on external indebtedness was an important reason. The true precariousness of the Latin American situation only became apparent when the second oil shock in 1979 coincided with an abrupt rise in real interest rates and developed country recession. Countries had chosen as badly by selecting their new style of adjustment through debt as they could have by following the original import-substitution and interventionist model. Asymmetric integration into the world economy through financial flows instead of exports took a heavy toll. When voluntary capital flows virtually ceased after 1982, the only immediate possibility was drastic reduction in imports and income. The rest of the decade was characterized by large resource transfers, accompanied in most countries by high real interest rates, large deficits financed by internal debt, accelerating inflation, and economic stagnation.[7]

This Great Depression of the 1980s, made more pointed by Asian success, has directed attention to structural deficiency. External agencies, on which almost all countries came to rely, conditioned their money on a greater commitment to liberalization. Plans to assist with the debt burden, whether Baker or Brady, required emphasis on the private sector. At the same time, more open politics and a regular electoral calendar in most Latin American countries have assured mounting domestic debate and pressure to redefine the state's role.

The outcome has been new emphasis on the virtues of the invisible hand. That commitment has been given greater force by two theoretical amendments to the standard Pareto efficiency argument. First, the rent-seeking literature has emphasized the additional distortion created by "directly unproductive profit seeking" in response to opportunities afforded by government intervention.[8] Second, special emphasis has been placed on outward orientation as the key source of successful economic development. A corollary proposition is also frequently added, implicitly or explicitly: liberalized domestic markets, as well as freer imports, are necessary to guarantee the competitiveness required for export growth.[9]

Despite their prominence, neither of these new criticisms of state intervention are decisive. They do not rule out the existence of externalities and imperfections which justified policy activism in the first place. The focus on rent seeking correctly highlights the importance of how intervention is implemented, but its special description distorts. Only the costs of response are reckoned, to the exclusion of positive benefits from public action, and even these costs are assumed without regard to institutional mechanisms such as auctions and performance-related subsidies that can do much to reduce the deadweight burden. The rent-seeking model posits a static competitive Eden as the counterfactual alternative, rather than the reality of powerful private interests and inadequate price signals.

If anything, modern economic theory has reinforced a more skeptical view of laissez-faire. Incomplete markets, imperfect information, strategic interactions, principal-agent problems, transactions costs, and bounded rationality take up a large part of the microeconomic literature. Stiglitz sees this new theory as the unifying element in tackling development issues.[10] Economies of scale, external economies, and path dependence are now at the heart of the new growth economics.[11]

The appeal of outward orientation is its empirical basis. The calculations of effective protection and the oft-replicated statistical linkage between export performance and economic growth lend support to the critique of *dirigiste* policy. Two cautionary notes are in order. The data do not speak with a single voice of the virtues of outward orientation; and the question of the contribution of liberalization to successful export growth remains contentious.

High effective protection levels frequently exaggerate actual productive inefficiency; tariff reforms are not followed by massive failures and significant resource reallocation. Multiple cross-section studies demonstrating a favorable impact of exports on aggregate performance do not fully satisfy in three dimensions.[12] First, causality remains an issue. Improved productivity yields greater international competitiveness, as does the converse. A majority of countries fail a Sims-Granger causality criterion. Second, the source of improved performance may be excessively attributed to exports by the production function framework used. Strong evidence suggests that access to imports is equally or more important. This means that exports partially count for their foreign exchange earnings, not their benefit of productive efficiency. Third, the favorable impact of export growth will be mediated by its form; export-led industrialization is different from specialization in exports that are resource based.

This is not an argument against fully exploiting international market opportunities. Latin American countries, and especially the smaller economies, have no doubt exaggerated the benefits of focusing on the internal market. But this does not make an export emphasis the appropriate universal alternative. Export growth of 10–15 percent a year may not be feasible. Rather than such an ambitious export-led process of development, the objective for many countries should be an export-adequate strategy in which diverse exports regularly keep up with product growth and earn needed foreign exchange. Unlike the econometric inferences of a .3 elasticity of output to export growth, computable general equilibrium models show the much smaller effect of .1.[13] Not that much may be at stake.

But a still more critical question is the relationship between market signals and successful export penetration. Overvalued exchange rates are prejudicial. But it may not be enough simply to get them right, without implementing other complementary policies that encourage investment and technological change. The response to the exchange rate depends not only on entrepreneurial capacity but also on the flexibility of the productive structure. The objective is not to get prices right in isolation, but to follow consistent policies long enough for productive transformation to occur. Liberalization of the financial system and trade may be the consequence of successful industrialization, rather than the cause of competitive efficiency.

In sum, no one has yet shown that intervention failure *necessarily* outweighs market failure. On the contrary, effective state action is widely regarded as an underlying feature of successful outward-oriented Asian economic performance. As many have argued, Korea and Taiwan did not succeed in exports due to simple liberalization but as a result of a conscious and state-directed development strategy. In Latin America as well, the steady record of Brazilian and Mexican economic growth was associated with technocratic policy design and implementation before this last dismal decade.

Even if implementation failure has prevailed in Latin America, this is an argument for correcting it, not for pursuing a second-best policy of laissez-faire in the presence of externalities that can be exploited to accelerate economic development. Paradoxically, the array of powerful private interests celebrated by the rent-seeking and related literature requires a strong state to manage successful reform. In the absence of state capacity, concentrated market and political power and other imperfections may make laissez-faire an nth-best choice.

The argument in favor of an altered state role has to come from the side of macroeconomic failure, not a debilitating sectoral misallocation. Despite a greater public presence in many countries in the 1970s, evidence suggests that more, not less, attention should be paid to market signals and international competitiveness. Despite the eloquence of Hernando de Soto in chronicling a stifling Peruvian mercantilism, the earlier tide of structuralism has been in retreat.[14] In most of the region, rent seeking was arguably less prevalent in the 1970s than it had been in the 1950s and 1960s. And export performance improved during the decade. Even in the dismal 1980s, "export activity has grown much more rapidly than the rest of the economy. . . . [It] increased by 32.3 percent between 1980 and 1987, while the rest of the economy did so by only 7.4 percent."[15]

Rather, the real villain is fiscal inadequacy.[16] This has made it more difficult for Latin American countries to adjust effectively to the less favorable external economic environment of the 1980s. The rise in world interest rates and an initially high external debt reflected themselves in increased public expenditures. For the region, external debt service rose from about 3 percent of GNP in 1977–78 to as much as 8 percent in 1984, before falling to around 6 percent in the late 1980s.[17] Because much of the debt was public or publicly guaranteed, it helped to elevate interest costs to significant fractions of public expenditures; for large debtors the amounts were a fifth and more. Real devaluations needed to adjust the balance of payments added to the domestic cost of debt service. Countries that successfully managed the export surpluses required to make the payment thus faced an internal transfer problem: how was the indebted public sector to acquire the foreign exchange?

The stylized answer is through increased domestic finance of an increased deficit. References to modest changes in Latin American debt service relative to gross product underestimate the true magnitude of the effect. Moreover, the reduction in noninterest governmental expenditure, principally for investment, did not fully compensate. Hence countries faced larger deficits and at the same time less access to foreign finance; this combination is what made it such a crisis. In aggregate, Latin American government deficits (after some correction for the inflation component of interest payments) rose from 4 percent of national product in 1980 to 7–8 percent between 1981 and 1987.[18] Longer-term comparable data are available for Brazil, where government deficits (excluding the central bank component) rose from approximate balance in the early 1970s to 5 percent and more in the early 1980s.

The options for financing this deficit were increases in real internal debt or a tax on financial intermediation: the inflation tax on base money plus indirect effects through reserve requirements and credit controls. In the absence of a capital market, the only resort for many countries was accelerated inflation; for others, principally Brazil and Mexico, increased domestic debt figured prominently. Neither was a viable solution. As private agents protected themselves against the inflation tax, higher rates of inflation were required, possibly extending well beyond the point of maximum revenue collection. As internal debt put pressure on domestic interest rates, not only was private investment crowded out, but interest payments themselves grew at faster rates than revenues. In the end, the financeable deficit compatible with stable inflation tended to decrease even while the actual deficit increased. Tax collections were eroded by accelerating inflation, directly through the Tanzi-Olivera effect, and indirectly by increased incentives for evasion. Indexing assured that past inflation rates reproduced themselves.

Under these conditions, the characteristic deterioration in Latin America's economic performance is no great puzzle. Investment declined on the supply side, and demand was stifled to try to dampen inflation. Uncertainty was fed by the considerable variability in real magnitudes as inflation levels climbed. Public policy floundered between efforts to stabilize by fixing exchange rates and public sector prices, and price liberalization to reduce subsidies and public enterprise deficits.

By 1985 inflation in several countries necessarily became a principal preoccupation as it exceeded all previous bounds. The array of special circumstances elicited a heterodox response, the first of a series whose most recent manifestation was Brazil's March 1990 program. These plans, in varying forms in different countries, have much to say about the critical fiscal problem and role of the Latin American state.

The Argentine Plan Austral and the Brazilian Plano Cruzado, launched in 1985 and 1986 respectively, were the first response. They started from a theory of inertial inflation. Both ended indexing arrangements that institutionalized adjustments to past inflation; wages were set to nominal levels corresponding to their real average over a previous period. Both promised more rigorous monetary and fiscal policy. Both anchored prices to a newly devalued and more realistic exchange rate. Both introduced new monetary units and froze prices and wages to create instantaneous disinflation. Both were launched in an overt political fashion by civilian presidents and gained initial widespread support. After initial successes, both soon unraveled, as price and wage controls eroded and repressed inflation became overt. Despite a series of new partial programs in the same spirit, inflation soared. In Argentina it was necessary to advance the inauguration of a new president in 1989, as speculation defeated all attempts to stabilize. In Brazil, inflation exceeded 80 percent a month in early 1990 in the last month of the lame duck government.

By contrast, the Bolivian stabilization plan put in place in 1985 and the Mexican effort initiated in 1987 have thus far been more successful and enduring. The Bolivian plan, under conditions of hyperinflation and increased use of dollar, relied on massive devaluation and a subsequently fixed exchange rate to anchor price stability. The latter was structured around a negotiated income policy to restrain inflation to lower levels of price and wage increase, with the exchange rate again serving as anchor. Import liberalization was also pursued in both countries to provide an external check on domestic prices.

What especially characterizes these successful stabilization programs are much greater underlying fiscal discipline and restraint on demand than in Argentina or Brazil. In Bolivia, significant dismissals of personnel occurred in state enterprises (in COMIBOL, the state mining company, the work force was reduced from 30,000 to 7,000) and public sector real wages were reduced. Revenues from increased taxes on petroleum rose sharply in the short term, while more wide-ranging reform has proceeded more slowly. In Mexico, the primary surplus (exclusive of interest payments) was already close to 5 percent of gross product in 1987; in both 1988 and 1989 the surplus continued to increase.[19]

Rational expectations theory has been a misleading guide by implying that inflation can be stopped at modest costs, something all too appealing to Latin American ears. Too much attention has been paid to changing expectations and establishing the credibility of fixed exchange rates and monetary restraint; too little has been focused on the need to remedy the underlying fiscal imbalance. The theory's future orientation works best when a memory of earlier stability exists to which to return. In Latin America, the gold standard was itself less the rule than the exception; high postwar inflation rates erased any residual memory.

Previous experiments with international monetarism in Chile and Argentina at the end of the 1970s foundered due to misplaced faith in an exchange rate anchor and the automatic nature of adaptive international flows. The later heterodoxy in Argentina and Brazil, although more drastic as inflation mounted to four digits, retained the deep fear of recession as a counterpart to stabilization, at least until the latest effort in Brazil. What the Bolivian and Mexican experiences suggest is that the check to inflation is far from costless. Instantaneous conversion to believing in future price stability was less important than a soft economy that discouraged wage and price increases. External reserves and even explicit coordination can help, but in the end credibility has been earned the hard way.

The lesson is clear. An effective state, not reliance on the market alone, is necessary to establish expenditure priorities and impose restraint. Inflation is symptomatic of a lack of command. Magic formulas don't work. They obscure the underlying lack of consensus within Latin American countries and the ineffective mobilization of elite opinion that made it impossible to raise taxes early in the debt crisis or cope adequately with a deteriorating fiscal balance in the 1950s and 1960s. External finance, and proliferation of the public sector, concealed the real weakness of the state during the 1970s.

Privatization may now be emerging as another panacea. It promises to satisfy the need for larger domestic finance, reduced public expenditure, and greater productive efficiency all at the same time. Foreign and domestic interests alike find it easy to criticize overblown bureaucracies and overextended state enterprises. But a closer look counsels caution.

First, the objectives may be inconsistent. Where the dominant motive is immediate finance, the striking government deficits compel the best managed and most efficient enterprises to be sold, reducing future net revenues. There is a trade-off between present and future, not a pure gain. Fire sales of money-losing public enterprises are not likely to bring in much money. Recording the proceeds as revenue rather than as a means to finance the deficit gives the benefits a too favorable impression.

Second, selling off the perpetual losers will only reduce future claims on public subsidies if macroeconomic policy is better conducted. Favored work rules, controls over prices, and high levels of indebtedness help explain poor bottom-line results. Two of these factors do not operate at the enterprise level. Even wages and employment are not set entirely independently by private firms. Change in ownership alone does not make the crucial difference. Note, moreover, that restructuring debt to make enterprises more attractive to new owners simply transfers the future interest payments to another portion of the government ledger.

Third, promises of privatization's increasing efficiency may be overstated. Measuring productive efficiency in parastatal activities is not easy because cash flow results can distort. The extremely rapid growth of state enterprises during the 1970s—they multiplied by a factor of two and three times in several Latin American countries—was associated less with a comprehensive expansion strategy in key sectors than with financing balance of payments gaps. That is, Latin American governments used guaranteed loans for such enterprises as a means of increasing capital flows and access to foreign exchange. State enterprises remained with specific financial liabilities, increased in real terms through devaluation and higher interest rates, although sometimes no counterpart real investment existed. This problem is further compounded by the general tendency to place controls on public sector prices as a way to check accelerating inflation. New private owners may not be better managers. What may count more than ownership is greater exposure to competitive forces, most effectively through import liberalization when the domestic market is small.

Fourth, it matters who buys and how. If credit is extended to finance purchases, the public deficit—not total demand—is reduced. If private wealth is further concentrated by acquiring new assets, pressures on public officials for special treatment will be increased rather than reduced. It is interesting that external debt holders have resisted conversion into equity of public enterprises; they prefer to use swaps for more attractive private assets.

In sum, the deep-seated deficit problem in Latin America and its attendant serious consequences permit no easy solution. The debt crisis of the 1980s has underlined the fragility of the state and its inability to respond to a less favorable external environment. Increasingly, the issue is not merely debt reduction but redesigning the Latin American state. In the last analysis, limited gain, both fiscally and in the balance of payments, is available under the Brady Plan.

4. Redesigning the Latin American Developmental State

There are two competing models of redesign. One starts by stripping away public functions and confidently assigning them to the market and private sector. The other begins by confronting the central challenge of the public deficit and defining a new development strategy. Their partial congruence in some particulars not only creates a false impression of consensus, but leads to inconsistent policy. For where the first model gives priority to a reduced state and slashed expenditure, the latter requires a stronger state and command over resources.

Although the multilateral institutions seem to favor immediate and wide-ranging liberalization, in conjunction with aggregate restraint, there is limited evidence to support such an approach, particularly where markets have been working. This shock therapy promises too much too quickly. One has to reduce inflation quickly when it has reached stratospheric levels, but it is only a first step. Initial success can help restore confidence, but it can also promote a misplaced euphoria that conflicts with the institutional underpinning of fiscal responsibility at the heart of effective governance and economic development.

Countries in the region have become committed to change, but most are groping toward the second of these models. They are doing so both because liberalism is still not widely seen as an attractive doctrine, and because they need to offer a developmental perspective to satisfy an increasingly frustrated populace. Pinochet's "Chilean miracle" is not an ideal that Latin Americans wish to emulate. Vargas Llosa's vision of a Peru radically transformed and democratized by deregulation is the exception that proves the rule, and it has not been rewarded at the polls. Salinas's Mexico, while moving to greater integration in the world economy and closer links to the United States, retains a strong and active public role. Underlying trade liberalization, moreover, presents a powerful macroeconomic logic: imports have dampened inflationary pressures, and it is necessary to attract capital inflows to avert a looming foreign exchange constraint.

Developing a stronger state is independent of political origins and campaign slogans. The Argentine Peronist, Menem, professes Manchester liberalism, while Brazilian conservative Collor embraces confiscation of wealth. Economic emergency compels strong measures and increasing recognition that the state is both too large and too weak. Not until and unless there is an increase in public revenues, as well as reduced expenditures, will control of inflation succeed long term. One can hope this lesson is being learned and that external advice will reinforce internal predispositions.

Once achieved, macroeconomic equilibrium will not by itself guarantee economic development. The length of the crisis has intensified uncertainty and rewarded private sector caution. Restarting and sustaining economic growth is where the public sector has a central and critical role. First, increased public investment is essential to larger private investment; deteriorating infrastructure and lack of adequate public services have reduced private returns. Increased spending also sends an important signal that the fiscal emergency is over. Second, larger social expenditures must be made to improve education and health, as well as expand programs targeted to the poor. Evidence suggests that significant increases in inequality and poverty occurred as a counterpart to the stagnation and accelerating inflation of the 1980s. Political stability requires more than rhetorical recognition. Third, the public sector must become a better regulator and subsidizer, even as it divests some of its productive activities and liberalizes trade. Natural monopolies in private hands will have to be overseen; financial activity cannot be left unattended; priority private investment will have to be encouraged. Industrial policy in developing countries starts from knowing what has gone before; it does not have to be, and especially for the smaller countries should not be, synonymous with an internal market emphasis.

In short, based on theory and practice, a constructive role for the state is still quite necessary. To perform the role effectively requires a new coalition of political support founded both on old and new realities: a heavily reduced external finance and larger domestic saving, especially of the public sector itself; an expanded, but more competitive, international market in manufactured products, based on diffusing technology and imports of capital goods; limits to the domestic tax base; and extremely high income inequality throughout the region. Political transformation is very much a component of state redesign; democratization is only a beginning.

Populism, with its primary focus on inequality and its predisposition to a very activist and inward-looking state, is not the principal constraint to such transformation in most of Latin America.[20] Raging inflation has weakened its appeal. Opposition to effective policies has not come from mass organization; the poor do not speak with a single, or very loud, voice. Labor unions are divided and less powerful than in the 1960s. Real wages have undergone significant decline in almost all countries.

Forces blocking the state's constructive involvement have held sway. One has been the absence of an effective structure of political parties. Another has been a private sector more interested in guaranteed benefits than in risk taking, and comfortable with a state providing transfers and assured order without threat from below. Technocrats were able to satisfy those demands as long as they had abundant resources; as these diminished, so did the quality of the policies.

The technocrats have been blamed for the failure, while the private sector has emerged in some eyes as the future savior. The conversion to a narrow market-oriented view risks discarding a three-decade-long process of increasing sophistication of Latin American public administration. Bureaucrats do not wear only black hats. Some have contributed to imaginative policies and defended the national interest against powerful private rent seekers. The heart of the matter is not simply taking the state out, but bringing the private sector, and civil society, back in more positively.

The challenge to the countries of the region is formidable. No simple blueprints exist. The Asian developmental state cannot be copied. That brand of corporatism—where authority was more centralized, resources more readily available to the state, and pressures from income inequality less salient—proved much more functional than the Latin American style of catering to all. The prospects for economic development during the decade ahead and beyond hinge on the outcome of the state redesign process now under way. The longer it takes to succeed, the more the last decade's cumulative forces of erosion will work against its achievement.

Notes

1. This piece draws together material from two earlier publications: Eliana Cardoso and Albert Fishlow, "The Macroeconomics of the Brazilian External Debt," in Jeffrey Sachs (ed.), *Developing Country Debt and Economic Performance* (Chicago: Univ. of Chicago, 1990); and Albert Fishlow, "The Latin American State," *Journal of Economic Perspectives* 4:3 (Summer 1990), 61–74.

2. World Bank, *World Bank Development Report, 1988* (New York: Oxford Univ. Press, 1988), 9.

3. Economic Commission for Latin America, *The Economic Development of Latin America and Its Principal Problems* (New York: United Nations, 1950).

4. Economic Commission for Latin America, *Series Históricas del Crecimiento de América Latina* (Santiago: [CEPAL] Naciones Unidas. Part of series: Cuadernos de la CEPAL, 1978).

5. Among the critical literature, Ian Malcolm, David Little, Tibor Scitovsky, and Maurice Scott, *Industry and Trade in Some Developing Countries: A Comparative Study* (Oxford: Oxford Univ. Press, 1970), was first. But note that back in 1964 ECLA's *Economic Bulletin for Latin America* carried two articles critical of excessive protectionism and recognizing the end of the import-substitution model.

6. Eliana Cardoso and Albert Fishlow, "Latin American Economic Development: 1950–1980," *Journal of Latin American Studies* 24 (Aug. 1992), part 3.

7. Albert Fishlow "Latin American Adjustment to the Oil Shocks of 1973 and 1979," in J. Hartlyn and S. Morley (eds.), *Latin American Political Economy* (Boulder, Colo.: Westview Press, 1986), 54–84; and Albert Fishlow, "From Crisis to Problem: Latin American Debt 1982–87," in R. Wesson (ed.), *Coping with the Latin American Debt* (New York: Praeger, 1988), 7–18.

8. Jagdish Bhagwati, "Directly Unproductive Profit-Seeking Activities," *Journal of Political Economy* 90 (1982), 988–1002; Anne Krueger, "The Political Economy of the Rent-Seeking Society," *American Economic Review* 64 (June 1974), 291–303.

9. For a summary of the arguments concerning outward orientation, and more extensive references, see Anne Krueger, "Import Substitution versus Export Promotion," *Finance and Development* 22 (1985), 20–23; Bela Balassa, "Outward Orientation," in Hollis Chenery and T. N. Srinivasan (eds.), *Handbook of Development Economics,* vol. 2 (Amsterdam: North-Holland, 1989), 1645–89.

10. Joseph Stiglitz, "Economic Organization, Information, and Develop-

ment," in Hollis Chenery and T. N. Srinivasan (eds.), *Handbook of Development Economics*, vol. 1 (Amsterdam: North-Holland, 1988), 39–71.

11. Brian Arthur, "Self-Reinforcing Mechanisms in Economics," in P. Anderson, K. Arrow, and D. Pines (eds.), *The Economy as an Evolving Complex System* (Redwood City, Calif.: Addison-Wesley, 1988), 9–31; and Andre Shleifer, "Externalities as an Engine of Growth" (mimeo, Univ. of Chicago, 1989).

12. Albert Fishlow, "Latin American Export Strategy in the 1990s" (mimeo, Inter-American Development Bank, 1989).

13. Hollis Chenery, S. Robinson, and M. Syrquin, *Industrialization and Growth: A Comparative Study* (Oxford: Oxford Univ. Press, 1986), 321–22.

14. Hernando de Soto, *The Other Path* (New York: Harper and Row, 1989).

15. Inter-American Development Bank, *Economic and Social Progress in Latin America Report* (Washington, D.C.: Washington Inter-American Development Bank, 1989), 4.

16. For recent treatment of, and extensive other references to, the fiscal problem, see Helmut Reisen and Axel van Tratsenburg, *Developing Country Debt: The Budgetary and Transfer Problem* (Paris: OECD, 1988); and William Easterly, "Fiscal Adjustment and Deficit Financing During the Debt Crisis," in I. Hussain and I. Diwan (eds.), *Dealing with the Debt Crisis* (Washington, D.C.: World Bank, 1989), 91–113. There is considerable difficulty in assembling the comparable comprehensive data on the consolidated public sector needed for analysis.

17. World Bank, *World Debt Tables, 1983–84* (Washington, D.C.: World Bank, 1984); and *World Bank, World Debt Tables, 1989–90* (Washington, D.C.: World Bank, 1990).

18. Economic Commission for Latin America, *América Latina: La Política Fiscal en los Anos Ochenta*, Serie Política Fiscal, 2 (Santiago: ILADES, 1989).

19. CIEMEX-WEFA, *Mexican Economic Outlook* 22:1 (March 1990).

20. See Jeffrey Sachs, "Social Conflict and Populist Policies in Latin America" (National Bureau of Economic Research Working Paper no. 2987, 1989); and Rudiger Dornbusch and S. Edwards, "Economic Crises and the Macroeconomics of Populism in Latin America," *Journal of Development Economics*, 32:2 (1990), 247–77. Both papers come perilously close to identifying macroeconomic failure with populism tautologically. Nominal wage demands obviously reinforce inflation and impede stabilization. What is needed, however, is careful analysis of the special force of wage demands and their channels of pressure under populist regimes rather than others, and a careful look at whether wages were the decisive causal factor in provoking initial macroeconomic disequilibrium.

4

The State of Revolution

MARGARET E. CRAHAN AND PETER H. SMITH

Latin America has been frequently regarded as a breeding ground for revolution. Socioeconomic inequity and deprivation of fundamental human rights would seem to provide ample reason for popular rebellion. Unconstitutional seizures of power have punctuated the region's history ever since the acquisition of independence, and violence has permeated a good deal of political struggle. The resulting impression of instability has given rise to a widespread stereotype: Latin America is a land of injustice and chaos, a "continent in ferment," a volcano about to erupt.

Exploration of this subject must begin with careful definition. For purposes of this discussion, revolution is defined as *an illegal seizure of political power, by the use or threat of force, for the purpose of bringing about a structural change in the distribution of political, social, or economic power.* According to this conception, revolutions are qualitatively different from barracks revolts or routine *golpes de estado,* which lead to the rotation of leaders but leave structures intact. Revolutions use at least the threat of force; in actual fact, they often take power through extensive campaigns of armed struggle or "internal war." They have far-reaching programs for socioeconomic change, but the ideological project need not necessarily be "leftist"—there could be right-wing revolutions too, just so long as they call for transformation of the social order. And, having attained political power, revolutions may or may not be able to carry out their social programs; there is thus such a thing as an "incomplete" or "unsuccessful" revolution.

Thanks are due to Bridget Welsh, Greg Speller, Charles Klimicek, and Hector Schamis for their assistance in the preparation of this essay, as well as to the Institute for Iberian and Latin American Studies of Columbia University and the Center for Iberian and Latin American Studies at the University of California, San Diego. Any errors are the responsibility of the authors.

In Latin America, revolutionaries have accorded central importance to the role of the state. It is the state that conditions the social order, it is the state that upholds and ratifies the distribution of power and benefits, it is the state that legitimizes and supports the status quo. If the state can do all these things, it can by extension undo them as well. Indeed, that is why the state is worthy of conquest. This *étatiste* presumption has been a central pillar of revolutionary ideology in contemporary Latin America.

Eastern Europe offers sharp differences. During the tumultuous transformations in Poland and Czechoslovakia, for instance, popular leaders—who may be considered "revolutionaries" in some senses of the term—at first set out to dismantle the state, not to seize and strengthen it.[1] Burdens of governance and of economic reform have prompted reassessment of this initial impulse, but deep suspicion of overpowerful states still lingers in the new democracies of Eastern Europe. And more generally, recent experiences in Asia, Africa, and Latin America have stimulated new ideas about the possibility of attaining revolutionary ends through nonrevolutionary means.

Revolution in Latin America has actually been a rare phenomenon. There have been numerous revolutionary movements since the achievement of independence, but only four genuine revolutions: Mexico in 1910, Bolivia in 1952, Cuba in 1959, and Nicaragua in 1979. Of course important differences exist among them. The Mexican and Bolivian revolutions took place relatively early in the twentieth century and were essentially "national" and indigenous; the Cuban and Nicaraguan revolutions erupted during the Cold War and, apparently because of their ideological predilections, became part of the international struggle between the United States and the Soviet Union. The difference in timing also produces variations in analytical perspective: we can pretty well assess the outcomes of the Mexican Revolution; the Bolivian Revolution came to an involuntary halt in 1964; the Nicaraguan revolutionary government relinquished power via elections in 1990; and, as of this writing, the Cuban Revolution appears destined for substantial revision or eventual demise.

Beyond these revolutions, an enormous amount of political transformation has occurred in Latin America through nonrevolutionary means—such as pre-emptive reform, reactive adaptation, co-optative strategy, and inclusionary policy. Numerous and varying experiments in populist and/or corporative organization have sought to achieve the *goals* of revolution without undergoing the *process* of revolution. In fact, a great deal of political activity throughout the region, from repression to reform, has been either explicitly unrevolutionary or implicitly antirevolutionary.[2] This helps explain the relative scarcity of the phenomenon. Paradoxically enough, it also testifies to the enduring importance of the theme, since the possibility, or threat, of revolution has been a continuing and crucial factor in Latin American politics.

This essay will explore the origins, courses, and outcomes of revolution in Latin America. To examine theoretical perspectives on these issues, we review changing conceptions of revolution in the scholarly community and attempt to identify conditions that explain the emergence of revolutionary movements. We then explore specifics of the revolutions in Mexico, Bolivia, Cuba, and Nicaragua to establish the degree to which they conform with theory. We conclude with brief reflections on recent developments in Latin America and Eastern Europe in an effort to suggest new directions in revolutionary theory and practice.

Views of Revolution

The decade of the 1960s was an era of great interest in and anticipation of revolution. Many scholars, journalists, and politicians sensed that Latin America was on the verge of upheaval. Richard Nixon's catastrophic 1958 tour through the region revealed the strength of pressures for change. The Cuban Revolution and social ferment elsewhere spread the conviction that Latin America was on the brink or in the throes of revolution. As *New York Times* journalist Tad Szulc wrote in 1963:

> The revolutionary theme—clarion-clear in some parts, still muted, uncertain, almost unconscious in others—is the dominant motif sounding among the restless, poverty-plagued, disoriented, and explosively expanding populations of Latin America in this decisive decade.
>
> It is a theme rich in variations, making itself heard in as many different tones as there are nationalities, cultures, ideologies, and special conditions in the twenty republics and the handful of colonies and foreign-controlled territories that make up the geographic and political concept known as Latin America.
>
> Yet all these variations do reflect a common theme: the demand for a better material life and, simultaneously, profound political and psychological changes that still remain largely undefined and only partially understood. The emphasis is on change, on experimentation, on adventure, and on a surging desire to upset the patterns of the old and to venture along the paths of the new.[3]

The combination of widespread injustice and inequality, together with the "demonstration effect" of the Cuban Revolution, was thought likely to stimulate additional radical revolutions. There would no doubt be more; the question was what kind.

According to the "modernization" theory prevalent throughout the early 1960s, the most desirable alternative to revolution was progressive reform. The choice was revolution or reform: the purpose of reform was to prevent revolution. Here was the ultimate rationale for the Alliance for Progress, so aptly captured by President Kennedy's oft-quoted remark: "Those who make peaceful revolution [reform] impossible will make violent revolution inevitable." In other words, Latin America would continue along its "natural" path toward revolution unless prophylactic steps were taken—particularly the implementation of peaceful reforms that could create the socioeconomic conditions for democratic rule. Without reform, the future would be Cuba.

This conviction received additional reinforcement from French journalist Régis Debray, among others, who argued that Latin America would not have to await the appearance of appropriate "material conditions" to embark on its revolutionary course. Visionary leaders, it was posited, could create the revolutionary cadres, or *focos,* that would eventually force a revolutionary solution. Challenging orthodox Marxist precepts, Debray and Ernesto (Ché) Guevara, the Argentine hero of the Cuban Revolution, maintained that the key to Third World revolution lay not in economic conditions, but in creating revolutionary consciousness and in applying moral rather than material incentives.

Throughout the United States, Europe, and Latin America, a predictable reaction took place. Conservatives were fearful, liberals were nervous, radicals were ecstatic. Despite their normative disagreements, all shared a similar view: Latin America was about to explode. And all were incorrect. Ché Guevara's 1966 expedition into Bolivia was not only defeated; it encountered resistance from the very peasantry expected to provide it with support. The Cuban Revolution encountered internal difficulties, particularly in the economic sphere, and became increasingly dependent on Soviet subsidies. And while the Alliance for Progress never amounted to much, its anticlimactic expiration did not give way to massive upheavals. Put another way, the absence of reform did not bring on revolution.

In this context *dependencia* literature began to appear. Social scientists began suggesting that the nature of Latin American economic development could contribute to revolution. Economist Paul Baran argued that economic development in the global periphery (Asia, Africa, and Latin America) was contrary to the interests of economic elites in the core (the United States and Western Europe). Consequently, alliances had emerged between elites in the core and periphery, resulting in a permanent state of dependence that precluded development in the Third World.[4] The implications of such dependence were more fully elaborated by scholars such as André Gunder Frank and Theotonio dos Santos. Frank argued that only by imposing socialism would countries such as Brazil and Chile have any possibility of economic development.[5] Dos Santos concluded that in the face of the threat of socialist revolution, capitalist elites in core countries would support military dictatorships in the periphery. The options for Latin America were, as a consequence, fascism via repression or socialism through revolution.[6] The Brazilian political scientist Fernando Henrique Cardoso, together with Enzo Faletto, qualified these observations by arguing that foreign capital could stimulate a form of "associated dependent development" in Latin America. But it was not realistic, they wrote in the mid-1970s, "to imagine that capitalist development will solve basic problems for the majority of the population. In the end, what has to be discussed as an alternative is not the consolidation of the state and the fulfillment of 'autonomous capitalism,' but how to supersede them. The important question, then, is how to construct paths toward socialism."[7]

By the 1970s events seemed to confirm that Latin America was heading not for revolution but for right-wing repression. This belief appeared to be supported by the emergence in the 1960s and 1970s in Brazil, Chile, Uruguay, and Argentina of regimes characterized by "bureaucratic authoritarianism." As conceptualized by the Argentine political scientist Guillermo O'Donnell, these regimes sought to stimulate economic growth by encouraging domestic and foreign private investment, in part through state intervention. While the economic policies of bureaucratic-authoritarian regimes might substantially alter the means of capital accumulation, they would not change the dependent nature of core-periphery relations.[8] Although many analysts at the time concluded that bureaucratic-authoritarian regimes reflected a logical outcome of economic and political processes specific to Latin America, more recently the Argentine political scientist Hector Schamis has argued that bureaucratic-authoritarian regimes bear "a striking similarity to the neoconservative projects of some advanced industrial countries. Issues such as 'ungovernability,' 'crisis of the state,' 'demand overload,' and others were part of the Southern Cone agenda even before Reagan and Thatcher engineered their own 'conservative revolutions.' "[9] While not revolutionary in any strict sense of the term, neoliberal strategies were bringing about profound socioeconomic transformations, most markedly in Chile.

Throughout the period it was commonly thought that the continent was headed not for revolution but for reaction. This view found support in a line of cultural interpretation that insisted that the Latin American ethos contained inherently authoritarian precepts that accepted and legitimized dictatorial rule. *Dependencia* analysts and cultural interpreters engaged in mutual recriminations, accusing one another of simple-minded determinisms. But they nonetheless concurred on the nature of Latin America's underlying trajectory—that the future belonged to the generals.

For all these reasons, the political destiny of Latin America in the 1970s was seen not as revolution but as repression. The only way to forestall this was not via reform, which would simply postpone or assure the inevitable, but by armed struggle. Such thinking helped stimulate the emergence of revolutionary movements in Nicaragua and El Salvador. But in general, the call to rebellion came to be regarded as the exception rather than the rule.

In the meantime, military regimes began giving way to civilian governments by peaceful means—in Peru, Argentina, Uruguay, Brazil, and eventually Chile. Academics and policymakers hailed the onset of "democratization," and those fearing revolutionary violence across the political spectrum were relieved. Analysts increasingly focused on processes of incremental change. Philippe C. Schmitter, Guillermo O'Donnell, and Laurence Whitehead argued that the skillful application of statecraft could exploit momentary opportunities to promote the installation and consolidation of democratic regimes.[10]

The trend toward democratization once again rearranged perceptions of political dynamics in Latin America. For the 1980s and 1990s the future no longer seems to be revolution: it is reform. But its content is qualitatively different from 1960s developmentalism. Most notably, it reflects a more pragmatic and less idealistic view of the capacity of free market capitalism to liberate masses of Latin Americans from poverty. The objectives of current reformist governments tend to be relatively modest, and their economic programs not always radically different from those of their authoritarian predecessors. Emphasis is on evolutionary, rather than revolutionary, change, in an era still smarting from memories of the brutal suppression of revolutionary movements and reformist tendencies. As in Eastern Europe, the trend may move toward what has come to be called "refolution"—reformism that may result in revolutionary outcomes.[11]

Within the last generation Latin America has undergone extraordinary transformation, as have scholarly perceptions of revolutionary processes. Dichotomies have shifted from reform versus revolution in the 1960s, with revolution as the norm; to revolution versus reaction in the 1970s, with reaction as the norm; to reaction versus reform in the 1980s and 1990s, with reform (or perhaps refolutions) now in the ascendant.

The Course of Revolution

Let us now turn to the revolutionary process itself. What have been the origins of revolution? What factors account for triumph and defeat? And what have been some of the outcomes of revolutionary policies?

Rising Up

Popular impressions often associate revolutionary uprisings with a charismatic leader. The image of the revolutionary *guerrillero*—a bearded, idealistic, romantic figure in quest of social justice—strongly supports this notion. Certainly the course of the Mexican Revolution was profoundly affected not only by Emiliano Zapata and Pancho Villa, but also by Venustiano Carranza and Plutarco Elías Calles. More recently, the predominant role of Fidel Castro in Cuba has encouraged analysts to place considerable weight on actor-oriented theories of social change. There are those, however, who insist that the critical actor in propelling the revolution was not Castro but Batista.[12] Through their personal charisma, individual leaders have at times played crucial roles in the creation of revolutionary movements and in the consolidation of their power.

But for the most part, contemporary scholarship explains the existence of revolutionary movements not through heroic leaders, but on the basis of economic, political, and social forces. This does not discount the importance of leaders. On the contrary, it asserts that leaders acquire prominence and power by responding to historical situations. In other words, social conditions facilitate the rise of the leader, not the other way around. What are some of these conditions?

Poverty. Analysts have stressed the inevitability of revolution due to social inequality and wretched living conditions. If this is true, what has not been clearly answered is why Latin America has not had a history of continuous turmoil. Poverty has always existed, but revolution, or even the emergence of revolutionary movements, has been a rare phenomenon. Why?

Classic Marxism does not offer much insight. The archetypical conditions for revolution—particularly the emergence of an industrial proletariat and the acceleration of class struggle—have not occurred in most of Latin America. Indeed, Marxist analysts have constantly had to cope with the fact that the "objective and material conditions" for social revolution have simply not been present.

Economic Change. In fact it appears that economic development, not stagnation, has created revolutionary potential in Latin America. Especially important has been the region's particular *form* of capitalist development and the social dislocation it has caused. Some political theorists have stressed the role of the "demonstration effect," arguing that disadvantaged masses would be likely to revolt only when they learned—from improved communications and mass media—that other people were better off than they. Focusing on the concept of "relative deprivation," for instance, Ted Robert Gurr has attempted to explain revolution in terms of collective psychology as a culmination of cycles of frustration and aggression that ultimately lead people to engage in armed struggle.[13]

One variation on this theme is James Davis's much discussed "J-curve," through which he argues that revolutionary movements are likely to break out when societies experience sudden economic downturns after a prolonged period of growth. The process of development tends to elevate aspirations, according to this view, and the frustration of these aspirations prompts people to rebel.[14] Applied to the political realm, this reasoning has a subtle and disturbing corollary: progressive change, like economic growth, could raise popular hopes, and a setback could trigger revolt. In other words, political reform could contribute to the conditions for revolution, rather than removing them.

The J-curve hypothesis appears to have some relevance for Mexico, Cuba, and Nicaragua. In all three countries prolonged, if unsteady, economic growth was interrupted by downturns prior to revolution. In Mexico, the impact of this reversal varied from region to region, as did levels of political volatility. Effects were more uniform throughout Cuba and Nicaragua, with less geographic extent and less differentiated economic structures, but the pattern was nonetheless present. By the late 1950s Cuba had achieved Latin America's highest per capita income, but unequal distribution of income led to frustration, particularly among the urban and rural proletariat. In Nicaragua, unemployment rose from 3.6 percent in 1971 to 20 percent in 1978.[15] In short, revolution tends to break out not in the most poverty-stricken countries, but in more advantaged countries that have undergone sharp and sudden economic decline.

Other approaches have concentrated on the social location of rebellious groups, not on their psychological attributes or cognitive perceptions. One study of this genre came from Eric Wolf, an anthropologist, who undertook to explain the origins of contemporary "peasant wars." Outraged by U.S. policy in Vietnam, Wolf sought to destroy the then official contention that hard-working peasants would not rebel without outside agitation. In a brilliant synthesis of struggles around the world, including Mexico and Cuba as well as Vietnam, Wolf focused attention on the "middle" or "free" peasantry. It was not the rich or most downtrodden peasants who made revolution. It was those in the middle, who could become tactically mobile:

> Yet this recruitment of a "tactically mobile peasantry" among the middle peasants and the "free" peasants of peripheral areas poses a curious paradox. This is also the peasantry in whom anthropologists and rural sociologists have tended to see the main bearers of peasant tradition. If our account is correct, then—strange to say—it is precisely this culturally conservative stratum which is the most instrumental in dynamiting the peasant social order. This paradox dissolves, however, when we consider that it is also the middle peasant who is relatively the most vulnerable to economic changes wrought by commercialism, while his social relations remain encased within the traditional design. His is a balancing act in which his balance is continuously threatened by population growth; by the encroachment of rival landlords; by the loss of rights to grazing, forest, and water; by falling prices and unfavorable conditions of the market; by interest payments and foreclosures. Moreover, it is precisely this stratum which most depends on traditional social relations of kin and mutual aid between neighbors; middle peasants suffer most when these are abrogated, just as they are least able to withstand the depredations of tax collectors or landlords.

Finally—and this is again paradoxical—middle peasants are also the most exposed to influences from the developing proletariat. The poor peasant or landless laborer, in going to the city or factory, also usually cuts his tie with the land. The middle peasant, however, stays on the land and sends his children to work in the town; he is caught in a situation in which one part of the family retains a footing in agriculture, while the other undergoes the "training of the cities." . . . This makes the middle peasant a transmitter of urban unrest and political ideas. The point bears elaboration. It is probably not so much the growth of an industrial proletariat as such which produces revolutionary activity, as the development of an industrial work force still closely geared to life in the villages.

"Thus," concludes Wolf, "it is the very attempt of the middle and free peasant to remain traditional which makes him revolutionary."[16] The emphasis, then, is on the authenticity of agrarian rebellion.[17]

The role of peasantry in revolution has prompted intense debate. In the case of Mexico, Friedrich Katz has shown that economic growth just prior to the revolution generally did not benefit *hacienda* workers in the Central Valley, while it improved the condition of agricultural workers in the North—and they proved more likely to rebel.[18] Indeed, Katz, John Womack, and others have found that it was often the more advantaged rural workers who were attracted to the revolution.[19] Together with small landowners, capitalist tenant farmers, middle sectors, and some elites, they composed the bulk of the revolutionary forces. Patron-client relations antedating 1910 were subsumed into relations among these groups, contributing to middle- and upper-class domination of the leadership. This fact, in turn, enabled leaders such as Venustiano Carranza to set limits on the extent of social revolution.

International Influences. Another source of revolution involves external or international factors—not so much through the presence of "outside agitators," a theme commonly invoked by antirevolutionary governments, but mainly in the form of structural influences. Ellen Kay Trimberger, for example, focuses on the relationships among social classes, the state, and foreign threats to national autonomy. When revolution occurs from above, she observes, "dynamically autonomous" bureaucrats (including military officers) seize and reorganize state power.[20] Using the state, they attempt to destroy the existing dominant class and reorient the national economy to respond better to foreign threats. They also seek to prevent upheaval from below. Strongly nationalist, the new elite tends to have few ties to traditional landed, commercial, or business groups and thus proceeds to impose sweeping reforms. Trimberger's scheme corresponds fairly well to military rule in Peru from 1968 to 1975 (which does not quite meet our definition of *revolution*), but does little to help explain the popular insurrections in Mexico, Bolivia, Cuba, or Nicaragua.

In spite of itself, U.S. domination has undoubtedly contributed to revolution in Latin America. With the exception of Bolivia, each of the region's major revolutions occurred in countries with long and painful histories of U.S. intervention. The United States seized half of Mexico's territory in the midnineteenth century, and during the regime of Porfirio Díaz (1884–1911), accumulated substantial control over the national economy by the early twentieth century. Newly independent Cuba was subjected in 1901 to the so-called Platt Amendment, essentially a license for the United States to intervene at will. Over time Washington managed to undermine the republic's legitimacy, stifle the 1933 revolution, identify itself with the noxious Batista regime, and stimulate nationalism. Nicaragua too had a long history of intervention by the United States, which helped bring to power Anastasio Somoza García in the 1930s. Close U.S. identification with the Somoza regime gave rise to strong nationalism and anti-imperialism, which became the hallmarks of Augusto César Sandino's campaign to expel U.S. marines and impose socioeconomic and political reforms during the 1920s and early 1930s. As a consequence, the 1979 Nicaraguan Revolution was defined to a considerable extent by a desire to reorder traditional political and economic relations with the United States.

Focusing on contemporary Central America, the historian Walter LaFeber has argued that revolution does indeed stem from outside influence—specifically from the influence of the United States. U.S. investment and intervention, LaFeber contends, created the region's agro-export economies; U.S. aid and encouragement, through the Alliance for Progress and the Central American Common Market, promoted a phase of rapid growth; and U.S. meddling sought to arrest processes of change in the 1970s and 1980s. In a sense, LaFeber takes the view of revolution—that it was prompted by outsiders—and turns it on its head. In his conception, ironically, it is antirevolutionary elements of U.S. policy that have promoted revolution in the region.[21]

Elite Fragmentation. One of the most important keys to revolutionary upheaval comes not from the middling or popular strata, but from the upper reaches of society. In revolutionary settings everywhere, from Russia to Mexico to Nicaragua, fragmentation of the dominant elite has served two critical functions: it has weakened the prerevolutionary order, and it has provided rebels with leadership. Elite fragmentation can occur for a variety of reasons, including economic or social changes that produce new claimants for power and prestige. Typically, it acquires revolutionary potential when the would-be elites find themselves excluded from or limited in their access to political power.

Research on Mexico has shown that the first wave of anti-Porfirian rebels, from Francisco Madero downward, came from discontented segments of the relatively privileged middle and upper middle classes.[22] This defection debilitated the regime and gave coherence to the initial phase of the rebellion. The phenomenon also illustrates the importance of viewing a revolution as a process over time. The Maderista period of the Mexican Revolution clearly did not embrace the more radical Zapatista and Villista demands for social redemption; but without the Maderista phase, the rest would never have happened.

Reasons for opposition to the Porfiriato varied by place as well as class. In Mexico's Central Valley, increased economic and social disparities afflicted "not only workers and peasants but small farmers, merchants, middle-sector intellectuals, and even leading members of the hacendado community. The owners of agriculture and industrial wealth were particularly affected by the increased susceptibility of the local economy to abrupt changes in the international economy."[23] And in many parts of the country, such discontent was exacerbated by exclusion from political office and/or influence not only in the federal government but also at state and local levels. Hence the strong response in distant provinces to Madero's call for free elections and an end to authoritarian rule. These factors helped transform the 1910 crisis of presidential succession into an insurrection and, ultimately, into a revolution.

Similarly, inspiration for the Cuban Revolution came from neither the peasantry nor the proletariat, though both groups benefited from its policies. Those who participated in the 26th of July movement in the 1950s and accompanied Fidel Castro into government came largely from the nation's bourgeoisie. In addition, financial support and tactical assistance for the rebellion came primarily from middle- and upper-class Cubans.[24] As in other revolutionary instances, fragmentation of the prerevolutionary elite proved to be essential.

This process was even more conspicuous in Nicaragua. In the aftermath of the 1972 earthquake, popular mobilization accelerated and divisions within the nation's elite increased. Opinion molders—church leaders, intellectuals, journalists, and students—joined the revolutionary forces; in so doing, they helped legitimate the Sandinista movement in the eyes of the Nicaraguan middle class and the international media. Bourgeois intermediaries proved especially effective in obtaining arms and other support for the Frente Sandinista de Liberación Nacional (FSLN) through such countries as Venezuela and Costa Rica. Somoza's short-sighted resistance to concessions further alienated the Nicaraguan bourgeoisie, thereby encouraging the United States to distance itself from the fading regime.

The role of the Nicaraguan bourgeoisie was critical. As Henri Weber has stated: "In Nicaragua the bourgeois opposition itself opened up the crisis of the Somoza regime and actually led the first phase of the revolution. It was only at the end of the process, with the help of Somoza's intransigence, that the FSLN captured the leadership of the struggle."[25] Weber suggests that the middle bourgeoisie, such as that represented by the Frente Amplio de Oposición (FAO), had credibility in

Nicaragua among the petite bourgeoisie and the rural and urban proletariat because it was not closely identified with the United States.
However, the Sandinistas ultimately proved more effective in exploiting nationalism and anti-imperialism to help consolidate their leadership, particularly in the face of the bourgeoisie's conviction that the
country's economic future required good relations with the United States.
The struggle within the governing junta in 1979 and 1980 helped portray the Sandinistas as stronger defenders of Nicaraguan sovereignty
than their bourgeois allies. It also helped discredit liberal democrats,
opening the way for the attempted imposition of Sandinista "popular
democracy," which rejected traditional democratic institutions and
practices. The FSLN moved on to create a strongly hierarchical party
that, in the opinion of some, including party members, ultimately came
to appear paternalistic, arrogant, and unresponsive to popular demands.[26]

As creators and interpreters of ideology, intellectuals have special
functions. Perhaps for this reason Antonio Gramsci, among all classical
theorists, may well have had the greatest impact on Latin American
revolutionary leaders, particularly the Sandinistas.[27] Like V. I. Lenin,
Gramsci believed the working class could successfully build revolution
only by long-term planning and organization via a vanguard party, itself a mechanism for the expression of the collective will. Gramsci adds
to Lenin's concept of party a middle layer of "organic intellectuals"
between the advanced theorists and the bulk of party members. "Organic intellectuals" would articulate "the first element with the second
and maintain contact between them, not only physically but also morally and intellectually."[28] This articulation was necessary to ensure the
party's viability as a social organization, and to forge agreement on
matters of fundamental ideology.

In practice, the participation of organic intellectuals has varied from
country to country. In Mexico there was no single source of ideological
inspiration, no clear-cut vanguard party à la Lenin or Gramsci. Nor did
the 26th of July movement or the Partido Socialista Popular assume
the role of a vanguard party in Cuba prior to 1961. Revolutionary ideology was rooted mainly in the thought of José Martí, the nineteenth-
century champion of independence, and in anti-imperialist and anticapitalist sentiments derived from Cuba's historical development. Part
of Fidel Castro's political genius came from his ability to articulate historical lessons and popular moods, somewhat in the style of a Grams-
cian organic intellectual, as in his landmark manifesto, *History Will Absolve Me.*[29]

Analysts of Nicaragua have suggested that the founder of the Sandinista movement, Carlos Fonseca, exemplified the organic intellectual.
Others have asserted that church people, students, poets, and journalists played important roles as organic intellectuals.[30] In any event,
Gramsci held special appeal for Nicaraguan revolutionaries of the 1970s

and 1980s, in part because he provided a justification for the FSLN's emphasis on the subjective, not objective, conditions of revolution and for its reliance on Christian belief as well as Marxist ideology.[31] Also important was his focus on "praxis," or the combining of theory and practice in an ongoing ideological struggle.[32] Hence the emphasis in Nicaragua on church, school, and party to change people's values and beliefs and thereby ensure revolution.

Seizing Power

Revolutionary movements face major obstacles in the quest for political power. They challenge entrenched sets of interests with near monopolies on economic and political authority. Notwithstanding occasional flights of rhetoric, there is nothing "inevitable" about the triumph of revolutionary movements. It is entirely possible, even likely, that the forces of reaction will prove to be stronger than the forces of change. Most revolutionary movements in Latin America have ended in defeat, despair, or extermination.

The Popular Base. One fundamental problem concerns the strength of the popular base. In most Latin American countries, neither the proletariat nor the peasantry alone has been strong enough to provide a decisive social base for revolution. As Marx defined it, the industrial proletariat has barely come into existence in many places; manufacturing has played a modest role in economic production, at least in comparison with Europe, so the working class has generally been neither large nor well organized. And where it has gained relative strength, as in Brazil and Argentina, the state has attempted to co-opt the laboring class by creating and controlling official union movements.

As we have already explained, the traditional peasantry has not been especially susceptible to revolution. Campesinos have often remained under the domination of local elites. They have so little land and so few material resources that they rarely can afford to take risks, precisely because of the misery of their objective circumstances. For logistical and political reasons peasants are difficult to organize, a trait that once led Marx to dismiss them as "a sack of potatoes." It is not the most downtrodden but the relatively advantaged campesinos—the "middle peasants," in Eric Wolf's language—who are most likely to participate in insurrections.

As a result, it is no simple task to cultivate a popular following among workers or peasants. It is even more difficult to forge horizontal, class-based, worker-peasant alliances. The undeniable fact is that workers and peasants tend to have differing agendas: workers want higher real wages and cheaper food, while peasants want higher prices for their food products. Workers want efficient agricultural production, which may mean economies of scale, while peasants want more equitable landholding systems, which may mean breaking up large *haciendas*; workers want state preferences for industry, peasants want support for agriculture; workers want political power for unions, peasants want power for cooperatives. While it might appear that common grievances and class interests would automatically forge worker-peasant, or "red-green," coalitions, the reality is that these two sectors have often stood in opposition. In the midst of the Mexican Revolution, for example, Venustiano Carranza was able to mobilize a "red brigade" of workers to help turn back the peasants under Zapata and Villa. This sort of disunity has led countless theoreticians of revolution to lament the absence, paucity, or underdevelopment of "class consciousness" in Latin America.

In spite of this, red-green alliances have supported revolution in some instances. Almost from the beginning, worker unions in Bolivia made common cause with discontented peasants. Partly because of the nature of sugar production, which meant that mill workers lived in semiurban settlements *(bateyes)* and many migrated back and forth to cities, considerable contact and communication existed between a "proletarianized" rural workforce and urban counterparts in Cuba. In Nicaragua, the extensive displacement of peasantry from rural landholdings created significant bonds between workers in the cities and the countryside. The consolidation of such alliances, however partial, was instrumental in the triumph and direction of these revolutions in two ways: it provided the movement with a powerful popular base, and it helped define the political agenda along social-class lines.

Red-green coalitions have proved important for the success of insurrectionary movements. They are probably not sufficient to assure victory for revolution, but they may well be necessary. Otherwise conservative forces may resort to divide-and-conquer tactics, pitting one sector against the other. Throughout modern Latin American history, in fact, ruling elites have systematically sought to prevent, prohibit, or forestall the consolidation of worker-peasant alliances. This alone testifies to their significance.

Power Structures. Although de-emphasized by orthodox Marxists, who focus more on class struggle than on politics, the capacity of the antirevolutionary state has an obvious impact on outcomes. Strong states have a good chance of resisting, or repressing, revolutionary movements. Weak ones do not.

In a critique of Marx, Theda Skocpol has observed that popular revolutions are more common in agrarian than industrial countries. She also asserts that political and military pressures have contributed more to the outbreak of revolution than have class struggles. Fundamentally, Skocpol diverges from Marx by arguing that revolutions have changed state structures as much as or more than they have changed class relations. In her view three factors are essential to understanding the incidence of revolutions: the relative autonomy of the state, the initiation of revolution by peasants with sufficient capacity to act against landlords, and the international dimensions of capitalist production.

For Skocpol, revolutions erupt when there is a concurrent weakening of the state structure and exacerbation of class contradictions. This applies to three of our cases: Mexico, Cuba, Nicaragua. She further argues that states are undercut by international pressures, which require that more resources be extracted from society. Forced to act as the administrative agent for the dominant class, often coercively, the state can lose legitimacy—as appears to have occurred in Mexico prior to 1910. It could even collapse, an event likely to unleash and intensify demands from peasants and other popular groups, as in Cuba and Nicaragua. The disaffected can then fill the power vacuum, take control of a new state, and bring about changes in class relations.[33] Here the Mexican case diverges, however, largely because of the great variety among revolutionary agendas for differing regional and social-class groups.

Within the state apparatus, the military assumes a major role. Historically, the armed forces in Latin America have assumed ultimate responsibility for maintaining domestic law and order, as well as for protecting national sovereignty. Often nurtured by oligarchic or dictatorial regimes, they have usually, but not always, developed a conservative, antirevolutionary outlook. One reason for this, in recent times, has been a network of professional and organizational links to the United States. Also crucial has been the social recruitment, ideology, and nationalism of the officer corps, usually men of middle-class background who identify themselves and their careers with the well-being of the military as an institution. Defining one of their principal missions as the preservation of internal peace, they have a profound antipathy for radical or "alien" ideologies.

Strong and cohesive military forces have often succeeded in defeating or repressing revolutionary movements. But where the armed forces are divided or ineffective, revolutionary groups have better chances for power. In Cuba, for example, Batista's army was more noted for its corruption than its fighting skill. Increased repression contributed to government's further delegitimation, and encouraged a March 1958 U.S. arms embargo. By August 1958 the army had withdrawn from the countryside to the cities. Within months Batista was on his way to exile.

Another key element in the power structure has been the Roman Catholic Church. In most Latin American countries, it has wielded enormous power and prestige, not only because of its moral suasion but also because of its secular influence. Since the 1960s church people have increasingly supported socioeconomic and political change. For some it has been an issue of justice, for others a means of avoiding Marxist revolution. Support from some priests, brothers, and nuns for radical social change has been encouraged by the "theology of liberation," which denounces the everyday injustices of contemporary capitalism and supports a "preferential option for the poor." This has led some to accuse liberation theologians of encouraging class warfare. In recent years the theology has been critical of the excesses of both capitalism and socialism while continuing to call for the restructuring of society to achieve higher levels of societal concord from greater equity and participation.[34]

Geopolitics and Superpowers. An additional variable affecting the likelihood of revolutionary change is geopolitics—particularly, but not exclusively, the hegemonic role of the United States. From the outset of the Cold War in the late 1940s, through the liberal heyday of the Alliance for Progress, to the interventionism of the Reagan era, the United States has maintained two cardinal principles: preference for stability, and opposition to Communism. As diplomat and analyst George Kennan once declared, the purposes of U.S. policy should be:

1. The protection of our [sic!] raw materials;
2. The prevention of military exploitation of Latin America by the enemy; and,
3. The prevention of the psychological mobilization of the hemisphere against us.

Under no circumstances, Kennan continued, should Communists be allowed to take power: "The final answer might be an unpleasant one, but . . . we should not hesitate before police repression by the local government. This is not shameful since the Communists are essentially traitors. . . . It is better to have a strong regime in power than a liberal government if it is indulgent and relaxed and penetrated by Communists."[35] The United States must therefore impose its own solutions: by covert intervention in Guatemala in 1954, in Cuba in 1961, in the Dominican Republic in 1965, in Chile in 1973, and in Grenada and Central America in the 1980s.[36]

Fidel Castro was able to take power in Cuba in 1959 partly because the Eisenhower Administration reduced its support of the dictator Fulgencio Batista. Ever since that time, Cuba has had to withstand intense pressures from the United States, including an invasion in April 1961. One of the principal strategies for Cuban self-defense was the cultivation of another then superpower, the Soviet Union. Some analysts have therefore argued that Castro's turn toward socialism stemmed essentially from U.S. actions.[37] Once the Castro regime had taken hold, the United States reaffirmed repeatedly that it would not tolerate "another Cuba" in the Western Hemisphere.[38]

This observation gives rise to a simple hypothesis: modern revolutions can succeed only if they can avoid or deflect hostility from hegemonic powers. In practical terms, this means Latin American revolutionaries should avoid the wrath of the United States. This was not much of a factor in Bolivia and was only an intermittent problem in Mexico, where the United States dispatched troops on more than one occasion, but these episodes predated the Cold War. An especially dramatic illustration came with the consolidation of the Nicaraguan Revolution after 1979. Under Ronald Reagan the United States waged unremitting war—economic, political, and military—on the Sandinista regime. It also caused the United States to pour millions of dollars in economic and military aid into El Salvador to snuff out the revolutionary movement there. The Cubans have managed to endure, largely because they were able to obtain protection from the USSR. The Sandinistas did not. Nor did the Salvadoran revolutionaries succeed in taking power, although in 1992 they reached a peace agreement with the government which allowed them some influence.

In sum, revolutionary movements in Latin America face daunting obstacles. Consolidation of a horizontal worker-peasant alliance may be a necessary condition for victory, but it is by no means sufficient. Even more instrumental has been the appearance of fissures, or fault lines, within the dominant establishment. Elite fragmentation weakens the rulers and provides opportunities for rebels. At critical moments, prospects for revolution require neutralization of the forces of reaction— particularly the military and the United States. In other words, the likelihood of seizing power depends not only on the strategy and tactics of the revolutionaries, but on the strength and cohesion of the antirevolutionaries.

Promoting Change

Whatever the causes of social revolution in Latin America, the undeniable fact is that the results have been limited. Indeed, much of the literature on Latin American revolution refers to revolutions that are "incomplete," "interrupted," "intervened," and so on. Part of the problem relates to the chronology of change. Some time ago there was much discussion in Mexico about whether its revolution was still alive. One leading Mexican intellectual, Daniel Cosío Villegas, argued that it had died by the 1940s but that the governing elites appreciated the utility of invoking the appearances of continuity.

> I sincerely believe that the Mexican people have long known that the Mexican Revolution is dead, although they do not know, or only half understand, why this fact is concealed instead of being proclaimed. Therefore, the question arose some time ago: If it is dead, why have the death notices not been circulated? Why, more exactly, has the Mexican Revolution not been buried in the Rotunda of the Great, or perhaps in the Monument to the Mexican Revolution, where two of its heroes, Francisco Madero and Venustiano Carranza, already lie? . . . The Mexican Revolution actually gave to the country, and especially to its leaders, an

ideology and a language and, so long as no new ideas and expressions appear, it is easier—and perhaps it has been indispensable—to continue governing with the old ideology and language. A popular saying is that it is better to endure a known evil than to risk an unknown good; so here it may be said that it is better to endure a known dead person than to risk an unknown live one.[39]

Another perspective has focused on the level of national development. Tracing the fate of the Bolivian revolution—"uncompleted," in his words—James M. Malloy asserts that the successful establishment of a new political and social order may in fact require a greater degree of socioeconomic development. As he explains it:

> Poverty and backwardness may create conditions which motivate men to rise up in violence. Such violent uprisings may successfully destroy the fabric of a pre-existent social order. But the question of "making the revolution" in the modern developmental context is a different kind of problem than the process of destroying the old. The modern revolution is a process of stripping previously dominant social groups (in some cases, not so dominant groups as well) and reorganizing them and their resources within a new political and economic framework with the avowed aim of national development. The ability to complete the process successfully depends, at least in part, on the previous level of development. . . .The Bolivian case appears to demonstrate . . . that *the prospects of completing a development-oriented revolution in countries below a certain level of development are, at best, extremely difficult.*[40] (emphasis added)

Revolutions can break out in lots of places, but can take hold only in a few. This, perhaps, explains the consolidation of the revolution in Cuba, one of the region's more "developed" countries.

The central question persists nonetheless: What have been the consequences of revolutions in Latin America? What difference have they made?

Posed in this fashion, such inquiries raise vexing conceptual and methodological issues. It is misleading to compare prerevolutionary and postrevolutionary conditions and conclude that the "differences" represent the "results" of revolutionary transformation. Indeed, at least three factors could be at work: (1) ongoing societal processes—alterations that would have occurred without a revolution; (2) changes resulting from upheavals associated with the fact of revolution, regardless of its ideological content; and (3) changes reflecting the ideological commitment and policy orientation of the resulting regimes. There is no unambiguous means of disentangling these effects; nor is there any self-evident criterion for establishing the chronological limits of a revolution. When do revolutions stop? How long do their impacts endure?

Considerations of this kind come forth in the Nicaraguan case. Sandinista ideology was an eclectic blend of principles, not a clear-cut program, and policy direction was the result of ongoing internal political struggle. Moreover, the revolutionary government did not have much time or opportunity to bring about long-lasting change, largely because of the Contras. We may never know what the Sandinista revolution might really have brought about.

Political Outcomes. Considerable work has been done on the outcomes of revolutionary change in Mexico, with specific focus on the social recruitment of political leadership. Research generally has found a slow and steady transformation in class background: the traditional upper class fading from the scene, the lower class making modest gains, and the middle class expanding and consolidating influence. Observable change thus occurred, much of it probably due to incremental changes that might have occurred without the revolution—and some perhaps resulting from the conflict itself. Outside of elite circles, there were substantial sectors that remained relatively unchanged.

While the Mexican Revolution signaled the triumph of the middle class, it gave most of the power to previously excluded fragments of the nation's middle class. Moreover, it had a decisive impact on the structure of political careers. The postrevolutionary "no re-election" rule and associated practices sharply reduced the level of elite continuity, cutting the degree of continuity roughly in half. And it thoroughly rearranged the shape of political careers, introducing an enormous amount of uncertainty into the lives of individual officeholders. In these and other ways recruitment and selection procedures came to strengthen centralized authority, concentrating power to a degree comparable to that under the Díaz regime. "Ironically enough," one study concludes, "the PRI has not really institutionalized the Revolution, as its name proclaims. What it has done is to find a new formula for reinstitutionalizing the essence of the Porfiriato."[41]

In addition, the period from 1917 to 1940 saw the consolidation of elite sectors of the revolutionary leadership in the face of unsuccessful protests from both the Right and the Left. Counter-revolutionary tendencies emerged with the Cristero revolt (1926–29), and radical demands erupted in periodic rural and urban protests. While some revolutionary promises were redeemed through an expansion of governmental services, labor rights, and sporadic land reforms, others were abandoned. The 1929 creation of the Partido Nacional Revolucionario (PNR) helped channel elite competition, while its transformation in 1938 into the Partido de la Revolución Mexicana (PRM) under President Lázaro Cárdenas (1934–40) helped broaden its base. This was accomplished largely through the absorption of four groups into the PRM as corporate units: peasants, laborers, the military, and the middle class. One prime objective was to ensure their support; another was to discourage the formation of opposition coalitions (including red-green worker-peasant alliances). This strategy continued under the

Partido Revolucionario Institucional (PRI), which has dominated electoral politics since 1940 and become synonymous with the congealing of the revolution.

Along similar lines, studies have shown that durable Latin American revolutions have also created strong states. Initially drawing much of its legitimacy from Fidel Castro's personal charisma, the Cuban state evolved in the 1970s into a powerful network of stable institutions. A Marxist constitution took effect in 1976, the Cuban Communist party became dominant, and the military became a modern professional force. Economic management was centralized and routinized. The Cuban state asserted thorough command of the national economy.

In Nicaragua the Sandinista directorate, never dependent on individual charisma, sought institutional legitimacy through national elections in 1984. It also established mechanisms for popular participation in governance, including the controversial Sandinista Defense Committees, and assumed a major role in the economy through nationalization of Somoza-held and other properties. These accomplishments were especially impressive, in view of the weakness of the prerevolutionary state apparatus and its dependence on a personalistic dictator. The task in both Nicaragua and Cuba was to create strong states, not just take them over. In this regard the Cuban and Nicaraguan revolutionary leaders bear a distinct resemblance to the "state-building elites" encountered by Theda Skocpol in other revolutionary settings.[42]

Indeed, many revolutionary leaders have attempted to construct more or less monolithic political systems. The tendency has been to establish a practical monopoly on power with or without token opposition. In Mexico and Cuba the revolutionaries managed to succeed; in Bolivia and Nicaragua they did not. There are many reasons behind these efforts to concentrate power, including:

1. The conviction that this is an essential prerequisite or accompaniment to the implementation of structural socioeconomic transformations
2. The strength and character of the opposition
3. The threat of foreign intervention
4. An ideological commitment to revolutionary "purity," a partisan (and possibly psychological) insistence on orthodoxy and discipline

Whatever the causes, results are apparent. All these revolutionary regimes have displayed authoritarian tendencies. All have demonstrated limited tolerance for political self-expression and opposition politics.

Social Outcomes. For reasons of social policy and state strategy, both the Cuban and Nicaraguan regimes inaugurated national literacy campaigns soon after taking power. The social goal was to "capacitate" workers and peasants, removing obstacles to their full participation in the national economy, and thereby eliminate a primary source of long-

TABLE 1.   Assessing the Impact of Revolution: Illiteracy and Education

Country	% Illiterate*	% Student Enrollment			
		Primary		Secondary	
		1960	1980	1960	1980
Cuba	5 (1979)	78	100	43	83
Dominican Republic	33 (1970)	67	82	39	64
		1965	1984	1965	1984
Nicaragua	43 (1971)	69	99	14	43
El Salvador	38 (1975)	82	70	17	24
Guatemala	54 (1973)	50	76	8	17
Honduras	43 (1974)	50	71	10	33

*Age 15 and over

Compiled from data in James W. Wilkie and Adam Perkal (eds.), *Statistical Abstract of Latin America,* 24 (Los Angeles: UCLA Latin America Center Publications, 1986), tables 900 and 901 (pp. 144–45); World Bank, *World Development Report 1987* (New York: Oxford Univ. Press, 1987), table 31 (pp. 262–63).

standing inequity. The political intent was to mobilize the population and inculcate values (through literacy and education) appropriate to a revolutionary society—in other words, to forge "a new socialist man."

Some of the effects of these campaigns appear in table 1, which presents data on levels of illiteracy and school attendance for both Cuba and Nicaragua—and to control for regional patterns and trends, for nearby nonrevolutionary countries as well. The implications are generally clear. Cuba virtually eliminated adult illiteracy by 1979, and Nicaragua, with a prerevolutionary rate of 43 percent, also made substantial progress. By contrast, the nonrevolutionary societies—the Dominican Republic, El Salvador, Guatemala, and Honduras—reveal distressingly high levels of illiteracy, ranging from 33 percent in the Dominican Republic to 54 percent in Guatemala. School attendance rates show a similar pattern, with Cuba claiming a 100 percent level for the primary-school-age population by 1980; Nicaragua moved to 99 percent by the mid-1980s and made notable progress in the secondary-school-age group, with the highest attendance in its comparison group. Largely because of the woeful legacy of the Somozas, Nicaragua had a lot of catching up to do, and this constituted a central preoccupation of the Sandinista government.

Economic Outcomes. The revolutionary socialist regimes of Latin America applied state power in singular ways. The nationalization of the Cuban economy, for example, eliminated the capitalist class and much of the petite bourgeoisie. In other revolutionary contexts—Mexico and Bolivia, for instance—political transformations tended instead to stimulate openings for nationally oriented segments of the entrepreneurial class.[43] Nicaragua came to occupy a special niche in this regard: originally intending to create a mixed economy, based on state control of the Somoza sector in collaboration with a nationalist private sector, the public-sector Sandinista leadership found itself increasingly alone. Nicaragua in this sense moved toward socialism not necessarily because of its initial design but because of the progressive withdrawal of the nation's private sector, together with the continuing exigencies of war.

Land reform generally constitutes a key demand of revolutionary movements, and land reform usually takes place in revolutionary settings (if only partially). According to one historian, James W. Wilkie, the land reform programs of postrevolutionary Mexico provided benefits for nearly half (46.5 percent) the economically active males employed in agriculture; for Bolivia the figure was 39.0 percent. In no other country—outside of Cuba—did the figure surpass 16 percent, and only in Venezuela was it higher than 10 percent. In all other instances the figures were less than 5 percent. In Nicaragua approximately 35 percent of agricultural land was held by cooperatives or state farms as of 1988.[44]

By the 1980s land reform was largely completed in Cuba. There it followed two basic phases: first, the "land to the tiller" program initiated in 1959, and subsequently, the nationalization of holdings over 67 acres—a step that left about 30 percent of the farm population in the private sector. This second stage was especially significant because it exuded a distinctly anticapitalist bias (in contrast to other programs in Latin America, including Nicaragua). "Only in Cuba," writes sociologist Susan Eckstein, "has the postrevolutionary leadership opposed large-scale market-oriented private producers. Castro and his *guerrillero* collaborators used state power differently than their counterparts in [Mexico and Bolivia]."[45] Overall, the land reform program in Cuba benefited nearly two-thirds of the rural male population, a much higher proportion than elsewhere in Latin America.

A similar picture emerges in regard to income distribution. By 1973 the top 5 percent of the Cuban population held 9.5 percent of the national income, compared with 28 percent in the prerevolutionary era. In comparison, the same segment of the population held 35.7 percent of the national income in postrevolutionary Bolivia, and 25–35 percent in postrevolutionary Mexico. Similarly, the bottom 40 percent in Cuba has improved its standing more than in other countries, controlling just over 20 percent of income in 1973, in contrast to 6.2 percent before the revolution. The differences between Cuba and other countries may in fact be understated because health care systems and social security arrangements provide additional nonwage sources of social equity under the Fidelista regime.[46]

The Nicaraguan Revolution is not directly comparable due largely to problems arising from the Contra war, the U.S. economic embargo, and Sandinista economic policies. Nicaragua did, however, reflect a similar pattern of concentration of wealth in the prerevolutionary period. In 1980, just after the Sandinista takeover, the poorest 20 percent of the population received approximately 3 percent of the national income, while the richest 20 percent received 58 percent. Despite massive increases in social investments by the Sandinista government, approximately 69.4 percent of the population was defined as poor by 1985; approximately 82 percent were at or below the poverty level by 1989. This was due in large measure to a precipitous decline in the gross domestic product. The impact of the Contra war cannot be overestimated here; as early as 1984 it had resulted in material and production losses of $380 million, while the military was absorbing about half of the government's budget. Although it had been one of the original goals, income redistribution under such conditions was virtually impossible for the revolutionary government.[47]

Comparison of the Latin American revolutionary experience with recent developments in Eastern Europe suggests the emergence of alternative routes to revolutionary ends, although prerevolutionary conditions displayed some similarities. In both Latin America and Eastern Europe, uprisings targeted authoritarian or totalitarian states that enjoyed considerable autonomy from social classes and interest groups. Economic policy-making was highly politicized and did not result in broadly distributed benefits. There was a high degree of superpower dependence. Both Latin American and Eastern European prerevolutionary regimes tended to repress dissident and opposition movements indiscriminately, thus contributing to the emergence of multiclass coalitions with relatively weak class consciousness. Given the identification of the party with the state in Eastern Europe and the identification of dictators with the state in Latin America, the seizure and transformation of the state was seen as a means of eliminating abuses by a party or by dictators.

External penetration by either the USSR or the United States caused insurrectionary movements to be highly nationalistic, and liberation from external domination to be a rallying cry. While not necessarily ideologically cohesive or class-based, the revolutionary leadership did contain its share of organic intellectuals. Popular discourse tended to focus on common goals, such as national liberation, human rights, popular participation, and the end of repression.

Once the old regimes were toppled, diversity within these coalitions contributed to conflict and fragmentation. In Eastern Europe long-standing ethnic rivalries became increasingly apparent; in Latin America economic and class interests reasserted themselves. In Latin America this contributed to the domination of the most ideologically cohesive groups, such as the PSP in Cuba and the FSLN in Nicaragua.

Differences between the Eastern European and Latin American revolutionary experiences include a lesser degree of military conflict in the former than in the latter. In addition, to date there appear to have been weaker counterrevolutionary movements in Eastern Europe in the 1980s and 1990s. Attitudes toward the state in Eastern Europe also differ sharply from those in Latin America. In Czechoslovakia and Poland, the emphasis is on reducing the state's size and power, privatizing the economy, and adopting capitalism. In Cuba and Nicaragua, the focus was on state building and increasing state intervention in the economy, substituting socialism for capitalism.[48] A related difference is Eastern Europe's suspicion of the identification of the state with a single party; in Mexico, Cuba, and Nicaragua revolution resulted in one-party states.

Such a comparison indicates that while the desire for radical change consitutes the core of revolutionary movements, their origins, courses, and outcomes are increasingly diverse and complex. This suggests the utility of comparative analysis. One intriguing hypothesis has already been posed by Jeff Goodwin and Valerie Bunce: "If 'proletarian' revolutions in the Third World have been impeded by the absence of a large factory-based proletariat, Eastern Europe's 'bourgeois' revolutions are likely to be impeded by the absence of a strong bourgeoisie."[49]

Legacies and Outcomes: Recasting Revolution

What now? What are the prospects for radical political change in Latin America? Will there be more revolutions in the future? We have no claim on prescience, but we can identify conditions likely to affect the probability of revolution within the foreseeable future.

The international political environment has undergone dramatic change. The end of the Cold War has concluded a 40-year East-West rivalry, transformed the terms of ideological discourse, and (at least temporarily) left the United States as the world's only military superpower. As of the early 1990s, a great deal of instability seems to exist on the international scene, as the distribution of effective power keeps moving and the challenge of collective security keeps shifting. There is no clear sign of a durable "new world order," so it is impossible to predict, with any degree of certainty, Latin America's place in the evolving global order.

Even so, we can begin to see some of the outlines. For one thing, the collapse of the Soviet Union and Eastern Europe has seriously damaged the socialist ideal. While theoreticians, and others, insist the Stalinist Soviet Union was a grotesque distortion of Marxist ideas, and the authentic goals of pure socialism should still command respect, the fact is that leftist ideology has lost credibility in much of the world. And since Marxism-Leninism has been a touchstone of revolutionary movements throughout contemporary Latin America, this development has stripped leftist radicals of much of their former appeal.

Political democracy, by contrast, has acquired new legitimacy. Long denounced by some critics as a "bourgeois" fiction, the idea of democracy—including respect for human rights—has taken hold throughout the world. This may partly be a reaction to the experience of Communist repression in Eastern Europe and military rule within Latin America. It may reflect a growing appreciation for the intrinsic value of human rights. It may show a recognition of the possibilities for achieving meaningful socioeconomic change through democratic action. For many it may well be a "second-best" alternative, an acceptable form of political compromise. In any event, democratic transitions in Eastern Europe and Latin America have led to the conclusion, however tentative, that nonviolent reform may be preferable to violent upheaval, that revolution is no longer necessarily desirable.

Within the Western Hemisphere, at least, the demise of the Cold War has led to an unequivocal reassertion of U.S. hegemony. The Soviet Union (once present, even interventionist) no longer is an actor. As a result, would-be revolutionaries no longer have substantial international sponsors or patrons. There is no major counterweight to the United States, no source of international balance. It is indicative, perhaps, that the most prominent insurrectionary movement in the hemisphere—Sendero Luminoso in Peru—has explicitly refused to identify itself internationally. In a sense, there are no friends for it to seek.

Sendero Luminoso raises additional questions about revolutionary processes in general and about the nature of revolution in contemporary Latin America. Its use of terrorism to a far greater extent than many revolutionary movements reflects its emphasis on annihilating the existing state, rather than attempting to capture it. The intent appears to be to create a new kind of state, based on a restructured society, with new concepts of citizenship and participation. This may explain the ferocity of Sendero's current attacks, not only on representatives of the state, but also on civic leaders, humanitarian aid workers, and church people, particularly those working at the grass roots. As a result, public officials and civic leaders have withdrawn not only from the highlands, where Sendero originated in the early 1980s, but more recently from working-class communities ringing Lima. Sendero seems strong not only because the state is increasingly circumscribed and weakened, but also because political parties, and other such actors, have also become debilitated. It is unclear whether Sendero presages substantial modifications in the nature of Latin American revolutionary processes, though it emerged in response to major alterations in the political, economic, and social environment of the region as a whole.

Overall, however, the asphyxiation of the Nicaraguan Revolution in the 1980s and the isolation of Cuba in the 1990s appear to have reduced the possibilities of the revolutionary alternative. In addition, the annihilation of the political left by military governments—often through physical liquidation—has in some countries eliminated entire generations of revolutionary leadership from the political scene. And with leftist radicals in retreat, technocrats have seized the advantage, proclaiming their adherence to market-oriented economics in order to undertake neoliberal strategies. From Mexico to the Southern Cone, the terms of public discourse have undergone a remarkable shift: there is no longer much contestation between liberal and radical beliefs. At times it seems the major question is how best to achieve the maximum benefits from neoliberal programs.

To date, however, neoliberal strategies have not demonstrated their capacity to reverse the trend of increasing immiseration and violence in countries such as Brazil, Haiti, and Peru. Levels of poverty have been steadily increasing throughout the 1980s and 1990s. Eventually, continuation of this trend could spawn new forms of radicalism that could result in revolutionary outcomes.

It is clear that a transformation in the definition and strategy of revolution has taken place. Throughout Latin America, citizens and activists have come to rethink the traditional concept of revolution—as a violent seizure of the state apparatus. They have not, however, surrendered the goal of structural alteration in the distribution of power. Thus, as in Eastern Europe, they may be devising new forms of revolution reflecting changed concepts of state and society.

In recent years, people in Latin America and around the world have chosen in increasing numbers to join "social movements" rather than armed struggle. Often working at the local level—whether teachers' unions, peasant cooperatives, women's groups, or base Christian communities—these grass roots movements seek to bring about structural change within the immediate domains of life and work. They focus on tangible results, rather than abstract philosophical principles. They deal with immediate concerns, not international alliances. Ideologically diffuse and socially diverse, they represent mounting challenges to socioeconomic injustice and indifferent or repressive political establishments.[50]

To a degree, the growth of such movements reflects a rejection of the classic revolutionary presumption about the centrality of the state. These movements are not attempting to take over the state apparatus: they are trying to bring about change *in spite of* the state. For them, the weakening of the Latin American state in the 1980s and 1990s has significantly modified long-standing perceptions about the nature and power of state institutions in society. Conquest of the state no longer seems to be the only strategy; the *étatiste* presumption appears to be in decline. Instead, the idea is to evade the state or, at least, negate its influence at local and regional levels. In contrast to their predecessors, contemporary social movements do not necessarily want a strong state.

In other words, it may be possible to pursue revolutionary purposes through new means. Classic revolution, as we have defined it, seems unlikely to occur in Latin America within the foreseeable future. So long as injustice and repression remain, however, revolutionary aspirations will thrive and aspirations will give rise to agitation. Popular struggle may assume a broad variety of forms, from the terrorism of Sendero Luminoso to the pragmatism of social movements and the far-reaching reformism of Eastern Europe. In one way or another, the struggle will no doubt continue.

Notes

1. Jeff Goodwin and Valerie Bunce, "Eastern Europe's 'Refolutions' in Comparative and Theoretical Perspective," ms., 1991.

2. John Mander, *The Unrevolutionary Society: The Power of Latin American Conservatism in a Changing World* (New York: Knopf, 1969).

3. Tad Szulc, *The Winds of Revolution: Latin America Today—and Tomorrow* (New York: Praeger, 1965), 3.

4. Paul A. Baran, *The Political Economy of Growth* (New York: Monthly Review Press, 1957); Paul A. Baran and Paul M. Sweezy, *Monopoly Capital* (New York: Monthly Review Press, 1966).

5. André Gunder Frank, *Capitalism and Underdevelopment in Latin America: Historical Studies of Chile and Brazil* (New York: Monthly Review Press, 1969).

6. Theotonio dos Santos, *Socialism o fascismo: dilema latinamericano* (Santiago: Editorial Prensa Latinoamericano, 1969).

7. Fernando Henrique Cardoso and Enzo Faletto, *Dependency and Development in Latin America*, trans. Marjory Urquidi (Berkeley: Univ. of California Press, 1978), xxiv.

8. Guillermo O'Donnell, *Modernization and Bureaucratic-Authoritarianism: Studies in South American Politics* (Berkeley: Institute of International Studies, Univ. of California, 1973).

9. Hector E. Schamis, "Reconceptualizing Latin American Authoritarianism in the 1970s: From Bureaucratic-Authoritarianism to Neoconservatism," *Comparative Politics* (Jan. 1991), 202.

10. See Guillermo O'Donnell, Philippe C. Schmitter, and Laurence Whitehead, (eds.), *Transitions from Authoritarianism*, 4 vols. (Baltimore: Johns Hopkins Univ. Press, 1986).

11. Timothy Garton Ash, *The Magic Lantern: The Revolution of '89 as Witnessed in Warsaw, Budapest, Berlin and Prague* (New York: Random House, 1990).

12. David D. Burks, *Cuba Under Castro* (New York: Foreign Policy Assn., 1964); Theodore Draper, *Castroism: Theory and Practice* (New York: Praeger, 1965); Andrés Suárez, *Cuba: Castroism and Communism, 1959–1966* (Cambridge: MIT Press, 1967).

13. Ted Robert Gurr, *Why Men Rebel* (Princeton: Princeton Univ. Press, 1971).

14. James C. Davis, "Toward a Theory of Revolution," *American Sociological Review* 27 (1962), 5–18, and "The J-Curve of Rising and Declining Satisfactions as a Cause of Some Great Revolutions and a Contained Rebellion," in Hugh

David Graham and Ted Robert Gurr (eds.), *Violence in America* (New York: Signet, 1969), 671–709.

15. Donald Schulz, "Ten Theories in Search of Central American Reality," in Donald E. Schulz and Douglas H. Graham (eds.), *Revolution and Counterrevolution in Central America and the Caribbean* (Boulder, Colo.: Westview Press, 1984), 16.

16. Eric R. Wolf, *Peasant Wars of the Twentieth Century* (New York: Harper and Row, 1969), 290, 291–92.

17. For additional theoretical statements on this general subject see Jeffrey M. Paige, *Agrarian Revolution: Social Movements and Export Agriculture in the Underdeveloped World* (New York: Free Press, 1975); Joel Migdal, *Peasants, Politics, and Revolution* (Princeton: Princeton Univ. Press, 1975); James C. Scott, *The Moral Economy of the Peasant: Subsistence and Rebellion in Southeast Asia* (New Haven: Yale Univ. Press, 1976); Samuel Popkin, *The Rational Peasant: The Political Economy of Rural Society in Vietnam* (Berkeley: Univ. of California Press, 1979); and Theda Skocpol, "What Makes Peasants Revolutionary?" *Comparative Politics* 14:3 (April 1983): 351–75. For a perceptive testing of the applicability of these theories to the Nicaraguan case, see Jeffrey L. Gould, *To Lead as Equals: Rural Protest and Political Consciousness in Chinandega, Nicaragua, 1912–1979* (Chapel Hill: Univ. of North Carolina Press, 1990).

18. Friedrich Katz, "Labor Conditions on Haciendas in Porfirian Mexico: Some Trends and Tendencies," *Hispanic American Historical Review* 54: 1 (Feb. 1974), 1–47.

19. Ibid.; John Womack, Jr., *Zapata and the Mexican Revolution* (New York: Knopf, 1969); Romana Falcón, *Revolución y caciquismo: San Luis Potosí, 1910–1938* (Mexico City: El Colegio de Mexico, 1984); Frans J. Schryer, "Peasant Politics in Latin America: Case Studies of Rural Mexico," *Latin American Research Review* 21:1 (1985), 272–77; Mark T. Guilderhus, "Many Mexicos: Tradition and Innovation in Recent Historiography," *Latin American Research Review* 22:1 (1987), 204–13.

20. Ellen Kay Trimberger, *Revolution from Above: Military Bureaucrats and Development in Japan, Turkey, Egypt and Peru* (New Brunswick, N.J.: Transaction Books, 1978). For an analysis of whether Peru under the military qualifies as a "revolution," see Alfred Stepan, *The State and Society: Peru in Comparative Perspective* (Princeton: Princeton Univ. Press, 1978).

21. Walter LaFeber, *Inevitable Revolutions: The United States in Central America* (New York: Norton, 1983).

22. Peter H. Smith, *Labyrinths of Power: Political Recruitment in Twentieth-Century Mexico* (Princeton: Princeton Univ. Press, 1979).

23. Barry Carr, "Recent Regional Studies of the Mexican Revolution," *Latin American Research Review* 15:1 (1980), 8.

24. Cole Blasier, "Studies of Social Revolution: Origins in Mexico, Bolivia and Cuba," *Latin American Research Review* 2:3 (1967), 45–46; Alfred L. Padula, "The Fall of the Bourgeoisie: Cuba, 1959–1961" (Ph.D. diss., Univ. of New Mexico, 1974).

25. Henri Weber, *Nicaragua: The Sandinista Revolution* (London: Verso, 1981), 35.

26. See Carlos M. Vilas, "What Went Wrong?" *NACLA: Report on the Americas* 24:1 (June 1990), 10–18.

27. Donald C. Hodges, *Intellectual Foundations of the Nicaraguan Revolution* (Austin: Univ. of Texas Press, 1986), 182–84.

28. Antonio Gramsci, *Selections from the Prison Notebooks* (New York: International Publishers, 1971), 153.

29. Fidel Castro, *History Will Absolve Me* (New York: Center for Cuban Studies, n.d.).

30. Roger N. Lancaster, *Thanks to God and the Revolution: Popular Religion and Class Consciousness in the New Nicaragua* (New York: Columbia Univ. Press, 1988); Steven Palmer, "Carlos Fonseca and the Construction of Sandinismo in Nicaragua," *Latin American Research Review* 23:1 (1988), 91–109.

31. Hodges, *Intellectual Foundations*, 183.

32. Antonio Gramsci, *The Modern Prince and Other Writings* (New York: International Publishers, 1957).

33. Theda Skocpol, *States and Social Revolutions: A Comparative Analysis of France, Russia, and China* (Cambridge: Cambridge Univ. Press, 1979).

34. For further discussion of the role of religion and the Catholic Church in contemporary Latin America, see "Religion: Reconstituting Church and Pursuing Change," by Margaret E. Crahan, in this volume.

35. George Kennan, as quoted in LaFeber, *Inevitable Revolutions*, 107.

36. The 1989 invasion of Panama was a classic demonstration of U.S. interventionism, but it had nothing to do with revolution.

37. Leslie Dewart, *Christianity and Revolution: The Lesson of Cuba* (New York: Herder and Herder, 1963).

38. Cole Blasier, *The Hovering Giant: U.S. Responses to Revolutionary Change in Latin America* (Pittsburgh: Univ. of Pittsburgh Press, 1976).

39. Daniel Cosío Villegas, "The Mexican Revolution, Then and Now," in Stanley R. Ross (ed.), *Is the Mexican Revolution Dead?* (Philadelphia: Temple Univ. Press, 1966), 115–16.

40. James M. Malloy, *Bolivia: The Uncompleted Revolution* (Pittsburgh: Univ. of Pittsburgh Press, 1970), 340–41. See also Jonathan Kelley and Herbert S. Klein, *Revolution and the Rebirth of Inequality: A Theory Applied to the National Revolution in Bolivia* (Berkeley: Univ. of California Press, 1981).

41. Smith, *Labyrinths of Power*, 187.

42. Skocpol, *States and Social Revolutions*.

43. Susan Eckstein, "The Impact of Revolution on Social Welfare in Latin America," *Theory and Society* 11 (1982), 44–45.

44. James Wilkie, *Measuring Land Reform*, supplement to *Statistical Abstract of Latin America* (Los Angeles: UCLA Latin America Center, 1974), 5; and Laura J. Enríquez, *Harvesting Change: Labor and Agrarian Reform in Nicaragua, 1979–1990* (Chapel Hill: Univ. of North Carolina Press, 1991), 93.

45. Eckstein, "Impact," 62.

46. Ibid., 69.

47. Claes Brundenius, "Industrial Development Strategies in Revolutionary Nicaragua," in Rose J. Spalding (ed.), *The Political Economy of Revolutionary Nicaragua* (Boston: Allen & Unwin, 1987), 88; Margaret E. Crahan, "Political Legitimacy and Dissent," in Jiri Valenta and Esperanza Durán (eds.), *Conflict in Nicaragua: A Multidimensional Perspective* (Boston: Allen & Unwin, 1987), 121; Oscar René Vargas, "Nicaragua: A Poor Country," *Envio* 10:123 (Oct. 1991), 12–13.

48. This comparison of revolution in Eastern Europe and Latin America draws on Goodwin and Bunce, "Eastern Europe's 'Refolutions,'" 6–61.

49. Ibid., 41.

50. See Susan Eckstein (ed.), *Power and Popular Protest: Latin American Social Movements* (Berkeley: Univ. of California Press, 1989); Joe Foweraker and Ann L. Craig (eds.), *Popular Movements and Political Change in Mexico* (Boulder, Colo.: Rienner, 1990).

PART II

New Voices/New Visions

5

Production, Reproduction, and the Polity: Women's Strategic and Practical Gender Issues

HELEN I. SAFA AND CORNELIA BUTLER FLORA

Women have always been a vital part of family and national survival in the Americas. They have been active, productive members of their families, communities, and nations. Their roles have varied tremendously, by age, social class, and ethnicity. Their contributions at times were influenced by an ideal of women active only in the home *(casa)*, while men were to be active on the outside *(calle)*. But women's participation in production and community life, as well as their work to ensure basic family reproduction, has grown more visible in recent years.[1]

The new importance given to women's active participation in Latin American life may be attributed both to internal changes in the roles women traditionally have performed and to external changes in the larger global economy. In the post–World War II expansionary period, women in many Latin American and Caribbean countries achieved substantial gains in educational and occupational levels, as well as dramatic declines in fertility. These changes enabled them to become more active participants in the political and economic lives of their countries, and to respond to the drastic reduction in economic opportunities and state support brought on by the debt crisis and structural adjustment policies starting in the late 1970s. Throughout the period of change, women of the Americas proved themselves agents and not simply victims of change.

This article is based in part on "Changing Gender Roles and Development in Latin America," by Helen Safa, in Hilda Kahne and Janet Giele (eds.), *Continuing Struggle: Women's Work and Women's Lives in Modernizing and Industrial Countries* (Boulder, Colo.: Westview Press, in press). Reprinted with permission of editors and publisher.

Socioeconomic transformations in Latin America and the Caribbean after World War II have had a special impact on women. As Latin American countries struggled to overcome dependency and develop their economies, women played important and, until recently, unrecognized roles. Both economic growth and decline depended to a large extent on women in the role of "shock absorber"—their efforts allowed labor to be highly mobile during times of economic opportunity, and filled gaps left in family income when the economy contracted. Understanding the period of growth and decline after the Second World War makes the importance of women in facilitating change more apparent.

Women's responses to these macrolevel changes were conditioned by their productive and reproductive responsibilities. Reproductive activities in the household have often been seen as women's sole function. But their equally critical productive activities for generating income have been ignored, until recently. Productive activities have thrust women into the public domain traditionally reserved for men and have made some women more conscious of the gender discrimination they face not only in the workplace but also as citizens of a state largely unresponsive to their practical needs for day-to-day survival.

Women's consciousness of gender subordination has been expressed largely through feminist movements, which address women's strategic needs. However, in Latin America there has been a long history of women acting on the community level to meet their practical needs, a phenomenon termed "community management" by Moser.[2] Nonfeminist women's groups have increasingly turned to collective public action to counter injustices women feel as they are blocked while trying to address their practical needs. This collective action has served to meet such basic necessities as food, water, and health care in the face of the region's growing economic crisis. Women have also struggled collectively for human rights to defend families against state repression in authoritarian military regimes, particularly in the Southern Cone in the 1970s and early 1980s.

These grass roots forms of collective action are distinguished by the widespread participation of poor women, who focus their demands on the state in their struggle for basic survival and against repression. These demands center largely on what Molyneux has termed women's "practical gender interests," those legitimized by women's traditional roles as wives and mothers and which respond to their immediate perceived needs. Molyneux distinguishes these practical gender interests from strategic gender interests, which are derived deductively by analyzing gender subordination and which challenge the traditional sexual division of labor from a feminist perspective.[3] The politicization of practical gender interests may transform them into strategic gender interests, which require a higher degree of gender consciousness. This transformation is aided by linkages between grass roots movements and more middle-class feminist movements present in many parts of Latin America, which generally work together more closely than those in North America. When the two movements do come together, both feminism and the grass roots movements are transformed.

This essay will explore the possibilities of this transformation among Latin American and Caribbean women by examining the extent to which women's changing productive and reproductive roles and their increased participation in the polity has been translated into greater gender consiousness. A central proposition of this essay is that women's increased participation in the public sphere—in order to resolve practical gender needs—has led Latin American and Caribbean women to formulate strategic gender interests aimed at redressing women's subordination to men. Our analysis will focus on poor women and their changing role in production, reproduction, and the polity, particularly since 1950.

Postwar Socioeconomic Changes

The period from 1950 to the mid-1970s was characterized by considerable economic growth in Latin America and the Caribbean. This growth was partly due to a worldwide economic expansion. In addition, national governments instituted policies of *import substitution,* aimed primarily at reducing the region's dependence on the export of primary products and increasing domestic manufacture for internal consumption.[4] Planned growth intended to create manufacturing jobs for men: the image of a developed society was one of nuclear families in which men supported women. From 1950 to 1980, total domestic product increased fivefold and per capita product doubled. Industry expanded and diversified, with manufacturing output increasing sixfold between 1950 and 1987. The tertiary sector, which increasingly employed women, grew at an even faster rate.

Rural Transformations

In order to generate capital to invest in new manufacturing enterprises, agriculture and mining exports had to increase. Much of the productive land was in the hands of *latifundistas* (large landowners), who devoted vast stretches of land to cattle-raising. Peasant families had use rights to enough land to raise food crops for their own consumption. Under traditional land tenure arrangements, peasant families had grazing rights for their livestock and access to land to raise crops and gather foods and medicines.[5] This land now had to generate foreign exchange through intensified production of export crops such as sugar cane, cotton, and tobacco.

Although land reform was implemented in part by modernizing urban elites to ensure that land use changed to export crops, the Cuban

Revolution underlined the need for greater equity, manifest in the agrarian reform programs of the Alliance for Progress. Most land reform laws in Latin America and the Caribbean were written to increase the efficiency of the land, not to redistribute it. When land was titled to the tiller, the tiller was assumed to be male. Although women in many parts of Latin America have historically been active agriculturalists, their participation was not reflected in land ownership.[6] Instead, as land titles became formal, women generally lost their usufructuary rights.

Migration

As land use became more export oriented and mechanized in areas of higher labor cost, permanent agricultural employment declined in favor of seasonal work. Women represented an increasingly important proportion of seasonal laborers. In Mexico, the proletarianization of peasant families led to whole families becoming engaged in seasonal agricultural work, while female migration since the 1970s shifted from urban areas to free-trade zones on the northern border and to the United States.[7]

Between 1950 and 1980 the percentage of the total population living in urban areas increased from 40.9 percent to 63.3 percent. Internal migration rates varied enormously by age and sex, but young women predominated in this flow due to the limited employment opportunities available to them in rural areas. Even after migrating, women have maintained long-standing ties to their native communities through periodic visits, which reinforce land rights and reciprocal exchange commitments.[8]

As men and younger women migrated out, older women became the de facto heads of households and main agriculturalists in some rural areas. Arizpe has documented the process of Mexican relay migration whereby the earning power of the migrant father is gradually replaced by that of his sons and daughters in order of age, as their remittances contribute to an impoverished peasant economy.[9] Yet not all married women with migrant spouses receive remittances. In a national sample of rural women in the Dominican Republic in the mid-1980s, only half the married women without spouses present had received remittances in the previous year.[10] Consequently, many women married to migrant workers were left with sole responsibility for maintaining their households in an impoverished rural economy.

Urban Growth and Change

Migration to urban areas is often motivated by a desire for education, since rural schooling is usually woefully inadequate. Further, rural women's heavy domestic load—gathering wood and water, carrying laundry long distances, raising crops and animals, and caring for younger children—means that girls rather than boys are more often needed at home and kept out of school. The lack of perceived job opportunities for women also seems to obviate their need for education. Thus, for women in particular, the move to the city means a chance for increased education, due both to the increased availability of schools and jobs and to the diminished need for their household labor. The result is that women's literacy rates are often higher than those of men in urban areas, while in rural areas women have higher illiteracy rates and lower school attendance.

Extended education for urban women has been accompanied by increased participation in the formal labor market and decreased fertility. In the early stages of rural-urban migration, women were primarily employed in domestic service or as market and street sellers.[11] This work often allows women to combine child care and income generation. Women who worked in the formal labor sector, which tended to require higher educational levels, were compelled to leave their children at home. The new incompatibility between productive and reproductive roles contributed to declines in fertility that occurred primarily among better-educated women.[12] Fertility declines became increasingly widespread as more women began to enter the formal urban labor market in white-collar and industrial jobs, as well as the service sector.

Despite lower fertility, higher educational levels, and increased labor force participation, poverty and income inequality continue to be major problems for Latin American and Caribbean women. The degree of poverty varies among countries and within countries. Poverty tends to be concentrated in rural areas and in black or indigenous Indian populations.[13] Despite an overall increase in average income from 1965 to 1975, economic growth primarily benefited the rich, while the number of poor actually increased.[14] The modern, urban sector was unable to absorb the large numbers of persons entering the labor force, resulting in persistently high rates of unemployment and underemployment in most countries. Although government expenditures on infrastructure and social services expanded in most Latin American and Caribbean countries during the period of economic growth in the 1960s and 1970s, attempts at income redistribution were limited.

The Economic Crisis

The economic crisis that hit most of Latin America and the Caribbean after 1973 threatened to overturn the progress of the previous three decades and halt all attempts at income redistribution. The crisis was brought on by rising import prices, particularly that of oil; a decline in both quantity and price of exports, especially agricultural products and minerals such as bauxite and nickel; and a sharp rise in interest rates on the foreign debt, which totaled U.S. $410 billion in 1987. The proportion of the population living in poverty grew during the crisis as a result of three developments: a steep decline in the gross domestic product (GDP), with negative growth rates in most countries; increased unemployment, which grew 48 percent between 1980 and 1985; and a decline of between 12 and 18 percent in real wages in the same period. Wages fell more precipitously among less organized workers who held less permanent agricultural, construction, and minimum-wage jobs, and who constituted the great majority of workers in the 1980s.[15]

Structural Adjustment

In desperation, several countries were forced to implement structural adjustment programs. The philosophy behind structural adjustment policies is to shift responsibility for survival from the state to individuals and families by forcing them to absorb a greater share of the cost of living. This is seen as reducing "the weight of the state." Such programs were designed by the International Monetary Fund (IMF) to cut government expenditures, improve the balance of trade, and reduce foreign debt. Yet these policies often resulted in greater hardship for the poor, since they included currency devaluation, which accelerated the inflation rate and increased the cost of living. These policies also resulted in the reduction of government subsidies for basic foods and subsidized credits to farmers; cuts in government expenditure, particularly for social services; and the decline of real wages.[16]

The pressure placed on balance of payments reinforced a new model of export-led economic development. Comparative advantage in the global economy, rather than import substitution, now determined development priorities. In Chile, Ecuador, and many Central American nations, this meant increased exports of nontraditional agricultural products, such as high-value fruits, vegetables, and shrimp. Women make up a large proportion of this new agricultural labor force. In other countries it meant the growth of assembly plants—*maquiladores*—which also employ primarily women.[17] In these cases, part of the comparative global advantage was the source of cheap and relatively skilled labor represented by young women (as well as the lack of environmental and labor protection laws). If the import-substitution model was aimed at creating a domestic market to purchase the products produced, the comparative advantage model represents an almost complete disarticulation between production and consumption, and a halt to all attempts at income redistribution.

The impact of the economic crisis has been particularly severe on women in Latin America and the Caribbean, and it threatens to undermine their newly won educational and occupational gains. Most analysts agree that women (along with children and the elderly) constitute a more vulnerable group than men because their occupational choices and access to resources are more limited. At the same time, the crisis is increasing the importance and visibility of women's contribution to the household economy, as additional women enter the labor force to meet the rising cost of living and decreased wage-earning capacity of men.

Women's Changing Productive Work

While Latin American and Caribbean women had long been involved in productive work that contributed to family income either in kind or in cash, the changing economic conditions of the 1980s made paid employment even more necessary. Practical needs motivated women's increased participation in the labor force. However, in some cases this participation also began to address women's strategic needs to increase their status vis-à-vis men. Paid employment does not automatically increase women's status, although it certainly increases their total work load. Nevertheless, paid work breaks women out of the isolation of the home and may give them a greater voice in the home and community.

The size of the female labor force increased threefold in Latin America between 1950 and 1980, with overall participation rates of women between the ages of 18 and 65 rising from almost 18 percent to over 26 percent in the same period. Participation rates for women grew faster than those for men, and included all age groups, although single women between the ages of 20 and 29 continued to be the most active.[18]

Wage Rates: The Continued Gap

Women in Latin America and the Caribbean continue to earn considerably less than men, despite their rising educational levels. The labor force throughout Latin America is highly segmented, which facilitates wage discrimination. Interestingly, agricultural work performed by women in Latin America is often done by Mexican and Central American male migrants in the United States. In both cases a segmented labor force allows wages to be kept low.

The demand for export crops and the expanding presence of international agribusiness have increased the number of female agricultural day laborers. In both traditional export crops, such as coffee and cacao, where women have always worked as unpaid family labor, and in new export agriculture, with such crops as flowers, fruits, and vegetables, women command lower wages, work harder, and are less unionized than men. Their situation illustrates the "comparative advantage of women's disadvantages," as Arizpe put it in a study of women workers in strawberry export processing plants in Mexico.[19]

The economic "advantage" of low wages for women is supported by an ideology that sanctions female dependence on men for economic survival. Indeed, this ideology often means that men will contribute little or nothing to household maintenance if their women are employed. For example, in Colombia, a women's income-generation project was brought to a halt when the men refused to contribute anything to the household budget if the women earned any income whatsoever. Further, Stolcke has documented the discontent of women and their resentment toward their husbands when the women had to engage in wage labor as *volantes,* or day laborers, on coffee plantations near São Paulo (even in the same tasks they previously performed as unpaid family labor on tenant farms).[20] This suggests that the ideology of dependence on a male breadwinner continues to influence women's as well as men's attitudes toward women's paid employment. For both men and women, the critical need for additional income, combined with traditional norms of male financial responsibility for the family, creates ambivalence. Men's power as sole or primary breadwinner is undermined, leading some women to question other realms of male authority as well.

Higher educational levels contribute to the increased participation of women in the formal labor force. Formal labor force participation offers some benefits and legal protection (although not against wage discrimination). It also requires specific credentials and training. Women's educational levels increased faster than those of men during the expansion in primary and secondary education, from 1950 to 1970. This contributed to an increase between 1960 and 1980 in the number of women in white-collar work, particularly in the more developed Latin American and Caribbean countries. However, even relatively privileged white-collar women face a highly segmented labor market and are found principally in such traditionally feminine occupations as clerical work, elementary school teaching, and nursing—all requiring special training but all poorly paid. Formal labor force participation outside the home made it more difficult for women to combine paid employment with child care than did work in either the informal or agricultural sectors.

Industrial Employment and Unemployment

The pattern of industrial employment varies tremendously among Latin American nations. The application of neoliberal economic policies in countries such as Chile and Argentina prior to the crisis led to deindustrialization and the decline of the male and female industrial labor force. Unemployment in Chile was consistently high in the decade following 1974 and reached one-third of the labor force in 1983, and 80 percent in the shanty towns surrounding Santiago.[21] In São Paulo, Brazil, however, the spectacular industrial boom of the 1970s led to an appreciable growth in female employment in manufacturing, increasing 181 percent between 1970 and 1980.[22] Despite this rise, women workers were largely concentrated in exclusively female and low-paying jobs, showing that the sexual division of labor in the workplace may be reinforced rather than weakened by development and industrialization.

The economic crisis of the 1980s in many Latin American countries marked a substantial increase in women's industrial work through export processing.[23] Export processing in Latin America and the Caribbean allows advanced industrial countries to cut labor costs by exporting the labor-intensive stages of the manufacturing process to low-wage countries, and paying only a low value-added duty when these assembled goods are re-imported. Export manufacturers have shown a preference for women workers because, like agricultural day workers, they are cheaper to employ, less likely to unionize, and have greater patience for the tedious, monotonous work involved in assembly line production of clothing and electronics, the most popular export-processing items.

Wage reductions resulting from currency devaluation during the economic crisis have increased the attractiveness of investment in export processing in Mexico, the Dominican Republic, and other areas. In the Dominican Republic, the number of workers increased between 1985 and 1992 to an estimated 135,000, approximately 70 percent of whom are women. At the rate of exchange prevailing in August 1986, the average wage in export processing was approximately U.S. $90 monthly.

Although not officially proscribed, no unions exist in the Dominican export-processing plants, and workers are fired and blacklisted with other plants if any organizing activity is detected. Workers complain of the lack of public transportation, proper eating facilities, adequate medical services, and child care in the free-trade zones in which these export-processing plants are located. The government offers little support to workers with grievances, and most women just quit when they can no longer withstand the pressure of high production quotas, strict discipline, and long hours. As a result, labor turnover is high, and factory managers have indicated a preference for women with children, because they feel their need to work ensures greater job commitment. A high percentage of Dominican women workers in export-processing zones are married or are female heads of households, a departure from the global pattern in which young, single women predominate in export processing.[24]

Growth of the Informal Sector

As a result of the formal sector's economic crisis and stagnation, substantial growth has occurred in the informal sector, which is characterized by small-scale, unregulated forms of production and distribution, requiring little capital or technological input. Because of the barriers they face in formal sector employment, women often predominate in the informal sector.

Without a formal wage labor contract, jobs in the informal sector lack protective labor legislation, minimum wages, social security, and other benefits. Many of the workers in the informal sector are self-employed or are employed as family labor. Among Latin American and Caribbean women, domestic service and street selling are two of the largest occupational groups in the informal sphere. Although the proportion of working women in domestic service has declined from more than 37 percent in some countries in 1960 to a maximum of 22.9 percent in 1980, it remains Latin America's largest occupational group. However, alternative employment opportunities for women and girls have forced the modernization of domestic service in the region's most developed countries, with a changeover from resident to nonresident employees. In some situations, women in domestic service actually have entered the formal sector with social security coverage, regulation of hours and days off, and paid vacations.[25]

Once women acquire a small amount of capital—and dependents— they move to other activities, such as street and market vending. Street traders range from rural indigenous women in Mexico and the Andes selling their own produce or craft specialties in the city, to Jamaican, Haitian, or eastern Caribbean "higglers," who travel among the islands, and even as far as Miami, buying and selling food, clothing, appliances, and other consumer goods. As the economic crisis worsens, more and more women and men seek to generate income by selling and reselling consumer goods.[26]

The informal sector is also expanding among women whom Portes has termed "disguised wage workers."[27] In an effort to cut labor costs and avoid unions and other labor legislation, manufacturers are increasingly subcontracting part of their production process to homeworkers, who are not entitled to benefits. Even service industries such as data processing are turning to subcontracting as a way to cut labor costs and meet international competition.

Most homeworkers are married women who must do piecework because of child care responsibilities or because their husbands forbid them to work outside the home. This piecework allows the women greater flexibility in working hours. Employers can also increase flexibility and scale work volume up or down with market fluctuations. There is thus no employment stability, and piecework rates generally fall below minimum wage, as a recent study of homeworkers in Mexico City demonstrated.[28] An added problem for homeworkers is the need to purchase or rent sewing machines, for which payments must continue whether or not they generate income.

Microenterprises and women's income-generation projects are also contributing to the growth of the informal sector.[29] Because of their potential for labor absorption and cost advantages in a highly competitive international market, microenterprises are receiving increased public and private sector support, access to credit, raw materials, foreign exchange, and other privileges formerly reserved exclusively for the formal sector. International donors and lenders are increasingly channeling loans through grass roots organizations, often organized by women in support of microenterprises. These programs have proliferated throughout the region and are generally set up by external sources with minimal funding, since the number of women involved in each project is small. As in the case of industrial homework, microenterprise products, including agricultural items, clothes, footwear, and crafts, may be marketed by multinational corporations. While microenterprises do provide markets for products created by women, they may simply be another mechanism for cutting labor costs.

Standing has argued that "global feminization through flexible labor" results from structural adjustment policies and the need to cut labor costs to meet greater international competition from developing and advanced industrial societies.[30] He cites a number of factors, including the growth of export processing, labor market deregulation through subcontracting and the informal sector, and cuts in government expenditure, which contribute to rising women's participation rates and declining men's participation rates.

Women are thus entering the formal labor market at the same time that organized labor in Latin America and the Caribbean has been seriously weakened. In Chile, union membership declined from 41 percent of the labor force in 1972 to 10 percent in 1987,[31] largely as a result of government repression and the deindustrialization policy. The decline in the region's union membership has also been partially attributed to the increased number of employed women who are difficult to organize because they work in sectors like seasonal agriculture, export processing, or white-collar jobs.

The labor movement has also tended to neglect women workers. Despite the increased participation of women in the labor force, organized labor continues to regard them as supplementary workers in comparison with men, and to focus on class rather than gender issues. As a result, women workers' specific problems—the need for day care and maternity leaves, for example—are rarely included in union demands. Union leadership continues to be largely male, with women concentrated in welfare departments and in secretarial positions.

Women's lack of bargaining power in the workplace thus lies less with women themselves than with the lack of support they receive from unions, the state, and political parties.[32] At present, most women workers have no adequate vehicles through which to express their grievances or transform their exploitation into greater class solidarity or gender consciousness. Until the claims of women workers are given the same legitimacy as those of men, labor's position as a whole will continue to deteriorate.

Labor force participation and other forms of income generation clearly meet women's practical needs. Projects that help women earn income are often legitimized internationally—as well as within the household. Yet because women still tend to be regarded as supplementary workers, their productive activities have had limited impact on addressing their strategic needs. In Brazil, for example, social movements have emerged among women agricultural and industrial workers around such strategic needs as equal job access by sex, or equal pay for equal work, but with little success.

Change and Women's Reproductive Roles

Women in Latin America are honored and respected for their reproductive roles, including childbearing, childrearing, and the many arduous tasks that go into maintaining a household and preparing the next generation to become productive members of society. Reproductive roles are both biological and social. Social reproduction for women includes household and social management, such as maintaining kinship linkages, developing neighborhood networks, and carrying out religious, ceremonial, and social obligations in the community. Social reproduction generally involves women's activities geared to meeting practical needs. Yet because reproductive roles, both biological and social, are embedded in gendered power relationships, women organizing collectively to carry them out often end up addressing strategic needs as well.

Upper- and middle-class women have been able to delegate many of their reproductive tasks to poor women in urban and rural areas.[33] And poor women have developed a number of household survival strategies—particularly mobilizing family labor—to assist them in carrying out household tasks. Yet in response to the increasing economic pressure of the 1980s and 1990s, women's reproductive roles have become increasingly difficult as government-funded systems providing water, electricity, health care, and education deteriorate. Further, the increased need to generate income leaves less time for reproductive tasks. Strategies to meet these increased reproductive demands include decreasing the number of dependents through decreased fertility, stretching family income by maximizing earnings and minimizing expenditures, restructuring the division of labor in the family, and collectivizing reproductive work through communal projects.

Fertility and Family Size

Decreasing fertility levels may be attributed to various factors, including women's increasing educational and occupational levels, rising age at marriage, high rates of marital instability, and greater availability of contraceptives. Because of this complex set of influences, fertility rates vary by country and development level (see table 1). Women in more

TABLE 1. Social Indicators of the Quality of Life for Females in Latin America and the Caribbean

Country	Life Expectancy of Females at Birth in Years		Total Fertility Rates		Females as Percentage of Total Enrollments in Primary Education	
	1970	1985	1970	1985	1970	1985
Argentina	69.30	73.10	3.04	3.38	49	49
Barbados	70.10	75.40	3.44	1.94	—	—
Bolivia	47.30	53.00	6.56	6.25	41	47
Brazil	59.90	66.00	5.31	3.81	50	48
Chile	63.80	72.90	4.12	2.59	50	49
Colombia	60.70	66.00	5.94	3.93	50	50
Costa Rica	67.50	75.70	5.80	3.50	49	48
Dominican Republic	57.20	64.60	7.01	4.18	50	50
Ecuador	58.20	66.40	6.70	5.00	48	49
El Salvador	57.80	67.10	6.62	5.56	48	50
Guadalupe	68.50	76.10	5.18	2.55	—	—
Guatemala	51.30	61.30	6.60	6.12	44	45
Guyana	64.70	70.80	5.30	3.26	—	—
Haiti	47.60	54.40	6.15	5.74	44	47
Honduras	52.70	61.70	7.42	6.50	50	50
Jamaica	68.10	75.70	5.43	3.37	50	49
Martinique	68.60	75.50	4.96	2.14	—	—
Mexico	62.20	68.10	6.70	4.61	48	49
Nicaragua	52.80	61.00	7.09	5.94	50	52
Panama	65.50	72.90	5.62	3.46	48	48
Paraguay	61.70	67.50	6.40	4.85	47	48
Peru	53.00	60.50	6.56	5.00	46	48
Puerto Rico	73.50	77.60	3.40	2.54	—	—
Suriname	65.70	70.60	5.94	3.59	—	—
Trinidad and Tobago	67.70	71.30	3.89	2.88	49	50
Uruguay	71.90	73.70	2.81	2.76	48	49
Venezuela	66.10	72.10	5.90	4.10	50	49
United States	74.1	78.1	2.55	1.85	49	49

From: Elssy Bonilla, "Working Women in Latin America," *Economic and Social Progress in Latin America: 1990 Report* (Washington, D.C.: Inter-American Development Bank, 1990). Sources: Mayra Buvinic, *Women and Poverty in Latin America and the Caribbean: A Primer for Policy Makers.* Washington, D.C.: Inter-American Development Bank, 1990, p. 31. Information on Cuba is not provided.

advanced and industrialized countries, such as Uruguay and Argentina, began to have lower fertility rates in the 1950s.[34] By 1970, the total fertility rate was below 4.0 in Uruguay, Argentina, Puerto Rico, and two countries in the English-speaking Caribbean: Barbados, and Trinidad and Tobago. Between 1970 and 1985, fertility had dropped dramatically in Barbados, Brazil, Chile, Colombia, Costa Rica, Cuba, the Dominican Republic, Guadalupe, Guyana, Jamaica, Martinique, Mexico, Panama, Paraguay, Suriname, and Venezuela, and had fallen somewhat in all other Latin American and Caribbean countries except Argentina, where it was already low. This decline was facilitated by government-sponsored family planning programs in some countries, which usually met with stiff opposition from the Catholic Church.

Falling Incomes and Survival Strategies

Women throughout Latin America and the Caribbean have adopted a variety of strategies to add income and cut expenditures. Women in poor Latin American and Caribbean households have commonly sought to stretch family income by producing goods at home rather than purchasing them in stores; adding additional wage earners to the household; and developing mutual aid networks among extended kin and neighbors. These patterns have intensified with the economic crisis.[35] In Mexico, newly married couples are doubling up with parents, and other adult wage earners are incorporated into the household. The result is an increase in household size, reversing the trend toward smaller households that occurred prior to the crisis. Incorporating adult wage earners into the household to pool expenses and income is occurring in several countries in the region, including Chile, Peru, and Brazil. The domestic burden is increased as household possessions such as refrigerators are sold to meet emergency needs, and as expenditures are reduced on transportation, utilities, clothes, and even food. These survival strategies have enabled consumption patterns in some households to remain relatively stable, although in many countries the nutrition and health situation of the poorest sectors is deteriorating.

In Chile, for example, high growth rates from 1977 to 1981 (facilitated by massive foreign loans) were dealt a severe below by deteriorating terms of trade and an increase in real interest rates. As in other countries, this resulted in declines in GDP and wages, and increases in unemployment, inflation, and income concentration from 1981 to 1985. Despite government programs focusing on maternal and child health and nutrition, which protected some of the poor, a 1983 budgetary cut in these programs produced an increase in child mortality and malnourishment among preschool children and pregnant women. (Malnutrition among school-age children increased from 4.6 percent to 15.8 percent between 1980 and 1983.) A 1983 national study concluded that 32 percent of the population could not purchase the minimum food basket defined by ECLAC (Economic Commission for Latin America and the Caribbean), reflecting a 105 percent rise in the consumer price index between 1981 and 1984.[36] However, the economy improved after 1985.

Division of Labor in the Family

Can meeting women's practical needs—particularly income and household maintenance—result in addressing women's strategic needs, specifically restructuring the division of labor within the family? In her comparative studies of women factory workers in export manufacturing in the Caribbean, where women are major contributors to the household economy, Safa found that women use their earnings and the family's increased dependence on them to bargain for greater household authority and shared household responsibility.[37] The changes are more marked in Puerto Rico than in the Dominican Republic, because the Puerto Rican industrialization process started earlier and offered more jobs to women than men, particularly in the garment industry (in the initial labor-intensive stage). Women's formal labor force participation is thus increasingly normative; their income is accepted as necessary for household maintenance. In Safa's sample of Puerto Rican garment workers, even single women's wages, though low, represent at least 40 percent of the household income. The percentage is even higher in the case of married women and female heads of households, who constitute a majority of Safa's respondents. Most men no longer feel threatened by their wives' working because they recognize that families can no longer survive on a single wage. For the same reason, most women now continue to be employed even if they are married with young children, despite the heavy burden this places on them.

Safa found that the increased employment of married women in Puerto Rico and the Dominican Republic, as in the rest of Latin America, has not led to any appreciable increase in the male share of domestic work. Housework and child care are still women's responsibility, even when women are also making a major contribution to the household economy. However, employed Puerto Rican married women now share more decisions with their husbands and have greater control over the family budget. In Dominican households, however, the man's authority within the family is much less affected by his wife's paid employment. Though most Dominican women agree that their wage is essential to family survival, the ideological dependence on a male provider is stronger than in Puerto Rico, where a longer tradition of formal female employment prevails. In addition, working women in Puerto Rico are entitled to unemployment insurance and food stamps, and unemployed female heads of households with young children can receive welfare payments, while no such transfer payments exist in the Dominican Republic. While female-headed households are poorer than male-headed households (even with these payments), Puerto Rican women have more income alternatives than Dominican women, which may contribute to the greater authority of Puerto Rican women within their households.

Declining male wages and increasing male unemployment are contributing to the increasing rate of female-headed households throughout most of the region during the past decade.[38] Either men leave of their own accord, because they are unable to support their family, or their wives force them out. Partial figures for 1982 show the percentage of female heads of households fluctuates between 18 and 23 per-

cent in Latin America, and between 24 and 46 percent in the Caribbean.[39] Historical and cultural differences between countries help account
for these variations, since a long tradition of female economic autonomy exists in the English-speaking Caribbean.

But throughout the region, socioeconomic factors—male unemployment, migration, urbanization, and the recent economic crisis—increasingly contribute to the formation of female-headed households. Households headed by women consistently fall into the lowest income
categories, even though these female heads are more likely to be employed than are married or single women. The low income of female-
headed households reflects the disadvantages faced by women in the
labor market and that such households often have fewer employed
members, due to the absence of a male partner. In rural areas of the
Dominican Republic, Rosado and Flora found female-headed households (20 percent of the sample) had fewer resources for generating
income than their male peers.[40] Female heads of household try to cope
with this problem by incorporating other adult kin, such as siblings or
cousins, as additional wage earners in the family, or as caretakers for
children to facilitate their own participation in the labor force.[41]

The extreme economic pressures that the poor in Latin America and
the Caribbean are now experiencing help explain why many women
continue to look to men as the principal economic providers. Safa found
that women realize their own serious disadvantages in the labor market
and are aware of the extreme poverty in which most female-headed
households live.

The social identity that women gain from their roles as wives and
mothers is also important in explaining women's attachment to their
domestic role. As Stolcke notes in her study of Brazilian agricultural
laborers, men have become more demoralized than women about the
transition to wage labor and their increasing difficulty in fulfilling their
breadwinning role.[42] While women are also poor, they retain their roles
as wives and mothers. Unlike men, they are not dependent on their
wage for status within the household. According to Stolcke, "Whereas
men have to, literally, 'earn' their rightful place in the household, wom-
en's 'natural' place is in the home." Men's reproductive roles are thus
more difficult to change than women's, not only because of their traditional privileges, but because of the ideology that men are incapable
of household tasks and lose their masculinity if they perform them.[43]

Women and Collective Action

The past decade in Latin America has witnessed a marked increase in
collective action by women, as workers in trade unions, as housewives
in squatter settlements, and as mothers defending human rights against
state repression. Women's collective action in the 1970s and early 1980s

commonly has been viewed as a response to authoritarian military rule and the economic crisis. In this perspective, women organized to defend their families against state repression and threats to their livelihood; women were seen in their traditional reproductive roles, seeking to fulfill practical needs. However, collective action can also be seen as an outgrowth of a breakdown in the traditional Latin American division between private and public spheres. In these terms, we can see new roles for women, as well as new implications for women's strategic needs.

Industrialization and urbanization from 1950 through 1980 weakened the family's role and strengthened that of the state. When the state was forced (or chose, as a result of the economic crisis) to withdraw from providing basic services and a safety net for its population, a huge vacuum was created. Women's traditional community responsibilities were greatly enlarged. The viability and sanctity of the private sphere, always considered women's domain, was threatened more and more by economic and political forces. In many situations, women organized to address their practical needs or to make their voices heard by an increasingly unresponsive state.

The poor have a long history of collective action in Latin America and the Caribbean, both through rural *mingas* (collective work groups) and land invasions and through squatter settlements in urban locales. Women have always played a prominent role in these neighborhood forms of collective action, though their importance has seldom been explicitly acknowledged. At the same time, women commonly resort to informal mutual aid networks—including extended family and neighbors—to help stretch family income and resolve community problems. With the economic crisis, these communal survival strategies have intensified and in some cases institutionalized into formal organizations, such as the *comedores populares* or *ollas comunes* (communal kitchens) for food distribution, or *talleres productivos* (production workshops) for garment production and other types of piecework. In Santiago's metropolitan region in 1986, there were an estimated 1,383 *organizaciónes económicas populares*, or OEPs (popular economic organizations), of which 1,208 were self-help organizations with almost exclusively female leadership and participants.[44]

Although food aid and public works programs exist in some Latin American countries, governments have done little to help the poor meet the rising cost of living. On the contrary, in the majority of countries, the share of the budget targeted to social services fell between 1980 and 1985. Educational deterioration throughout the region has manifested itself through teacher attrition and declining primary school enrollments. The closure of public health facilities, lack of medical personnel, medicine and vital equipment, and growing health care costs have also contributed to a sharp increase in infant mortality rates in some Latin American countries. These cuts in government services add to the cost of living, increase women's reproductive work, and put more pressure on women to join the labor force. Thus, at the same time that more responsibility is turned back to women and the community, fewer state resources are available to them. The cuts also reflect the pressure on Latin American and Caribbean governments to reduce state programs to redistribute income and alleviate the poverty resulting from structural adjustment and other neoliberal economic policies.

One of the most successful and unique collective consumption strategies aimed at combating the growing economic crisis is the *comedores populares,* or communal kitchens, organized by women in Lima, Santiago, and other Latin American cities. Groups of 15–50 households buy and prepare food collectively for the neighborhood, with each family paying according to the number of meals requested. Many of these *comedores* sprang up spontaneously, while others have been started or at least supported by the Church, state, and other local and international agencies. In 1985, their number in Lima was estimated at 300; more recent estimates give the figure as 1,000–1,200.[45] Their growing number is evidence of women's collective response to the increasing severity of the economic crisis in Peru and other Latin American countries in the last few years.

Such collective public activity to meet individual private needs has helped women recognize the societal dimensions of what had previously been defined as totally private. These organizational efforts have been aided at times by church groups and other private voluntary organizations, including middle-class feminists. As a result of grass roots organizing originally in response to practical needs, a growing number of women's groups throughout Latin America are addressing women's strategic needs as well. Women's grass roots groups are increasingly addressing domestic violence and sexual abuse of women and girls, key women's strategic needs. For example, one women's group in Lima bought whistles for each group member. When a husband started to beat his wife, she blew her whistle, and the entire group gathered to confront the aggressor. The women are very proud of the decline in domestic violence—although they also say that by confronting their husbands, they risk having them leave the house altogether. Only women in strong solidarity support groups can take such great risks to maintain personal health and safety.

Women's self-help organizations have been criticized by feminists because the organizations were initiated to help women fulfill traditional domestic roles. It is clear that their formation is motivated by women's practical gender needs. In urban areas, women's organizations have addressed inadequate public services, such as running water, electricity, and transportation. Women's reproductive role as housewives and mothers has tended to push them into the foreground as champions of collective consumption issues, and includes protests against the high cost of living and lack of adequate day care, health services, and schools.

However, the collectivization of private tasks—such as food preparation and child care—is transforming women's roles, even though it is not undertaken as a conscious challenge to gender subordination. Poor women use their domestic role as a base of strength and legitimacy in their demands on the state.[46]

Latin American women are also demanding participation in the polity to make governments more responsive to basic human needs. In the process they are redefining and enlarging their domestic role from private nurturance to collective public protest, and thus challenging women's traditional confinement to the private sphere. To meet women's practical needs effectively through collective action requires strategic changes in their status as second-class citizens.

Traditional avenues of protest have failed to address meaningfully women's issues, in part because authoritarian military regimes in the 1970s and early 1980s created a vacuum by repressing trade unions and opposition political parties.[47] Even after democratization, these institutions have neglected women and continue to regard men as the primary spokespersons to the outside world. Political parties are seen as a male sphere, in which the poor—male and female—play essentially a client role, exchanging votes for political favors, such as improving roads or setting up day care centers. This fosters *asistencialismo* (charity dependency) and may lead to the co-option of women's groups for partisan political ends, as occurred with the *Centros de Madres* under the Pinochet government. The *Centros* were run by a staff of volunteers (largely wives of military officers) appointed by the government and headed by Pinochet's wife, who offered women training courses to improve their domestic role. As a result, *Centros* membership declined drastically in this period, and new nonofficial women's groups—supporting both human rights and collective consumption—arose. These unofficial groups provided the base for the women's movement mobilized against Pinochet, starting in 1983.[48]

Women's human rights groups, such as Chile's Association of Democratic Women *(Agrupación de Mujeres Democráticas)* and the Chilean Association of the Relatives of the Detained and Disappeared, were formed as early as 1973 in solidarity with political prisoners and their families, and to aid in the search for victims. Some members of these human rights groups were middle- and working-class housewives with no previous political experience. As in the case of the well-known Mothers of the Plaza de Mayo in Argentina, these groups generally refused any identification with political parties or feminism. Catholic doctrine played an important role in women's self-definition and quest for legitimacy, and women rarely questioned their traditional gender roles as wives and mothers. On the contrary, to legitimize their protest these women often appealed to Catholic symbols of motherhood and family—values authoritarian states also proclaimed but destroyed in the name of national security. Women themselves were often victims of repression, sought out for violent sexual torture designed to destroy their feminin-ity and human dignity. Human rights movements mobilizing women as wives and mothers, similar to those in Chile and Argentina, have also arisen in Uruguay, Brazil, Honduras, El Salvador, Guatemala, and other Latin American countries under military rule.[49]

The transforming potential of women's social movements in Latin America has been questioned by those who feel the movements cannot outlive immediate crisis situations, such as opposition to military rule or economic crisis. Jelin maintains that women participate more in short-term, sporadic protest movements than in long-term, formalized insti-tutional settings.[50] In Argentina, the Mothers of the Plaza de Mayo, who played such an important role in defeating the military dictator-ship, have lost popular support and have split into two groups. The split is due partly to the conflict regarding the democratically elected government's human rights policy and prosecution of the military, both of which fell far short of the Plaza de Mayo goals.

With the transition from military to democratic rule in countries such as Argentina, Brazil, Uruguay, and Chile, most social movements, both male and female, have lost strength as the locus of power has shifted back to political parties. Elections rekindled old political divisions and fragmented social movements and political coalitions that had arisen, not only among women, but among youth, the urban poor, and broader-based human rights groups. This can be seen in Chile in the fragmen-tation of MEMCH 1983, an umbrella organization that originally united 24 women's organizations and was active in defeating the military re-gime. While the state and political parties have integrated some wom-en's demands into their platforms, women have not assumed decision-making positions within the political parties. The number of female candidates placed high on the electoral lists in the first democratic elec-tions in 1989 was likewise very low, resulting in the election of only two women senators and seven women deputies out of 120. No woman held a position in the first cabinet of President Patricio Aylwin, although a woman was later appointed to the cabinet to head SERNAM *(Servicio Nacional de la Mujer).*[51]

The Brazilian liberal democratic state that supplanted military rule has been more successful in addressing women's needs and electing women to public office, including 26 women in the 1986 congressional elections.[52] Although divided on such issues as family planning, both the Church—through its support of Christian base communities—and feminist groups—through legitimizing women's concerns—gave crucial initial impetus to women's widespread grass roots organizing. Women also gained greater representation through the government-appointed Council on the Status of Women in São Paulo, which was subsequently established in 23 other states and municipalities, and through the Na-tional Council on Women's Rights, which played a critical role in de-veloping women's proposals for the new Brazilian constitution. Despite pressure put on the council by an active grass roots constituency operating outside the state, the National Council is no longer responsive to women's needs. The recent election of a conservative president and the continuing economic crisis weakens the possibility of implementing women's demands, both because of budgetary constraints, and the election and appointment to the council of women whose identification with women's interests is diminished.

Nevertheless, certain gains have been achieved and even institutionalized into legal codes. The Brazilian constitution adopted in 1988 facilitates divorce, extends maternity leave, and eliminates the prohibition on abortion (without legalizing it). Argentina has also legalized divorce and modified *patria potestad* (male kin's legal control of women) to give women more power in the family and joint custody of children.

Women's social movements, generally begun as an extension of family and community roles to meet practical needs, serve strategic needs as well. Women have acquired greater self-esteem and recognition of their rights as women, and greater legitimacy in the public sphere. Such ideological changes are the best guarantee that these women will resist attempts to re-establish the old order and will continue to press for their rights.

Conclusion

Has there been a growth of gender consciousness among poor Latin American and Caribbean women? Have women been able to translate their increased participation in the public sphere into strategic gender interests that directly challenge women's subordination? Or do women's recent setbacks in the economic and political spheres spell a return to the past and a fundamental obstacle to further advancement?

We would argue that Latin American and Caribbean women collectively have inserted themselves too decisively into the public sphere to retreat into the private domestic domain. Women have become increasingly important members of the labor force and contributors to the household economy; they have mobilized their households in response to economic crises; and they have organized social movements for human rights and social welfare.

As a result of attempting to meet these practical needs, some women are beginning to see the need for strategic changes, and they are trying to voice their demands in labor unions and political parties. Women's demands were less of a threat when confined to domestic issues, including public services and the rising cost of living. Such continuation of their traditional reproductive roles did not directly attack male interests in more established power structures—labor unions or political parties, for example. As women move away from these "private" issues of practical gender interests into more strategic gender interests that attempt to restructure gendered relationships, they will undoubtedly meet greater resistance. They thus must acquire not only a greater degree of gender consciousness, but the political will to overcome the resistance of patriarchal power structures.

In part, this resistance reflects an ideological debate over the primacy of class or gender. Women carry on this debate among themselves, as well as with men. Marxists have long assumed class consciousness to be the primary avenue of structural change and mobilization in capitalist society and have viewed the women's movement as weakening the class struggle. However, we would argue that gender consciousness does not invalidate the Marxist theory of class struggle, but calls for its reinterpretation to accommodate new political voices. By politicizing the private sphere, women have redefined rather than rejected their domestic reproductive roles and extended the struggle against the state beyond the workplace into home and community. While class consciousness arises primarily in the workplace through men's and women's productive roles as workers, gender consciousness is based primarily on women's reproductive roles as wives and mothers. Marxists must recognize that inequality in capitalist society is not limited to class, but intersects with inequalities of gender, race, ethnicity, and region. These are proving to be increasingly important avenues of mobilization and collective action in Latin America and the Caribbean.

Changes in women's role in production, reproduction, and the polity in Latin America and the Caribbean also pose a challenge to prevailing feminist theory, which argues that the family is "the central site of women's oppression." In Latin America and the Caribbean, however, it would appear that women have been more successful in challenging their subordination in the home and neighborhood than at work or in the polity. Working women have a greater role in decision making; many no longer look to their husbands as sole heads of household or economic providers. Further male migration—temporary and permanent—has left rural women in de facto charge of their communities, while urban housewives organize to press their demands on the state for adequate public services. In these areas their status vis-à-vis men is changing.

In contrast, women's increased labor force participation has not enhanced their status in the workplace; society continues to regard them as supplementary workers. The profits from a segmented labor force, coupled with developing countries' desperate need for foreign exchange, has meant that unions, political parties, and national governments see no need to improve women's wages and working conditions, or meet their special needs for day care, maternity leave, and so forth. State cuts in social services—health care, education, water, and electricity—have added to women's domestic burden and threatened their families' survival. Therefore, the greatest resistance to gender equality in Latin America and the Caribbean appears to lie at the level of workplace and state, rather than the home.

Women's heavy responsibility for domestic tasks restricts their participation in the formal labor market and in traditional political parties. But women's ability to define collective action as a logical extension of their domestic role has enabled them to gain some legitimacy in the public sphere. These communal activities arise less out of a need to reduce gender subordination than out of women's struggle to fulfill traditional reproductive roles. Women's concern for their families propels many of them to increase their household income and struggle for human rights and economic justice. Thus the family is a contradictory institution for women, serving both as a source of subordination and legitimacy in the public sphere. When women join together to meet practical needs through collective action, they may find the strength to address strategic needs arising out of gender subordination.

The economic crisis now endangering the entire Latin American and Caribbean region undoubtedly poses a threat to further advances in women's equality. The economic crisis has increased the importance of women's contribution to the household, but it has also placed a heavy burden on women to meet the rising cost of living, cuts in government services, and high unemployment levels. In many countries, foreign debt payments consume half or more of government revenues and undermine the government's ability to stimulate economic growth or relieve poverty and income inequality. Under these circumstances, it is not too surprising that most governments in the region have been largely unresponsive to women's demands, leading to women's disillusionment and, in some cases, withdrawal.

But women can no longer be ignored by the polity in Latin America and the Caribbean. Women have passed beyond the stage in which their needs were largely invisible, to one in which they are now heard, even if some have been co-opted for partisan political ends. Women have been joined by other protest groups concerned with ecology, urban poverty, and the rights of indigenous peoples, which suggests the widespread need for greater participation in the region's polity.

As Kirkwood reminds us, the issue is not simply one of women's incorporation into a male-defined world, but of transforming the world to eliminate the hierarchies of class, gender, race, and ethnicity that have so long subordinated much of the Latin American population, men as well as women.[53]

Notes

1. When we refer to reproduction and reproductive activities of women, we do not mean only bearing and rearing children, as the terms are commonly

used. Instead, we base our use on the tradition of analysis from political economy, which refers to the process by which society replaces the material goods it has consumed through production for use in the household, maintains the labor force, and reinforces or recreates the institutional structure—including cultural norms and values. Janet Henshall Momsen, in *Women and Development in the Third World* (New York: Routledge, 1991), describes reproduction as including biological reproduction and social reproduction. Social reproduction includes care and maintenance of the household, and social management, such as maintaining kinship linkages, developing neighborhood networks, and carrying out religious, ceremonial, and social obligations in the community. Others choose to refer to what we call reproductive activities as the domestic mode of production, as Ken Kusterer does in his essay "The Imminent Demise of Patriarchy," in Irene Tinker (ed.), *Persistent Inequalities: Women and World Development* (New York: Oxford Univ. Press, 1990), 239–55.

2. Recently, the community management activities of women have been increasingly acknowledged, and for some this becomes a separate category of female roles. Caroline Moser discusses the importance of these activities in "Gender Planning in the Third World: Meeting Practical and Strategic Gender Needs," *World Development* 17:11 (1989), 1799–1825.

3. Maxine Molyneux originally formulated the concept of practical and strategic gender *interests* in an article on women's role in postrevolutionary Nicaragua, "Mobilization Without Emancipation? Women's Interests, State and Revolution," in Richard Fagen, Carmen Diana Deere, and Jose Luis Corragio (eds.), *Transition and Development Problems of Third World Socialism* (New York: Monthly Review Press, 1986), 280–302. Although writing in reference to socialist states, Molyneux and others have not confined their application of this concept to these states. In a more recent article, "Gender Planning in the Third World," Caroline Moser applies the concept, which she terms gender *needs,* to policy and practice programs worldwide. According to both authors, practical gender needs are those needs that are formulated from the concrete conditions women experience in their engendered position within the sexual division of labor. Strategic gender needs address the structure and nature of the sexual division of labor and women's subordination to men. We use the terms *gender interests* and *gender needs* interchangeably.

4. See Celso Furtado, *Economic Development of Latin America: Historical Background and Contemporary Problems* (Cambridge: Cambridge Univ. Press, 1970), and Raúl Prebish, *Nueva Politica Comercial para el Desarrollo* (Mexico City: Fondo de Cultura Economica, 1964), as two classic import-substitution theorists.

5. Cornelia B. Flora, "Public Policy and Women in Agricultural Production: A Comparative and Historical Analysis," in Wava Haney and Jane Knowles (eds.), *Women and Farming: Changing Roles, Changing Structures* (Boulder, Colo.: Westview Press, 1988), 265–80.

6. Carmen Diana Deere discusses the lack of attention to women in Latin American agrarian reform in "The Latin American Agrarian Reform Experience," in Carmen Diana Deere and Magdalena Leon (eds.), *Rural Women and State Policy* (Boulder, Colo.: Westview Press, 1987), 165–90.

7. Lourdes Arizpe, "Effects of the Economic Crisis on the Living Conditions of Peasant Women in Mexico," in *The Invisible Adjustment: Poor Women and the Economic Crisis* (Santiago: UNICEF Regional Office, 1987), 111–30.

8. Susan C. Bourque, "Urban Development," in K. Lynn Stoner (ed.), *Latinas of the Americas: A Source Book* (New York: Garland Press, 1989), 581–94.

9. Lourdes Arizpe, "Relay Migration and the Social Reproduction of the Peasantry," in Helen Safa (ed.), *Toward a Political Economy of Urbanization in Third World Countries* (New Delhi: Oxford Univ. Press, 1982), 19–46.

10. Lucila Rosado and Cornelia Butler Flora analyzed a national survey of rural women on the impact of remittances on rural households in "Economic Survival Strategies in the Rural Dominican Republic: The Impact of Gender and Remittances," paper presented at the Fourty-seventh International Congress of Americanists, New Orleans, 1991.

11. Ximena Bunster and Elsa Chaney have written a classic study of this phenomenon in *Sellers and Servants: Working Women in Lima, Peru* (New York: Praeger, 1985).

12. Stanley K. Smith, "Determinants of Female Labor Force Participation and Family Size in Mexico City," *Economic Development and Cultural Change* 30 (1981), 129–52.

13. The Latin American and Caribbean region is marked by great ethnic diversity, resulting from the subjugation of indigenous Indian populations by Spanish, Portuguese, and other European colonists and from the importation of enslaved Africans, chiefly into the Caribbean basin and Brazil. These oppressed indigenous and African-American populations continue to be concentrated at the bottom of the socioeconomic ladder. Indian groups are found primarily in the rural areas of Bolivia, Peru, Ecuador, Guatemala, and Mexico, where indigenous populations developed the highly complex, preconquest civilizations of the Inca, Aztecs, and Maya. At the same time, because of extensive racial mixing between white European and these indigenous and African-American populations, the rigid color bar found in the United States is replaced by a fluid color/class continuum, with darker-skinned people at the lower end of the socioeconomic scale. While Indian communities were often traditionally characterized by more egalitarian relationships between the sexes than non-Indian communities, women's high illiteracy rates, low educational levels, and lack of knowledge of Spanish or Portuguese have limited their access to the larger society, and thus "modernization" has tended to lower the status of women in indigenous communities vis-à-vis men. The primacy given to gender difference is due to space limitations and does not imply neglect of these important ethnic and cultural differences.

14. Economic Commission for Latin America and the Caribbean (ECLAC), *Latin American and Caribbean Women: Between Change and Crisis* LC/L.464 (CRM. 4/2), (Santiago, Chile: ECLAC, 1988), 9.

15. Elssy Bonilla discusses these trends and their impact on women in "Working Women in Latin America," *Economic and Social Progress in Latin America: 1990 Report* (Washington, D.C.: Interamerican Development Bank, 1990), 208–56.

16. See Giovanni A. Cornia, "Economic Decline and Human Welfare in the First Half of the1980s," in Giovanni Cornia, G. R. Jolly, and F. Stewart (eds.), *Adjustment with a Human Face*, vol. 1 (New York: Oxford Univ. Press, Clarendon Press, 1987), 11–47; and ECLAC, *Latin American and Caribbean Women*, as examples of the research on the impacts of structural adjustment.

17. See Maria Patricia Fernández Kelly, *For We Are Sold, I and My People: Women and Industry in Mexico's Frontier* (Albany: State University of New York

Press, 1983), for the first major study of the *maquiladora* industry in Latin America.

18. ECLAC, *Latin American and Caribbean Women*. It is important to note that labor force statistics have consistently underrepresented the productive work of women, as they are biased toward formal labor force participation. Part of the large increase in women's labor force participation reflects changes not in performance of productive work, but in where it is performed and the labor relations involved. In the rural area alone, Bonilla estimates that nearly 50 percent of family income in the region's small-farm subsector comes from women's activities. See Elssy Bonilla, "Working Women in Latin America."

19. Lourdes Arizpe introduces this term in her article "The Comparative Advantage of Women's Disadvantages," *Signs* (special issue edited by H. Safa and E. Leacock) 7 (Winter 1981), 453–73.

20. Verena Stolcke, "The Exploitation of Family Morality: Labor Systems and Family Structure on São Paulo Coffee Plantations, 1850–1979," in Raymond T. Smith (ed.), *Kinship, Ideology and Practice in Latin America* (Chapel Hill: Univ. of North Carolina Press, 1984), 264–96.

21. Claudia Serrano, "Pobladoras en Santiago: Algo mas de la crisis," in *Mujeres, crisis y movimientos: America Latina y el Caribe* (Santiago: Isis Internacional, 1988), 73–92.

22. See John Humphrey, *Gender and Work in the Third World* (London: Tavistock, 1987), for a discussion of women and industrial development in São Paulo, Brazil, in the 1970s.

23. Export processing refers to the unskilled assembly line work carried out largely by women in certain developing countries, and it results from the fragmentation of production brought on by increasing international competition. Because of its emphasis on exports, export processing is the reverse of import substitution, which was designed to build up domestic industry to meet the country's internal needs. See Helen I. Safa, "Runaway Shops and Female Employment: The Search for Cheap Labor," in Eleanor Leacock and Helen I. Safa (eds.), *Women's Work: Development and the Division of Labor by Gender* (South Hadley, Mass.: Bergin and Garvey, 1986), 58–71.

24. See Susan Joekes, *Employment in Industrial Free Zones in the Dominican Republic: A Report with Recommendations for Improved Worker Services* (Washington, D.C.: International Center for Research on Women, 1987); and Helen I. Safa, "Women and Industrialization in the Caribbean," in S. Stichter and J. Parpart (eds.), *Women, Employment and the Family in the International Division of Labor* (London: Macmillan, 1990), 72–97, for a discussion of women in duty-free zones in the Dominican Republic.

25. See Elsa Chaney and Mary Garcia-Castro, *Muchachas No More: Household Workers in Latin America and the Caribbean* (Philadelphia: Temple Univ. Press, 1989), for an extensive discussion of changes in domestic service.

26. For a discussion of various types of street sellers, see Bunster and Chaney, *Sellers and Servants;* Lourdes Arizpe, *Indigenas en la Ciudad de Mexico. El Caso de las Marias* (Mexico: Ed. Sep. Setentas, 1975); and ECLAC, *Women in the Inter-Island Trade in Agricultural Produce in the Eastern Caribbean* L. 465 (CRM. 4/9). (Port of Spain, Trinidad: ECLAC, 1988).

27. Alejandro Portes, "The Informal Sector: Definition, Controversy, and Relation to National Development," *Review* 7:7 (1983), 151–74.

28. Lourdes Beneria and Martha Roldan, *The Crossroads of Class and Gender* (Chicago: Univ. of Chicago Press, 1987).

29. See Cornelia Butler Flora, "Income Generation Projects for Rural Women," in Deere and Leon (eds.), *Rural Women and State Policy*, 212–38; Helen I. Safa, "Urbanization, the Informal Economy and State Policy in Latin America," in M. P. Smith and J. Feagin (eds.), *The Capitalist City: Global Restructuring and Community Politics* (London: Blackwell, 1987), 252–72; and Marguerite Berger and Mayra Buvinic, *Women's Ventures: Assistance to the Informal Sector in Latin America* (West Hartford, Conn.: Kumarian Press, 1989), for analyses of income-generating projects and the informal sector in Latin America.

30. Guy Standing, "Global Feminization through Flexible Labor," *World Development* 17:7 (1989), 1077–96.

31. Patricia Chuchryk, "Feminist Anti-Authoritarian Politics: The Role of Women's Organizations in the Chilean Transition to Democracy," in Jane Jaquette (ed.), *The Women's Movement in Latin America* (Winchester, Mass.: Unwin Hyman, 1989), 149–84.

32. This is discussed by Safa, "Women and Industrialization."

33. Middle- and upper-class women in Latin America and the Caribbean usually have domestic servants, but the only assistance poor women can draw on are female relatives living with them, or nearby or occasionally neighbors, who are not always willing or able to help. Only in Cuba is there a nationwide government program to provide child care centers for working mothers.

34. Women in Argentina, Chile, and Uruguay already had fairly high educational levels and labor force participation prior to 1960, due to more developed forms of urbanization and industrialization which preceded the rest of the region, as well as earlier support for female public education in these countries. Another factor in the level of development of these countries is the predominantly European nature of their populations, compared with countries with large indigenous populations, where the problems of educating these groups have been compounded by their lack of knowledge of Spanish or Portuguese. Educational and occupational gains made by women (and men) in Cuba are due largely to the conscious effort of the socialist revolutionary government that took power in 1959.

35. See Mercedes Gonzalez de la Rocha, "Economic Crisis, Domestic Reorganization and Women's Work in Guadalajara, Mexico," *Bulletin of Latin American Research* 7:2 (1988), 207–23 and Cornia, Jolly, and Stewart (eds.), *Adjustment with a Human Face*, for a discussion of changing reproductive strategies in light of the crisis and structural adjustment.

36. Dagmar Raczynski, "Social Policy, Poverty and Vulnerable Groups: Children in Chile" in Cornia, Jolly, and Stewart (eds.), *Adjustment with a Human Face* vol. 2. (New York: Oxford Univ. Press, Clarendon Press, 1988), 57–92.

37. See Safa, "Women and Industrialization," 72–97; and Helen I. Safa, "Female Employment and the Social Reproduction of the Puerto Rican Working Class," in J. Nash and H. Safa (eds.), *Women and Change in Latin America* (South Hadley, Mass.: Bergin and Garvey, 1985), 84–105, for a discussion of her studies of women factory workers in the Caribbean.

38. Elssy Bonilla, "Working Women in Latin America," 216.

39. ECLAC, *Latin American and Caribbean Women*, 15.

40. Rosado and Flora, "Economic Survival Strategies."

41. A. Lynn Bolles, "Economic Crisis and Female-Headed Households in Urban Jamaica," in Nash and Safa (eds.), *Women and Change,* 65–83.

42. See Stolcke, "The Exploitation of Family Morality," 264–96, for a fascinating discussion of gender relationships under shifting relations of production.

43. Geoffrey Fox, "Honor, Shame, and Women's Liberation in Cuba: Views of Emigré Men," in Ann Pescatello (ed.), *Female and Male in Latin America: Essays* (Pittsburgh: Univ. of Pittsburgh Press, 1973), 273–90.

44. Teresa Valdes and Marisa Weinstein, *Organizaciónes de pobladoras y construcción democrática en Chile,* Documento de Trabajo 434 (Santiago: FLACSO-CHILE, 1989).

45. See Giovanni A. Cornia, "Adjustment at the Household Level: Potentials and Limitations of Survival Strategies," in Cornia, Jolly, and Stewart (eds.), *Adjustment with a Human Face* vol. 1, 90–104; Cecilia Blondet, "Women's Organizations and Politics in a Time of Crisis," paper presented at workshop at the Helen Kellogg Institute for International Studies, Univ. of Notre Dame, Notre Dame, Ind., 1989; Maruja Barrig, *De vecinas a ciudadanas: a mujer en el desarrollo urbano* (Lima: CENTRO, 1988); and Violeta Lafosse, "Los comedores y la promoción de la mujer," in N. Galer and P. Nuñez (eds.), *La mujer y comedores populares* (Lima: SEPADE, 1988) for discussions of this form of collective reproductive activities.

46. Teresa Caldeira, "Mujeres, cotaneidad y politica," in E. Jelin (ed.), *Ciudadanía e identidad: Las Mujeres en los movimientos sociales Latinoamericanos* (Santiago: UNRISD, 1987), 75–128.

47. Elizabeth Jelin, "Introduction," in Jelin (ed.), *Ciudadanía e Identidad,* 1–18.

48. Valdes and Weinstein, *Organizaciónes de pobladoras.*

49. See Chuchryk, "Feminist Anti-Authoritarian Politics," 149–84; and Ximena Bunster, "Surviving Beyond Fear: Women and Torture in Latin America" in Nash and Safa (eds.), *Women and Change,* 297–325, for a discussion of women's human rights organizations in Chile. See also Maria del Carmen Feijoo and Monica Gogna, "Las Mujeres en la transicion a la democracia," in Jelin (ed.), *Ciudadanía e identidad,* for a discussion of such groups in Argentina.

50. Jelin, "Introduction," in Jelin (ed.), *Ciudadanía e identidad,* 1–18.

51. See Maria Elena Valenzuela, "Mujeres y política: Logros y tensiones en el proceso de redemocratización," in *Proposiciónes 18: Chile Sociedad y Transición* (Santiago: Ediciónes Sur, 1990); and Valdes and Weinstein, *Organizaciónes de Pobladoras,* for a discussion of women in Chilean politics in the 1980s.

52. See Sonia Alvarez, "Women's Movements and Gender Politics in the Brazilian Transition," in Jaquette (ed.), *The Women's Movement in Latin America,* 18–71, for a discussion of the transition to democracy and women in Brazil.

53. Julieta Kirkwood, *Ser politica en Chile: Las Feministas y los partidos* (Santiago: FLACSO, 1986).

6

The Construction of a Latin American Feminist Identity

MARYSA NAVARRO-ARANGUREN

Latin American and Caribbean feminism is a vibrant movement of continental proportions. It is politically and socially heterogeneous, and in contrast to most feminist movements in other parts of the world it has a broad social base built on long-standing and intense interaction—at times marked by friction—between grass roots activists and feminists.

The interaction has given an unusual characteristic to the mobilization of women in Latin America. It encompasses a wide spectrum of groups, involved in very different activities. Some are identified with the *movimiento de mujeres* (women's movement), a name that describes grass roots organizations created by urban women in shantytowns or squatters' neighborhoods to protest the rising cost of living, to feed the community, or to obtain health care.[1] The *movimiento de mujeres* also includes new organizations founded by peasant women, especially indigenous women in the Andean region; workers trying to articulate and negotiate gender-specific demands with male-dominated unions; and groups formed by women, frequently mothers, who searched for "disappeared" relatives in the 1970s, and, since the return to democratic rule, continue to function as human rights organizations.

The feminist groups range from magazine collectives and battered women's centers to networks created to decriminalize abortion and combat violence against women. The members of the groups define their political activism by their participation in feminist groups and call themselves *feministas independientes* or *autónomas* ("independent," "autonomous"). The movement also includes women who insist on calling themselves Catholics *and* feminists, as well as women who maintain a dual commitment to political parties and to feminism, and therefore belong to feminist organizations that may or may not be connected to political parties. More recently, an increasing number of feminists are redefining their oppression and participation in the feminist movement because they are lesbian, Indian, or black.[2] A large number do not necessarily call themselves feminists but see their activities increasingly connected to issues raised by feminists and participate in campaigns organized by feminists. This group includes a growing number of activists from the *movimiento de mujeres* who find that so-called bourgeois radical feminist issues—sexuality, birth control, or violence against women, for example—are as relevant to them as the bread-and-butter issues that initially mobilized them.

Feminism has been growing steadily in the last two decades. Beginning with a few scattered groups in Mexico, Argentina, Puerto Rico, and Peru in the early 1970s, it made inroads in Colombia, the Dominican Republic, Venezuela, Chile, and Brazil in the second half of the decade. In the eighties, it has gained supporters in still other countries, including Paraguay since the demise of General Alfredo Stroessner, and all the Central American nations, including Nicaragua and El Salvador.

In the late sixties, however, while the women's liberation movement exploded in the United States, Canada, and several European countries, *Latin American* and *feminist* appeared to be contradictory terms. Attacked by the Left, ignored by the Right, usually ready to accept the latest fashion from Europe or the United States, and ridiculed by the press on both sides of the political spectrum, second-wave feminism seemed unable to gain a solid foothold on the continent. At a time when the hegemonic revolutionary rhetoric of the New Left made the Cuban model appear virtually inevitable, the ideal of the New Man a reachable paragon, and guerrilla warfare the preferred option, "woman's oppression" was at best defined as a secondary contradiction easily solved within the "correct" revolutionary process, as Cuba demonstrated. Feminism was dismissed as the product of capitalist contradictions, inapplicable to underdeveloped or dependent capitalist societies. Feminists were attacked as frivolous dupes of Yankee imperialism, misguided petites bourgeoises, or upper-middle-class women indifferent to serious national problems. They were accused of being like their turn-of-the-century foremothers, an elite interested in issues irrelevant to most of their countrywomen, burdened by poverty and illiteracy.[3]

While the hegemonic rhetoric of the New Left retarded feminism's development in the early years, the emergence of the movement in individual countries was shaped by specific conditions. In Mexico, the proximity of the United States was a significant factor because it permitted Mexican women to follow the development of the U.S. women's liberation movement without relying on the generally biased accounts of the mainstream press. Mexican feminists still remember their sense of discovery and joyous enthusiasm when they read an article by journalist Marta Acevedo in the magazine *Siempre!* describing a massive feminist rally in San Francisco celebrating the fiftieth anniversary of the Nineteenth Amendment.[4] In a country still shaken by the 1968 Tlatelolco massacre, young women who had participated massively in the student movement organized the first of many groups, MAS (Mujeres en Acción Solidaria, "Women in Solidary Action"), in 1971. Their first public action was to protest the celebration of Mother's Day. They went on to create other groups, research gender issues, participate actively in the debates preceding the 1975 United Nations meeting in Mexico City, and organize a well-attended parallel meeting. The following year, they founded two feminist publications, the short-lived newspaper *La Revuelta,* and the monthly *FEM,* which still appears today, now joined by *Debates Feministas.*

In Peru, the first feminist organization was ALIMUJER (Acción para la Liberación de la Mujer, "Action for Women's Liberation"), created in 1973 by a group of Trotskyist party militants who defined themselves as an autonomous group within the PRT. It was followed by other groups: Centro de la Mujer Peruana Flora Tristán ("The Flora Tristán Center for Peruvian Women"), Movimiento Manuela Ramos ("Manuela Ramos Movement"), Mujeres en Lucha ("Women in Struggle"), and Mujeres y Cambio ("Women and Change"), created in Lima in the late seventies. Most emerged during the second phase of the military dictatorship (1975–80), in the aftermath of the widespread strikes and riots prompted by the severe austerity plan launched in 1975 by General Francisco Morales Bermúdez.[5]

Argentine feminists also began to meet in the early seventies, in a country divided by the Peronist/anti-Peronist frenzy. The first organization was UFA (Unión Feminista Argentina, "Argentine Feminist Union").[6] Despite the country's growing violence, UFA managed to survive, together with a few other groups, until the 1976 military coup forced all political organizations and parties to interrupt their activities. Although new feminist groups emerged toward the end of the military dictatorship, the years of military rule did not produce a strong feminist movement, contrary to what occurred in Chile and Brazil, for example. In the case of Argentina, the rebirth of feminism was stunted by the pervasiveness of the Peronist/anti-Peronist dychotomy and its violent consequences, and by the hegemony of the "Peronist revolutionary" discourse and its contradictory nature for women, exemplified in the figures of Evita and Isabel Perón.

For most of the 1970s, Latin American feminist groups remained few, small, and weak. They were mostly composed of young, educated, middle-class women, the new beneficiaries of the significant educational expansion that took place in the 1960s. Some of the women were already in the labor force, especially in the service sector, competing for jobs with other women, not men, and relegated to positions where advancement was limited. Most, however, were still university students, enrolled in increasingly large numbers in the so-called feminine professions—nursing, teaching, the humanities, and so forth. They lived in a context in which men systematically occupied positions of power and exerted control and authority in political parties, the state bureaucracy, trade unions, and the student movement. A comparatively small number realized that the issues that galvanized North American feminists also affected their own lives and became feminists without prior involvement in traditional party politics. The large majority, however, joined the feminist movement after participating actively in left-wing politics, including guerrilla organizations, particularly urban guerrilla groups.

The incorporation of these young women was crucial for the definition of Latin American feminism. Challenging the left hegemonic discourse, however, proved to be a slow process. It began among Mexican and Peruvian feminists but gradually extended to most countries, even Nicaragua. The young women who undertook this task were the first generation of *militantes*. They were modern, and above all liberated— they had challenged paternal authority and were committed to a political cause. They worked long hours in the shantytowns, *barrios nuevos,* or *villas miserias,* wore blue jeans, shunned makeup, attended *festivales de canción protesta,* and, having discovered their sexuality, engaged in premarital sex.

Their transformation began when they realized that fraternity did not mean sisterhood, when they recognized and accepted that while feeling liberated and committed to the liberation of peasants, workers, and the poor, they denied their own identity as women and were therefore blind to their own oppression. The transformation implied developing a critique of left-wing parties and organizations from a feminist perspective, without falling into Cold War rhetoric, and generating a discourse that would embrace all women, especially the most disadvantaged, and protect them from becoming another vanguard or elite. It encompassed a redefinition of class struggle, incorporating personal and domestic issues traditionally considered irrelevant by the Left, though they are central to women's lives, such as sexuality, abortion, reproductive rights, violence against women, and day care centers.

Furthermore, having rejected leaderships, hierarchies, democratic centralism, party discipline, and, in the words of Chilean feminist Julieta Kirkwood, the logical consequences of patriarchy—authoritarianism and militarism—they needed to find new ways of being political and doing politics. Kirkwood, a sociologist by training, was one of the founders of Círculo de Estudios de la Mujer ("Women's Studies Circle"), the first second-wave feminist group created in Chile during General Augusto Pinochet's dictatorship. Before her tragic death in 1985, she published several influential essays and cofounded other feminist organizations, including the socialist feminist collective that began publishing the magazine *Furia* ("Fury") in 1981, MEMCH83, the umbrella group that coordinated the activities of opposition women in the early eighties, and Centro de Análisis y Difusión de la Condición de la Mujer, La Morada ("Center of Analysis and Information on Women's Condition").[7] In her attempt to understand and define what feminism could and should be under authoritarianism, she looked into the past, searching for the history of Chilean women and analyzing the relationship of the Left to women's struggles. In an essay entitled "The Feminist Questions," she pointed out that

> paradoxically, living under the dictatorial authoritarian system has demonstrated to many sectors that authoritarianism is something more than an economic or political problem; that its roots are deep, that it is imbedded in the social structure, and that many elements and contents heretofore not considered political because they were identified with the domestic sphere must be questioned and rejected. Today people are beginning to say that the family is authoritarian, that children's socialization is authoritarian and rigid in its assignation of sexual roles; that education, factories, intermediate organizations, and political parties are structurally authoritarian.[8]

For many *militantes,* becoming a feminist also meant rethinking and rearticulating activism outside traditional party structures. Some decided they could reconcile gender concerns with left-wing activism by developing a feminist praxis inside the parties, and they therefore advocated what they called *doble militancia.* Others demanded organizational separation and independence from political party control and created *organizaciónes autónomas.* Most, tired of their failure to reconcile feminism with left-wing politics, abandoned party membership to join or found feminist organizations.

The *militantes* feminist consciousness was awakened by the contradictions women experienced in male-dominated political parties, whose platforms did not address their specific needs, and where they found themselves relegated to demeaning auxiliary roles or silenced in women's commissions that refused to question hierarchies or leaderships. Feminist consciousness was also fueled in Church organizations passionately committed to social change for *los sectores populares,* within a revolutionary discourse that refused to address women's oppression inside or outside the Church, reiterated the most conservative views on such vital issues as reproduction and sexuality, and ignored Church complicity in perpetuating a double standard of sexual behavior. It was sparked by discussions prompted by the United Nations Decade for Women, various regional projects connected with it, goals of "equality, development, and peace," the 1979 adoption by the General Assembly of the United Nations of the Convention for the Elimination of All Forms of Discrimination against Women, and especially the call for the 1975 meeting to be held in Mexico, a country where women had voted for the first time in a national election in 1958 but where illiterate males had been given the vote in 1917. In preparing for the 1975 meeting, Latin American governments, the press, and civil society in general were compelled to assess women's status and to take note of discriminatory legislation affecting them. While this process did not necessarily result in the correction of such legislation, it legitimized the discussion of gender issues, even in countries under authoritarian military dictatorships where politics were highly circumscribed.

Unwittingly, the process stretched the limits of the political debate and in so doing created space for the rebirth of feminism. In Brazil, taking advantage of the new policy of *distensão* inaugurated by General Ernesto Geisel, in June 1975 women were able to meet in a week-long seminar to discuss gender issues, under the sponsorship of the United Nations Information Center and the Brazilian Press Association. They went on to create the Centro da Mulher Brasileira ("Brazilian Women's Center") in Rio de Janeiro, the Centro de Desenvolvimento da Mulher Brasileira (CDMB, "Center for the Development of Brazilian Women") in São Paulo, and two additional groups, which published newspapers, *Nós Mulheres* and *Brasil Mulher*. Ironically, in Argentina, where María Estela Martínez de Perón was president in 1975, feminists were prevented from bringing up gender issues during preliminary discussions and were refused admission to the United Nations–sponsored meeting in Buenos Aires on August 25.[9]

Feminist consciousness was spurred by heated international confrontations with First World feminists, as in the Conference on Feminine Perspectives held in Buenos Aires in 1974 and the 1975 International Conference on Women and Development at Wellesley College; by polemics focusing on new research on women published in the United States and Europe; by the availability of funds to pursue this type of research; and by participation in professional meetings, such as the Latin American Studies Association.

The development of feminist consciousness was eased by changing family patterns and values fostered by the new urban culture that resulted from the massive urbanization of recent decades; by greater freedom from paternal authority, acquired by women through increased educational levels and/or entrance into the labor force; by the rediscovery of sexuality and sexual pleasure; and, despite the opposition of the Church, by greater access to contraceptives, at least among the middle class.

Feminist consciousness was also spurred by the expansion of communications, especially the availability of cheap portable radios, cassette tapes, and television sets. As the refrigerator had somewhat earlier, the television set began to occupy a privileged place in the home, and even among the poorer sectors, ownership of a set became a priority, together with food and shelter. In countries under military dictatorships, where censorship was particularly rigid, national radio and television networks transmitted daily official reports of resounding triumphs in the struggle against subversion, complete with pathetic mug shots of "subversives." But the broadcasts also pushed consumerism, fashions (including the quintessential gringo outfit at the time, Bermuda shorts and T-shirts), international news, rock and roll, and reruns.

Other significant changes in communications included the expansion of transnational publicity campaigns originating on Madison Avenue; the proliferation of best-sellers first published in New York; Hollywood movies opening simultaneously in New York, Los Angeles, Rio de Janeiro, and Buenos Aires; and the unprecedented access—at least for the middle class—to what was once a luxury reserved for an oligarch: the trip to Europe, and, increasingly, to Miami or New York, *en cómodas cuotas mensuales* ("in easy monthly installments"), despite inflation and falling wages.

Ironically, the retreat of the Left and the rise of brutally repressive military regimes in such countries as Brazil, Uruguay, Argentina, and Chile also contributed to the growth of feminism in these countries. The conversion of many *militantes* to feminism was a consequence of their participation in sexist guerrilla organizations, where women were seen as equal to men because they participated in military operations and "packed a .45," yet were often given an additional "double shift," performing traditional menial feminine tasks for the revolutions and rarely promoted to leadership positions. In Uruguay, for example, women composed 25 percent of the MLN (Tupamaros) membership, but not a single woman held a leadership position in the organization. "In general," recalls a Tupamara, "the organization scorned personal problems. They were perceived as secondary, and a bit bothersome. Especially during the last period, when they were considered—I repeat—'symptoms' of ideological weakness." [10]

When military regimes took over the Southern Cone and stepped up repression, thousands had to flee their countries, settling in Mexico, Canada, or Europe, at a time when the feminist movements mobilized large numbers of women. During their exile, the *militantes* realized that confronting the leadership of a left-wing party with gender issues, as the French Trotskyist and Italian Communist feminists were doing, could no longer be dismissed as frivolous or treasonous to the working class. They discovered their oppression in consciousness-raising groups, confronted the leadership of their organizations, created feminist collectives, established contact with feminists in their countries, and became powerful advocates for the movement after they returned from exile. [11]

In other Latin American countries, however, women did not break their ties with the guerrillas. In Peru, they have continued to swell the ranks of Sendero Luminoso ("Shining Path"), where they reportedly hold some leadership roles and representation on the central committee. In the last stage of the insurrection in Nicaragua, women represented some 30 percent of the FSLN ("Sandinist Front of National Liberation") combat forces, and after 1979, six women were awarded the rank of *Comandantes Guerrilleras.* On the other hand, in the mid-eighties, the Sandinista leadership was surprised to discover that Nicaraguan women considered important issues generally dismissed by the Left as bourgeois feminists' preoccupations—that is, abortion, rape, sexism, and violence against women, among others.[12]

The incorporation of women who had participated in left-wing parties and organizations signified the rejection of left-wing tenets and practices, but did not imply abandoning commitment to radical social change. Latin American women's resolve not to separate their struggle from that of society's most exploited sectors was strengthened by the women's mobilization in neighborhoods and shantytowns, which got under way as feminist groups began to multiply.

While feminists needed to find a "voice" to describe and analyze their oppression and *un espacio de reflexión* ("a space for reflection") in which they could develop a new identity, delve into the past, read feminist texts, create new forms of interaction, and dream of a utopian future, they were pressed to act by the reality in which they lived. In Chile and Brazil, for example, they had to redefine themselves while their top priority was to participate in the struggle against dictatorship and strengthen the opposition movement, demanding "Democracy in the Country and Democracy in the Home" in the streets of Santiago, participating in the Women's Movement for Amnesty in Brazil, and marching in the streets of São Paulo in support of a "complete, general, and unrestricted amnesty."

Unlike feminists in the United States and some European countries, most Latin American feminists did not create consciousness-raising groups but instead *grupos de reflexión,* reading and discussion groups. By the time Latin American feminism got under way, some feminist literature was already available in Spanish or Portuguese—works by Simone de Beauvoir and Betty Friedan, for example. However, much was not available, and participants in discussion groups had to labor over poorly mimeographed, makeshift translations of materials published in French, Italian, or English, brought by travelers or sent by friends in exile. In these groups, Latin American women, like their counterparts in the United States and Canada, also discovered that "the personal is political," but they did it by discussing texts and seeking to define what was specifically Latin American in the "political." When they found themselves ready to act, their activities were directed toward issues uncovered in their reading groups and those raised by women of the popular sectors. Feminists were pressured to define gender oppression of women of different classes and ethnic/racial origins, in an interaction at times complicated by the interference of the Church or left-wing parties, especially over such issues as reproductive rights, sexuality, or rape.

Despite the deepening economic crisis and the serious financial difficulties of the last decade, Latin American feminists have succeeded in organizing international gatherings, known as *encuentros*, approximately every two years.[13] The first was held in the outskirts of Bogotá, Colombia, in July 1981, sponsored by a coalition of Colombian feminists interested in learning whether other feminists existed in Latin America, meeting them, and exchanging information with them. Since then, there have been four more *encuentros*, in Lima, Peru (1983), Bertioga, Brazil (1985), Taxco, Mexico (1987), and San Bernardo, Argentina (1990). The last *encuentro* was attended by some 2,800 women representing all Latin American countries, including Nicaragua, Haiti, and, for the second time, Cuba. The organizers scheduled its conclusion, a march in downtown Buenos Aires, for November 25, the day feminists throughout the continent take to the streets to denounce violence against women, as they have done since the first *encuentro* in 1981.

While convened by feminists, the *encuentros* are open to all women; in fact, they consistently attract large numbers of activists from the *movimiento de mujeres*. They are usually chaotic gatherings, in which participants engage in heated political debates and plan strategies that have shaped Latin American feminism for the last decade. The organizers of each *encuentro* have managed to publish a *memoria* of each meeting.

The texts included in the *memorias* and issues discussed in the *encuentros* have had a direct impact on the movement because they are taken up in national meetings, which are also divided in *encuentros nacionales de mujeres* and *encuentros nacionales feministas* (national women's *encuentros* and feminist *encuentros*).[14] In Bogotá, for example, the main debate was whether feminists should pursue an independent path (autonomy) or retain an ideological commitment to a left-wing political party and to feminism *(doble militancia)*. At the last two *encuentros*, the main topic of discussion was the relationship between feminism and the *movimiento de mujeres*; tensions disappeared only on the last day, when everybody proclaimed, "Somos todas feministas!" ("We are all feminists!"). In San Bernardo, Argentina, significant new developments were the presence of congresswomen from several Latin American countries and the founding of several continental networks—of black women, mental health workers, and women supporting the right to abortion, among others.

Organizations created by feminists in the past two decades vary greatly. In almost every country, theater, film, magazine, and video collectives thrive, and feminists everywhere have access to the magazine *mujer/ fempress*, an "alternative communication network for women," founded in 1981 by Adriana Santa Cruz and Viviana Erazo. Published in recent years in Santiago de Chile, it is an effective feminist network because it has correspondents in most Latin American countries and it carries news about women throughout the continent. In Mexico City and other capitals, feminists have founded support groups for domestic workers, prostitutes, and, more recently, for AIDS patients. Montevideo, Uruguay, is the Latin American headquarters of Católicas por el Derecho a Decidir ("Catholics for Free Choice")—as the name indicates, a group that supports free choice from a Catholic perspective. But other Catholic groups exist throughout the continent, such as the Peruvian Círculo de Feministas Cristianas "Talitha Cumi" ("Feminists' Christian Center 'Talitha Cumi' "). Many groups have radio programs: in Mexico City, the Centro de Comunicación Alternativa "Alaíde Foppa" ("Center for Alternative Communication 'Alaíde Foppa' ") produces feminist radio programs addressed to women, and in São Paulo the group Comunicacão Mulher ("Communication/Woman") creates audiovisual materials for women and children. La Morada, in Santiago de Chile, is the only Latin American feminist group that owns and operates a radio station. On the other hand, Delegacias de Defesa da Mulher, women's police stations where victims of domestic violence receive psychological and legal counseling, can be found only in Brazil. First created in the state of São Paulo, in 1985, a total of 74 women's police stations had opened throughout the country by 1990.

In recent years, feminists in many countries have organized women's studies courses and programs, most often outside the university. In the Caribbean they have founded CAFRA (Caribbean Association for Feminist Research and Action), a network of English-, French-, and Spanish-speaking researchers and activists. Most countries have documentation and research centers. Two of the oldest are Centro Flora Tristán and CIPAF (Centro de Investigación para la Acción Femenina, "Research Center for Feminine Action"), in Santo Domingo, Dominican Republic, where participants produce books as well as magazines and audiovisual materials for workshops involving urban and rural women.[15] Since 1982, in Lima, Peru, the Movimiento Manuela Ramos ("Manuela Ramos Movement") has used the popular medium of the *fotonovela*—photo-illustrated romances—to communicate a different kind of message among women's grass roots organizations. Its *fotonovelas,* entitled "Manuela Ramos," focus on such issues as adolescent pregnancy, rape, family planning, sexual harassment, premarital relations, and organizing techniques among women.

Many groups rely exclusively on European or U.S. funding for their support, while others, such as the Argentine ATEM 25 de Noviembre Asociación de Trabajo y Estudios de la Mujer, ("Association for Work and Study on Women, November 25"), refuse to accept any foreign financial aid.

Feminists have organized a variety of campaigns: for nonsexist education, to obtain the *patria potestad* (paternal/maternal authority), against domestic violence, in support of divorce, for the ratification of the United Nations Convention for the Elimination of All Forms of Discrimination against Women, and for access to contraceptives, and for day care centers. Although the first feminist groups tended to be located in the capitals, the numbers in the provinces are growing. In Brazil, feminist organizations have expanded from São Paulo and Rio de Janeiro to the northeastern states and even Goiás. In the town of San Cristóbal, Chiapas, Mexico, for example, a group of women founded in 1990 the Colectiva de Mujeres Autónomas en Lucha "Citlalmina" ("Collective of Autonomous Women in Struggle 'Citlalmina' "). Its purpose is to hold workshops with indigenous women and discuss such issues as human reproduction, menstruation, fertility, and organizing techniques.

In several countries, feminists have succeeded in incorporating gender-specific concerns into public policy issues. They have entered traditional politics while remaining firmly committed to feminism and have affected campaign platforms. After lengthy and heated discussions, they have overcome their deep reluctance to cooperate with the state—perhaps a remnant of their commitment to vanguard politics—and have supported the institutionalization of women's demands as well as the establishment of national and local women's councils.

In all these respects, the record of Brazilian feminists has been exceptional. In the last stages of the military dictatorship, they succeeded in making issues such as violence against women, day care, contraception, and sexuality "prominently included in the platforms and programs of many individual candidates and national political parties," writes Sonia Alvarez. "For the first time since the Brazilian suffrage movement in the 1920s and 1930s, gender became the basis for widespread electoral mobilization and gender inequality the object of generalized political debate." [16] Brazilian feminists were the first to enter the political structure and create state councils on women (Conselho Estadual da Condicão Femenina) to promote women's interests, initially in São Paulo in 1983, and later in Minas Gerais. It was a real "astronaut step," recalls Jacqueline Pitanguy (who went on to preside over the National Council for Women's Rights in 1985), because feminists had "to get into the government, while maintaining a fundamental commitment to the social movement." [17] In 1986, with the election of the Constitutional Assembly, which had the task of drafting a new constitution, feminists were ready with a list of recommendations, many of which found their way into the 1988 constitution. However, the proposals for maternity and paternity leaves and decriminalization of abortion were not included.

By contrast, feminists in Colombia failed to organize themselves to participate directly or indirectly in the 1991 constitutional convention. Though indigenous people were represented and the assembly was presided over by the former guerrilla leader Antonio Navarro Wolff, women were conspicuously absent from among the 74 delegates, and the document ratified in July 1991 includes civil reforms already adopted by many other Latin American nations. The failure of Colombian feminists in this instance should be attributed in part to the weaknesses of the feminist movement, as well as to Colombia's endemic political violence, its 30-year-long guerrilla warfare, and the more recent violence connected with drug trafficking.

In Brazil, on the other hand, while the new constitution guarantees equality before the law for men and women, and establishes the government's obligation to prevent violence in the home, a recent report by the Women's Rights Project of Human Rights Watch indicates that

> over 70 percent of all reported incidents of violence against women in Brazil take place in the home. In almost all the cases the abuser was either the woman's husband or her lover. Over 40 percent involved serious bodily injury caused by, among other things, punching, slapping, kicking, tying up and spanking, burning of the breasts and the genitals, and strangulation . . . Moreover, female victims still have little reason to expect that their abusers—once denounced—will ever be punished.[18]

Furthermore, as Alvarez points out, since the return to civilian rule, the successes achieved by the feminists during the transition to democratic rule have not been translated into greater effective power and influence.[19] In this respect, however, the Brazilian situation is unfortunately not unique. In Chile, women were also crucial players in the long struggle against Pinochet's dictatorship, feminists were forceful participants in that struggle, and gender issues gained prominence in the final stages of the opposition campaign, but all this did not lead to increased political power or influence in the government once President Patricio Aylwin took office.

Everywhere in Latin America, feminist groups continue to be small, sometimes bitterly divided, yet usually ready to come together to support a specific issue, participate in a particular campaign, or work with women from the *movimiento de mujeres*. They remain a minority, but their political impact is by no means negligible. They have insisted that sisterhood must be real for brotherhood to exist; that *sisterhood* is a word encompassing all women—especially the poorest, who suffer most from regressive economic policies; that racial and sexual diversity is desirable; that sexual and gender differences exist; and that women must reject old hierarchies, old leaderships, blind obedience, discipline for discipline's sake, and authority as a prelude to authoritarianism. Through their writings and courageous actions, they have insisted on equality, diversity, pluralism, and economic, racial, and social justice. They have given new meaning to the concept of democracy in Latin America.

Notes

1. Within the recent scholarship on social movements, the topic of women's grass roots organizations has received a great deal of attention. See the essay by Helen I. Safa and Cornelia Butler Flora in this volume; Helen I. Safa, "Women's Social Movements in Latin America," *Gender and Society* 4:3 (Sept. 1990), 353–59; Elizabeth Jelin (ed.), *Women and Social Change in Latin America*

(London: Zed Books, 1990); Joe Foweraker and Ann L. Craig (eds.), *Popular Movements and Political Change in Mexico* (Boulder, Colo.: L. Rienner, 1990); Jane S. Jaquette (ed.), *The Women's Movement in Latin America. Feminism and the Transition to Democracy* (Boulder, Colo.: Westview Press, 1991); and Sonia E. Alvarez, *Engendering Democracy in Brazil. Women's Movements in Transition Politics* (Princeton: Princeton Univ. Press, 1991).

2. See Lélia Gonzalez, "Por un feminismo afrolatinoamericano," in *Mujeres crisis y movimiento. América Latina y el Caribe* (Santiago: Isis Internacional–Mudar 1988), 133–41.

3. Second-wave feminism is not a privileged topic among Latin Americanists, perhaps because many still believe in the once prevalent notion that Latin American women do not define themselves as feminists. That notion, which in many respects coincided with the views of the Old and New Left, was articulated in the seventies in the work of Elsa Chaney, *Supermadre: Women in Politics in Latin America* (Austin: Univ. of Texas Press, 1979); June Nash and Helen Safa (eds.), *Sex and Class in Latin America* (New York: Praeger, 1976), and Evelyn P. Stevens, "Marianismo: The Other Face of Machismo in Latin America," in Ann Pescatello (ed.), *Female and Male in Latin America* (Pittsburgh: Univ. of Pittsburgh Press, 1973). It was strengthened by works that fall within the field of "testimonial literature." For example, Domitila Barrios de Chungara with Moema Viezzer, *Let Me Speak!* (New York: Monthly Review Press, 1978); and Elisabeth Burgos-Debray (ed.), Ann Wright (trans.), *I . . . Rigoberta Menchú: An Indian Woman in Guatemala* (London: Verso, 1984). For recent examples of scholarship on second-wave feminism from a different perspective, see Cornelia Butler Flora, "Socialist Feminism in Latin America," *Women and Politics* 4:1(Winter 1984), 69–93; Marianne Schmink, "Women in Brazilian Abertura Politics," *Signs,* 7:1 (Autumn 1981), 115–34; Magdalena León (ed.), *Sociedad, Subordinación y Feminismo* (Bogotá: Asociación Colombiana de Estudios Populares, 1982); Susan C. Bourque, "Urban Activists: Paths to Political Consciousness in Peru," in Susan C. Bourque and Donna C. Divine (eds.), *Women Living Change* (Philadelphia: Temple Univ. Press, 1985), 25–56; Marysa Navarro, "First Feminist Meeting of Latin America and the Caribbean," *Signs* 8:1 (Autumn 1982), 154–57; Virginia Vargas, "El Aporte a la rebeldía de las mujeres," in Coordinación de Grupos de las Jornadas Feministas (ed.), *Jornadas feministas: Feminismo y sectores populares en América Latina* (Mexico, D.F.: Ed. Electrocomp, 1987), 13–39, "Movimiento de mujeres en América Latina: Un Reto para el análisis y para la acción," and Margarita Pisano, "Pasos críticos y deseos de cambio," in *Mujeres, crisis y movimiento. América Latina y el Caribe* (Santiago: Isis Internacional–Mudar, 1988), 83–90; Alvarez, *Engendering Democracy in Brazil;* June E. Hahner, *Emancipating the Female Sex. The Struggle for Women's Rights in Brazil, 1850–1940* (Durham: Duke Univ. Press, 1990), has an epilogue that covers the second wave; and Nancy Saporta Sternbach, Marysa Navarro-Aranguren, Patricia Chuchryk, and Sonia E. Alvarez, "Feminisms in Latin America: From Bogotá to San Bernardo," *Signs* 17:2 (Winter 1992), 393–434.

4. For additional background on Mexican feminism, see also Ana Lau Jaiven, *La Nueva ola del feminismo en México* (Mexico City: Grupo editorial Planeta, 1987), and *Otro modo de ser. Mujeres Mexicanas an Movimiento* (Mexico, D.F.: Centro de comunicación Alternativa Alaide Foppa, 1991).

5. See Bourque, "Urban Activists"; Virginia Vargas, "Movimiento feminista

en el Peru: Balance y perspectivas," in *Década de la mujer: Conversatorio sobre Nairobi* (Lima: Centro Flora Tristán, 1985), and *El movimiento de mujeres en el Perú: Vertientes, espacios, nudos* (Lima: Ed. Flora Tristán, 1990); and Maruja Barrig, "The Difficult Equilibrium between Bread and Roses: Women's Organizations and the Transition from Dictatorship to Democracy in Peru," in Jaquette (ed.), *The Women's Movement in Latin America*, 114–48.

6. See Leonor Calvera, *Mujeres y feminismo en la Argentina* (Buenos Aires: Grupo Editor Latinoamericano, 1990).

7. See especially "La Formación de la conciencia feminista en Chile," *Materia de Discusión*, no. 7 (Santiago: Programa de FLACSO, 1980); "Chile: La Mujer en la formulación política," *Documento de Trabajo*, no. 109 (Santiago: Programa de FLACSO, 1981); Julieta Kirkwood, *Ser política en Chile: Las Feministas y los partidos* (Santiago: Programa de FLACSO, 1982); and "El Feminismo como negación del autoritarismo," *Materia de Discusión*, no. 52 (Santiago: Programa de FLACSO, 1983). See also Patricia Crispi, *Tejiendo rebeldías: Escritos feministas de Julieta Kirkwood* (Santiago: Centro de Estudios de la Mujer y La Morada, 1987).

8. Julieta Kirkwood, *Ser política en Chile. Los nudos de la sabiduría feminista* (Santiago de Chile: Editorial Cuarto Propio, 1990); 202–3.

9. Calvera, *Mujeres y feminismo*, 79–80.

10. Ana Maria Araújo, *Tupamaras* (Paris: Des Femmes, 1980), 161.

11. See Angela Neves-Xavier de Brito, "Brazilian Women in Exile: The Quest for Identity," *Latin American Perspectives* 13:2 (Spring 1986), 58–80; and Albertina de Oliveira Costa, Maria Teresa Porciuncula Moraes, Norma Marzola, and Valentina da Rocha Lima, *Memorias das mulheres do exílio*, vol. 2 (Rio de Janeiro: Paz e Terra, 1980).

12. See Maxine Molineux, "Mobilization without Emancipation? Women's Interests, State and Revolution," in Richard Fagen, Carmen Diana Deere, and José Luis Coraggio (eds.), *Transition and Development: Problems of Third World Socialism* (New York: Monthly Review Press and the Center for the Study of the Americas, 1986), 280–302; and Norma Stoltz Chinchilla, "Revolutionary Popular Feminism in Nicaragua: Articulating Class, Gender, and National Sovereignty," *Gender and Society* 4:3 (Sept. 1990), 370–97.

13. Marysa Navarro, "El Primer encuentro de Latinoamérica y el Caribe," in León (ed.), *Sociedad*, 309–18; Virginia Vargas, "El Movimiento feminista latinoamericano: Entre la esperanza y el desencanto (Apuntes para el debate)," paper written for the Fifth *Encuentro*, 1990; and Saporta Sternbach et al., "Feminisms in Latin America."

14. See Eleonora Menicucci de Oliveira's account of the Brazilian *IX Encuentro Nacional Feminista* held in Guaranhuns, Sept. 1987. Eleonora Menicucci de Oliveira, "Reflexiónes a partir del IX Encuentro Nacional Feminista," in *Mujeres crisis y movimiento. América Latina y el Caribe*, 97–107.

15. See Carmen Barroso and Cristina Bruschini on doing feminist research on the sexuality of poor women living in São Paulo's periphery, "Building Politics from Personal Lives: Discussions on Sexuality among Poor Women in Brazil," in Chandra Talpade Mohanty, Ann Russo, and Lourdes Torres (eds.), *Third World Women and the Politics of Feminism* (Bloomington: Indiana Univ. Press, 1991), 153–73.

16. Alvarez, *Engendering Democracy in Brazil*, 176.

17. Jacqueline Pitanguy, "Políticas públicas y ciudadanía," in Regina Rodrí-

guez et. al., *Transiciónes. Mujeres en los procesos democráticos* (Santiago: *Isis Internacional*, 1990), 15.

18. *Criminal Injustice. Violence Against Women in Brazil. An Americas Watch Report* (New York: Human Rights Watch, 1991), 4–5.

19. Alvarez, *Engendering Democracy in Brazil*, 223.

7

Religion: Reconstituting Church and Pursuing Change

MARGARET E. CRAHAN

From Quetzalcoatl to Gustavo Gutierrez

Latin America is a continent in which religion has historically played a major role in molding peoples and cultures. Well before the arrival of the Spanish and Portuguese, the indigenous civilizations were rooted in belief systems that gave meaning and order to life. Political leaders and religious leaders were sometimes the same, or were closely identified with one another, as in the Aztec and Inca empires. The economic and social organization of communities and states was often influenced by religiously sanctioned values. In some instances, religion even helped facilitate the conquest, as in the case of the Aztecs' identification of Hernando Cortés with the god of life, Quetzalcoatl.[1]

The conquest of America was justified by the Spanish and Portuguese, in part, on the grounds that it was their responsibility to see to the salvation of the Native Americans by converting them. Beginning in 1514 the conquistadors were obliged to read a document known as the *Requerimiento* prior to attacking those who resisted conversion to Catholicism and subjugation to the Spanish Crown. It was full of legal and theological explanations of divine right monarchy and Catholicism. When the *encomendero*-turned-Dominican-friar, Bartolomé de Las Casas first read it, he reported that he could not decide whether to laugh or weep.[2] It reflected the conviction of the monarchs that they were acting not only legally and morally, but also in the best interests of the inhabitants of America.

This confidence had been stimulated by the 1492 victory of Ferdinand and Isabella over Granada, the last of the Moorish strongholds, which facilitated the geographical and political consolidation of Spain.

Concerned with establishing royal authority as paramount, in the face of an ethnically and culturally heterogenous population, the monarchs used religion as one means to promote loyalty to the Crown. The expulsion of the Jews in the same year and the use of the Inquisition to impose religious as well as political orthodoxy, were intended to reinforce the power of the monarchy. While accepting some of the Moors and Jews fleeing across the border, Spain's neighbor, Portugal, was also disposed to use religion to ensure loyalty, particularly in its overseas colonies. Hence, religion from the outset was utilized as a prime instrument of imperial control.

Both countries had extracted from Rome concessions that allowed the Crown to exercise considerable authority over the Catholic Church in America.[3] In return for assistance in maintaining the Church, the monarchs enjoyed certain patronage rights involving appointments, offices, and finances. This agreement was known as the *Patronato Real* in the Spanish colonies and as the *Padroado Real* in the Portuguese. Nevertheless, tension between church and state in the colonies was a constant, given the Crowns' tendency to grant dual jurisdiction to civil and ecclesiastical officials in hopes of maintaining royal authority supreme and unthreatened by local interests. This strategy was not entirely successful and gave rise to constant tension between church and state in the colonial period.[4]

Another prime source of conflict between royal and ecclesial officials was the exploitation of Native Americans. While some church people and institutions abused them, others were in the forefront of their defense. As early as 1514 clerics such as Las Casas began denouncing Native American exploitation and maltreatment as being against both royal and God's law. Subsequently Las Casas succeeded in convincing the Crown to issue the New Laws (1542) to protect Native Americans, but it was virtually impossible to enforce them. Other priests and religious leaders, such as the Franciscans in Brazil, sought to protect Africans brought to the colonies as slaves. Throughout the colonial period, church people played a substantial role in focusing attention on critical moral issues, particularly those related to the poor and exploited. This occurred at the same time that the Church, as an institution, served as a principal support for continued imperial control and was identified with local elites.

Secular elites were largely educated by the Catholic Church, which was instrumental in disseminating European Enlightenment thought, with its revolutionary implications. In addition, the "education" of a good number of church people in the realities of life—particularly parish priests in rural areas—contributed to support for the wars of independence. Hence, the involvement of Miguel Hidalgo and José Maria Morelos as leaders of the Mexican struggle for independence. In Quito the head of the revolutionary junta was Bishop José Cuero y Caicedo, who personified the identification of some of the Church leadership with America rather than with Spain. In Brazil, which gained its independence in 1821, increasing alienation between the Crown and the Catholic Church contributed to the erosion of support for the monarchy, thereby contributing to the declaration of a republic in 1889. Overall, however, the Church as an institution in both Spanish and Portuguese America was identified with maintaining the status quo.

With the advent of independence in the 1820s, the Catholic Church faced substantial challenges. European liberalism had brought with it strong strains of anticlericalism and secularism. In some countries, such as Chile, this contributed to the separation of church and state, while in others, such as Mexico, it resulted in the forced divestment of Church property. In Brazil the Catholic Church was also faced with an erosion of its influence. The nineteenth century throughout Latin America was one of substantial readjustment for the Church, which no longer enjoyed as pre-eminent a place within society. While some church people continued to distinguish themselves through their concern for the poor and exploited, the Church, as an institution, continued to be identified with the elite. This was partially due to the cultivation of elites in an effort to ensure the well-being of the institution, without which, the leadership felt, the Church's mission of the salvation of all could not be accomplished.

The issuance by Pope Leo XIII in 1891 of the encyclical *Rerum Novarum,* which contained a strong critique of the exploitation of workers by industrial capitalism, did not cause any immediate major readjustments in the Catholic Church's alignments. It did, however, stimulate increased ecclesial focus on labor, which was beginning to organize and mobilize. The growing appeal of secular and religious competitors in the 1920s, particularly for the working and middle classes, led the Church to increase its efforts to maintain their loyalty, as they constituted the majority of the faithful. This resulted in a proliferation of organizations, including Catholic worker and student groups, as well as political parties such as the Christian Democrats. While they did have some success, it was not sufficient to prevent the inroads of Marxism, secularism, and Protestantism.

The worldwide economic depression in 1929 and its contribution to political instability encouraged additional rethinking of the social doctrine of the Catholic Church, particularly with respect to the morality of capitalism and liberal democracy. The upshot was that some church people began investigating other political and economic forms. Dom Helder Camara, who gained fame in the 1960s and 1970s as Brazil's most outspoken progressive bishop, was attracted to experiments such as Mussolini's in the 1930s. On the fortieth anniversary of *Rerum Novarum* in 1931, Pope Pius IX issued the encyclical *Quadragesimo Anno,* which suggested that in view of the obvious deficiencies of capitalism, liberal democracy, and socialism, corporatism might be an alternative. Such a posture had resonance in Latin America, where the political instability and economic dislocation in the 1930s had deepened the suffering of the majority of the population and encouraged the corporatist experiments of Getúlio Vargas in Brazil and Juan Perón in Argentina.

As pressures for change increased in Latin America, particularly in the post–World War II period, the Catholic Church felt increasingly challenged to be responsive. This inclination was reinforced by the decision of Pope John XXIII to call the Second Vatican Council, which opened in 1962. Aimed at revitalizing the Catholic Church so it could exert more moral leadership in responding to such problems as the arms race, the Cold War, repressive governments, and gross socioeconomic disparities within and between nations, this meeting resulted in theological, pastoral, and bureaucratic reforms that had unanticipated consequences.

While prelates from Asia, Africa, and Latin America were in the minority, they did succeed in increasing the focus on poverty and unequal relations between industrialized and industrializing countries. The Brazilian bishops, in particular, lobbied their colleagues for more attention to social justice issues. As a consequence, the prelates gathered in Rome concluded that the Church should commit itself more forcefully to promoting peace, justice, and human rights, as well as to modernizing the institution theologically, bureaucratically, liturgically, and pastorally. In 1968 the Latin American bishops met in Medellín, Colombia, for the Second General Conference of Latin American Bishops (CELAM II) to translate the conclusions of the Vatican Council into Latin American realities.

Influenced by position papers drafted largely by social scientists and progressive theologians—notably the essay "Teología de la liberación" by the Peruvian Franciscan Gustavo Gutierrez—the prelates concluded that the promotion of peace, justice, and human rights required a "preferential option for the poor," that is, greater identification with and involvement in the struggle of the majority of Latin Americans for liberation from exploitation and repression. This initiated a major shift in the institutional Church's traditional identification with the bourgeoisie.[5] The Medellín conclusions, cast in the general terms of consensus statements, stimulated a great deal of debate both within and without the Church and were interpreted by some as justifying support for revolutionary movements, including Marxist ones. Critics began to organize, coalescing around the Colombian bishop Alfonso López Trujillo, who succeeded in 1972 in being elected secretary-general of CELAM by a narrow margin. From that time until the next general conference in Puebla, Mexico, in 1979, there was intense debate focusing on the implications of the preferential option for the poor, the use of Marxist concepts and analysis in liberation theology, new pastoral forms such as base Christian communities (CEBs), and the direct involvement of priests in politics.

Liberation theology and base Christian communities are two of the most innovative religious developments in the twentieth century. The former emphasizes the need to analyze reality, reflect upon it in terms of the biblical message and other religious sources, and act in accordance with the divine will to recreate the Kingdom of God on earth— that is, societies characterized by peace, justice, and respect for human rights. Its methodology focuses on analysis, reflection, and praxis, or informed action for justice. Liberation theology has been used by some base Christian communities, but does not appear to be as prevalent among them as sometimes presumed.

CEBs are generally constituted by fifteen to thirty people who come together, ordinarily without a priest or minister, to reflect on the Bible or other documents in terms of their applicability to daily life and to the problems of society in general. In some instances, as in El Salvador and Nicaragua in the 1970s, some CEBs served to generate support for revolutionary movements. Studies indicate, however, that base Christian communities range across the spectrum politically, ideologically, and theologically. Liberation theology, which has been adopted by some CEBs, appears to be most influential among church personnel, intellectuals, and university students.[6]

In 1979 the third conference of Latin American bishops (CELAM III) at Puebla in Mexico reasserted the Catholic Church's commitment to a preferential option for the poor, avoided taking a stand on liberation theology, supported CEBs as a useful tool for evangelization, but warned against their politicization, and condemned clerical involvement in politics. The latter was held to be the responsibility of an evangelized laity. Since Puebla debate has continued, stimulated in part by the attempted imposition by Pope John Paul II (1978–) of greater theological and doctrinal orthodoxy and more centralized control. He has repeatedly insisted that the teaching authority of the Church (*magisterium*) resides exclusively in the hierarchy, and that developments such as liberation theology which encourage more individual biblical and doctrinal interpretation are not valid. In addition, the use by liberation theologians of some aspects of Marxist analysis, including the concept of class struggle, has aroused considerable concern on the part of the pope. The depth of this preoccupation was revealed by the issuance in 1984 and again in 1986 of critiques of liberation theology by the Vatican's Congregation for the Doctrine of the Faith. The first of these generated considerable negative response from progressive Latin American Church elites, and hence the second took a more moderate view, conceding that there were some positive aspects of liberation theology, particularly the necessity for societal restructuring to liberate the poor majority.[7]

The involvement of priests in the revolutionary government in Nicaragua from 1979 until 1990 was also viewed by Pope John Paul II as a challenge to the Church's stated position of political nonpartisanship.

Visiting Managua in March 1983 the pope took the occasion to scold publicly Ernesto Cardenal, one of four priests then holding ministerial posts who had refused to abide by a 1981 Vatican directive to resign. Cardenal and his colleagues had argued that their faith mandated that they participate directly in the struggle for socioeconomic justice and that the implementation of socialism was the only way to accomplish that in the Nicaraguan case. He was supported in his position by sectors of the clergy and laity commonly referred to as the "popular church" or "people's church." While this group constituted a minority of Nicaraguan church people, its visibility and discrepancy from positions of the institutional Church caused John Paul to single it out for criticism in 1982 and 1983. The pope's action reflected his deep distrust of the Marxist government of Nicaragua and his concern for maintaining hierarchical authority and doctrinal orthodoxy within the Catholic Church.[8] Such conflicts indicated the extent of the ongoing tension between those within the Church who tended to regard it as a community of believers committed to revolution and those who accepted a more hierarchical and traditional concept of the Church. Some observers have characterized the conflict as being between those who conceive of the Church as having a largely "prophetic" mission and those more concerned with the Church as an institution.

John Paul's attention has also been focused on what he appears to regard as the unwarranted politicization of theology and the Catholic Church in Brazil. As a consequence, he is thought to have named as bishops individuals who are generally more conservative than their predecessors.[9] In addition, the theologian Leonardo Boff has been silenced on two occasions by the Vatican's Congregation for the Doctrine of the Faith for his use of some aspects of Marxist analysis, especially in his critiques of the governance of the Church.[10] These disputes reflect differences of opinion stimulated by competing models of church within the Catholic Church, reflecting the tension between historical continuities and pressures for change.

Continuity versus Change

Since the 1960s debate within the Catholic Church has been intensifying over three principal models of church, commonly designated as the Christendom, neo-Christendom, and people's or popular church models. Nowhere has the discussion been as intense as in Latin America. These models are clearly ideal types that are not necessarily mutually exclusive, and a good number of church people and analysts hold that in reality the models coexist. The Christendom model, which is rooted in the Catholic Church's constitution and historical evolution, conceives of the Church as strongly hierarchical and molded by undeviating religious principles. Such a church is inclined to cooperate with the state and is suspicious of movements predicated on struggle for radical change. The neo-Christendom model views society as broadly infused with Christian beliefs and values. The Church serves as the sacramental mediator between the individual and God, and has considerable influence over secular institutions, but is not allied with the state. Change should properly come about in a peaceful, evolutionary fashion. The third model is that of the popular or people's church, in which the Church is allied with the poor majority in a struggle for liberation that will transform society. In this process the Church itself becomes more communitarian and egalitarian.

The Christendom model is most closely identified with the colonial and nineteenth-century Catholic Church, while the neo-Christendom model describes more accurately the twentieth-century Catholic Church. The people's church model flows out of the ferment of the last thirty years and emphasizes the Church as a community of believers, over the Church as an institution.

Such models help determine the actions of church people at all levels within the institution, with the neo-christendom model being more prevalent among the clergy and hierarchy, and the people's church model more prevalent among the intellectual elite of the clergy and religious, as well as some grass roots laity. This can have substantial bureaucratic and other consequences, for as one analyst has noted, "The view of the church . . . that predominates among bishops and Catholic activists at all levels shapes the priorities they set for the institution, the kinds of organizations they build, and the activities they see as necessary and proper extensions of their religious role."[11]

Both the Christendom and neo-christendom models are concerned with the exercise of power within society and the maximizing of ecclesial influence. There are two prime goals: to infuse society with Christian principles to achieve the salvation of all, and to protect the institutional Church, without which the aforementioned transcendental objective could not be carried out. The people's church model is also concerned with power, focusing on its radical redistribution in order to reduce substantially socioeconomic injustice and exploitation. It is commonly identified with socialism and by implication also assumes a redistribution of power within churches such as the Catholic.

Beginning in the late 1960s and early 1970s the Christendom and neo-Christendom models were challenged by theologians such as the Peruvian Gustavo Gutierrez, the Uruguayan Juan Luis Segundo, and the Brazilian Leonardo Boff, as well as by the Argentine Protestant theologian José Míquez Bonino.[12] They questioned the Catholic and mainline Protestant churches' historical strategies for promoting the salvation of all and institutional preservation as leading to an acceptance of the status quo and hence the exploitation of the poor. The traditional distinction between temporal and spiritual spheres was seen as false, since churches were in and of the world. Consequently their actions and those of their members could not be politically neutral. As a result the Christian was morally obligated to act in the face of sin, including that resulting from societal structures that allowed for or encouraged poverty, repression, and gross violations of human rights. To challenge the status quo was to discharge one's moral duty. The people's church model was regarded as overcoming a false dichotomy between the sacred and profane, thereby allowing churches to promote effectively both temporal liberation and spiritual salvation. Consequently, it was necessary for churches and church people to engage directly in the struggle to liberate themselves and others from oppressive structures.

To those who charged that such a position encouraged class struggle and hence was antithetical to the churches' ideal of nonconflictual societies, Gustavo Gutierrez replied:

> Those who speak of class struggle do not "advocate" it—as some would say—in the sense of creating it out of nothing by an act of (bad) will. What they do is to recognize a fact and contribute to an awareness of that fact. And there is nothing more certain than a fact. To ignore it is to deceive and to be deceived and moreover to deprive oneself of the necessary means of truly and radically eliminating this condition—that is, by moving toward a classless society. Paradoxically, what the groups in power call "advocating" class struggle is really an expression of a will to abolish its causes, to abolish them, not cover them over, eliminate the appropriation by a few of the wealth created by the work of the many and not to make lyrical calls for social harmony. It is a will to build a socialist society, more just, free, and human and not a society of superficial and false reconciliation and equality. To "advocate" class struggle, therefore, is to reject a situation in which there are oppressed and oppressors. But it is a rejection without deceit or cowardliness; it is to recognize that the fact exists and that it profoundly divides men, in order to be able to attack it at its roots and thus create the conditions of an authentic human community. To build a just society today necessarily implies the active and conscious participation in the class struggle that is occurring before our eyes.[13]

Such disclaimers did not quiet the fears of those both in and out of the churches who feared socialism as inimical to Christianity. In the 1970s and 1980s disagreements between those who supported reform of capitalism and those who supported socialist revolution intensified in some Church organizations, theological schools, and within dioceses, parishes, and CEBs. While virtually all sectors accepted the necessity of change and the desirability of a preferential option for the poor, there were sharp debates over how best to achieve more just societies. The calls by some Church leaders for support of socialism helped legitimate revolutionary organizations, including Marxist ones, in such countries as Nicaragua and El Salvador. The direct participation of clerics and religious, as well as lay leaders, further legitimated these movements. While the Catholic Church historically has been anti-Marxist, this has not prevented it from cooperating with Marxist movements for change in extremely repressive situations.

In Nicaragua, for example, on June 2, 1979, the Catholic bishops issued a statement that held that the insurrection then under way to overthrow the dictatorship of Anastasio Somoza was moral and licit, since all avenues for peaceful change had been exhausted. However, the prelates subsequently made clear that their acceptance of the necessity of insurrection was not to be interpreted as carte blanche for the new government that took power in July of that year. Indeed, the episcopacy warned that care should be taken to avoid the importation of foreign "isms" and the massification of society. In addition, a multiparty system that encouraged popular participation was considered to be the most moral and conducive to the common good of society as a whole.[14] The subsequent attempted imposition of a one-party state by the Frente Sandinista de Liberación Nacional (FSLN) was considered by the hierarchy to be inimical to democracy, as well as to the welfare of the Catholic Church.

The growing animosity between the Sandinista government and the Catholic episcopacy, as well as a number of Protestant churches, in the early 1980s highlighted the tension between historical positions of the institutional churches and Marxist movements on how to achieve socioeconomic justice. The tension was epitomized by splits within churches, with some priests and ministers serving within the Sandinista government, and others seeking to delegitimize it. The Moravian Church, which was predominant on the Atlantic coast of Nicaragua, contributed some leaders not only to the armed opposition, but also to the National Assembly.

Some Catholics and Protestants incorporated themselves into government organizations, while many remained uncomfortable with both the strongly pro-Sandinista and anti-Sandinista sectors. Fundamentalist groups tended to be suspicious of the Marxism of the Sandinistas, and a number of their leaders were outspoken in their opposition.[15]

Many church people struggled to integrate their commitment to the revolution with their religious principles. In Estelí, a rural community where Catholic and Protestant groups had been active in support of the insurrection to overthrow Somoza, abuse of power by the Sandinista government, together with the U.S.-backed contra war to dislodge it, caused a great deal of agonizing.[16] Base Christian communities and other religious groups struggled with the application of religiously founded moral principles to an exceedingly complex situation, while the national and international press focused on the charges and countercharges of a handful of priests and bishops at the national level.

By 1983 church people not identified with either the radical Right or the radical Left had begun asserting themselves at all levels of the churches. These included ordinary laypersons, together with parish priests and ministers. In addition, the Vatican's secretary of state, Agostino Casaroli, encouraged the episcopacy to seek ways to defuse tensions with the government.[17] The government responded in kind, and by the late 1980s tensions had declined sufficiently so that the Sandinista government asked one of its chief critics, Cardinal Miguel Obando y Bravo, to chair the Committee of National Reconciliation, which was mandated by the peace process initiated by the Central American presidents at their August 1987 meeting at Esquipulas in Guatemala. Reportedly Obando was more impressed by the Sandinistas' commitment to seek a negotiated settlement to the contra war than by that of their opponents.[18]

This apparent change in the cardinal's stance is reflective of a not uncommon phenomenon even in the highly charged atmosphere of political, ideological, military, and religious struggle that has afflicted a good number of countries in Latin America in recent years. Church leaders, like others, modify their views over time, even though some of their supporters or critics do not always take note. This is indeed a phenomenon that merits more attention by scholars.

Such was the case with the Protestant community in Nicaragua, which has been portrayed by some as universally opposed to the Sandinista government. In reality it was divided over the issue, and the views of individual church people and institutions evolved, as did the government's attitudes toward them. At the outset of the revolution some fundamentalist Protestant denominations were strongly opposed to the Sandinista government, largely because of fear of Marxism. Between 1981 and 1983 some Pentecostal pastors were detained by the government and expelled from the country. By the mid-1980s this situation had improved. In 1987 the Assemblies of God, one of the largest such denominations, invited the Vice-Minister of the Interior to address its national conference. The superintendent of the denomination, the Reverend Saturino Cerrado, described this as a clear indication of improved communication between his church and the government.[19]

Evidence from Nicaragua, as well as other countries, suggests that contrary to what might be expected, fundamentalist groups do not always support conservative positions in religion and politics.[20] Nor do bishops, as witness the cases of Paulo Evaristo Arns in São Paulo, Brazil; Raúl Silva Henríquez of Santiago, Chile; and Samuel Ruíz of Chiapas, Mexico. They, and other church leaders, have challenged the status quo and encouraged others to do so, particularly in times of crisis.

In Brazil under the military government (1964–85), when repression by the state was high and organizations such as labor unions were unable to function freely, Cardinal Arns promoted the documentation and publication of human rights violations and provided an institutional base for proscribed activities.[21] The return to civilian government did not diminish his commitment, nor that of the majority of his episcopal colleagues, to condemn injustices, particularly those suffered by the poor. There was, however, some reassessment of Church priorities and strategies due to the changing circumstances and pressures from Rome for less political activism.[22]

Cardinal Raúl Silva Henríquez of Santiago, Chile, took the lead in that country in the aftermath of the September 11, 1973, military coup in providing assistance to the thousands of individuals who suffered human rights violations. Joining with Protestant and Jewish colleagues, he helped form the Committee for Peace, which began providing legal, medical, and other assistance to victims and their families, as well as documenting and publicizing violations nationally and internationally. In 1976 these services were taken over by the Vicariate of Solidarity as an office of the Archbishopric of Santiago. The efficacy of its work helped make it the most trusted institution in Chile by the late 1980s, along with the Catholic Church as a whole.[23]

Bishop Samuel Ruíz of Chiapas, Mexico (the area where Bartolomé de Las Casas tried unsuccessfully to establish a community in which Native Americans could live without fear of exploitation), has distinguished himself for his defense of landless peasants, as well as Guatemalan refugees who have fled across the border as a result of government repression and guerrilla warfare in that country. Ruíz's work emphasizes grass roots organization and empowerment and epitomizes a progressive interpretation of the mandates of Vatican II, Medellín, and Puebla.[24] Some tensions among progressive clerics, religious, and laity have arisen, however, over the most effective strategies for liberation. Such a situation highlights not only the complexity of the problems being confronted, but also the degree to which churches in the modern world are rarely monolithic. Nevertheless, it is true that church people at the grass roots level generally have more liberal positions than those at the top.

This has been confirmed by a number of studies, including those of the Centro Bellarmino in Chile. Surveys have indicated that only 13.1 percent of bishops in the 1970s felt that liberation theology had a substantial role to play in the country, while 34 percent of lay leaders, 36.4 percent of nuns, and 40.6 percent of priests believed so. Two-thirds of lay leaders and the majority of nuns surveyed preferred a more democratic church, while 70 percent of the bishops surveyed favored a centralist one. Three-quarters of nuns and lay leaders favored an emphasis on smaller, more socially involved Church organizations.

One of the most important differences concerns the role of women in the Church. While approximately one-half of the nuns and two-fifths of the laity surveyed were open to women serving as priests, only one-fifth of the priests and less than 7 percent of the bishops were open to such a development. Finally, the vast majority of priests, nuns, and laity surveyed were receptive to a married priesthood, while the majority of the bishops surveyed did not feel it was a real possibility.[25] Such questions take on considerable importance given the traditional scarcity of priests in Latin America, which has led to dependence on foreign missionaries and, particularly since Vatican II, to nuns and laypeople increasingly assuming functions of priests. This is especially evident in pastoral and social welfare work at the local level in virtually all of Latin America. The increased visibility of women, at least at the grass roots, has not necessarily resulted in substantially greater input for them into ecclesial decision making or policy formation.[26] Change in this respect would have worldwide repercussions, as the majority of Catholics are concentrated in Latin America.

Nor have developments such as liberation theology necessarily resulted in greater equality for women in church or society. As was noted at the Second Latin American Feminist Conference in 1983: "While liberation theologians recognize that women are marginalized within society as *poor people*, they did not address patriarchal structures as such, either within society as a whole or within church structures. It is imperative that liberation theologians actively challenge the structure of patriarchy in both their own practice and their methodology, and make a specific option for women among the poor and the oppressed."[27] Additionally, Elsa Tamez, a Methodist theologian from Mexico, argues:

> Liberation theology, when done from women's perspective, not only deals concretely with daily experience, but it is the basis, the point of departure for their theological work. Thus, not only is daily experience integral to their theology, but theology is transformed by the incorporation of women's life experience, especially that of poor women. We believe that the theological point of departure is not only the praxis of justice and the experience of God, but also "the praxis of caring," which is to say that there must be collegial relations between men and women, older and younger people and children, between all peoples. The praxis of caring includes daily interpersonal experience. Theology which takes this into account opens its horizons to make room for other perspectives, such as women's perspectives.[28]

Other church women have asserted that those of them who incorporated themselves into liberation movements prior to the late 1980s were required to abandon their feminism, for it was commonly regarded as an "imperialist theory calculated to divide and weaken the popular sector." Believing that it was "morally wrong, to make any claims in our own behalf,"[29] women did not identify themselves as feminists and continued to subordinate their objectives to those of the male-dominated liberation movements. The upshot was that women frequently attempted to copy men in their thinking and action, as well as in their spirituality. Only through the experience of struggle within the liberation movements did some women eventually begin to feel empowered to act as women in terms of their participation.[30]

Most Latin American women's relationship to religion is not as con-

sciously articulated. For many it serves primarily as a psychological outlet for the frustrations and pain of their daily lives or it is regarded as
a luxury for which they do not have time.[31] In addition, as religious
options in Latin America have increased, laypeople are more able to
choose the faith community that appears to serve best their spiritual
and secular needs. Hence, while the Catholic Church and the mainline
Protestant denominations have looked to such innovations as the CEBs
to make them more responsive to the problems of daily life of the ordinary laity, other groups, including Pentecostals and spiritists, appear
to have more appeal in some contexts.

In Brazil, for example, even long-term leaders of CEBs have turned
to what they regard as more hospitable religious groups. One such recent convert to a Pentecostal group explained her decision to join the
Assembly of God on the grounds that "there everyone supports us; in
the Catholic Church, everyone just comments and criticizes. In the Assembly of God, everyone prays together, because everyone suffers together."[32] Spiritist cults such as Umbanda and Candomblé are also seen
by some as more responsive to personal concerns than institutional religion. While CEBs are intended to focus on generalized societal problems, spiritism provides an outlet for anger and resentment, as well as
the possibility of divine intervention via the spirits to remedy problems.[33]

It is at this level of society that religious ferment is perhaps greatest.
Pressures for societal change have intensified in recent years as the poor
have become more organized and intent on political participation and
socioeconomic justice. The greater involvement of the Catholic and
Protestant churches among the poor has not only facilitated this mobilization, it has also had tremendous impact on the internal workings of
the institutional churches and more generally on the role of religion in
Latin America. While institutional churches have provided some resources and a degree of leadership, much of what has occurred at the
base is the result of the use of a wide variety of elements, including
religion, as part of a culture of resistance to exploitation. As research
has increasingly confirmed, the degree of resistance dating back to the
colonial period, particularly among Native Americans, has been obscured by the necessity for secrecy.[34] As this resistance has become more
visibly expressed, religions and churches have become useful vehicles
for its expression. Ecclesial support for peace, justice, and human rights
has provided individuals and communities with a degree of moral purchase to their critiques of society.

The "people's church," in reality, is not necessarily that described in
some of the literature and linked to leftist clerical elites.[35] Rather, it
may very well be more the creation of an ongoing process in which
ordinary individuals come together to define the content and intent of
their religious beliefs themselves. Given this, even with a religion as
pervasive as Catholicism in Latin America, the results of official man-

dates are not easily implemented. In addition, studies have suggested that the stated policies of Church leaders do not often result in societal change.[36] What Catholicism is definitionally and what it is in reality in Latin America reflects the degree to which any religion takes on different realities according to context. The diversity of Catholics has infused the Catholic Church in recent years with a great deal of dynamism and ferment. It has not necessarily resulted in major progress in realizing the Church's stated agenda of promoting peace, justice, and human rights.

The Catholic Church Faces the Future

Quite clearly the Catholic Church in Latin America today is operating in a context substantially different from its traditional one. Secular and religious competitors abound, and the complexities and problems of modern life present challenges that test it daily. In response to such pressures the Catholic Church as an institution has committed itself to supporting substantial societal and ecclesial change. The challenge of this decision is epitomized by the extent of change required to achieve the level of societal concord the Church deems desirable.

In order for an organization as complex and as historically weighted as the Catholic Church to promote change effectively, certain conditions are necessary. These include a relatively high degree of internal consensus; a clearly defined set of policy goals and sufficient autonomy from special interests to legitimate them; the resources necessary to convince a critical mass within society to accept change or at least not to be strongly opposed; the expertise to devise recommendations and strategies adequate to the effective promotion of change; and the maintenance of commitment over time in the face of changing circumstances, both within and without the institution.

The task the Catholic Church, as well as some other churches, has set itself is nothing less than the reordering of society to ensure the common good. As defined by the Brazilian Episcopal Conference, the common good is "that combination of specific conditions which permit all people to reach standards of living compatible with human dignity, thus the essential characteristic of the common good is that it be common for everyone, without discrimination of any kind whether it is cultural, social, religious, racial, economic, political or partisan."[37] Such an undertaking implies major structural change that could undercut the interests of some sectors of society. This appears at odds with the Church's desire to maintain the universality of its appeal. As a consequence, it has attempted to promote change, while at the same time reasserting the importance of building community, solidarity, and reconciliation within society. The difficulties involved make the maintenance of some degree of consensus within the Church critical to achieving its objectives.

In sum, for the Catholic Church, or indeed any church, to promote change, it must maintain a level of internal consensus and commitment sufficient to convince a critical mass of the populace, although not necessarily a majority, of the necessity and desirability of such change. If the agenda involves major structural changes perceived by some influential sectors of society to prejudice their interests, then the Church's impact will be limited. Some of these sectors may be within the Church or have allies within the Church, owing to the tradition of cultivating political and economic elites. Opposition may also come from non-elites who perceive their interests as more likely to be advanced by achieving greater influence within existing structures. Given the complexity of modern societies, opposition to any agenda for major changes will probably be substantial, cutting across class as well as other categories. The promotion of change may also be impeded by socioeconomic conditions. Churches will, as a consequence, calculate the impact of such a position on their institutional well-being. This may give the appearance that the Church's commitment to change is waning.

In Latin America the moral authority of the Catholic Church has historically been substantial and has had a major role in influencing normative values. These values, however, do not necessarily generate support for a change-oriented agenda, particularly since the Church has historically promoted nonconflictual societies as an ideal. The Church must therefore transcend part of its own heritage if it is to support change strongly.

Catholicism, as well as many other religions, roots its authority in a divine mandate, that is, the salvation of all. This makes the definition of salvation critical. The reformulation of the concept of salvation at Vatican II and Medellín to emphasize more strongly communal and temporal elements has given rise to sharp debates. These require the Church to expend considerable energy on defending reconceptualizations that underpin its change-oriented agenda. Given the complexities of the theological, political, and ideological issues involved, differences of opinion are substantial and have given rise to diverse opinions being expressed by Church leaders at all levels. Since the 1960s there has been a growing sense that the Church is speaking in multiple voices, thereby allowing individuals and groups within and without the Church to opt for the view that reinforces their stance. This has undercut the cohesion of the Church, thereby weakening its ability to maintain consensus on the means to promote societal change. Such differences of opinion have also contributed to an erosion of hierarchical authority.

For any church's agenda to transcend class and other interests, it must be informed by the historical experience of a critical mass within society. This necessitates resources and expertise to diagnose adequately the roots of societal problems and legitimate the changes being recommended. It also requires that the Church as an institution and church people be trusted by a broad cross section of society. In the post–World War II period, and particularly since the 1960s, Catholic personnel have become more highly educated and cognizant of specialized disciplines, including those in the social sciences. They have also become more focused on influencing public opinion. While the Church has developed more professionalized cadres and technical expertise, it has also had changing and, at times, conflicting policy and programmatic emphases. Some groups and programs have even appeared to be working at cross-purposes.

In addition, it must be remembered that policymakers frequently tend to opt for feasible, rather than stated, goals. Even when an objective is aggressively pursued it may not be achieved, or it may have unintended consequences. These factors place a premium on consistent administrative control, the loyalty and skill of personnel, and access to substantial resources, including money. Church officials also need to be able to revise and jettison policies and programs when necessary. This is not always easy for individuals imbued with a high degree of moral certainty. Obviously such institutional and personal issues help determine the Church's capacity to promote change effectively in society.

The Catholic Church does have some advantages. It has considerable internal cohesion and a tradition of incorporating diverse sectors and adapting to changing circumstances. The very ferment and pressures for change affecting it, as well as Latin American society more generally, can serve as a stimulus to its leaders to take the initiative and thereby increase the institution's influence. Crises can encourage actions that transcend traditional ecclesial patterns of behavior, as well as supplant the roles of temporal actors unable to exercise effective leadership roles. This is what happened in Brazil in the 1960s and Chile in the 1970s with the emergence of authoritarian regimes, as well as in Central America in the 1980s with the intensification of oppression. In such situations, the Catholic Church helps fill the vacuum created by the repression or suppression of political parties, labor unions, and civic organizations. In this respect the Church has been favored by the stability of its leadership and bureaucracy, as well as its willingness to incorporate some displaced secular leaders. This has helped create a critical mass of experts and policy strategists who, under the protection of the Church, challenged authoritarian governments with a view toward establishing more democratic systems.

The incorporation into a church of individuals from the secular sphere cannot avoid having an impact on a church's analysis of society and modus operandi, potentially contributing to more internal dynamism and diversity, with potentially modernizing and democratizing results. In highly repressive situations it also tends to increase trust in the church among diverse sectors, including some who were traditionally irreligious or anticlerical. On the other hand, the role of a church in opposing authoritarian governments can alienate sectors that benefit from the latter's policies or are fearful of instability. This may lead to challenges to the authority of the church's leadership and the legitimacy of its policies, as well as to actual attacks on ecclesial personnel. Nevertheless, crises in Latin America since the 1960s have tended to mobilize the churches and reduce divisions within them.

What is remarkable is that up to the present the Catholic Church in Latin America has continued to support societal change in the face of such problems. In so doing, it has reasserted its moral leadership, with all the inherent risks. Recognizing this and the fact that religious institutions are not substitutes for secular organizations that represent class or other interests, the Church has generally attempted to retire to a less partisan role when crises have subsided. This has been regarded by some as evidence of a reassertion of conservatism within the Church, particularly in view of the fact that it has sometimes supported partisan groups in its efforts to eliminate authoritarian regimes.

Some within the Catholic Church feel it should continue to engage in partisan politics during transitions to democracy or during the consolidation of revolutions thought to be beneficial to the common good. This was the case with the Nicaraguan priests in government during the Sandinista period. The Church's official position—that to promote peace, justice, and human rights effectively, it must function in a non-partisan and politically neutral way to maximize the appeal of its agenda—is regarded by some as an avoidance of moral responsibility. For those who believe that no common agenda is possible, the institutional Church is regarded as failing to live up to its commitment to a preferential option for the poor. This epitomizes the ongoing tension within the Catholic Church, and indeed, within religion and society in Latin America more generally, concerning how to effect change. In its attempt to create change the Catholic Church has been stimulated to reconstitute itself, as have some other churches, thereby contributing further to the transformation of Latin American society.

Notes

1. Miguel Leon Portilla, ed., *The Broken Spears: The Aztec Account of the Conquest of Mexico* (Boston: Beacon Press, 1962), vii.

2. An *encomendero* was a colonist whose service to the Crown was rewarded by a grant of Native American labor. Lewis Hanke, *Selected Writings of Lewis Hanke on the History of Latin America* (Tempe: Center for Latin American Studies, Arizona State Univ. Press, 1979), 3.

3. Because of constraints of space, this essay will emphasize the Roman Catholic Church, with which approximately 80–90 percent of Latin Americans identify. Since the 1950s, fundamentalist groups such as the Assemblies of God, Church of the Open Door, Jehovah's Witnesses, Seventh Day Adventists, and Four Square

Gospel Church have grown substantially, as have African- and European-derived spiritist groups, particularly in Brazil and the Caribbean. Fundamentalist and spiritist communities often offer religious certainty and psychological release from societal pressures. It should also be noted that Catholic and mainline Protestant congregations, such as the Methodists, Presbyterians, and Baptists, which have dynamic leadership and are responsive to community needs, have also experienced growth. Accurate statistics on current denominational membership are difficult to establish, in large measure because they are often based on claims rather than actual censuses. In addition, there is considerable variation as to what constitutes a member, sometimes defined as anyone who may have participated in any activity of the church (for example, visited a clinic). Furthermore, recent research on fundamentalist growth suggests that there are substantial retention problems, with many "members" leaving within a year or two. See, for example, Timothy E. Evans, "Percentage of Non-Catholics in a Representative Sample of the Guatemalan Population," paper presented at the sixteenth International Congress of the Latin American Studies Association, Washington, D.C., April 4–6, 1991. More optimistic estimates of fundamentalist growth are contained in David Martin, *Tongues of Fire: The Explosion of Protestantism in Latin America*, foreword by Peter Berger (Cambridge: Blackwell, 1990); and David Stoll, *Is Latin America Turning Protestant? The Politics of Evangelical Growth* (Berkeley: Univ. of California Press, 1990). On spiritism, see Diane DeG. Brown, *Umbanda: Religion and Politics in Urban Brazil* (Ann Arbor: Univ. Microfilms International Research Press, 1986); David Hess, *Spirits and Scientists: Ideology, Spiritism and Brazilian Culture* (Univ. Park: Pennsylvania State Univ. Press, 1991); Jim Wafer, *The Taste of Blood: Spirit Possession in Brazilian Candomblé* (Philadelphia: Univ. of Pennsylvania Press, 1991); Peter H. Fry. "Reflexões sobre o crecimento da conversão à Umbanda," *Cadernos do ISER*, 1:29–40; Paula Montero and Renato Ortiz, "Contribuiçâo para um estudo quantitativo da religião Umbandista," *Ciência e Cultura* 28:4 (1976); 407–16; América Moro and Mercedes Ramírez, *La Macumba y otros cultos Afro-Brasileños en Montevideo* (Montevideo: Editora Oriental, 1981). The sources commonly used for general statistics on religion in Latin America are the *World Christian Encyclopedia*, as well as the *Anuario Pontificio* and *Statistical Abstract for Latin America*, published annually.

4. Margaret E. Crahan, "Civil-Ecclesiastical Relations in Hapsburg Peru," *Journal of Church and State* 20:1 (1978); 93–111; Margaret E. Crahan, "Church-State Conflict in Colonial Peru: Bourbon Regalism Under the Last of the Hapsburgs," *Catholic Historical Review* 62:2 (April 1976); 224–44; Nancy M. Farriss, *Crown and Clergy in Colonial Mexico, 1759–1821: The Crisis of Ecclesiastical Privilege* (London: Athlone Press, 1968).

5. A revised version of Gustavo Gutierrez's essay was published in Spanish in 1971 as *Teología de la liberación: Perspectivas* (Lima: CEP, 1971), and in English in 1973 as *A Theology of Liberation: History, Politics, and Salvation*, trans. and ed. Sister Caridad Inda and John Eagleson (Maryknoll, N.Y.: Orbis Books, 1973) .

6. William Bole, "Conclusions of 1987 U.S. Information Agency Study Contradicted Official Government Line on Liberation Theology," *Religious News Service*, June 25, 1990, 1. For an analysis of liberation theology and criticisms of it, see Arthur F. McGovern, *Liberation Theology and Its Critics: Toward an Assessment* (Maryknoll, N.Y.: Orbis Books, 1989). For reflections on CEBs by some

actual participants, see Sergio Torres and John Eagleson (eds.), *The Challenge of Basic Christian Communities* (Maryknoll, N.Y.: Orbis Books, 1982).

7. Congregation for the Doctrine of the Faith, "Instruction on Certain Aspects of the 'Theology of Liberation,'" *Origins* 14 (September 13, 1984); 194–204; Congregation for the Doctrine of the Faith, "Instruction on Christian Freedom and Liberation," *Origins* 15 (April 17, 1986); 115–28.

8. John Paul II, "Carta de Juan Pablo II a los obispos de Nicaragua, 29 de junio de 1982," *Informes CAV* 15–16 (Sept. 1982); 1–3; John Paul II, "Threats to the Church's Unity," *Origins* 12:40 (March 17, 1983); 633–36.

9. Ralph della Cava, "Vatican Policy, 1978–1990: An Updated Overview," *Social Research* (forthcoming 1992).

10. Paul E. Sigmund, *Liberation Theology at the Crossroads: Democracy or Revolution?* (New York: Oxford Univ. Press, 1990), 158–62.

11. Daniel H. Levine, "Church Elites in Venezuela and Colombia: Context, Background and Beliefs," *Latin American Research Review* 14:1 (1979); 74–75.

12. Gutierrez, *A Theology of Liberation*; Juan Luis Segundo, *Faith and Ideologies,* trans. John Drury (Maryknoll, N.Y.: Orbis Books, 1984); Leonardo Boff, *Church. Charisma and Power: Liberation Theology and the Institutional Church,* trans. John W. Diercksmeier (New York: Crossroad, 1985); José Míguez Bonino, *Doing Theology in a Revolutionary Situation* (Philadelphia: Fortress Press, 1975).

13. Gutierrez, *A Theology of Liberation,* 274.

14. Conferencia Episcopal de Nicaragua (CEN), *Presencia Cristiana en la revolución: Dos mensajes—Momento insurreccional, 2 de junio 1979; Iniciando la reconstrucción; 30 de julio 1979* (Managua: Cristianos en el Mundo, Comissión Justicia y Paz, Documento, 1979).

15. Margaret E. Crahan, "Cuba and Nicaragua: Religion and Revolution," in Thomas M. Gannon, S.J., (ed.), *World Catholicism in Transition* (New York: Macmillan, 1988); 265–82; Philip J. Williams, *The Catholic Church and Politics in Nicaragua and Costa Rica* (Pittsburgh: Univ. of Pittsburgh Press, 1989).

16. Elizabeth Quay Hutchinson, "Entre Cristianismo y revolución, no hay contradicción! Catholic Activism in the Insurrection of Estelí, Nicaragua" (thesis, Harvard and Radcliffe Colleges, March 1986).

17. Interview with an official of the Catholic Nunciatura, Managua, Nicaragua, Aug. 2, 1984.

18. Interviews with Foreign Ministry officials in Mexico and Panama, Jan. 1988.

19. Central American Historical Institute (CAHI), "Pentecostals in Nicaragua," *Update* 6:8 (March 10, 1987); 4–5.

20. Margaret E. Crahan, "Religion, Revolution and Counterrevolution: The Role of the Religious Right in Central America," in Douglas Chalmers, Maria do Carmo Campello de Souza, and Atilio Borón, (eds.), *The Right and Democracy in Latin America* (Westport, Conn.: Praeger, forthcoming 1992), pp. 163–182.

21. Maria Helena Moreira Alves, *Estado e oposicão no Brazil (1964–1984),* trans. Clovis Marques (Petrópolis: Editora Vozes, 1984); Scott Mainwaring, *The Catholic Church and Politics in Brazil, 1916–1985* (Stanford: Stanford Univ. Press, 1986).

22. Scott Mainwaring, "Grass-roots Catholic Groups and Politics in Brazil," in Scott Mainwaring and Alexander Wilde (eds.), *The Progressive Church in Latin America* (Notre Dame, Ind.: Univ. of Notre Dame Press, 1989), 151–92.

23. CERC, *Informe preliminar sobre primera encuestra nacional* (Santiago: CERC, 1988).

24. Martín de la Rosa, "Iglesia y sociedad en el México de hoy," in Martín de la Rosa and Charles A. Reilly (eds.), *Religión y política en México* (Mexico City: Siglo Veintiuno Editores, 1985), 282–84.

25. Brian H. Smith, *The Church and Politics in Chile: Challenges to Modern Catholicism* (Princeton: Princeton Univ. Press, 1982), 41–47, 341–45.

26. Katherine Ann Gilfeather, M.M., "Women Religious, the Poor and the Institutional Church in Chile," *Journal of Interamerican Studies and World Affairs* 21 (Feb. 1979), 143–44.

27. Mary Judith Ress, "Feminist Theologians Challenge Churches," in Alfred T. Hennelly, S.J. (ed.), *Liberation Theology: A Documentary History* (Maryknoll, N.Y.: Orbis Books, 1990), 387–88.

28. Elsa Tamez, "The Power of the Naked," in Elsa Tamez (ed.), *Through Her Eyes: Women's Theology from Latin America* (Maryknoll, N.Y.: Orbis Press, 1989), 4–5.

29. Ana María Bidegain, "Women and the Theology of Liberation, " in Tamez, *Through Her Eyes*, 28.

30. Ibid., 28–29.

31. Ximena Bunster and Elsa M. Chaney, *Sellers and Servants: Working Women in Lima, Peru* (New York: Praeger, 1985), 159.

32. John Burdick, "Gossip and Secrecy: Women's Articulation of Domestic Conflict in Three Religions in Urban Brazil," *Sociological Analysis* 50:2 (1990), 163.

33. Ibid., 167–68.

34. Nancy Farriss, *Maya Society Under Colonial Rule: The Collective Enterprise of Survival* (Princeton: Princeton Univ. Press, 1984); Jeffrey Gould, *To Lead as Equals: Rural Protest and Political Consciousness in Chinandega, Nicaragua, 1919–1979* (Chapel Hill: Univ. of North Carolina Press, 1990); Kay B. Warren, "Interpreting la Violencia in Guatemala: The Many Shapes of Kaqchivel Silence and Resistance, 1978–1985," in Kay B. Warren (ed.), *The Violence Within: Cultural and Political Analysis of National Conflicts* (Boulder: Westview Press, forthcoming).

35. Manzar Foroohar, *The Catholic Church and Social Change in Nicaragua* (Albany: State University of New York Press, 1989); Roger N. Lancaster, *Thanks to God and the Revolution: Popular Religion and Class Consciousness in the New Nicaragua* (New York: Columbia Univ. Press, 1988).

36. Cornelia Butler Flora and Rosario Bello, "The Impact of the Catholic Church on National Level Change in Latin America," *Journal of Church and State* 31 (Autumn 1989), 527–42.

37. Brazilian Episcopal Conference, "Christian Requirements of a Political Order, February 17, 1977," *LADOC "Keyhole" Series,* 16 (Washington, D.C.: United States Catholic Conference, n.d.), 57.

8

Remapping Culture

JEAN FRANCO

Until recently Latin American culture was identified predominantly with literary culture. To study literature was to evaluate "autonomous" works of verbal art. In this essay, I shall discuss the emergence of a new field of cultural studies and the changes in contemporary culture and thinking that help account for its emergence.

What formerly underpinned literary criticism as a discipline was the tradition of close readings practiced by Anglo-American New Criticism, Latin American stylistics, and French "explication de texte." But while these methods encouraged attentive reading, they ignored historical scholarship and the material conditions that accounted for the varying evaluation and canonization of texts at specific historical periods. They also ignored the aesthetic ideologies that underpinned literary innovations, and the different audiences, implied or real, to which works are addressed. Even more crucial given the present postmodern condition, traditional literary criticism was unable to deal with what Walter Benjamin has called "the work of art in the age of mechanical reproduction"—the transformation of works of art that occurs when the aura of uniqueness and originality is destroyed by transposition to other media, translation into other languages, recycling, and pastiche.

Cultural criticism, on the other hand, not only engages with texts formerly considered "nonliterary" but is, of necessity, interdisciplinary. For instance, in her book *Signs, Songs and Memory in the Andes*, Regina Harrison, whose "field" is literature, studies Quechua oral culture and particularly the problem of translation, using a methodology drawn from philology, anthropology, linguistics, literary criticism, and history, and based on field work as well as archival study. In referring to his book *Colonial Encounters: Europe and the Native Caribbean, 1492–1797*, Peter Hulme describes it as a study of "colonial discourse,"—that is, the production of a non-European world through "a discourse that imbricated sets of questions and assumptions, methods of procedure and analysis, and kinds of writing and imagery, normally separated out into the discrete areas of military strategy, political order, social reform, imaginative literature, personal memoir and so on."[1] Like many contemporary studies, Hulme's work spills over linguistic boundaries to focus on English and Hispanic texts of discovery and conquest.

Of course, this cross-disciplinary work is not confined to literary studies. Political science, anthropology, and history now draw on the resources of literary criticism. As early as the 1950s, Kenneth Burke had seen the potential for describing political events in terms of dramatic structure and tropes. But at that time, Burke was writing against the current for in the 1950s disciplines were establishing boundaries. Science, with its clearly defined object of study and goals, was the model for all academic research; indeed, with the advent of structuralism even literature succumbed to the prevailing scientific model. Underwritten by the science of linguistics, terms like *narratology* began to proliferate.

But this disciplinary consolidation came to seem crippling to scholars in both social sciences and the humanities. Thus, following Hayden White's pioneering *Metahistory*, many historians became interested in the way history had traditionally been narrated, and hence in textual criticism. Material once thought suspect—folktales, popular poetry, literary texts, religious beliefs and practices—enlarged the idea of the historical document and focused attention on areas formerly outside the realm of historical inquiry. Much the same can be said of anthropology. James Clifford's *The Predicament of Culture* drew attention, among other things, to the powerful connection between surrealism and ethnography in France. Anthropology has become self-reflexive, examining the very procedures and discourses on which it was founded.[2]

Indeed, disciplines are using common methodologies more and more. In Latin America, research teams now often include political scientists, anthropologists, and literary critics working on contemporary cultural and political phenomena. For instance, the study of the cultural consequences of privatization recently undertaken by Nestor García Canclini seems to call for the expertise of economists, political and social scientists, and art critics, not to mention scholars with a comparative perspective. In the Southern Cone, the focus on cultural studies began under the military governments and was pioneered by independent research organizations such as CENECA in Chile, CEBRAP in Brazil, CEDES in Argentina, and FLACSO. It was the FLACSO journal, *Cabeza de Goliat*, that took up the debate on postmodernism, and the journal of the Federación Latinoamericana de Asociaciones de Facultades de Comunicación Social, *Dia-logos de la comunicación*, that has consistently explored new forms of reception and subjectivity.[3] These tendencies clearly indicate that topics such as media politics, the globalization of culture, and modernization cannot be studied within a purely national framework, and call for increasing transnational and interdisciplinary collaboration.

In sum, we are witnessing not only the emergence of a new field, shared by the social sciences and humanities, but one that requires new forms of scholarship.[4] What we are now witnessing are the initial stages of a development that is not universally welcomed. In Latin America, many literature departments seem impervious to these changes, and in the United States, the changes have become a source of public controversy around the issue of multiculturalism.

This development owes much to postmodernism and the poststructuralist revolution. Poststructuralism liberated thinking from the old disciplinary boundaries and crippling dichotomies such as originality/imitation, modern/traditional, public/private, national/cosmopolitan, and so forth, and had a lasting effect not only on the study of culture but on the writing of literature. What is Roa Bastos's novel *Yo el Supremo (I the Supreme)* but a revisionary version of nineteenth-century Paraguayan history from a poststructuralist perspective? Indeed, all the names—from Roland Barthes to Foucault and Derrida—appear in the novel. Would it have been possible, asks Roa Bastos in this book, to have maintained national autonomy in the years following independence without sacrificing democratic participation? The novel's Dr. Francia is literally the dictator who wants to shape and control a destiny that will be lost in the labyrinths and slippages of language.

Roa Bastos's story brings into conflict the foundational discourses of post-Enlightenment Latin America, discourses of national autonomy and originality, and the attempt by Dr. Francia to preserve the nation's purity and boundaries, to control the language and even the opinion of posterity. What the novel creates is not the "character" of a dictator, but the Enlightenment's clashing and incompatible discourses and their transformation in Latin America. The form of the novel is quite different from the same author's earlier book, *Son of Man,* and registers with extraordinary virtuosity the deconstruction of historical discourse while indicating the limits of discourse itself.

Yo el Supremo is not an isolated example. Contemporary novels pose questions not dissimilar to those asked by critics and historians. What does it mean, asks Vargas Llosa in *La Guerra del fin del mundo (The War of the End of the World)*, when the modern state is founded on the violent suppression of heterogeneity? What are the consequences, asks García Márquez in *El Amor en los tiempos del cólera (Love in the Time of Cholera)*, of the gendered separation of public and private spheres? What kind of author, asks Clarice Lispector in *A hora da estrela (Hour of the Star)*, can possibly claim to know and represent the other? What does it do to the testimonial when the "witness" is not a militant or exemplary but a marginalized and paranoid bum, as in Diamela Eltit's *El Padre mío*? And what happens to old pieties, such as commitment to revolutionary change and responsibility toward the underprivileged, when some writers define that responsibility not in terms of leftist militancy as in the sixties but in terms of neoliberalism?

If poststructuralism's effect has been to undermine many of the truisms that used to inform any essay on Latin American culture—the continent's originality and the intellectuals' role as the "voice" of the silenced masses—it is also true that contemporary literature challenges more recent history, forcing us to rethink the literature of the "boom."

Revisionary Criticism

This remapping of culture features several different aspects. The most obvious is perhaps the disappearance, except in journalistic criticism, of evaluative judgments. Critics are no longer interested in separating "good" literature from "bad," nor are they concerned exclusively with traditional literary genres such as the novel, theater, or lyric poetry. The boundaries between popular and high culture have definitively been eroded. In addition, new kinds of texts, once devalued or ignored, begin to assume importance, especially those written by or intended for women, for instance, the sentimental novels of the twenties and thirties studied by Beatriz Sarlo in her book *El Imperio de los sentimientos*. The interest in nation formation has led critics to explore hitherto ignored novels and poetry by women and to examine feminine concepts of citizenship and nationhood. By going beyond canonical genres, critics have discovered in the colonial period an extraordinary range of religious writing and autobiography by women, which has allowed them to reevaluate the apparently isolated figures of Sor Juana Inés de la Cruz and Madre Castillo.[5]

The interest in this hitherto devalued writing goes far beyond the sociological, however. For instance, autobiographies and testimonies of nuns in the colonial period and Inquisition records not only provide us with a rare insight into everyday life but are sources for the study of a vernacular language far removed from the language of what the late Angel Rama termed "the lettered city." As is the case with black and Hispanic literatures in the United States, the study of minority culture, whether of different ethnic groups or of women, has opened up forgotten archives and yielded new sources of documentation that undermine what has formerly been represented as "tradition."[6]

Poststructuralism stands or falls on its ability to provide contestatory new readings of texts that will unsettle old boundaries and periodizations.[7] But the new scholarship inevitably implies new areas of inquiry; rather than the study of colonial literature, the study of colonial discourse; instead of studying national culture, an inquiry into how the nation has been narrated; instead of autonomous literary movements, exploring the confrontation with modernity and modernization that finds its representation in modernism, postmodernism and the avant-garde.

Colonial Discourse

Colonial discourse is the study of Europe's "othering" of the rest of the world; it focuses on texts as "systems of forces institutionalized by the reigning culture at some human cost to its various components."[8] As developed recently and in subtle fashion by Homi Bhabha, it also involves discussion of the colonial "subject"—the technology of mastery and subjection.[9] In any such formulation, the conquest and discovery of the Americas must have a privileged position. Indeed the modest proposal of Todorov's *La Conquête d'Amérique (The Conquest of America: The Question of the Other)* is that "the conquest of America prefigures and founds our present identity . . . . We are all direct descendants of Columbus."[10] In parallel fashion, Rolena Adorno describes her study of Guamán Poma de Ayala as an act of decolonization. Recent works by Beatriz Pastor, Martin Lienhard, and Serge Gruzinski adopt a similar critical attitude, one evident in much of the discussion around the quincentennial and arguments regarding whether the reference ought to be to a conquest, discovery, or encounter.[11]

The study of the discourse of discovery and conquest represents an acknowledgment that discourse is also a practice, that it is formed by and attempts to regulate social action. Clearly Europe's "discovery" of the New World and its peoples, the invention of discourse that would accommodate this new reality, and the repertoire of myth, legend, empire, and dissidence thus created, cannot be taken as one historical event among others, as Todorov rightly points out.

According to this revisionary scholarship, documents such as Columbus's and Cortés's letters, the chronicles of conquest, the account of Nuñez Cabeza de Vaca's captivity among the Indians, and the information gathered by Sahagún are not simply acts of communication or referential documents. They are also complex fields in which older medieval theocentric systems are gradually displaced, transformed, and annexed by new discourses. Further, colonial discourse clearly extends beyond the colonial period itself. Mary Pratt's book *The Imperial Eye* deals with the colonial discourse on Africa as well as Latin America and identifies a new "invisible" form of colonialism in the writings of eighteenth- and nineteenth-century scientists, botanists, and travelers.[12] In this second stage, the organization and cataloguing of American nature is considered an essential preliminary to the domination of commerce.

As a corollary to all this, attention has also shifted to the hitherto unexamined problem of translation. The discovery and conquest of America was above all powered by a process of translation, as Todorov shows; a new kind of social subject—the native informant, translator, and mediator—emerges on the boundaries of this discourse.[13] The question, then, of how new concepts were translated and coined has become central. For instance, Peter Hulme, noting the identification of Caribe and cannibal in a letter written by Columbus's physician, writes, "Obviously in 1493 the word 'caribe/canibal' had no independent or transparent meaning in Spanish. Dr. Chanca's letter is probably the first indication that the gloss 'who eat human flesh' would attach itself so persistently to the word that it would, in time, become its meaning in Spanish."[14] An entire chapter of Regina Harrison's book is devoted to the translation and history of the word *supay* in Quechua culture, for in missionary texts it became associated with the word *devil*, though for the indigenous it also has positive connotations of strength. Of her experiences with Peruvian Quechua, she wrote that her encounter "thrust me back into the moment of conquest, forcing me to question the nature of how things were said in Quechua, the meaning of specific words in specific situations, and in instances their transformation in the mouths of Iberian priests and newly titled landholders. I saw that, though the pronunciation remained intact, meaning was altered so that *viracocha* became synonymous with 'Spanish master' as well as retaining its ancient meaning of a supreme, perhaps invisible spiritual force."[15]

Thus translation also has its history, as students of pre-Columbian texts know only too well. Indeed, one of the problems inherent in the study of "colonial discourse" is that by concentrating on the victors researchers may ignore less accessible sources—especially the indigenous themselves. Regina Harrison attempts to correct this by conducting present-day field work that will help her understand the past as well as the present of indigenous societies. However, in his provocative discussion of native American texts, *Book of the Fourth World, Reading the Native Americas Through Their Literature,* Gordon Brotherston takes a yet more radical position, pointing out that Western scholarship has rendered indigenous writing so invisible that "in the Library of Congress system . . . the category native America or Fourth-World literature is simply absent." Moreover,

the concept of the Fourth-World text and literature in general has been especially fragmented as a result of having had imposed upon it imported notions of literary medium. For a start, jejune western pronouncements on what does and does not constitute script, and the categorical binary that separates "oral" from "written," have proved especially inept when applied to the wealth of literary media in native America, for instance, the scrolls of the Algonkin, the knotted strings *(quipus)* of the Inca, Navajo dry-paintings and the encyclopaedic pages of Mesoamerica's screenfold books. Whole modes of representation have as a result been simply ignored, along with the configuring of space and time whose reason is assumed in the placement and enumeration of every native detail.[16]

Literary History and Nation Formation

Older literary histories tended to consider literature primarily as national literature. However, in his book *Imagined Communities. Reflections on the Origins and Spread of Nationalism,* Benedict Anderson argued that the nation responded to the Enlightenment's need for a "secular transformation of fatality into continuity, contingency into meaning."[17] It is this imagined nation, its "ambiguity" (for Homi Bhabha) that has brought into question much literary history, in which national character or national originality (*Argentinidad, Mexicanidad,* and so forth) were taken for granted. The constitution of citizenship through a process of exclusion and discrimination, the honor role of exemplary founders and citizens, and the composition of utopian narratives and national iconography clearly suggest that nations are made and that literature and art have been complicitous in national formation. Thus the study of nation and narration focuses on literary forms, such as romance (Doris Sommer), or gauchesque poetry (Josefina Ludmer), that negotiate ethnic and class differences and bring them to a fictional but satisfactory conclusion.[18] The regional novel of the beginning of this century similarly reflects the problems of cultural definition, in which "nature," "land," and "woman" were fictionally brought under control and civilized.

Most Latin American countries still teach national literatures at high school and university levels, which has contributed not a little to the paucity of comparative studies. The national project too often meant the exclusion of minority and local literatures and indigenous cultures. Multiculturalism, now an issue in the United States, is beginning to surface in Latin America as indigenous groups and nonmetropolitan regions exert their autonomy from the center. In Mexico, for example, Chicano literature was ignored until recently, for quite clearly groups such as Chicanos, Hispanics living in the United States, Japanese in Brazil, or Jewish writers in many Latin American countries were simply not included within the concept of the nation. But little by little, nation is becoming simply one of several "imagined" communities and literature no longer seems inseparably bound to national identity.

Modernity, Modernism, and Postmodernism

The third focus of revisionary scholarship is modernity and modernization, and particularly what might be termed the "postmodern condition," or, to use Andrew Ross's term, "universal abandon." Like the nation, modernity is a concept that has powered Latin American literature from Spanish American and Brazilian modernism onward, although attitudes toward it have been ambiguous. Spanish American modernism inscribed Latin American literature into "universal culture" while rejecting the materialism of the age. As in nineteenth-century Europe, the aesthetic bridged the gap between the abstract and the particular, ideal and material life, public and private.

Much revisionist criticism starts from Perry Anderson's thesis that modernity is the individual's lived relation to modernization and that modernism is the aesthetic expression of modernity. Certainly the experience of urban life is reflected in Hispanic modernism, Brazilian modernismo, with its celebration of the modernity of São Paulo, Argentinean ultraismo and its claim that the world axis would soon pass through Buenos Aires, not to mention the twenties avant-garde, the novel of the "boom" and art movements such as constructivism. Yet as Beatriz Sarlo stresses, this is *"una modernidad periférica."* Her own study of modernity substantially departs from traditional criticism by focusing on the diverse cultural practices in Buenos Aires during the 1920s and showing the multiple and contradictory tendencies to which writers, journalists, and artists responded. Her focus is on the transformation of sensibility brought about by urban life as inflected by Buenos Aires's ex-centricity.[19]

One literary response to modernity had been nostalgia for the lost golden age. Beginning in the late forties and fifties, the new novel, while not altogether negating this nostalgia, provided a critical view of the unsophisticated form in which it had been expressed. The much touted "magical realism" of Alejo Carpentier, Miguel Angel Asturias, José María Arguedas, and Juan Rulfo was, as Vargas Llosa pointed out, a creative move away from the "primitive" and simplistic realism of earlier days. The writers of the "boom" generation would stress their technical sophistication, command of language, and narrative techniques. Not surprising, at least one critic would emphasize their desire for "mastery"; certainly, virtuosity of style made Latin America culturally visible to the rest of the world for the first time.[20] Although this can be regarded as an achievement of the "boom," the fact that writers now consciously address an international public has affected the very form of the novel itself, as I mention below.

The boom of Latin American literature is now history. *Magic realism,* the term coined by Alejo Carpentier in the 1940s, has become an advertising gimmick, a word synonymous with "exoticism." Reviewers routinely describe Latin American literature as "magical realism" whether it is or not. Joan Didion described violence in El Salvador as "magical realism," and Bloomingdale's fashion ad for Sybilla's clothes is headed ONE HUNDRED YEARS OF SOLITUDE: SYBILLIA'S ROOTS. Have we, in Octavio Paz's words, reached the end of the "modern era," and with it, the end of the idea of art and literature?[21]

Revisionist criticism is only just beginning to grasp the fact that the literary institution itself has been profoundly affected by mass culture and globalization. Indeed, in his book *Journeys Through the Labyrinth*, Gerald Martin suggests that the midseventies marks the closure of a period of literary history.

> Something was completed during the period 1967–75 which had com-
> menced half a century before with the Mexican Revolution. That some-
> thing was a literary cycle which began with the novels of the Mexican
> Revolution—turning "naturalism" into "realism," or perhaps "epic real-
> ism"—and ended with the Cuban Revolution and its historical aftermath.
> It is obvious enough that these two progressive historical events mark
> Latin America's concrete historical emergence into the modern world and
> the opening of consciousness, which did not produce the "New Novels"
> but certainly helped to make and shape the "boom" before as suddenly
> contributing to its curtailment. Thus Fuentes, Cortázar, García Márquez
> and Vargas Llosa were able to complete the exploration of the relation-
> ship between America and Europe, Indian and European, country and
> city, labor and capital . . . and thus comprehend the meaning of Amer-
> ica in world history and the direction of its trajectory of the past 50, 150,
> or 500 years.[22]

But is it really an end? Isn't it rather the unfamiliarity of the contemporary world that disconcerts both writers and critics, and perhaps accounts for the lure of the past?

If contemporary fiction is any guide, there certainly has been an extraordinary turn from the utopian predictions that characterized many
novels of the nineteenth and early twentieth centuries to a fixation on
rewriting historical events in terms of fiction. García Márquez's *El General en su laberinto (The General in His Labyrinth)* is only one example of
the vast corpus of new writing in Latin America dedicated to the revision of history. Roa Bastos's novel *Yo el Supremo* draws on the hundreds
of travel accounts and histories that describe the rule of Dr. Francia in
early nineteenth-century Paraguay; García Márquez's *El Amor en los
tiempos del cólera* painstakingly reconstructs the spirit of nineteenth-century
liberal reform, and, in a different mode, Eduardo Galeano's "poetic"
revision of historical documents in *Memoria del fuego (Memory of Fire)* is
intended to respond to the lies of official history. In *La Guerra del fin
del mundo (The War of the End of the World)*, Vargas Llosa addresses the
extension of state power in nineteenth-century Brazil in terms that speak
to the present. Fernando del Paso's *Noticias del imperio* rewrites the story
of Carlota and Maximilian. *La Campaña (The Campaign)*, by Carlos
Fuentes, views the whole Independence period through the adventures
of a hero in search of his ideal woman. These and many other "historical" novels, too numerous to cite, actually represent skepticism about
both history and the public sphere.

What is striking about these novels, with the exception of Roa Bastos's *Yo el Supremo*, is that although they are written in very different
styles, they are all nevertheless "readable" rather than experimental texts

and are clearly intended for an international public. They mark the transition from the boom writer's stated "responsibility" to a national public, to whom he stands in vanguard relationship, to the writer as superstar in a global culture. Such texts signal the end of avant-garde experiment.

The Reconversion of Culture

Both literary critics and novelists of the boom generation seem more comfortable revising the past than confronting contemporary culture, with its frenetic recycling and preference for performance—national rock, salsa, performance art—over traditional genres, such as poetry or novels. Nevertheless, the novel has increasingly emphasized private space over public responsibility. For instance, in his novel *El general en su laberinto,* García Márquez represents a public figure—and not any public figure, but Simón Bolívar—withdrawing from public life and undertaking his final journey to solitude and death. Regarded by many people as a "social" writer, García Márquez can now retrospectively be understood as a writer who represented public space in order to valorize the private space of literature.

But this attention to the personal and private takes on new significance in an era of privatization, especially given the poverty of the public sphere. For *private* is a multilayered word, used not only to designate individual as distinct from social life, but also private enterprise as distinct from the state.

The contemporary enthusiasm for privatization extends into culture in many ways. The most obvious effect is on cultural production itself and the change of patronage from state-subsidized art projects and publications (particularly in Mexico) to other forms of patronage, for instance, by television monopolies. Whereas in the past a novel's reputation depended on favorable criticism or word-of-mouth recommendations, nowadays it depends on aggressive marketing. *The General in His Labyrinth* was a best-seller even before it hit the bookstores—although in fact the Colombian publisher, La Oveja Negra, overestimated demand and the competition of pirate publishers and went into bankruptcy. Nevertheless, this kind of marketing represents a marked contrast to the old-style artisan publishing that predominated until the seventies.

Not only marketing but also the way in which García Márquez wrote his novel represented a new departure, for he employed a team of historians to check on its historical accuracy. The writing of the novel is no longer an individual effort but more like film production, which depends on teams of technicians. Finally, in contrast to García Márquez's earlier work, praised for its fantasy, this novel was said to have rescued Simón Bolívar from myth and made him real.

García Márquez is a special case—few writers have reached such a huge public. Nevertheless, his conversion into entrepreneur and the diversification of his writing, which now includes *telenovelas,* can be considered symptomatic of a new era. In this new era, the separation of history from fiction has been blurred; a Nobel Prize winner turns to popular literature aspiring to make the novel a form of mass communication addressed to a serialized public, yet at the same time, he emphasizes through his protagonists and plots the process of withdrawal into private life.

The postmodern era has transformed genres. Television has adapted melodrama, rock has taken over the lyric, theater barely survives in the era of cinema and video, modern classical music has no public, modern art has a public of investors, and corporations, such as Mexico's Televisa, increasingly support art galleries. In postmodern culture, copying, imitation, and outright piracy are no longer considered blameworthy. Indeed, these produce hybrids, a form now prized. Furthermore, the public has become stratified in new ways that depend on habits of consumption rather than social class.

It is in this environment that formerly "marginalized" peoples have "permission to speak." Whereas the narrative of national identity has tended to marginalize the indigenous, blacks, and women, contemporary pluralism seems to embrace everyone. Yet as even a cursory survey of contemporary writing by women reveals, this pluralism, while creating spaces for women, also reaffirms the power of the center. Nothing illustrates this better than the marketing of Frida Kahlo as an icon of suffering womanhood. The political implications of her work have been obscured by this emphasis on her personal life and on paintings that supposedly "speak" to women. Kahlo herself cannot be blamed, of course, for what gallery owners and promoters have done to her work (she is the first Latin American artist whose work has been sold for more than a million dollars).

Yet the success of the iconization of woman as victim obscures the more difficult task of creating a critical space for women. Marginalized by the often macho sentiments of the sixties' avant-garde, torn between the contradictory demands of middle-class feminism and popular movements, women intellectuals began to redefine their position in the light of international feminism in the midseventies, a redefinition that has been monitored in several important journals. *Fem* of Mexico counted among the initial collective group the poet Alaide Foppa de Solórzano, whose radio broadcasts on women's issues in the seventies were a pioneer endeavor. More recently, the Mexican journal *debate feminista* has focused both on theory and new forms of creativity. In Buenos Aires, the journal *feminaria* has similarly brought together the work of social scientists, theoreticians, culture critics, and producers. There is thus an increasingly important space for women's writing that combines criticism with creation and theory. In traditional genres—poetry, drama, and the novel—women have increasingly focused on the body and sexuality, which was often treated in stereotyped fashion by even the best male writers.

Women's writing is not at all homogenous, however, for it involves both a seizure of "public" themes, as in Elena Poniatowska's *La Noche de Tlatelolco (The Night of Tlatelolco)*, and the "reinhabiting of the private,"—that is, redefining the so-called private sphere in ways that upset older patriarchal family romances.[23] Yet it is interesting to note that women writers have also been innovative with respect to genres. For example, Elena Poniatowska's lyrical essay *Women of Juchitán*, which accompanies a collection of photographs by Graciela Iturbide, offers a utopian vision of subaltern women's power. Other innovative genres are the performances of Astrid Haddid, and Jesusa Rodríguez, who has satirized some of Mexico's major national myths—the Malinche, Coatlicue, and the president himself.

Middle-class women, of course, have a choice whether to write hermetic fiction that defies market appeal or to act as intermediaries to subaltern voices, as Elena Poniatowska did in her novel *Hasta no verte Jesus mío*. It is too easy to dismiss as "elitist" middle-class women writers who have chosen to write difficult or self-reflexive prose, since frequently (as in the case of Diamela Eltit and Cristina Peri-Rossi) they address questions of women's sexuality or the definition of aesthetic desire and pleasure, which generally have been represented in masculine terms. On the other hand, to consider their testimonials as major alternatives to the prevailing literary institution is problematic.

The best-known work of testimonial literature is *I . . . Rigoberta Menchú, An Indian Woman in Guatemala*, which was transcribed from tape-recorded notes by Elizabeth Burgos-Debray. What accounts for this testimonial's popularity is that an Indian woman was presented for the first time as an active agent rather than victim. Yet few other testimonials are as compelling, and very few are self-conscious about the process of editing and form. This is why testimonial is not so much the expression of the subaltern as an intermediary genre, an alliance between a middle-class recorder and a subaltern speaker.

What may displace the testimony is the increasing intervention of subaltern women and indigenous peoples in forging their own cultural identities. In Colombia, for example, the national indigenous organization CRIC has undertaken to provide texts for the teaching of writing and reading in indigenous languages. There has been a continent-wide movement of the indigenous to impose their own meanings and interpretations on the 1992 quincentenary. Also, an increasing number of indigenous intellectuals aim not to cede literature and interpretation to representatives of Western culture, but to use all available repertoires. In this context, the testimonial is likely to become one form among many for the expression of subaltern experience, which is more and more likely to reflect contemporary cultural heterogeneity.

In the past, heterogeneity and the hybrid were regarded as problems, as obstacles to national cohesion. Nowadays both writers and critics celebrate cultural hybridity. In Alejo Carpentier's novel *Concierto Barroco,* a black slave visiting Venice with his master disrupts the classical conventions of seventeenth-century Europe. Cultural hybridity is here embraced as desirable. It has become a distinguishing mark of Latin America, making the continent postmodern *avant la lettre.*[24]

The irony is that the belated celebration of cultural heterogeneity has come at a time when the media presents less cultural diversity than ever before and when even traditional cultures are globalized: Ecuadorean musicians play, for example, outside Columbia University and in Mozart's birthplace, Salzburg. Under these circumstances, it is possible that the traditional music they play will become standardized or be transformed into "salsa." Culture critics have increasingly focused on the inventiveness of popular culture, its ability to transform and appropriate styles, the dynamic and often "wild" forms of dissemination and reception.[25] Nonetheless, as the world becomes more hybrid, it is possible that Latin America is becoming less so.

Nowhere is heterogeneity more apparent than in the United States, which, with a Latino population much bigger than that of most Latin American countries, can no longer be left out of any account of hemispheric culture. Latino culture in the United States first attracted international attention as a subaltern style—that of the Californian *pocho* whose zoot suits so angered the Anglo-American servicemen in the 1940s. At first Latino culture developed around identity or political struggles, such as the Farm Workers movement of the fifties and sixties, which stimulated the Teatro Campesino of Luis Valdés. The novels of Tomás Rivera and Rodolfo Hinojosa, and the poetry of Alurista, Raulsalinas, José Montoya, and many others, as well as the Chicano muralist movement, were bound up with the emphasis on Chicano identity and community. In parallel fashion, Newyorricans such as Victor Hernández Cruz and Tato Laviera also embraced cultural hybridity, in defiance of island purity, while insisting on the specificity of barrio culture.[26] Both Chicanos and Newyorricans occupied a new social and cultural space that was neither purely Hispanic nor assimilationist. In the last decades another wave of immigrants—Cubans, Central Americans, Colombians, and even Brazilians—has in turn faced the identity questions formerly faced by Chicanos and Puerto Ricans. But now these immigrants have arrived into a culture that prizes hybridity rather than purity, an era in which alliances are being formed to combat "English only" teaching. Not surprisingly, this new Latino culture is less bound to nationalism.

The performance artist Leguizamo, who satirizes a Latino assimilated into the dominant "Japanese" culture, speaks to every Latino drilled in ways of imitating the dominant culture. The performance artist Guillermo Gómez Peña divides his audience into "English only" and those who speak Spanglish, Nahuatl, and other exotic languages.

In her book *Borderlands/La Frontera,* Gloria Anzaldúa emphasizes that the issue for Chicanas is no longer a question of assimilation or lost identity. Rather, Chicanas and other "minorities" have been forced to fashion original and plural personalities. No doubt this represents something new: the beginning of a Latino culture that refers to national origins without being imprisoned in nationality, a culture that can travel across national boundaries and adopt the tactics of Cuban *choteo,* Mexican *albur,* or Argentine irony to make a cultural space at once recognizably "latino" yet mobile and flexible. Latino artists and performers are now the vanguard voices in the American context, members of a global border culture no longer confined to the U.S./ Mexican border.[27]

Whereas poststructuralism has resulted in new readings of the past, what goes by the name of postmodern theory—for instance, the writings of Baudrillard and Jameson—has signally failed to provide a satisfactory theory of the global. In large part this is because, despite "global culture," our knowledge is not yet global; in any case, the global is inflected differently in every locality, and new cultural configurations are constantly being formed. Not surprisingly, Latin American critics have claimed that in any case Latin America was postmodern *avant la lettre,* since its culture has always been formed from a complex transaction between other cultures and regional specificities. The hybrid, copy, pastiche that have always been features of Latin American writing are now commonplaces of contemporary culture, which is engaged in a perpetual recycling of a new global repertoire.

At the same time, new and more threatening aspects of contemporary culture go unnoticed. Two examples that come to mind are the uneasy relationship between pluralism and censorship, and the role of culture in democratization. The two problems are indeed closely connected, since market forms of pluralism—the expression of different opinions, tolerance of different life-styles—censor out the unpopular, marginal, and merely unpleasant.

Culture both here and in Latin America confronts the problem of media and general publics intolerant of innovation and unconventional behavior. This is why a performance artist such as the Mexican Jesusa Rodríguez sees her greatest antagonist in Televisa, which lists words that cannot be uttered, situations that cannot be represented, and blacklists those who do not conform.[28] Of course we cannot equate this kind of self-censorship with the old-style repression of free speech in dictatorships. But neither should it be ignored. Contemporary emphasis on the accessible, popular, and global leaves little room for nuanced criticism, and, as I have already argued, it tends to restore the power of the center by reproducing stereotypes on an international scale. As nations lose some of their autonomy, nationalism is on the rise; now that all races are represented in culture, racial hatred comes to the fore. And all this is happening at a time when literature seems to have ceded its critical position or become marginalized.

Culture is still a powerful force that acts against facile globalization and the reassertion of hierarchy, though we cannot expect it will always assume the traditionally valorized forms of poetry and the novel. In the age of mechanical reproduction people increasingly turn to public performance, to forms of interaction outside the scope of the small screen. These cultural interactions, which range from the mime on the street to the public at a rock concert, from student storytellers on university campuses in Colombia to Mexico's satiric cabarets of the Teatro de la Capilla, are perhaps no more than random samples. Sadly, they are the minor spaces that remain open, even as the larger public sphere of political discussion shrinks. More positively, they suggest the potential of new political and cultural communities.

Notes

1. Peter Hulme, *Colonial Encounters: Europe and the Native Caribbean, 1492–1797* (London and New York: Methuen, 1986). On the problem of "translation" and cultural contact, see Regina Harrison, *Signs, Songs and Memory in the Andes. Translating Quechua Language and Culture* (Austin: Univ. of Texas Press, 1989), and Mary Louise Pratt, "Arts of the Contact Zone," *Profession* 91 (New York: Modern Languages Association of America, 1991). In this essay I will include the English title in the first citation of those works that have been translated into English.

2. James Clifford, *The Predicament of Culture. Twentieth-Century Ethnography, Literature, and Art* (Cambridge: Harvard Univ. Press, 1988). Hayden White's *Metahistory. The Historical Imagination in Nineteenth Century Europe* (Baltimore: Johns Hopkins Univ. Press, 1973), opened the way to the study of history as discourse. In geography, David Harvey, *The Condition of Postmodernity: An Enquiry into the Origins of Cultural Change* (Cambridge, Mass.: Blackwell, 1989), was symptomatic of the increased focus of geographers on culture, as well as on spaciality and urbanization.

3. Nestor García Canclini, *Culturas híbridas. Estrategias para entrar y salir de la modernidad* (Mexico City: Grijalbo, 1989). See also the work of José Joaquín Brunner, especially *Un Espejo trizado: Ensayos sobre cultura y políticas culturales* (Santiago: FLACSO, 1988).

4. The field of cultural studies was developed in Great Britain by Stuart Hall in the 1970s. See his essay "The Emergence of Cultural Studies and the Crisis of the Humanities," *October* 53 (Summer 1990). There is a program in Latin American cultural studies at King's College, London University. City College, New York, is also planning a Latin American cultural studies program.

5. For a cultural studies approach to literature by women, see Seminar on Feminism and Culture in Latin America (ed.), *Women, Culture and Politics in Latin America* (Berkeley: Univ. of California Press: 1988); Jean Franco, *Plotting Women. Gender and Representation in Mexico* (New York: Columbia Univ. Press, 1990); Beatriz Sarlo, *El Imperio de los sentimientos* (Buenos Aires: Catálogos, 1985); and Doris Sommer, *Foundational Fictions: The National Romances of Latin America* (Berkeley: Univ. of California Press, 1991). For the colonial period, see the anthology compiled by Electa Arenal and Stacey Schau, *Untold Sisters. Hispanic Nuns in Their Own Words* (Albuquerque: Univ. of New Mexico Press, 1989).

6. Besides its usefulness as a study of Sor Juana's life and times, see the third edition of Octavio Paz's book *Sor Juana Inés de la Cruz o las trampas de la fe* (Mexico City: Fondo de Cultura Económica, 1982) for a recently discovered letter by Sor Juana Inés de la Cruz. This book is translated into English by Margaret Sayers Peden as *Sor Juana or the Traps of Faith* (Cambridge: Harvard Univ. Press, 1988).

7. Roberto González Echevarría, *The Voice of the Masters. Writing and Authority in Modern Latin American Literature* (Austin: Univ. of Texas Press, 1985), was one of the earliest contributions to the deconstructive enterprise in Latin America. Deconstruction's main contribution is probably to have shown how much of the discourse on identity is bound up with the myths of origins. See, for instance, Carlos J. Alonso, *The Spanish American Regional Novel. Modernity and Autochthony* (New York: Cambridge Univ. Press, 1990). One of the problems faced by Latin American poststructuralist criticism, however, is how to claim Latin American difference without falling into claims of originality. In a recent book, *Myth and Archive. A Theory of Latin American Narrative* (New York: Cambridge Univ. Press, 1990), Roberto González Echevarría solves the problem by developing the Foucauldian idea of the archive as a repository of fictions and generator of difference between discourses.

8. Edward Said, *Orientalism* (London: Routledge and Kegan Paul, 1978).

9. For a discussion of colonial discourse, see Robert Young, *White Mythologies. Writing History and the West* (London and New York: Routledge, 1990). Colonial discourse was primarily developed in relation to French, British, and German constitutions of Eurocentric knowledge. The pioneer work is, of course, Said's *Orientalism*. Homi Bhabha's interesting theories are based on English colonialism. See, for instance, his essay "Sly Civility," *October* 34 (1985). The notion of colonialism that is disseminated in "postcolonial discourse" has been challenged by J. Jorge Klor de Alva, though this critique has not yet been published.

10. Tzvetan Todorov, *La Conquête de l'Amérique. La Question de l'autre* (Paris: Seuil, 1982), 14. This book has been translated into English as *The Conquest of America: The Question of the Other* (New York: Harper & Row, 1987).

11. See, for example, Beatriz Pastor, *Discursos narrativos de la conquista: Mitificación y emergencia* (Hanover N.H.: Ediciones del Norte, 1988), Rolena Adorno, *Guamán Poma: Writing and Resistance in Colonial Peru* (Austin: Univ. of Texas Press, 1986), and Martin Lienhard, *La voz y su huella. Escritura y conflicto étnico-social en América Latina* (Havana: Casa de las Americas, 1990).

12. To be published in early 1992 by Methuen.

13. Tzvetan Todorov, "Cortés et les signes," *La Conquête d'Amérique*, 104–29.

14. Hulme, *Colonial Encounters*, 69.

15. Harrison, *Signs, Songs, and Memory*, 3–4.

16. I read this preface in manuscript. See, however, Gordon Brotherston's *Image of the New World. The American Continent Portrayed in Native Texts* (London: Thames and Hudson, 1979).

17. Benedict Anderson, *Imagined Communities. Reflections on the Origin and Spread of Nationalism* (London: Verso, 1983), 19. See also Eric J. Hobsbawm, *Nations and Nationalism since 1780. Program, Myth and Reality* (New York: Cambridge Univ. Press, 1990).

18. Doris Sommer, "Irresistible Romance: The Foundational Fictions of Latin America," in Homi K. Bhabha (ed.), *Nation and Narration* (New York: Methuen,

1990), pp 71–98. Josefina Ludmer, in her book *El Género gauchesco. Un Tratado sobre la patria* (Buenos Aires: Sudamericana, 1988), studies "gauchesque" poetry in relation to the consolidation of the Argentine state.

19. Beatriz Sarlo, *Una Modernidad periférica. Buenos Aires 1920 y 1930* (Buenos Aires: Nueva Visión, 1988). See also Perry Anderson, "Modernity and Revolution," *New Left Review* 44 (March–April 1984), 96–113. Gerald Martin's book on the contemporary novel, *Journeys through the Labyrinth. Latin American Fiction in the Twentieth Century* (London and New York: Verso, 1989), is influenced by Anderson's view of modernity and modernism.

20. González Echevarría, *Voice of the Masters* .

21. Octavio Paz, *The Children of the Mire. Modern Poetry from Romanticism to the Avant-Garde* (Cambridge: Harvard Univ. Press, 1974).

22. Martin, *Journeys through the Labyrinth.*

23. For a fuller account, see Jean Franco, "Going Public. Reinhabiting the Private," in Juan Flores, Jean Franco, and George Yudice (eds.), *On Edge. The Crisis of Modern Latin American Culture* (Minneapolis: Univ. of Minnesota Press, forthcoming).

24. This is one of the arguments of José Joaquín Brunner in "¿Entonces existe o no la modernidad en América Latina?" *Punto de vista* 31 (1988), 1–5.

25. For a discussion of mass culture that departs from the usual outcry against manipulation, see Jesús Martín Barbero, *De los medios a las mediaciones. Comunicación, cultura y hegemonía* (Mexico City: Gustavo Gili, 1987).

26. See interview with Tomas Ybarra Fausto in Flores, Franco, and Yudice, *On Edge.* Also, see José David Saldívar, "The Dialectics of Our America," in Gustavo Pérez Firmat (ed.), *Do the Americas Have a Common Literature?* (Durham, N.C.: Duke Univ. Press, 1990).

27. Gloria Anzaldúa, *Borderlands/La Frontera* (San Francisco: Spinsters/Aunt Lute, 1987).

28. She states this is an interview to be published in *Tulane Drama Review.* An extract from Jesusa Rodríguez's work can be seen in the British Broadcasting Corporation film *Love and Power,* one of a series on Latin America.

PART III

American Identities in Formation

9

Transforming Memories and Histories: The Meanings of Ethnic Resurgence for Mayan Indians

KAY B. WARREN

This essay makes problematic a set of frequently evaded issues in social scientific research on the Americas: the changing significance of ethnic identities for "Indian" populations; the cultural politics of religious beliefs initially imposed during colonial missionizing; the interplay of national and local culture in patterns of assimilation and resistance; and the growing importance of ethnic nationalist movements in the transformation of civil society. This essay also examines what is purposefully obscured in much social research: the cultural processes through which observers produce their knowledge of other cultures. The goal of this very specific analysis of particular cultures, communities, and researchers is to challenge views of indigenous populations as either passive victims of colonial domination or distinctive cultures outside the flow of history. As an interpretive anthropologist and ethnographer, I take entry into issues of identity and change through a consideration of cultural memory and remembering.

Continuities and ruptures, histories and counterhistories, conquests

This essay was initially conceptualized for the 1991 Cultural Anthropology meetings and further refined as a result of stimulating seminars with members of the Americas Advisory Board. My thanks to Bobby Paul for the initial invitation, to Larry Rosen, Jim Boon, and Al Stepan for energizing questions; to Rosann Fitzpatrick, Agatha Andrews, and Jeff Himpele for insightful suggestions and discussions in our Latin American Studies Reading Group at Princeton; to June Nash, Luis Enrique Sam Colop, John Watanabe, Charles Hale, Rubén Rumbaut, Jean Franco, Helen Safa, Cornelia Butler Flora, Meg Crahan, Nancy Stepan, and Vanessa Schwartz for critical readings and discussions of the analysis. The ethnographic research for this analysis was supported by grants from the MacArthur Foundation and the Princeton Program in Latin American Studies and Humanities and Social Sciences Faculty Grant Fund.

and revitalizations are of central concern to Mayan Indians in Guatemala's climate of continuing personal and political flux. For contemporary rural communities and Indian ethnic nationalists alike, remembering a Mayan past—something in fact demeaned and dismissed by many Mayas only 15 years ago—is now seen as uniquely valuable and important. This analysis describes issues played out and debated in current Mayan expressions of memory and history. For Mayas living in rural communities and ethnic nationalists working at urban research centers, remembering involves specialized knowers of the past, volatile continuities and discontinuities, appearances that require unmasking, and growing concerns about who authors and who owns the past.

Before the Spanish conquest in the sixteenth century, indigenous Mayan populations lived in a Mesoamerica with its own complex history of empire building, interregional trade, warfare, cultural exchange, and conquest. Mayan culture sprang most probably from Olmec roots some 3,000 years ago, leaving traces of its southward expansion in glyphic accounts on stone monuments erected in what centuries later was to become southern Mexico and Guatemala. From A.D. 300 to 600, Mayan political and religious centers were established at such lowland sites as Tikal, Palenque, and Copan, which featured temple complexes, expansive plazas, intricately carved and painted calendrical histories, and striking sculptures. For reasons still not completely clear, but most likely involving the overcultivation of fragile lowland ecologies and escalating political demands for labor and tribute, these centers faded in importance after A.D. 900. Mayan culture then came to thrive in highland Guatemala and northern Yucatán, outside the early core. It was influenced by Toltec invasions from the Mexican north, which over time brought trade, culture change, and immigrant elites who were absorbed into Mayan society.

In the Guatemalan highlands, lineage-based communities, confederacies, and states emerged, along with continuing tensions among Mayan groups, as the rapidly expanding K'iche' state sent colonizing lineages to resettle among Kaqchikel, Tz'utujil, Mam, Ixil, Poqomam, and Pipil populations. Shortly before the Spanish conquest, the Kaqchikels, Tz'utujils, and other smaller groups broke away and established their own regional spheres of influence and states.[1] Not surprisingly, historic cleavages and conflicts among Mayan groups proved significant when the Spaniards, along with their indigenous allies from central Mexico, invaded the highlands in 1524. The Spaniards found the Kaqchikels eager to send forces to assist in conquering their rivals. Later, when the Kaqchikels openly rebelled against escalating Spanish demands for tribute and labor, the already conquered K'iche's and Tz'utujils were successfully mobilized to subdue them.[2]

The Spanish conquest was not a singular event that reduced heterogenous and stratified indigenous populations into a homogeneous subservient underclass. Rather, it is best seen as a complex and uneven process that created new political geographies that sometimes echoed older cultural divides, favored culture brokers from indigenous as well as European backgrounds, and sparked a long history of rebellions and other acts of cultural resistance.[3] Yet European colonization also brought waves of change that could not be absorbed as before: epidemics of European diseases against which indigenous populations were immunologically defenseless, the forced resettlement of rural populations subject to Catholic missionizing, and the fragmentation of indigenous states into localized communities providing compulsory labor and tribute for Spanish colonizers and their cultural descendants, who came to be called "Ladinos" in Guatemala.[4]

By 1821 Guatemala achieved political independence from Spain as a ladino-dominated society with a Westernized Latin American culture. The nation continued to depreciate and marginalize the vast majority of its population, composed of impoverished agriculturalists who had been renamed *indios* (Indians), *naturales* (natives), and *indígenas* (indigenes). Each rural community entered the twentieth century with its own sense of ethnic identity, expressed through localized religious brotherhoods and diviners; dialect of one of the 21 Mayan languages; and special relations with neighboring Ladino plantations.[5] As Guatemala became an exporter of coffee, bananas, and cotton. Mayan communities continued to be seen as sources of seasonal farm workers recruited through governmentally mandated systems of compulsory labor, conscripts for the military, and migrants to growing urban centers. Small numbers of Ladinos settled in many Indian communities, generally forming less than 15 percent of the local population, and worked as appointed governmental administrators, merchants, landowners, plantation managers, and teachers. Local ethnic divisions of labor reflected the national pattern: ladinos dominated nonmanual occupations, while Indians were channeled into heavy manual labor in agriculture, construction, and road building.

What impresses observers of contemporary Guatemala is the persistence of localized Mayan culture, along with the increasing assimilation of national, Ladinoized culture through schools, mass media, migration, and continuing involvements of local communities in national affairs. In a country of 9 million people, major ethnolinguistic groupings exist, including the Kaqchikel, K'iche', Mam, and Q'eqchi', each of which has between 260,000 and 658,000 speakers, as well as smaller groups, including the Poqomchi', Q'anjob'al, Tz'utujil, Chuj, each of which has between 50,000 and 100,000 speakers. Each language community contributes to the significance of Mayan culture in contemporary society.[6] In a country in which Mayas make up 44 percent of the population and more than half of the people still live in rural communities, cultural anthropologists are interested in tracing the meanings and implications of Mayan cultural persistence and transformation. The interrelation of political marginalization and poverty is a live issue in

Guatemala, which has the lowest "physical quality of life" index in Central America and the third lowest, after Haiti and Bolivia, in all Latin America.[7]

This essay begins in the Kaqchikel Mayan community of San Andrés Semetabaj, a community of 3,500 people in the highland Department of Sololá, where I did fieldwork as a cultural anthropologist in 1970–72 and 1989. The community illustrates the range of situations in which memory is an issue for Mayas experiencing the erosion of traditionalist authority; the success of proselytizing groups such as Catholic Action and the Evangelicals; the ascendancy of Mayas at the expense of Ladino elites in local politics; and the conflicting aims of national and international groups seeking to revitalize or destroy Mayan culture.[8] In communities such as San Andrés we can follow local responses to clashes between guerrillas and the military, between Catholics and Evangelicals, and between alternative economic development agencies—groups all fighting for the hearts and minds of impoverished rural populations. Mayas respond to these clashes with their own forms of cultural mediation and agendas for identity.

The analysis then turns to a national movement for the creation of pan-Mayan identity, cross-cutting local differences in language and community identification. As part of this movement, Mayan scholars and professionals have created the new academic discipline of Mayan studies, which promotes linguistic and anthropological research. In publications, lectures, workshops, and widely copied cassette tapes, these scholars are disseminating Mayancentric critiques of Ladino racism and foreign colonialism, drawing on other anthropological traditions with little concern for theoretical debates driving North American and European anthropology. As will become apparent, local and national ethnic projects, while distinctive, are becoming increasingly interconnected as Mayas circulate their cultural and political analyses through a variety of communication channels. Among their joint concerns are Mayan reappraisals of the Columbus quincentenary celebrations and imaginings of a unified, nationalist community.

Doing justice to Mayan rememberings raises issues about the contingent and constructed character of the analyst's memory. Like all social scientists, anthropologists make historically contingent choices, as they attempt, on the one hand, to survive fieldwork in politically difficult situations and, on the other, as they craft ethnographic descriptions that contribute to social theory and cross-cultural research. As this analysis will show, anthropological assumptions have sometimes misdirected research on the culture and politics of memory, but these disciplinary conventions are neither hegemonic nor static. My own selective memories of Mayan culture, products of my initial theoretical interests and fourteen months of fieldwork recorded in several thousand pages of field notes, undoubtedly influenced how I perceived change upon my return 17 years later. Perhaps even more important, innovations in in-

terpretive anthropology and Mayan scholarship now highlight alternative voices in traditionalist rituals I taped years ago (yet imply that others are less important), legitimize what were once unpopular questions
(while marginalizing other concerns), and raise additional political issues for the practice of North American anthropology (at the same
time as the murder of a Guatemalan anthropologist has discouraged
research on politics and violence).[9]

Greater self-awareness has been urged not only by recent experiments in self-reflexive anthropology, but also by Mayan anthropologists
and linguists in their critiques of North American researchers. All non-
Mayan anthropology is now labeled "foreign," whether or not the researcher supports indigenous rights and criticizes racism. Mayan observers argue that foreign field-workers politically reveal themselves in
gaps common between research rhetoric and practice,[10] a criticism that
has caused some anthropologists to re-evaluate their field methods and
ethics.[11] In pursuing these issues, the final section of this analysis con-
siders the interplay of Mayan and North American anthropologies,
specifically, the shifting constructions of legitimate research.

Mayan *Costumbre* as Memory

Both memory and its various embodiments—recalling, forgetting, de-
nying, repressing, erasing, revitalizing, replacing, veiling, rejecting, re-
enacting—are preoccupations in Mayan communities. Classical North
American studies of the Mayan worldview tended to essentialize and
conflate memory-continuity as "Mayan culture" and decry change as
"culture loss." Such ethnographic descriptions noted that what Mayas
called *costumbre*—re-enacted continuities in community religion and social organization—was central to traditionalist Mayan culture. "Why do
you do this?" asked the ethnographer. "Because of *costumbre*," was the
inevitable reply, which was taken as self-evident consensus and continuity within the Mayan community.

Costumbre was mandated by high-status elders *(principales)*, narrated
by ritual guides *(k'amol b'ey,* "takers of the path") at religious brotherhood ceremonies, and evoked by diviners *(aj q'ij)* at rituals for individual and community welfare. *Costumbre* was closely associated with activities and rituals of the civil-religious hierarchy, the dominant social
organization of many Mayan communities, which until the 1960s defined elders' moral authority, community membership, access to communal resources, and obligations to work in civil and religious affairs.[12]
In describing *costumbre* before its erosion, North American anthropologists often adopted a language of Durkheimian metaphors: continuity, cohesiveness, solidarity, consensus, integration. In this cultural system, ethnicity was condensed into each community, with its own
ancestors, lands, saints, religious brotherhoods, and Mayan dialect.

But two issues complicated this analysis of memory-continuity. In towns such as San Andrés, the elders spoke of religious brotherhoods *(cofradías)* as alternatively invented by the Mayan ancestors long before the conquest *and* the Spanish conquerors. Moreover, prayers offered at rituals spoke of *costumbre*'s tenuousness, as fragments only partially remembered, an echo of a different but not completely knowable past. In fact, ruptures, rather than a simple continuity of memory, were commemorated at key rituals during Holy Week and the celebration of the patron saint.

In the rush to document continuities—an ironic process since ethnographers and Mayas alike are well aware of the sixteenth-century Spanish conquest—most anthropologists overlooked anxieties expressed in the prayers of the exemplar of continuity, the civil-religious hierarchy's ritual guide. The *k'amol b'ey* narrated rituals with the following thoughts:

> Our fathers came, our mothers came,
> Our grandmothers, our grandfathers,
> In ancient times, with ancient expressions.
> They had good words,
> Good words were in their thoughts.
> They knelt before the Earth.
>
> Perhaps the word will continue,
> Perhaps the voice will continue.
> But now we cannot express ourselves well
> Before the Earth.

The *k'amol b'ey*'s prayers described rituals as an imperfect mimesis because ancestors had "better words, better expressions," which they used before Mayan authorities and God. "Ours is another generation," they concluded. These prayers named other ruptures: the alienation of youths from elders they were supposed to respect, and the community's lack of empathy for others in pain.

In effect, the *principales* and *k'amol b'ey* continually reinvented religious practices "first invented"—this is their metaphor—by the ancestors. A few of the most active elders were known as human archives of prayers, narratives, and explanatory details representing the past. Remembering was a specialized activity in a system in which religious participation in processions and rituals was of primary importance for most individuals. In San Andrés, specialized knowledge, and generosity in time and devotion to religious brotherhoods, translated into great personal respect and authority in religious matters, but few specific political powers. Financial incentives, particularly access to communal lands and harvests, were generally available to participants. Given the nature of Kaqchikel authority, knowledge, and religious practice, "we do this out of *costumbre*" could not be an idealized affirmation of continuities, consensus, common knowledge, integration, or even the coercive moral force of the closed corporate community.

Just as the past is not fully recoverable in Kaqchikel culture, so other individuals are not regarded as transparently familiar or knowable. Central to Kaqchikel cultural constructions of the person are beliefs that individual minds are different worlds, and that some individuals have the capacity to transform themselves, sometimes benignly but most often disruptively, into other beings. Because of built-in limitations to people's knowledge of others and the fact that other selves may not have stable existences, appearances are not necessarily what they seem to be.[13] "Each mind is a world" is used by San Andrés Mayas to explain that one cannot know with any great certainty another's actual motivations and internal thoughts.[14] In the civil-religious hierarchy, "each mind is a world" meant that people were assumed to have very different reasons for serving, all of which were acceptable as long as people participated. Some participants were personally devoted to a particular saint, others made pledges to a saint and were obligated to pay them back in service. Still others only cared about access to communal lands. Imputing motives was not important, only the outcome: what mattered was that different wills managed to converge to celebrate the commonality of place that defined their community.[15]

As the 1970s progressed in San Andrés, it became increasingly apparent that individual wills might not come together, that the Mayan hierarchy might falter in the face of several decades of aggressive evangelizing by Catholic and Protestant groups. In fact, after several years of frustrating difficulties, the civil-religious hierarchy collapsed in 1974. A politicized younger generation successfully challenged the legality of unpaid community service and the right of religious brotherhoods to hold communal lands for their own benefit. These actions fulfilled the *k'amol b'ey*'s worst fears: that the youth would refuse to follow traditionalist constructions of authority.

Moreover, local evangelizing groups, including Catholic Action and several Evangelical denominations, challenged the religious brotherhoods' hegemony by converting traditionalists, who were then barred from participating in activities associated with *costumbre*. The high cost of service and heavy time demands were often-cited reasons for abandoning *costumbre*, though there were myriad others. Ultimately, "each mind is a world" was used by traditionalists to explain individual defections, which led to Catholic Action's early gains. Later, "each mind is a world" was used by traditionalists and Catholic Action members to discuss conversions and the growth of Evangelical congregations.

Evangelical conversions introduced a new rationale for autobiographical remembering: the personal conversion story—told at services or in evangelizing conversations with others—relaying how an individual found Christ. In witnessing, individuals denigrate their past in order to demonstrate the magnitude of their personal transformation in the present, proudly recasting the significance of their former lives. At first hearing, these autobiographical commentaries might appear alien to traditionalist Kaqchikel religion, which called for diviners to interpret the past's relevance to the present and offered tales of moral unmasking, which individuals could personalize with allusions to current circumstances.[16]

In practice, however, religious cleavages described by analysts as mutually exclusive are not necessarily honored by Mayan traditionalists, Catholic Action catechists, or Evangelicals. Evangelical conversion stories, for instance, evoke traditionalist Kaqchikel constructions of the person. One early leader appropriated the traditionalist *la llorona* story, which tells of an adulterer enticed by a magical being that appeared as his lover and called him through the night. As the couple secretly embraced and the monster revealed its true nature, the husband shrieked his awful discovery. All that was needed was a consultation with a diviner to confirm the man's guilt before his knowing wife.

In borrowing this narrative and embedding it into an encompassing story of personal religious transformation, the new Evangelical found a novel way to escape his past: he used the story to allude to his life before conversion. In effect, his religious transformation heightened the value of his moral unmasking, a move thought to be particularly entertaining and clever by others, including those outside his church.

The *la llorona* narrative is one of many stories in traditionalist and new variants of Kaqchikel culture which represent the instability of the individual self. Themes of transformation and appearances, which cannot be trusted, saturate Kaqchikel stories of humans: the *rajav a'a'* is a family member who becomes a magical animal and harasses the town at night; the *rajav yab'il* takes the form of a stranger who brings disease and death from neighboring towns; the *sub'unel* neighbor is suspected in oblique accounts of being a deceiver and collaborator with political enemies. Such narratives are anchored in the past and told as histories with direct implications for the present. In emphasizing the stories' veracity and relevance, a Catholic religious leader explained, "My niece saw the woman as she was transforming herself; this happened."

The moral is that some unknown individuals have the capacity to become spiritual animals or animal-like enemies to deceive, bring sickness and death, or betray others. Other transformers, such as the convert, are not considered inherently dangerous because they are not secretive or deceptive.[17] In fact, the capacity of humans to transform themselves or have spiritual counterparts is basic to ancient, as well as contemporary, Mesoamerican "mythistories" and religions.[18]

That the connection between appearance and reality is never transparent for this Kaqchikel Mayan community was heightened by the political violence of 1978–85, when the Guatemalan countryside was overwhelmed with army sweeps, disappearances, threats of civil war, and the recruitment of government and guerrilla informers in rural com-

munities.[19] Knowing other minds and predispositions continues to involve anxieties and uncertainties, which are not only products of a difficult political present but also legacies of a traditionalist Mayan past.

Given these constructions and histories, it should not be surprising
that Mayan culture generates leaders who are intermediaries and specialized interpreters. As guides, diviners, or contemporary religious and
political leaders, these intermediaries take on the never completed work
of making sense of other minds and intentions. In the past, the *k'amol
b'ey* of the civil-religious hierarchy celebrated moments of connection
for diverse minds and focused the problem of disrespect for authority
on the younger generations' inner states. Diviners interpreted illness,
accidents, misfortunes, and family deaths as consequences of an individual's own moral failings, or the result of another's envy and anger.
In the narratives, diviners help unmask the transforming *rajav a'a', rajav kab'il*, and adulterers.

Contemporary leaders continue these practices, focusing their ener-
gies on people's capacities to transform themselves into political threats,
and the deceits this may involve. In fact, today's leaders are proud of
working well with people they feel cannot really be trusted. The problem of unstable selves—people who may not be what they appear—is
an ever present subtext to the town's political life. Unmasking draws
on the past to expose and interpret the present, thus keeping Kaqchikel constructions of the self alive in a world of competing religious and
political loyalties.

Catholic Action: Memory and the Revitalization of Identity

The Catholic Church fostered the development of Catholic Action groups
throughout Latin America in the 1950s to promote grassroots sacramental orthodoxy. Scholars have tended to judge this movement by the
depoliticizing intentions of its conservative founders.[20] It would be a
mistake, however, to see religion and other cultural forms as imposi-
tions by elites on passive populations. Rather, one must examine how
local communities appropriate and rework dominant ideologies. In
Guatemala, Catholic Action was introduced by conservative religious
and political leaders to promote religious devotion and counteract what
was anticipated by the Right to be the radicalization of impoverished
Mayas by "communists" involved in the revolutionary governments of
Arbenz and Arévalo from 1945 to 1954. This decentralized religious
movement—which may be seen as a precursor of, rather than a depoliticizing alternative to, liberation theology's social concerns[21]—trained
local catechists to run their own religious study groups, with continuing
supervision and sacraments from priests stationed elsewhere.

Over time, Mayan catechists turned to antiracism work in cooperatives and schools, and became active in other political groups. For their

this-worldly activism and because of the fear that they would contribute to rural populations' further politicization, many catechists (and other Mayan leaders) were persecuted during Guatemala's genocidal civil war between leftist guerrillas and the military. The war engulfed the highlands from 1978 to 1985 and left between 50,000 and 70,000 dead; 500,000 internally displaced; and 350,000 in exile as refugees in Mexico and the United States.[22] Mayan attempts to revitalize their culture and identity must be seen in the context of national political ambivalence toward wider Mayan political participation.

The young Mayan families who founded the San Andrés movement in the 1950s offered distinctive historical explanations for their actions. On the one hand, they stressed continuities with early Mayan Catholic communities at the time of Spanish missionizing hundreds of years before. In this light, Catholic Action was a revitalization of Catholicism as practiced by Mayas, a return to sacramental orthodoxy, which had been lost over time as the scarcity of priests forced communities to pursue their own forms of worship through religious brotherhoods. As a result, religion became closely identified with processions rather than masses and sacraments; images of the saints were taken as powerful divinities rather than as representations; and diviners perpetuated beliefs in God the Earth-World rather than the spiritual God the Father. Religious continuity was used by Catholic Action to encourage joint collaboration with the civil-religious hierarchy in support of Catholic orthodoxy's revival in the community.

When traditionalist Mayas and Ladinos in San Andrés violently rejected the new group and its nontraditionalist Mayan leadership, Catholic Action pulled apart and established its own congregation. Thereafter, the new congregation's goal was to destroy *costumbre* through direct competition rather than collaboration, to deprive the religious brotherhoods of willing participants by demanding that converts avoid processions, brotherhood ceremonies, and community festivals.

An alternative history was formulated to justify Catholic Action's new militancy, one that denounced the heterodoxy and "impurity" of the civil-religious hierarchy, whose celebrations involved drunkenness and sexual license at liminal dances during Holy Week and the feast of San Andrés. Religious brotherhoods were pictured as impoverishing individuals economically, by requiring heavy financial commitments to sponsor festivals, and morally, by "causing men and women to think impure thoughts" during drunken celebrations. This history, as well as years of work to create counter-celebrations for all major holy days, called for ruptures and discontinuities from the traditionalist past to create a moral future.

I returned to San Andrés in 1989 to find that the civil-religious hierarchy—an organization hundreds of years old in its preconquest and postconquest transformations[23]—had indeed died 15 years before. Statues of the saints were stored in private homes, the *k'amol b'ey* was no longer choreographing hierarchy meetings and reciting prayers before sacred meals at brotherhood shrines, and the *principales* no longer called on everyone to serve the community in the brotherhoods, community church, or municipal offices a year at a time. These changes represented the worst-case scenario predicted by the elders in the early seventies. What astounded me most, however, was the recent revival of brotherhood rituals: amazingly, Catholic Action was dramatizing them as *actos culturales*—as community theater—to audiences of hundreds of Mayas who were absolutely entranced by the productions. Moreover, a particularly dedicated leader and catechist, who in the past had done everything he could to undermine traditionalists' legitimacy, enthusiastically described some of his duties as the work of a *k'amol b'ey*.

Catholic Action in San Andrés and other Mayan communities now sees its role as revitalizing *costumbre*. What accounts for this turnabout, this sudden interest in cultural continuity? It became clear in interviews that the Catholic leadership sees these activities—which, for example, were an integral part of their new *salón social*'s two-day inauguration in 1989—as opportunities to rekindle memories for adults and teach young people about their ethnicity. The rituals are no longer sacred ceremonies. Rather, they are plays in which young people, always in male-female pairs, dressed in newly acquired traditionalist outfits instead of their everyday Western clothing, play the parts of the *k'amol b'ey*, the brotherhood head, his assistants, and their wives. As the catechists pointed out, the plays were not held in sacred space—never in the church's sanctuary—but in the new hall, which they anticipated would be the center of active youth programming.

Catholic Action has organized a selective remembering of brotherhood rituals, with the explicit goal of affirming what has now become problematic: the continuity of Mayan ethnicity. Although anthropologist Renato Rosaldo associates "imperialist nostalgia" with foreign missionaries, colonial administrators, and anthropologists,[24] in this instance the irony belongs as much to Mayan cultural *insiders*. For clearly, in challenging *costumbre* and promoting nontraditional education, the activities of Catholic Action's local members eroded the very commitments to ethnicity they now nostalgically re-enact. Nevertheless, the authenticity of *actos culturales* for Catholic Action rests in the immediacy of their connection to traditionalist rituals in San Andrés. Knowledgeable grandparents, along with a retired *k'amol b'ey*, have been consulted so rituals would be just right. As one leader put it, "We are doing our own ethnography for these rituals."

The 1989 *actos* feted young couples who marched in their own procession to the stage; re-enacted the *cofradía*'s preparations for the titular town feast; and celebrated the harvest ceremony, including crop storage and the hand-grinding of corn for tortillas, a process long ago replaced by machines. Notably missing were the high points of earlier practices: the hierarchy's fraternal meals, during which the *k'amol b'ey* offered commentaries; images of the saints as the focus of shrine activities and processions; drunken nights of music and liminal dancing at the close of major celebrations; and diviners. The selectivity of these plays is driven in part by the perceived compatibility of certain traditionalist activities with Catholic orthodoxy and the continuing unacceptability of other activities and icons. In a striking way, historical tensions between Catholic Action and religious brotherhoods are reflected in this remembrance and its accompanying forgetfulness, even as the plays are now explicitly about recapturing loyalties of the ever problematic youth.

The focus on youth is strategic, given two current fears: one, that youths who associate Mayan culture with agrarian poverty and marginalization will abandon their ethnicity altogether and use their educations to disappear into Ladino society. In response, leaders are looking to modernize *(modernizar)* Mayan culture to make it more attractive to young people. This means recognizing that young adults—especially those with educations and nonagricultural aspirations as teachers and office workers—need social recognition and a respected place in the community. They, not the elders, are the new narrators, the microphoned hosts and inventors of cultural activities. The second fear is that the Catholic Church will lose the next generation to the Evangelicals. *Actos culturales* are therefore designed with an eye to countering the Evangelicals' alleged lack of interest in maintaining Kaqchikel culture.

These concerns may well explain the focus on couples and the interest in reviving traditionalist marriage negotiation rituals, called *pedidas*. The *pedida*—involving *k'amol b'ey* intermediaries who acted as go-betweens representing the families of the groom and bride, where community endogamy was the valued norm—is a prolonged and stylized set of rituals expressing heightened respect for parental authority. Narrative tension, one of the most enjoyable parts of the ritual in people's personal and historical accounts, is introduced into the encounters as the bride's family feigns disinterest or asks for more time to deliberate.

The *pedida* was another focal point of Mayan traditionalism (although I did not understand its importance in the early 1970s because of my own internalized anthropological bias against research on devalued "private" family issues or women).[25] Traditionalist marriage negotiations were part of a discovery procedure, another variant of unmasking, to see if the girl's parents opposed the union. Initial refusals on the part of the girl's parents were expected; if serious impediments existed, it was said the family would throw chiles on their cooking fire or bring hot water to the door to signal an unacceptable match. Rituals called for gift giving and a marriage ceremony, after which the couple lived together.

The emphasis is now on the use of the *pedida* to promote continuity of religious congregations and Mayan ethnicity, ensuring that young people can marry within their church and town.[26] As memories of the past are filtered through the needs of the present, it is not surprising that Catholic Action elders now see themselves as *k'amol b'ey*, yielding to young adults the "modern" role of hosting public entertainment, but keeping for themselves the equally contemporary work of neotraditionalist marriage negotiation. The line between Catholic orthodoxy and brotherhood heterodoxy is remembered in novel ways.

Anthropology's essentialism for Mesoamerica—that real Mayan culture consists of continuities in remote highland areas, in contrast to corrupted culture elsewhere, which cannot be authentic after being muddied by bilingualism, foreign religious movements, and national politics—ignores the cultural processes described in this analysis of memory, history, and the production of local culture. James Clifford argues that ethnicity is cultural montage, taking different forms, intensities, salience, and substance as individuals reinvent themselves and respond to wider politics and economics.[27] This analysis of local culture has attempted to go a step further in tracing the recycling of ethnic memory by showing how Kaqchikel Maya constructions of memory influenced invention and reinvention; offered metaphors for change; interweaved discontinuity and continuity; and crystallized and dissolved differences between ideologies and groups. In the process, the Mayas of San Andrés see themselves as self-conscious observers of their own cultural system, as producers of knowledge—"we are doing our own ethnography"—for their own consumption and ends.

I now turn to the national movement for ethnic revitalization to consider ways in which educational elites are forging a unifying pan-Mayan culture, in part through the creation of a new academic field, Mayan studies. Again, I will show how memories and the politics of selectivity collide and reveal one another across important divides, in this case across the uncharted divide between Mayan and North American researchers.' This historic moment of ethnic intensification in both societies shapes the continuing dialogue.

A Dialogue on Identity between Anthropology and Mayan Studies

On returning to Guatemala, I was excited to hear about the growing numbers of Mayan teachers, linguists, and social scientists—combinations of professions and ethnicities that did not exist in the early 1970s—and was particularly interested in presenting some of my recent work to these audiences. Mayan studies had come into being, focusing on Mayan languages at the Proyecto Lingüístico Francisco Marroquín,[28] Academia de Lenguas Mayas, and Asociación de Escritores Mayances[29]; Mayan development priorities and critiques of Western development ideologies as neocolonialism, at the Coordinadora Cakchiquel de Desar-

rollo Integral (COCADI[30]); research archives at the Centro de Docu-
mentación Maya (CEDIM); survey research at the Centro de Investigaciónes Sociales Mayas (CISMA); and exchanges of research findings
through lecture series at the Seminario Permanente de Estudios Mayas[31]
and the annual Talleres Mayas conference[32].

While diverse in histories, agendas, and politics, these centers share
a common concern with fostering Mayan autonomy; revitalizing local
Mayan culture and languages; promoting pan-Mayan loyalties; and cri-
tiquing Guatemalan racism and U.S. neocolonialism, which have politically marginalized and impoverished indigenous populations. The resulting scholarship is a diverse, fluid paradigm-rejecting field of cultural
studies. The various research centers are attempting to unite Mayas
across language groups and localized ethnicities, and build a national
movement seeking wider cultural and political participation.

Believing it was extremely important for North American scholars
working on Guatemala to present their research to Mayan studies fo-
rums, I eagerly, if nervously, accepted invitations to lecture to Mayan
anthropologists and linguists on the topic "Indian Identity in Guatemala and Peru: A Critique of the Concept of Ladinoization." I decided
to focus on two issues: how contemporary North American research
has analyzed Mayan ethnicity and how my collaborative work on Quechua Indian communities in Peru raised interesting comparative issues
for Mayas in Guatemala.[33]

I was explicitly challenging anthropological analyses of change as *lad-
inización,* a linear model of cultural assimilation, which argues that economic mobility will inevitably lead Mayas to become the ethnic other;
that is, to pass as Ladinos outside their original communities. Mayan
scholars question this formulation—which they associate with the early
work of Richard N. Adams and other North Americans, as well as with
Guatemalan Ladino scholars who argue from a historical materialist
perspective—because there appears to be no place for Mayan culture
in these visions of the future.[34] Mayas see assimilationist images of change
as academic ethnocide. I hoped my critique of North American literature and presentation of an alternative nonlinear model of change, underscoring Mayan agency, would be a useful contribution.

I began the lecture with a critical reading of North American anthropology unavailable to most Mayas because it is published in English.
Here I considered my role as translator and critic of dominant trends
in North American anthropology.[35] Although the lecture focused on
Indian ethnicity in Mesoamerica, I structured the presentation to explore the general range of approaches available in studying ethnicity
and race. The talk also involved an ethnographic case study of tensions
between transregional ethnicities and the state's restrictive definition of
rural populations in national policy, drawn from my Peruvian field research. I argued a progressive constructionist position on ethnicity, and
illustrated individual and community activism in the face of domination

by discussing successful rural resistance to national reforms, which had endangered crucial rural-urban economic networks largely ignored by policymakers.[36]

Let me summarize my conceptual critique of North American scholarship on ethnicity and then discuss the strikingly different responses I received from two Mayan audiences of scholar-activists. My goal is to show how the past is problematic for both North American and Mayan anthropologies and to explore convergences as well as tensions in our projects.

The Four Fallacies of "Indianness"

The first common fallacy in North American formulations of ethnicity involves the assertion that "Indianness" is the product of a singular historical period. Variants of this argument locate different moments of ethnogenesis. One essentializing line of reasoning holds that Indianness is the cultural core predating the Spanish conquest which has been carried into the present in particular practices, such as divining and the authority of Mayan *principales*.[37] Another version finds that Indianness is largely the product of the sixteenth-century ethnic divisions of labor created when Spanish colonists set up land trusteeships (*encomiendas*) and other forms of forced labor, and communities were resettled into *reducciónes* for missionization and the organization of religious brotherhoods.[38] Still another version points to the creation of Indianness in the nineteenth century, when commercial expansion for the international market and liberal nationalist ideologies justified a new round of forced labor policies, the state's negation of collective Mayan land claims, and the shift from small-scale plantation agriculture to export-oriented commercial production. This period created a class of impoverished, landless, laboring Mayas, dependent on seasonal migration for economic survival.[39]

A second common fallacy argues that change in culturally plural systems inevitably means "culture loss."[40] The assumption is that cultural distinctiveness is culture, and that national society is somehow the opposite of "the cultural." This reasoning parallels the common Western view that Third World societies are distinctively cultural, while the West transcends these particularities through economic and scientific rationality. Unfortunately, the resulting distinction between "self" and "other" often obscures the mutual impact of societies on each other, as well as the contested and ideological aspects of dominant cultures, whether "national culture" in Guatemala or "Western culture" in and outside the Third World.

Another version of this fallacy holds that ethnicity means a hegemonic worldview or nothing.[41] In this case, an individual's choice is either to embrace or reject a given construction of ethnicity. This is the conclusion of much Mesoamerican research. The construction of polar, mutually exclusive choices—Indian or Ladino—ignores overwhelming evidence that individuals and communities continually rework identities, and that *costumbre*'s constructions have promoted diversity among Mayas.

A third common fallacy holds that ethnicity will wither away with the emergence of individualism and the transformation of agrarian class relations that accompany capitalist development. Modernization theorists phrase the argument in terms of growing freedom for individualistic entrepreneurship and democratic participation with the decline of collective and coercive traditionalism.[42] The withering of ethnicity is also a neo-Marxist prediction for those who see ethnicity as a barrier to the class-based politicization of newly proletarianized populations, or for those who view culture as derived or epiphenomenal to start with. The modern market economy, in its quest for consumers as well as wage laborers, is portrayed as inevitably undermining ethnic identities.[43] This is seen as a necessary if painful process, revealing underlying class conflicts and the necessity for structural change. Cultural distinctiveness is dismissed as an impediment, the product of colonial domination, which perpetuates a false consciousness of the systemic nature of oppression for agrarian underclasses.

Finally, a fourth common fallacy holds that the substance of an ethnic identity is uniformly derived from defensive, oppositional reactions to the dominant group's culture. This is a recent culturalist answer to economic determinism.[44] Unfortunately, in its extreme form this becomes another top-down formulation, in which the dominant Ladino culture is portrayed as creating the terms of reference to which Mayas can only react by defining themselves as the devalued opposite. Thus, Mayas value work in the fields, in contrast to those who despise manual labor. Mayas are pictured as isolated, in contrast to the ethnic other who seeks wider influence through personal contacts; they seek prestige through community service, in contrast to Ladinos who do so through material accumulation.

In this paradigm, Mayas react as prisoners of a grammar of ethnic dichotomies. The dominant group's ethnicity and ideology is portrayed as uncontested, unproblematic, and self-authored. The only way to change in this system is to conform by passing as a Ladino without challenging the structural hierarchy of the two groups.

The Constructionist View as an Alternative

After identifying and criticizing these approaches in the lecture, I made the case for an interactive view of identity as a collage of conflicting meanings, simultaneously advanced by different actors in social systems. In this formulation, ethnicity becomes the practice, representation, negotiation, resistance, and appropriation of identity for all parties.[45] Clearly, it would be inaccurate to see identity formation as an open choice of self-definition, a free market of personal identities, due to the very real structural economic, cultural, and political constraints on individual and collective actions. Inevitable tension between ethnicity's experience and representation for individuals, communities, national society, state authorities, and trans-state groups raises further questions about the politics of who defines ethnic cleavages.

Wherever they study, analysts need to make the terms of domination and subordination problematic by showing how power is exercised and subverted in different settings, while subordination is always more than passive submissiveness.[46] Moreover, nation-states and emerging regional associations need to become issues of anthropological study, not as monolithic abstractions but as systems of cultural production with their own conflicting ideologies and agendas.[47] In short, this approach advocates the study of cultural process—the "how" rather than merely the "why" of change—which has preoccupied modernization theorists and historical materialists.

The constructionist approach notes that the Guatemalan categories *indígena, natural,* or *maya* may be contrasted with *ladino.* But in practice both the significance of the contrast and the labels used to mark "self" and "other" are tremendously variable over events, lifetimes, and recent history. From this viewpoint, there is no Mayan or Ladino except as these identities are constructed, contested, negotiated, imposed, imputed, resisted, and redefined in action.[48] Other identities are always salient: in San Andrés there is a constant interplay of ethnicity, generation, religion, education, family history. The process is never-ending because identity never quite coalesces. Even the Mayan-Ladino contrast may be challenged by the diversification of contemporary Mayan identity arising from ethnic nationalism and the diaspora of political and economic refugees.

The constructionist view does not inevitably negate the importance of economic and political transformations, as historical materialists have complained, but argues that the process of determining their salience for local culture is not predetermined. It makes more sense to assume that a different periodicity may prevail for the history of Mayan communities, a different shape to ethnic time, rather than assume their historical experience is determined by national economic transformations accompanying the expansion of foreign investment and commercial agriculture for the world market. We can only know this, of course, by understanding Mayan constructions of time and history. This view also argues against any particular historical moment of ethnogenesis, stressing culture as continually reworked understandings of the world. In this sense, culture is not "lost" but transformed.

Thus, ethnicity is not assumed to give way to class or individualism in a linear narrative of progress toward a utopian future, as in liberal democratic or socialist visions. First of all, notions of "class" and "individual" have been culturally constructed in a variety of ways by Mayan communities. Moreover, the concept of ethnicity appears to be very much a product of the modern world; it is not just a temporary hold-over from the traditional past, as we are learning in Canada, Iran, Israel, Northern Ireland, South Africa, Southeast Asia, Sri Lanka, the Baltic States and elsewhere. If anything, it has become clear that nationalism and ethnicity are explosive political combinations, which, though their mix is incredibly various, often appear to influence each others' constructions. Studies of nationalism and ethnicity pose challenges to contemporary social science precisely because both are modern struggles with identity and otherness.[49]

Finally, this view argues against theories of meaning that focus on distilling a unified master worldview, identifying core symbols with definitive meanings, interpreting texts divorced from their use and contexts, or assuming meanings are always packaged in structuralist contrasts. As anthropologist Edward Bruner so forcefully observed for Native American identities, narratives of cultural struggle have the potential to carry many messages and their political significance can change dramatically as a counterpoint to the experiences and lessons of change.[50] It is in the creation and transformation of particular communities and groups that we understand the significance of narratives of ethnicity. Ethnicity, like race, is continually reinvented.[51]

Mayan Studies Replies

The lectures in which I presented this analysis were given at the Mayan Studies Permanent Seminar (Seminario Permanente de Estudios Mayas) and the North American sponsored Center for Mesoamerican Regional Investigations (CIRMA). Mayan responses were very different: at the CIRMA talk the Mayas were virtually silent, though just at the public event; participants at the Mayan Studies Seminar, in contrast, wanted to debate the politics of North American anthropology in general. The seminar was a university audience, conversant in the give-and-take of academic seminars. Their response was a complex counterpoint to my seminar presentation: while I described constructionist transformations of ethnicity, they wanted to talk about anthropology and colonialism. This led to lively discussions of the politics of anthropological analysis. Clearly Mayas were in control of this medium and its conventions, and were certainly in control of defining the visitor. They effectively subdued my constructionist approach with their own essentialist political critique of North Americans as neocolonial academics.

One of the most telling parts of the Mayan studies seminar was the closing remark by Professor Demetrio Cojtí of the Universidad de San Carlos who said the appropriate role for North American anthropologists should be one of helping to identify continuities in Mayan culture, the essential characteristics that make Mayas Mayan. This stood in stark contrast to what I had just concluded in my review of North American formulations of ethnicity and descriptions of Peruvian communities: that being Quechua in Peru or Mayan in Guatemala was whatever the populations were doing; that there was no essential Quechua or Mayan, no constant core, but rather a complex, ever changing self-authorship, sometimes reweaving the past, sometimes rejecting it.

I made my empirical case by analyzing Quechua Indian culture in Peru. Local populations there have recently extended ancient social networks linking families across ecological zones in the Andes to newer migration routes leading to coastal cities. Urban Peruvian life is associated with non-Indian nationals, with *mestizos*[52] who look to national society for their cultural identity. The conundrum for Andean populations is how to participate in national *and* rural societies.

In fact, urban migrants have used their social networks to maintain footholds in traditionalist communities where agriculture and animal husbandry predominate, along with Quechua religion and collective commitments to land and work. Depending on economic and family situations, participants in rural-urban networks position themselves to exchange resources: agricultural surpluses, access to higher education, housing, job opportunities, day care, and moral support.[53]

Have Quechua populations lost their ethnicity with migration and urban involvements? No. In this case, as my research with Susan Bourque has shown, it would be more accurate to argue that they have found a new idiom to express their sense of self: regionality. Now, instead of being *indios,* as Peruvian Indians are called, and rather than falling into the *mestizo* or a depreciated intermediary category, *cholo,*[54] these populations call themselves *"serranos"* (people of the sierra), in contrast to their coastal kin, or *"costeños"* (people of the coast).

This transformation is really part of a populist development strategy. Rather than being total strangers when they come to urban centers, migrants are now considered kin from the same locale and background as earlier migrants who are now settled urbanites. Young women and men have internalized these new understandings, while the grandparent generation is still ill at ease on the coast, overwhelmed by the alien environment and grateful when they can stand as rural outposts of their networks. In the capital, community heritage is often transformed into regional loyalty, linking still wider ranges of people who live in the same squatter settlements, belong to urban associations that nostalgically construct common *sierra* origins, and discuss the kinds of change to support in their home communities. How different is Guatemala, where similar paths of migration have compelled mutually exclusive ethnic choices, where children in urban centers can betray their parents by passing as Ladinos.

I was thrilled by the discussions at the seminar—no doubt by my apparent survival in the politicized forum—and energized by the intensity of the audience.

Though the second lecture was more polished and included more information on Mayan culture (from the 1970s when I first did research in Guatemala), the response to it was complicated by setting and format. The audience at the Center for Mesoamerican Studies was overwhelmingly foreign, full of visiting anthropologists, linguists, geographers, and language students. The Mayas were teacher-linguists in the Kaqchikel language school. I was worried when the Mayas remained quiet during the question-and-discussion period since I knew they would have their own reactions. After I finally turned to the Mayan scholars for their responses, one young linguist blurted with great intensity, "What are you doing here in Guatemala, what benefit does your research have for the Mayas of San Andrés?" Although I then discussed these issues in detail, I felt the Mayas had been inhibited and frustrated by the lecture format on someone else's turf. Furthermore, there were no Mayan professionals, such as Professor Cojtí, to empower younger students, who, in the case of these applied linguists, had little exposure to university lectures and seminars.

Later that night I talked to a friend among the Mayan linguists who said the lecture had indeed provoked much private discussion. Basically the Mayas were saying: "Even though her politics sound fine, how can we know who this anthropologist is? How can we know she is who she presents herself to be?" I was devastated, hurt, and angry, since I had gotten to know several of the teacher-linguists during the previous five months. I felt I had been plunged into another version of the transforming selves argument, that I had been captured in such a way that was hopeless to escape. How could I prove I was just myself, that there was nothing menacing to unmask?[55] Somehow this critique, though one Mayas would likely extend to one another in their own home communities, was much more difficult for me to shake than if I had been politely categorized as a North American academic colonizer.[56]

I talked to my applied linguist friend again the next day and asked if there was anything to do about the Mayan suspicions. I suggested we meet again, just the Mayan linguists and myself to discuss the lecture and any related issues. The small group meetings were very useful. I found that the applied linguists wanted basic definitions of "identity" and other anthropological concepts I had used. They also wanted to know more about doing research, how they might go about accomplishing community studies for their own concerns. Finally, they wanted to know about resources, specifically, how one might get small amounts of money to pay for travel, housing, tapes, and tape recorders to do more work in their communities. We also talked about research dissemination since it was the problem I also faced with my work in San Andrés. Could one set up tape libraries? How could people use these tapes? What anthropological training would be useful for researchers? What research projects would Mayas pursue?

Clearly, there are recognized class and ethnic differences in education, income, and rural-versus-urban residence between these two research groups. That the applied linguists were especially interested in taping oral narratives of an older generation—which is dying without passing on their knowledge of *costumbre*—reflects how rooted their identities are in specific places and communities. They realistically see Mayan university groups gaining greater support and recognition for research projects. For their part, university academics are seeking to build a more abstract and transcendent ethnicity, one not intimately tied to particular places and people.[57]

In different ways, however, both groups had similar messages. Foreign anthropologists, no matter how supportive of Mayan rights, have returned relatively little of their research to the communities studied. This is one facet of colonialism that Mayan ethnic nationalists criticize in North American academics. Why do foreign anthropologists study us? What do they do with their findings? What are their intentions? Are they who they present themselves to be? Or are they really Evangelical missionaries, detractors, or secret collaborators with other governments?[58]

Repatriating research is particularly important because the traditionalist archive, the specialized knower in the form of the *k'amol b'ey*, has disappeared in many communities, and *costumbre* is being revitalized by various groups with their own political agendas.[59] Yet here again, a revealing difference appears in the two groups' definition of "community" to which research and resources should be returned. For the applied linguists, the issue was a local and personal one; for the university scholars, community is not the old *municipio* but a new community ethnic nationalists are striving to build.

One irony that stood out after these lectures is that North American anthropology is exploring social constructionist perspectives on ethnicity at the very moment Mayas have rediscovered essentialism. Professor Cojtí wanted me to do what I could not: be a cultural archaeologist or ethnohistorian who finds continuities, whatever their current significance, and argues that they are the Mayan culture core. How odd, I thought, that one would trust a North American's judgment on these issues. On this point, the ethnic projects of U.S. anthropology and Mayan studies seemed impossible to reconcile.

On further reflection, however, I now believe I failed to understand fully Mayan motivations for their essentialist arguments. For Mayas—who are in actuality creating all sorts of novel ethnicities and levels of identity—essentialism is a powerful rejection of the Ladino definition of Mayas as the negative or weaker other. Thus, Mayan ethnic scholars are challenging my fourth fallacy, not with a constructionist solution, but with an essentialist alternative to seeing ethnicity as a self-denigrating reaction to domination.[60] Mayan languages, calendrics, priest-diviners, and community elders' authority antedate the Spanish conquest; they are examples of Mayan cultural genius that were not completely eroded with the passage of time or with Spanish, and later Ladino, domination.

Mayan scholars are arguing they must be revalued and revitalized before the past slips beyond the grasp of memory.

It would be a mistake, however, to see this essentialism as a definitive
or unitary resolution to the problem of characterizing Mayan ethnicity.
It certainly is not a resolution for ethnic nationalists who, as new intellectual elites, are also actively fighting discrimination in education, employment, politics, and social life. Other dimensions of Mayan identity
and roles for foreign anthropologists have been articulated at recent
conferences in the United States and Latin America.[61] Increasingly, Mayas
are calling on foreign anthropologists and historians to document Mayan
resistance to racism and domination. Like essentialism, resistance highlights a sense of identity independent of the dominant culture's definitions. In this instance, Mayas want to document a heroic rather than
complicit sense of their relation to the racism attempting to subdue
them.

Resistance is another way to deny that change represents a linear
erosion of distinctiveness through ladinoization. Mayan resistance challenges narratives on both right and left that speak of the definitive
"conquest" of indigenous populations in 1524, or the "reconquest" of
Mayan populations during the genocidal violence of 1978–85. On the
one hand—like descendants of other populations in the Americas who
were displaced, involuntarily brought over as slaves, or marginalized in
the colonial process—Mayas have challenged plans for the 1992 commemoration of the 500th anniversary of the "discovery" of the New
World. Mayas wonder what there is to celebrate: certainly not their
own conquest, population collapse through smallpox and influenza epidemics, and brutal exploitation as forced laborers for the colonial
economy.

On the other hand, Mayas urge attention to the human rights abuses
that accompanied the militarization of the Guatemalan countryside in
the late seventies, and forced displaced populations to face continual
persecution, flee the country, or resettle in military-controlled "development poles." But they do not want national violence portrayed as a
defeat of Mayan culture.[62] In their critiques of the language of conquest and reconquest, Mayas are arguing against disempowering narratives that obliterate Mayan culture and resistance to domination. Perhaps, they argue, there is a possible convergence of foreign and Mayan
cultural studies with the goal of documenting resistance as well as essentialism.

Final Thoughts: Dilemmas in Local and
National Ethnic Projects

Strategic essentialism, cultures of resistance, and ethnic nationalism are
the hallmarks of a politicized Mayan studies designed to articulate con-

cerns of cultural resurgence, criticize disempowering national narratives, and coordinate ethnic projects nationally and locally. It would be a mistake to see local and pan-Mayan ethnicities and cultural studies as developing independently of each other. Many Guatemalan organizations, some run by Mayan researchers and cultural critics, others by the Catholic Church, development groups, or tourism-oriented entrepreneurs, are interested in promoting Mayan ethnicity and cultural distinctiveness. Local populations have been exposed to a landslide of workshops, radio programs, religious tracts, and educational materials in Mayan languages. Educated youths eagerly tape and circulate recordings of lectures and other presentations by Mayan cultural critics and linguists, along with marimba favorites and rock music. The proliferation of *doble caseteras* (tape copiers) means everyone can copy and exchange tapes.

On a local level in San Andrés, the youth—many of whom have teaching certificates and some of whom are now pursuing university educations to join the community's first generation of Mayan professionals—echo ethnic nationalist critiques of North American anthropology as colonialism. "How will your research benefit our community?" they ask, even though they know the researcher's history of local support. Educated Mayas now criticize their community's school textbooks for racist bias, much like advocates for multiculturalism in the United States. The examples they discuss, however, are not so much from their own childrens' texts as from ethnic nationalist critiques. Individuals are also displacing some of their own cultural experience, particularly memories of rituals and calendrics, with knowledge gained from taped lectures. And young people are going to language institutes to learn the languages their fathers still speak. Experience-based memories are being replaced by ethnic nationalist explanations in building a wider ethnic revitalization.

The most difficult dilemma now is the successful invention of a pan-community Mayan identity, since virtually all Mayas identify with their home communities as their primary ethnic unit or more diffusely with their language groups. Wider identifications are crucial, ethnic nationalists argue, if Mayas are to avoid modern forms of the divide-and-conquer strategy historically used by dominant groups.

First in importance is the creation of research institutes and archives so Mayas rather than "foreigners" are in charge of memories. Mayas want to know what others have written about them, unmask foreign researchers' politics and identities, discuss among themselves the psychological scars of racism, and generate their own cultural knowledge. A daunting project is the writing of a Mayan history to counter official histories that justify Ladino domination. Mayan scholars see this as a critical project, and local populations, who have heard tapes or attended workshops, are now aware that existing histories teach children ethnic inferiority. Many histories effectively end their portrayals of Mayas

as historical agents at the Spanish conquest, describing the collaboration of some Mayan groups with the Spaniards and the defeat of the
Mayan leader Tecún Umán by Alvarado. Mayas are erased from the
historical creation of the modern nation-state. Given the current emphasis on preconquest calendrics, it will be interesting to watch how
Mayan periodicities give shape to time in the counterhistories to the
official national history.

Second is the problem of promoting Mayan languages to populations
who are rapidly switching to Spanish. For ethnic nationalists, this is a
clear example of cultural "loss," not a simple transformation. Mayan
linguists affiliated with the Academia de Lenguas Mayas initially had to
wrest the official alphabet for transcribing Mayan languages from
Evangelical groups, such as the Summer Institute of Linguistics, which
had been the major publisher in Mayan languages. In developing their
own alphabet, Mayan linguists want ways of representing sound systems that do not use Spanish as a frame of reference, as has been the
case since the colonial period.[63] In a country where only 50 percent of
the population is literate, the goal is to teach local populations how to
read and write in their own languages. Creating pan-community publications is difficult because in Guatemala there are 21 variously related
Mayan languages, with approximately a hundred dialects. The scholarly issue currently before linguists is how to portray this language diversity, which, by associating distinctive dialects with local settlements,
reinforces ethnic identification at the community level.[64] As Mayan nationalists attempt to constitute "community" on a translocal level, so
they imagine a future with greater linguistic unification. Mayan linguists now call for research that demonstrates the unity of Mayan languages, and cast doubt on the motives of foreign researchers who would
see substantial differences among dialects. In effect, dialect divergence
is being viewed as an index of cultural and ethnic cleavage, used to
subdivide and thus control Mayan populations.[65]

Finally, ethnic nationalists hope to revive Mayan calendrics and religious associations with the environment as culturalist commitments that
will transcend rather than reinforce religious differences.[66] Dilemmas
exist here as well, because Mayas have diverse, sometimes conflicting
religious loyalties. In San Andrés the ironies are clear: ethnic nationalists are promoting Mayan priest-diviners for major calendric events at
the same time that local groups such as Catholic Action are revitalizing
Mayan *costumbre* without diviners to minimize tensions with sacramental
orthodoxy.[67] The challenge is to create rituals, as in the past, that will
allow for a multiplicity of individual wills, as well as emerging styles of
ethnic leadership and interpretation. As in the re-enactments of traditionalist rituals as community theater in San Andrés, it will be important to watch how the selective process of re-presenting the past is used
to make the case for cultural resurgence, rather than extinction in the
present. As for other ethnic populations in the Americas, the issue for

Mayas in Guatemala is how to live in the modern world without re-
nouncing memory, identity, or wider claims on civil society.

Notes

1. John W. Fox, *Maya Postclassic State Formation: Segmentary Lineage Migration
in Advancing Frontiers* (Cambridge: Cambridge Univ. Press, 1987).

2. Robert M. Carmack, *Quichean Civilization: The Ethnohistoric, Ethnographic,
and Archaeological Sources* (Berkeley: Univ. of California Press, 1973); and
Christopher Lutz, *Historia sociodemográfica de Santiago de Guatemala 1541–1773*
(Guatemala: CIRMA, 1984). For Mayan accounts of the pre-Hispanic period
and the conquest, see Dennis Tedlock's translation, *Popol Vuh: The Definitive
Edition of the Mayan Book of the Dawn of Life and the Glories of Gods and Kings*
(New York: Simon and Schuster, 1985); and Adrián Recinos and Delia Goetz's
translation, *The Annals of the Cakchiquels* (Norman: Univ. of Oklahoma Press,
1953).

3. Nancy Farriss, *Maya Society under Colonial Rule: The Collective Enterprise of
Survival* (Princeton: Princeton Univ. Press, 1984); Grant Jones, *Maya Resistance
to Spanish Rule: Time and History on a Colonial Frontier* (Albuquerque: Univ. of
New Mexico Press, 1989); George W. Lovell, *Conquest and Survival in Colonial
Guatemala: A Historical Geography of the Cuchumatán Highlands, 1500–1821*
(Kingston: McGill-Queen's Univ. Press, 1985); Steve Stern, *Peru's Indian Peoples
and the Challenge of the Spanish Conquest: Huamanga to 1640* (Madison: Univ. of
Wisconsin Press, 1982); Steve Stern (ed.), *Resistance, Rebellion, and Consciousness
in the Andean Peasant World: 18th to 20th Centuries* (Madison: Univ. of Wisconsin
Press, 1987); and Karen Spalding, *Huarochirí: An Andean Society under Inca and
Spanish Rule* (Stanford: Stanford Univ. Press, 1984).

4. Christopher Lutz presents a historical analysis of the interplay of race,
culture, and class in the colonial capital, as well as a discussion of transformations in the significance of the term *Ladino* in *Historia sociodemográfica*, esp. 433–
34.

5. The community *(municipio)* for the Guatemalan highlands is best understood as a county, in some cases dominated by a county seat or, in others,
composed of dispersed population clusters that outshine the center in activism.

6. Guillermina Herrera, "Las lenguas indígenas de Guatemala: Situación actual y futuro," in Nora England and Stephen R. Elliot (eds.), *Lecturas sobre la
lingüística Maya* (Guatemala: CIRMA, 1990), 27–50.

7. James Painter, *Guatemala: False Hope, False Freedom* (London: Catholic Institute for International Relations (CIIR) and Latin America Bureau, 1987).

8. The loss of rural Ladino populations to urban centers was an unanticipated consequence of the national violence between the military and guerrilla
forces from 1978 to 1985. The terror and silence forced on Guatemalan populations during *la violencia* gave rise to narratives of anxiety and uncertainty,
veiled languages for expressing the existential dilemmas of violence, and subtle
forms of resistance. Issues of memory, especially representations of the explosive surrealism of violence as experienced in Mayan communities, are raised in
Kay B. Warren, "Interpreting *la Violencia* in Guatemala: The Many Shapes of
Kaqchikel Silence and Resistance, 1978–1985," in Kay B. Warren (ed.), *The*

Violence Within: Cultural and Political Opposition in Divided Nations (Boulder, Colo.: Westview Press, 1992).

9. Myrna Mack, a Guatemalan researcher associated with AVANCSO, was killed outside her office in September 1990 by the Guatemalan military.

10. Luis Enrique Sam Colop, "Foreign Scholars and Mayas: What are the Issues?," and Nora England, comp., "Questions for Foreign Linguists: Panel on the Role of Foreign Linguists in Maya Linguistics," from the Taller Maya, June 1989, Quetzaltenango, Guatemala, in *Guatemala Scholars Network News,* coordinated by Marilyn Moors (Washington: Guatemala Scholars Network, Feb. 1990).

11. See Nora England, "Doing Mayan Linguistics in Guatemala," *Language* (1992). Anthropology itself has a history of ethical concerns and a formal code of ethics for its field-workers.

12. There are many interpretations of the role of the civil-religious hierarchy, and particularly the *cofradías,* in Mayan communities. One can see the brotherhoods as a transformation of pre-Hispanic ideology in Robert Carmack, *The Quiché Mayas of Utatlán: The Evolution of a Highland Guatemala Kingdom* (Norman: Univ. of Oklahoma Press, 1981), as the social glue that holds Mayan communities together and mutes incipient class differences in Frank Cancian, *Economics and Prestige in a Mayan Community* (Stanford: Stanford Univ. Press, 1965), or as a colonial and neocolonial attempt to control Mayan populations in Waldemar Smith, *The Fiesta System and Economic Change* (New York: Columbia Univ. Press, 1977). Also see Kay B. Warren, *The Symbolism of Subordination: Indian Identity in a Guatemalan Town,* 2d ed. (Austin: Univ. of Texas Press, 1989), for a view of brotherhoods as a social form appropriated and subverted by local communities to create cultural and political space that nevertheless may have inadvertently supported Ladino domination.

13. Kay B. Warren, "Each Mind Is a World: Dilemmas of Feeling and Intention in a Kaqchikel Maya Community," in Lawrence Rosen (ed.), *Other Intentions: Culture and the Attribution of Inner States* (Cambridge: Cambridge Univ. Press, 1993).

14. This notion is expressed in the bilingual community as *jun jolomaj jun ruch'ulew* in Kaqchikel, *cada cabeza es un mundo* in Spanish, and *cada jolomaj jun mundo,* an interweaving of both languages.

15. See John Watanabe, *Maya Saints and Souls in a Changing World* (Austin: Univ. of Texas Press, 1992).

16. Catholic confession is seen as an individual accounting to the priest. Diviners interpret the nature of the problem in dialogue with the individual, their pulsing blood, and divining seeds and crystals; cf. Barbara Tedlock, *Time and the Highland Maya* (Albuquerque: Univ. of New Mexico Press, 1982).

17. Deception can also become an issue in situations where anthropologists hide intentions that are interpreted as religiously motivated.

18. See Ana Erice, "Reconsideración de las creencias mayas en torno al nahualismo," *Estudios de Cultura Maya* 16 (1985), 255–70; L. Marie Musgrave-Portilla, "The Nahualli or Transforming Wizard in Pre- and Post-conquest Mesoamerica," *Journal of Latin American Lore* 8:1 (1982), 3–62; Tedlock, *Popul Vuh.*

19. Rigoberta Menchú, with Elisabeth Burgos-Debray, *I . . . Rigoberta Menchú: An Indian Woman in Guatemala* (London: Verso, 1984); Victor Montejo, *Testimony: Death of a Guatemalan Village* (Willimantic, Conn.: Curbstone Press, 1987).

20. Daniel Levine, *Religion and Politics in Latin America: The Catholic Church in Venezuela and Colombia* (Princeton: Princeton Univ. Press, 1981).

21. Menchú, *I. . . Rigoberta Menchú*; Kay B. Warren, *The Symbolism of Subordination*; José Luis Chea Urruela, *Guatemala: La cruz fragmentada* (San José: DEI and FLACSO, 1988).

22. For details, see Beatriz Manz, *Refugees of a Hidden War: The Aftermath of Counterinsurgency in Guatemala* (Albany: SUNY Press, 1988); Robert Carmack (ed.), *Harvest of Violence: The Maya Indians and the Guatemalan Crisis* (Norman: Univ. of Oklahoma Press, 1988); and Michael McClintock, *The American Connection: State Terror and Popular Resistance in Guatemala* (London: Zed Press, 1985).

23. Flavio Rojas Lima, *La Cofradía: Reducto cultural indígena* (Guatemala: Seminario de Integración, 1988); Carmack, *The Quiché Mayas*.

24. Renato Rosaldo, *Culture and Truth* (New York: Basic Books, 1990).

25. I remember making this decision quite purposefully in 1970–72 as I cut off interviewees eager to discuss *pedidas* in favor of what I saw as more important public rituals and formal institutions. In the mid-1970s, feminist anthropology made the distortions of this selectivity increasingly clear to me by demonstrating the androcentric bias common to North American research. See Susan C. Bourque and Kay B. Warren, *Women of the Andes; Patriarchy and Social Change in Two Peruvian Towns* (Ann Arbor: Univ. of Michigan Press, 1981), and Kay B. Warren and Susan C. Bourque, "Women, Technology, and Development Ideologies: Analyzing Feminist Voices," in Micaela di Leonardo (ed.), *Gender at the Crossroads of Knowledge: Feminist Anthropology in the Postmodern Era* (Berkeley: Univ. of California Press, 1991), for conceptual critiques.

26. Another veiled concern may be the high rate of unwed mothers, something that is said not to have been a problem in the past as marriages were arranged as soon as young people showed any interest in the opposite sex.

27. See James Clifford, *The Predicament of Culture: Twentieth-Century Ethnography, Literature, and Art* (Cambridge: Harvard Univ. Press, 1988).

28. See Margarita López Raquec, *Acerca de los alfabetos para escribir los idiomas Mayas de Guatemala* (Guatemala: Ministerio de Cultura y Deportes, 1989).

29. Demetrio Cojtí Cuxil, *Configuración del pensamiento político del pueblo Maya* (Quetzaltenango: Asociación de Escritores Mayances de Guatemala, 1991); and María Luisa Curruchich and Rafael Coyote Tum, *Nimawa'in* (Quetzaltenango: Asociación de Escritores Mayances de Guatemala, 1990).

30. *El Idioma, centro de nuestra cultura* (Guatemala: COCADI Departamento de Investigaciónes Culturales, 1985); *Maya Kaqchikel Ajlab'al: Sistema de Numeración Maya Kaqchikel* (Guatemala: COCADI Departamento de Investigaciónes Culturales, 1988); and *Cultura Maya y Políticas de Desarrollo* (Guatemala: COCADI Departamento de Investigaciónes Culturales, 1989).

31. Luis Enrique Sam Colop, "Jub'aqtun Omay Kuchum K'aslemal: Cinco Siglos de Encubrimiento," *Seminario Permanente de Estudios Mayas Cuaderno:* no 1 (Guatemala: Editorial Cholsamaj, 1991).

32. Nora C. England and Stephen R. Elliot, comps., *Lecturas sobre la lingüística Maya* (Guatemala: CIRMA, 1990).

33. Susan C. Bourque and Kay B. Warren, "Denial and Reaffirmation of Ethnic Identities: A Comparative Examination of Guatemalan and Peruvian Communities," Program in Latin American Studies, Occasional Papers no. 8 (Amherst: Univ. of Massachusetts, 1978), and *Women of the Andes*.

34. Much like Mario Vargas Llosa's portrayal of change for Peru, "Inquest

in the Andes," *New York Times Magazine,* July 31, 1983, 18, and "Questions of Conquest: What Columbus Wrought, and What He Did Not," *Harper's Magazine,* Dec. 1990.

35. The following is, obviously, a very distilled presentation of the lecture, reprinted as "Identidad indígena en Guatemala: Una Crítica de modelos norteamericanos," *Mesoamerica* (Guatemala: CIRMA, forthcoming). The point of my analysis was to identify alternative, abstract ways in which identity has been modeled in Mesoamerican studies by North Americans. Clearly each of the works I cite deserves a less reductive reading in its own right as well as the historical contextualization of its contribution.

36. No doubt my choice of presenting a Peruvian case study was tactical in several ways. First, I did not want to talk about the current situation in Guatemala since I was still in the middle of my fieldwork. Second, I felt that another culture would allow issues to surface without politically charging the discussion.

37. Elements of this view are reflected in the important studies of Mayan traditionalism by Barbara Tedlock, *Time and the Highland Maya*; Robert Carmack, *The Quiché Maya*; and Robert M. Hill and John Monaghan, *Continuities in Highland Maya Social Organization: Ethnohistory in Sacapulas, Guatemala* (Philadelphia: Univ. of Pennsylvania Press, 1987). A similar range of models can be found in studies of ethnically and racially stratified systems such as that of the United States.

38. See William L. Sherman, *Forced Native Labor in Sixteenth-Century Central America* (Lincoln: Univ. of Nebraska Press, 1979).

39. For examples of this very influential view in Mesoamerican scholarship, see Marvin Harris, *Patterns of Race in the Americas* (New York: Norton, 1964); Manning Nash, "The Impact of Mid-nineteenth Century Economic Change upon the Indians of Middle America," in Magnus Morner (ed.), *Race and Class in Latin America* (New York: Columbia Univ. Press, 1970), 170–83; Rodolfo Stavenhagen, "Classes, Colonialism and Acculturation," in Irving Louis Horowitz (ed.), *Masses in Latin America* (New York: Oxford Univ. Press, 1970), 235–88; Robert Wasserstrom, *Class and Society in Central Chiapas* (Berkeley: Univ. of California Press, 1983); and Jim Handy, *Gift of the Devil: A History of Guatemala* (Boston: South End Press, 1984).

40. Judith Friedlander, *Being Indian in Hueyapán: A Study of Forced Identity in Contemporary Mexico* (New York: St. Martin's Press, 1975), and Carmack, *The Quiché Maya,* are examples from very different theoretical orientations.

41. For an elegant example of the Mayan worldview as hegemonic, see Gary Gossen, *Chamulas in the World of the Sun: Time and Space in Mayan Oral Tradition* (Prospect Heights, Ill.: Waveland Press, 1984). For a subtle analysis of Indian subethnicities from this common view, see Douglas E. Brintnall, *Revolt Against the Dead: The Modernization of a Maya Community in the Highlands of Guatemala* (New York: Gordon and Breach, 1979).

42. Joel S. Migdal, *Peasants, Politics, and Revolution* (Princeton: Princeton Univ. Press, 1974), represents the comparative argument; Frank Cancian, complicates the model in *Change and Uncertainty in a Peasant Economy* (Stanford: Stanford Univ. Press, 1972) and *Economics and Prestige in a Mayas Community* (Stanford: Stanford Univ. Press, 1965).

43. Given the dominance in the 1960s and 1970s of historical materialism and dependency theory in social scientific research done by Latin Americans and North Americans on Central America, this has been a very influential view.

For example, see Rodolfo Stavenhagen's classical formulation, "Classes, Colonialism and Acculturation" and Susanne Jonas and David Tobis (eds.), *Guatemala* (Berkeley, Calif.: North American Congress on Latin America, 1974).

44. See John Hawkins, *Inverse Images: The Meaning of Culture, Ethnicity and Family in Postcolonial Guatemala* (Albuquerque: Univ. of New Mexico Press, 1984), for a fully elaborated example of this perspective.

45. In the lecture, I did not pursue the issue of multiple identities given the tensions around different religious affiliations and the dismissal of gender as a major issue by many, but certainly not all, Mayan scholars. My very presence may have raised some of these issues. "Why," asked my Ladina language coach, "would university scholars listen to a woman lecture? It's only that you are a North American that anyone would bother." It never occurred to her that the university audience would be Mayan.

46. See Richard N. Adams, "Ethnic Images and Strategies in 1944," in Carol A. Smith (ed.), *Guatemalan Indians and the State: 1540 to 1988* (Austin: Univ. of Texas Press, 1990), 141–62.

47. Richard N. Adams, *Crucifixion by Power: Essays on Guatemalan National Social Structure, 1944–1966* (Austin: Univ. of Texas Press, 1970); Merilee S. Grindle, *State and Countryside: Development Policy and Agrarian Politics in Latin America* (Baltimore: Johns Hopkins Univ. Press 1986).

48. See Carol Hendrickson, "Images of the Indian in Guatemala: The Role of Indigenous Dress in Indian and Ladino Constructions," in Greg Urban and Joel Sherzer (eds.), *Nation-States and Indians in Latin America* (Austin: Univ. of Texas Press, 1991), 287–306.

49. Clifford Geertz, *The Interpretation of Cultures* (New York: Basic Books, 1973); Remo Guidieri, Francesco Pellizzi, and Stanley J. Tambiah (eds.), *Ethnicities and Nations: Processes of Interethnic Relations in Latin America, Southeast Asia, and the Pacific* (Austin: Rothko Chapel/Univ. of Texas Press, 1988); Benedict Anderson, *Imagined Communities: Reflections on the Origin and Spread of Nationalism*, 2d ed. (London: Verso, 1991); Warren (ed.), *The Violence Within*.

50. Edward M. Bruner, "Ethnography as Narrative," in Victor Turner and Edward M. Bruner (eds.), *The Anthropology of Experience* (Urbana: Univ. of Illinois Press, 1986), 139–55.

51. Both race and ethnicity are constructions, and current scholarship is interrogating the accepted distinctions between these phenomena. Even *putative physical difference* as the central organizing principle for race is differentially constructed and contested across cultures, as Caribbean migrants learn when they come to the United States.

52. *Mestizo* is often taken literally as a metaphor for a mixture of Spanish and Indian blood. But in practice the term more accurately refers to participants in the mainstream of Latin American society with its distinctive New World culture.

53. More recently migration has surged with the clashes between the Shining Path guerrilla movement (Sendero Luminoso) and the Peruvian military; See Susan C. Bourque and Kay B. Warren, "Democracy Without Peace: The Cultural Politics of Terror in Peru," *Latin American Research Review* 24:1 (1988), 7–34.

54. See Pierre L. van den Berghe and George P. Primov, *Inequality in the Peruvian Andes: Class and Ethnicity in Cuzco* (Columbia: Univ. of Missouri Press, 1977).

55. On reflection, there are interesting ironies here. My reaction is shaped by a belief in an essential "self," a real and constant Kay Warren, whom others should find accessible. Here I am a native informant (so my innocence is part of the message), not the anthropologist (who would pursue the transformation of Kay Warren from one situation to another in her daily life). For me, constructionist fluidities are located in the realms of ethnicity and gender. By contrast, Mayan constructions involve an interesting mix of essentialist and constructionist attributions for the self and an essentialized core for ethnicity.

56. On reflection, the theoretical and comparative language of my talk (as well as my own preferred teaching style) may have contributed to their fears. I wanted to avoid politically charged issues and also to allow Mayas to respond in an open-ended way to the talk. So purposefully there was no closure, no definitive comparison of Peru and Guatemala. In this sense I was evasive, calling for an interactive dialogue. Their public silence and private concerns can be seen as responses to the talk as a veiled language requiring further interpretation and avoidance of comments that would reveal personal politics (cf. Warren, "Interpreting *la Violencia*" in *The Violence Within* and "Each Mind Is a World" in *Other Intentions*). If talking about Quechua resistance to Peruvian reforms were by chance a veiled commentary on the Guatemala situation, then the audience would have had to worry about who was listening, especially at CIRMA, where there were many strangers. We shared reservations about talking about anything politicized; by convention no one mentioned the violence that had dominated recent Guatemalan politics.

57. My thanks to John Watanabe for this insight, which flows from his analysis of place, soul, and ethnicity in a Mam community, *Maya Saints*.

58. Note that their concerns did not take the variant of skepticism that dismisses anthropology as the study of the anthropologist's own reflection in another culture. Hidden forms of control, not narcissism, was the worry.

59. Evangelicals, for instance, publish in Mayan languages with the singular goal of promoting conversions; the Catholic Church promotes cultural revitalization to slow the erosion of their official religious monopoly. The tourism industry and North American and European development groups have other stakes.

60. My thanks to Rosann Fitzpatrick for the initial insight. See Gayatri Chakravorty Spivak's discussion in *In Other Worlds: Essays in Cultural Politics* (New York: Routledge, 1988), 197–221.

61. Including, among others, notable panels at the 1990 and 1991 American Anthropological Association Meetings, the 1990 Mesoamerica Conference at SUNY-Albany, the 1991 Latin American Studies Association Meetings, and the 1991 *Segundo Encuentro Continental* in Guatemala.

62. See W. George Lowell, "Surviving Conquest: The Maya of Guatemala in Historical Perspective," *Latin American Research Review* 23:2 (1988), 25–27.

63. López Raquec, *Acerca de los alfabetos*.

64. Demetrio López Cuxil, "Lingüística e idiomas Mayas en Guatemala," in *Lecturas sobre la lingüística Maya*, 1–25; Nora England, "Language and Ethnic Definition Among Guatemalan Indians," paper presented at the 1988 American Anthropological Association Meetings, Phoenix.

65. This puts foreign linguists, who believe that linguistics is an objective science and do not see the linkage as a focus of concern, in an awkward position. But as Bruce Mannheim, *The Language of the Inka Since the European In-*

vasion (Austin: Univ. of Texas Press, 1991), shows for the Andes, linguistics like cultural studies operates in the realm of politics as well as science.

66. See Michael Hanchard, "Culturalism Versus Cultural Politics: Afro-Brazilian Social Movements Since the 1970s," in Warren, ed., *The Violence Within*, for an analysis of the dilemmas of culturalism and racial politics in Brazil.

67. For some Mayan professionals, Catholicism presents a paradox: it is an inescapable symbol of the impact of the Spanish conquest and, thus, is inappropriate for Mayan resistance. Yet, Catholicism has been an important source of social criticism and mobilization for change. For a comparative case, see Begoña Aretxaga, "Striking with Hunger: The Cultural Meanings of Political Violence in Northern Ireland," in *The Violence Within*.

10

Race, Color, and Class in the Caribbean

ANTHONY P. MAINGOT

Introduction: The Central Debate

Nearly four centuries stretch between the Spaniards' arrival in the Caribbean and the abolition of slavery in 1886 in the region's last hold-out, Cuba. All the other major colonial powers—Great Britain, France, the Netherlands, Denmark—had already substituted free, wage-earning labor for slavery. By the end of the nineteenth century, however, virtually every Caribbean island had become a plantation society—that is, a society in which white ownership and management and black labor—first slave and then wage-earning—raised specific crops for export. Almost everywhere the crop was sugar, an extremely labor-intensive industry. But it was the racial aspect of the enterprise that made the plantation a different type of capitalist venture from the European factory. Because master and slave were of different races, power relationships developed a specific social dimension more closely associated with caste than with social class relations. In plantation societies, conceptions of racial superiority and inferiority became the essential ideological underpinnings of what otherwise would have been simple exploitation of labor. As the eighteenth-century French aristocrat Chastellux noted, "It is not only the slave who is beneath the master, it is the negro who is beneath the white man."[1]

Attempts to understand this dual dimension of race—that is, class and caste—within the political context of colonial and class oppression have dominated intellectual and scholarly discussion on Caribbean race relations. The debate has always had enormous psychological and ideological significance, and, not infrequently, political and social consequences. It could not be otherwise, given the importance of race in the life of Caribbean societies.

In addition to philosophical and moral arguments that provided the grand sweep, discussions of race and class relations have also been carried out on historical and sociological levels. These did not address questions about the ultimate fate of humanity and civilization but dealt, rather, with the everyday, ongoing nature of social relations in the Caribbean.

In many ways the Caribbean has become a laboratory for the study of race relations, with many of the concepts developed there used in the examination of race relations elsewhere. And yet, intellectual or theoretical closure has always been lacking in the Caribbean debates; there simply are no definitive answers. In part this is because the scholarship has not been able to answer convincingly these persistent questions: If the Caribbean as a whole was shaped by ideas and practices characteristic of sugar plantation society, how do we explain the wide variety of "styles" and expressions persevering in Caribbean race relations? Was there more than one type of "plantation society"? Did other forces transcend the plantation's institutional and material conditions? If the answer is yes, what were these forces? Even though debates over the role of race in the Caribbean were common in the nineteenth century, the issue took on special relevance in the late 1930s because both in the United States and the Caribbean black citizens were stirring politically and economically. Ultimately, of course, the real quest was to explain race relations in the United States, hoping that comparative research would throw light on the subject.

By the mid-1940s, two scholars held center stage. Both focused on slavery and the plantation, singling out the varying degrees of cruelty or humaneness in the workplace and so, presumably, the subsequent evolution of race relations. Their radically different explanations of the origins of race relations in the Caribbean and Latin America soon had significant scholarly defenders and detractors.

The first thesis followed a strict historical materialist interpretation. Its author, Trinidadian Eric Williams, had written a doctoral dissertation at Oxford University in 1938 on the relationship between English capitalism and the abolition of slavery in the West Indies, a dissertation he published in the United States in 1944.[2] His argument was theoretically straightforward and unequivocal: history's decisive forces are developing economic powers; any age's political and moral ideas (including those on race and slavery) are to be examined in "the very closest relation to the economic development." As such, it was not the efforts and ideas of the well-meaning abolitionists that forced Britain to abolish the abominable institution, it was the development of an industrial bourgeoisie that preferred the buying power of wage earners to the penury of slaves. The bourgeoisie's economic interest differed radically from that of the plantocracy, and economic changes in England gave the bourgeoisie the political advantage. The thesis was powerful and cogently argued.

In 1946 Williams's determinism was challenged by anthropologist Frank Tannenbaum, who was already well acquainted with Williams's work. Like Williams, Tannenbaum presented his argument forcefully and with crisp simplicity. In what became known as the "Tannenbaum thesis" he maintained that slavery was never purely an economic relationship but also a moral one.[3] In other words, Tannenbaum believed, the existence of the totally incorporating and dehumanizing institution called slavery never went unchallenged, and the particular moral and religious challenges and stipulations did help shape the society's attitude toward race. Accepting this as historical fact, Tannenbaum and those who accepted his thesis asserted that where the moral status of the slave as a person was officially and culturally accepted—as in the Catholic Hispanic variant—social change took place in an "elastic and friendly milieu." Where the slave was denied such moral status, but regarded as mere chattel—as in the Protestant "northern" plantation society—mores hardened and "the historical outcome was violence and revolution."

In 1956 these two scholars met in a historic debate.[4] It was a time of enormous change in the Caribbean, with island after island moving toward self-government under newly elected parties appealing to newly enfranchised black masses. Not surprisingly, Caribbean study was also generating great excitement among national and foreign scholars alike. The debate was hardly academic, since the question of racial identity was central to the issue of national identity. Predictably, both Williams and Tannenbaum stuck to their theses.

Williams reiterated his belief that the distinction in race and color was "only the superficial visible symbol of a distinction which in reality was based on the ownership of property." Thus, Caribbean race relations must be studied in terms of property relationships, not necessarily across similar time periods. In Caribbean terms, this would mean comparing eighteenth-century race relations (that is, master-slave relations) in Jamaica and Barbados, when sugar cultivation was at its peak, with nineteenth-century Cuba. The Cuban sugar plantation—and therefore the large-scale importation of enslaved Africans—did not reach full development until after the Haitian economy's collapse and the decline of sugar production in the British islands. Similarly, it made no sense to compare nineteenth-century master-slave relationships in Cuba with those in Puerto Rico. Both were Spanish colonies, but Puerto Rico was an imperial backwater, with no significant development of the plantation system. Whereas in Cuba slaves composed 25 percent of the labor force in 1872, in Puerto Rico they made up only 2 percent of the labor force.

Tannenbaum repeated his dissatisfaction with what he considered Williams's indifference toward custom and mores and his denial of the role of customary law and religion in understanding race relations. In this, Tannenbaum spoke for a widely held Latin American emphasis on culture and acculturation, a focus that received a tremendous boost with the 1946 translation of the Brazilian Gilberto Freyre's 1933 work, *Casa-Grande & Sensala*. To Freyre, social and racial differentiations created by the economic system were ameliorated by culture, and specifically by a culturally based predisposition toward miscegenation. More than anything else, this created the "plastic compromise" between master and slave in Brazil, according to Freyre. The assumption was that the same applied in all areas where Iberian culture predominated.

The historical materialist versus cultural or moral influences debate was critical in generating interest in the comparative study of race relations on the plantation and in the wider society. Clearly, however, the debate had not been settled.

After a detailed study of slave society in nineteenth-century Cuba, Franklin Knight concluded that Tannenbaum's approach was inadequate to a comparative understanding of the slave plantation in tropical America.[5] This was a major failing since comparison and generalization were fundamental to understanding race relations. Legal frameworks, slave laws, and the moral and humanitarian traditions of the colonial metropolis were certainly important, said Knight, but his Cuban case study clearly indicated they were of limited value in understanding the island's day-to-day race relations. "It is knowledge of the society as a whole with all its economic ramifications," said Knight, "rather than of narrower segments of legal and cultural heritage, which will lead to a better understanding of conditions during and after slavery."[6]

As Williams had earlier, Knight believed that comparisons should be made at equivalent stages of plantation development. When this was done, he asserted, it was evident that plantation slavery systems everywhere in the Caribbean "bore a strong resemblance and were comparable." This was a clear statement of what became known as the "plantation society" thesis.[7] The plantation, said Knight, was a distinctive economic system that did not lend itself to a great deal of flexibility; society's common structural organization followed the sugar plantation's common organization.

The plantation society thesis did not go unchallenged. Rebecca Scott, for instance, doubted that broad generalizations about plantation societies could be made.[8] She was wary of facile comparisons between slave "societies." Consequently, she rejected both Williams's historical materialist and Tannenbaum's cultural thesis. She focused first on the slave, not slavery, and, second, on a specific event—emancipation in Cuba—rather than on a whole historical period. With abundant documentation, Scott demonstrated that rather than being passive witnesses to the collapse of slavery, slaves maneuvered and made choices in response to options available in society. By showing their continued initiatives—collective and individual—Scott reintroduced the role of values and the spirit of freedom, and emphasized the existent overarching legal and religious systems.

But beyond that, Scott paid particular attention to how individuals responded to legal and religious systems, as well as to the spirit of freedom ingrained in human nature, of the slave as much as the freeman. So, she explored significant aspects of the everyday life of slaves, long ignored by Caribbean scholarship, including male-female relationships and the importance of family ties; the persistence of friendship and loyalty toward still enslaved individuals by those who had gained their freedom; and the capacity of illiterate Africans to understand and use the law, manipulate the state, and rely on friendly allies of all types, white, *mulatto*, and black. To Scott, then, the slave acted purposively and in rationally determined self-interest.

Borrowing from this fundamental and cumulative literature, it appears that the development of Caribbean race relations can be said to have varied according to two sets of factors or processes. The first involved the particular legal and religious institutions, as well as cultural and social attitudes toward social stratification and differentiation (that is, the system of deference) introduced by the metropolitan power. The second set of factors focused on the ways individuals and groups responded to changing material and political interests by reinforcing or weakening the system established. The latter point is critical because it makes clear that both ideology and interests operate in social change, and both give shape to perceptions. Along with material capabilities, perceptions are the mainspring of action.

This debate's vivacity and scholarly level indicate that the Caribbean, with its rich variety of colonial legacies and wide array of responses to colonial systems, is an extraordinary laboratory for the study of continuities and changes in race relations. Both continuities and transformations are evident in the race, color, and class relations of five Caribbean societies of quite different sizes, colonial histories, and contemporary political situations (see table 1). The comparisons are matched: the Dominican Republic and its contiguous neighbor, Haiti; the much smaller Trinidad, an ex-British colony; Martinique, a present-day French Department d'Outre Mer; and Curaçao, an autonomous part of the Kingdom of the Netherlands.

The Colonial Heritages of Santo Domingo and Haiti

Among the many ideas and practices the conquering Spaniards transferred to the New World, the idea of racial differences was crucial. The belief in or concept of racial purity—*limpieza de sangre*—had been an integral part of the *reconquista*, the 800–year struggle to regain Spain for the Catholic kings. The definition of *"limpio"* was *"el cristiano viejo sin raza de moro ni judío."* The opposite of *limpio* was to be *"de mala*

TABLE 1. Land and Population: Six Caribbean Cases

	Colonial Heritage	Independence	(Km²) Size	% of land Carib. Islands	Pop. (mil.)	% of Pop. Carib. Islands	% white	% black	% colored	% other
Cuba	Spain	1902	110,992	47.4	10	48	66	12	21.9	0.1
Dominican Rep.	Spain	1865	48,734	20.8	6.9	16	16	11	73	—
Haiti	France	1804	27,750	11.9	6.3	16	—	90	10	—
Trinidad	Great Britain	1962	5,128	2.2	1.2	4	1.0	43	16	*40
Martinique	France	—	1,080	0.5	0.32	1.5	3.0	70	26	1
Curaçao	Netherlands	—	443	0.2	0.13	0.6	3.0	50	46	1

Note: Data on race are approximations.

*East Indians

raza."[9] Similarly, the corollary of natural aristocracy was natural servi-
tude, "since the more perfect should hold sway over the less." This
emphasis on racial purity and its association with a "natural" leadership
class was not invented in the New World; it had deep roots in medieval
Spain, indeed in medieval Europe. To be a *caballero*, a *hidalgo* (*hijo de
algo,* literally), you had to have a singular or particular demeanor, a
life-style that became known as *decoro.* Because it was a form of ceremonial behavior intended to reflect on both the individual and the group
to which he belonged, *decoro* was surrounded by both positive and negative rules of deference. The positive rules were meant to show explicit
appreciation, the negative proscribed and set taboos on relationships
with others. This corporativist association of the individual with the
social order was the essence of medieval stratification—rooted in
Thomistic doctrine—and it was passed intact to the New World.

It would be a mistake to assume that the age of discovery and reconnaissance was a liberating age. Even among humanists, it was conservative and extremely respectful of formal authority. Besides, to the extent
that the conquest of the New World was an extension of the *reconquista,*
and especially the vanquishing of the Moors at Granada, it perpetuated
the racial and religious prejudices of the Spanish crusade.[10] The unprecedented harshness with which the queen dealt with the Moors of
Granada, says J. H. Parry, "represented a deliberate rejection on the
Queen's part of the African element in Spanish culture."[11]

Racial distinctions and grading were an integral part of the Spanish
mentality. They had been the basis of the discrimination and social distance established between *gente decente* (decent people) or *gente pensador*
(thinking people), on the one hand, and Jews and Moors on the other.
In similar fashion it was used in the New World to put Indians, Africans, and their mixed-blood progeny in a subordinate position. Eventually, the system of stratification extended, with different degrees of
prejudice, to everyone born in the colonies—the *criollos.* Suspicions of
being tainted with "impure blood" could be overcome only through
proofs of purity that were "minutely examined, without any possibility
of trickery."[12] Certainly there was some "passing," as there is even in
the most rigid caste system, but it was the exception. Franklin Knight
discovered in nineteenth-century Cuba a large number of applications
for royal permission to breach the color gap so as to enter universities,
professions, or the all-white bureaucracy. He does not indicate the rate
of approvals, but does explain that "there must have been tens of thousands whose obvious handicap of skin color or lack of the socially valuable *limpieza de sangre* completely deterred [them] from any attempt to
break out of their artificially narrowed world."[13] There was, says Knight,
a built-in inequality in the system upheld by all whites in the Spanish
overseas colonies.

Naturally, in a colonization experience composed mostly of males,
race mixing was not to be inhibited by laws. Demographics and human

nature assured considerable race mixing. This sexual and biological democracy, however, did relatively little to minimize the emphasis on social status and the critical role race and color played in the assignment
of status. As Jean Descola put it, perhaps overstating the case, "The
Colour of [an individual's] existence depended on the colour of his
parents' skin."[14] The important point is that there tended to be a close
relationship between race and socioeconomic status. The dominant ideology secured the maintenance and exclusivity of that status. The
mechanism was invariably endogamy, and generally loyalty toward family
and group. As François Chevalier notes, in societies where written contracts are not customary, blood ties and personal bonds are the only
contracts with real importance.[15] In these situations race and ethnicity
are synonymous.

The combination of official discriminatory legislation and the reality
of race mixing had become so complex that by 1735 two Spanish en-
gineers discovered a bewildering array of "castes" or "tribes" in the
cities of Cartagena de Indias, Lima, Panama, and Santo Domingo. They
began with simple descriptive categories, *mestizo*, *mulato*, and *sambo*, followed by categories indicating biological proportions. An individual with
one-third African blood was known as a *tercerón*; *cuarterón* indicated
one-fourth African blood; *quinterón*, one-fifth; and *octarón*, one-eighth.
Following such finely calibrated categories were descriptive ones such
as *tente al aire* (mixture of a *cuarteron* and a *mulato*). The term *salto atrás*
(literally, a "jump back") was reserved for anyone suspected of even
the minutest degree of mixing.[16]

The two Spaniards were struck by the punctiliousness of the social
etiquette surrounding interpersonal relations, and of the *fueros* (legal
privileges as well as deference) due each: "Every person is so jealous of
the order of their tribe or caste, that if, through inadvertence, you call
them by a degree lower than what they actually are, they are highly
offended, never suffering themselves to be deprived of so valuable a
gift of fortune."[17]

The struggle was always to be or approximate being white, especially
among those whose mixture was not apparent. Race was supreme, for
"the conceit of being white alleviates the pressure of every other calam-
ity."[18]

Such was Spanish colonial society on the eve of Independence. The
same social classes that in 1810 proclaimed the Rights of Man and other
ideas absorbed from the North American and French revolutions had
only a decade earlier protested a royal edict (*Real Cédula de "Gracias al
Sacar"*) allowing an individual to purchase improved status. The edict
specified that the title of "Don" could be purchased by *blancos de orilla*
(lesser whites) for 1,400 *reales*, that free blacks could move up to the
rank of *pardo* (another term for *mulatto*) for 700 *reales*, or to *quinterón*
for 1,100 *reales*.

For the royal house the edict was a well-established way of raising funds without doing violence to the fundamental aspect of the existing order: the distinction between whites and nonwhites. Among nonwhites, the barrier was especially strong against those with African blood. To the local *criollo* aristocrats, however, the edict was a definite threat, and in much of Spanish America they refused to enact it. Venezuelan aristocrats *(mantuanos)* complained that by allowing the royal hand to "pen puerile and superficial principles," the edict had described a situation quite different from the reality of the province and the thinking of its distinguished and pure *(limpias)* families. They insisted on continuing the traditional "total separation, in daily life and in commerce, from mulattoes and *pardos,* [not] forgetting the insult and injury a white person feels merely by being told that he mixes with them."[19]

Similarly, Franklin Knight describes the Cuban planter class's vehement opposition to any Spanish legislation (often engendered under British pressure) to abolish the slave trade. He indicates the continuities between the language used by the planters and the midsixteenth century "tradition of the racist and ethnocentric propositions."[20] As Verena Martínez-Alier's study of marriage, class, and color in nineteenth-century Cuba demonstrates, the metaphysical notion of blood as the vehicle of lineage equalities was very much part of the white Cuban's attitude, "a legacy of the much older Spanish concern over purity of blood reinforced by the special socio-economic conditions obtaining in the colonies."[21] Interracial marriages were very infrequent; race mixing resulted from consensual unions.[22]

Even as many of these planters sought independence from Spain—as their counterparts on the continent had done half a century earlier—their attitudes often tended to be more anti-black than anti-Spanish. The white *criollo* resented the Spaniard for his unwillingness to show deference and the accompanying demeanor, precisely the deference he demanded—without expectations of reciprocity, of course—from his nonwhite fellow citizens. As Simón Bolívar complained to an English friend in his famous 1815 Jamaica Letter, "We should also have enjoyed a personal consideration [from Spain], thereby commanding a certain automatic respect from the people."[23] It is illusory to think that independence in itself could change such an entrenched and comprehensive legal and behavioral system. Indeed, that slavery was not abolished in Venezuela until 1840, in Cuba until 1886, and in Brazil until 1888 reflected the permanence not only of attitudes but indeed of the economic structure sustaining them.

These attitudes were not different among the Spaniards who inhabited the two-thirds of the island of Hispaniola. Indeed, they were not different on the one-third that Spain had ceded to France in 1697, Saint Domingue. If anything, the plantation system's extraordinary development in the French portion had created an extremely high consciousness about social distance and the role of race therein.

As David Nicholls has clearly documented, racialism, as related to

TABLE 2. Racial Categories in Saint Domingue
Late Eighteenth Century

	Parts White	*Parts Black*
noir (black)	0	128
sacatra	16	112
griffe	32	96
marabou	48	80
mulâtre	4	64
quarteron	96	32
métis	112	16
mamelouc	120	8
quarteronne	124	4
sang-mêlé	126	2
blanc (white)	128	0

Source: M. L. E. Moreau de Saint Méry, *Description topograp-
hique, civile, politique et historique de la partie française de l'Ille Saint
Domingue* (Paris [1798], 1958). Cited in Micheline Labelle, *Idéologie de couleur et classes sociales en Haiti* (Montreal: Les Presses de
l'Université Montréal, 1987), 49.

color prejudice, was the abiding feature of everyday colonial life in French Saint Domingue.[24] Nonwhites were categorized even more minutely than in Spanish colonial America. The degree of calibration, as related by colonial historian Moreau de Saint Méry, boggles the mind. It starts out with *noir* (black) and ends with *sang-mêlé*, literally, mixed blood (see table 2).

The Spanish notion of *limpieza de sangre* had its French equivalent and was implemented everywhere the French governed, including Louisiana, where such distinctions remained law well into the twentieth century. Indeed, the emphasis on race and color was such that a *mulatto* slave would enjoy more consideration than a free black. At the center of the idea of race was the notion of the African's intrinsic inferiority— biologically, culturally, and socially. Again, even such deeply rooted racist ideas did not stop race mixing either in Saint Domingue or its Spanish neighbor. The proportions, however, were radically different. On the eve of Haiti's first military invasion of its neighbor (1801), their respective population compositions were as shown in table 3.

Quite evidently, any society as conscious of race and color as Spanish Hispaniola would look with alarm on such a neighbor. As it turns out, Dominicans, as they began to call themselves, had other reasons as well to be in a veritable panic about their recently liberated neighbors.

Race and Color in Haiti

David Nicholls begins his seminal study of race and color in Haiti by asking what appears to be a paradoxical question to anyone accustomed

TABLE 3.   Race in Dominican Republic and Haiti
End of Eighteenth Century

	Dominican Republic (1794)	Haiti (1789)
Whites	35,000	40,000
Slaves	15,000 to 30,000	450,000
Freed/mixed	38,000	30,000

Sources: 1. Pedro Andrés Pérez Cabral, *La Comunidad mulata* (Caracas: Gráfica Americana, 1967), 106–7; David Nicholls, *From Dessalines to Duvalier: Race, Colour and National Independance in Haiti* (Cambridge: Cambridge Univ. Press, 1979), 19.

to a bifurcated "black-white" system: "How is it that racial pride should have been among the principal causes of Haitian independence, while colour prejudice should have been one of the chief factors undermining this independence?"[25]

The response is that each emphasis—on race or color—served a different strategic purpose. In the confrontation with white colonial domination, for instance, the emphasis was race. This made sense not only in terms of alliances, which all nonwhites found necessary to combat the external enemy, but also in terms of the way the white enemy classified all nonwhites. Whites certainly recognized shades of difference, but in the final analysis black and colored alike were "soiled" by Africa. This explains why the first Haitian constitution defined the nation as black *(noir)* and all its citizens as black. It also explains why, during the U.S. military occupation of 1915–34, the nationalist reaction among otherwise divided black and *mulatto* elites was couched in terms of a rediscovering of their collective African past. In the Haitian resistance to North American racism, ethnography became the central organizing discipline: nationalists of all shades of color drank at its font. Perhaps the most impressive of these nationalists was Jean Price Mars, a middle-class black whose *Ainsi parla l'oncle* was a call to his countrymen, especially *mulattos*, to come to grips with their African past and context. The racial principle—as biology, but also as cultural protest—made sense in the face of evident North American racism, which was both biological and cultural. However, once the racial protest was made and the North Americans withdrew, color differences took hold just as they had after the independence struggles of the early nineteenth century.

The material and political context, however, had changed. While the U.S. occupation forces showed a distinct bias toward the educated *mulatto* elite, even creating a new army *(gendarmerie)* staffed with their sons, they had also helped create a new black middle class. Through various technical schools and other practical social and public programs, a generation of black lawyers, doctors, teachers, and agricultural extension technicians soon rose to challenge the power of the *mulâtres*. Not surprisingly, differences in color and culture (fundamentally language differences) reappeared as the operative aspect of social, economic, and political competition.[26] Micheline Labelle discovered a precise and nuanced color classification scheme, not unlike Moreau de Saint Méry's, which survived from colonial days. But a "color ideology" came into full operation only around economic, and especially political, competition. Labelle maintains that it is the Haitian variant of class conflict.[27]

Nicholls's question is answered, therefore, by noting that in Haiti one has to differentiate between intrinsic ethnic identities of color and strategically varying identifications, which can be of race and/or color. No scholar has claimed that during any of the crises that called for a joining of all Haitian forces on the basis of African race against a common enemy, any of the groups abandoned their original sense of in-group feelings and attachments—that is, their ethnic allegiances. The constant racial tensions and clashes evident in all multiethnic armed forces gathered in the Caribbean—from Bolívar's liberating army to José Martí's Cuban army of liberation—show the persistence of early race and color identities.[28]

In Haiti, strength against an outside white enemy lay in organizing around race, specifically the black race, even as internal strife was organized around color. This does not mean, however, that color conflict is an absolute predictor of Haitian political behavior. Haitians, like all other Caribbean peoples, have a capacity strategically to highlight or mute racial and color divisions in the pursuit of a desired goal. The 1991 election of Haitian president Jean Bertrand Aristide is generally recognized as the first truly democratic poll in the island's history. It was also the first major political campaign in which race and color played no major part, at least not explicitly. Aristide's cabinet also reflected an indifference to color distinctions. The island's historical and debilitating caste division did appear to be a factor behind the September 30, 1990, overthrow of Aristide. But even then, the divisions were presented as conflicts of social class, not of color. Aristide's populism was quite different, thus, from that of the Duvalier regime, a dynasty that made color distinction a central piece of its existence for 26 years. With Duvalier followers attempting to revive the black versus mulatto strife during the 1990 campaign, it became strategically important that the opponents of Duvalier not make color an issue, as indeed they did not, with enormous electoral success.[29] Whatever other weaknesses and failures were evident in the Aristide government, that interlude indicated that color strife does not have to be the basis of a national mobilization.

This fact has also been evident in the Dominican Republic, except there the organizing principle was nationality, a concept that transcended race and color.

Race and Color in the Dominican Republic

In his social history of the Dominican Republic, H. Hoetink traces variations in race and color emphases over the half century following the
Haitian occupation.[30] He found that the essentially aristocratic-patriarchal
society, with clearly established criteria of stratification and social distance, demonstrated a remarkable adaptability during that half century. While the Haitian occupation increased the black and *mulatto* populations (by Haitian settlements and white flight), and reinforced the
African dimensions of Dominican culture, it also "softened" race relations among Dominicans themselves. Given their reduced numbers (on
the eve of the Haitian occupation only 63,000 inhabitants resided on
18,712 square miles), the elite attempted to unite all Dominicans in a
national liberation struggle against the Haitians. This effort to create a
strong national identity was not totally successful: in 1860 important
sectors of the white elite invited the Spaniards to reoccupy the island.
Fear of the Haitians overwhelmed any sense of national sovereignty.

By 1865, however, independence-minded Dominicans again called
on Dominicans of all colors, in the name of nationality, to defeat the
Spaniards. The Spaniards' defeat, and the flight of many whites who
had supported them, further democratized the stratification system. This
explains how a black of Haitian descent, Ulysses Heureaux, could govern for the last twenty years of the nineteenth century. As soon as the
fear of foreign occupation, Haitian or otherwise, abated, however, Dominicans returned to divisions of race and color. Heureaux was persistently hounded with racial epithets and accused of favoring Haitian
settlement. When he showed an inclination to concede to a U.S. naval
base, his enemies warned that North American racism would oppress
Dominican blacks and *mulattos.* The political use of racial fears could
go in all directions. Even during the U.S. occupation (1916–24), the
Dominican white elite refused to cooperate in certain reforms, opening
the doors to members of the colored middle class. This was especially
true in the military, where Rafael Leonidas Trujillo used U.S. sponsorship to catapult himself—and his many relatives and friends—into a
29–year dictatorship.

Again, the Dominican capacity to use race and color identifications
when convenient was evident in the Trujillo years. The dictator simultaneously became the most ferocious enemy of the traditional white
aristocracy (which on more than one occasion snubbed him in his re-
quests for membership in their clubs) and the greatest promoter of
Hispanic white identification. The combination of a democratization of
social mobility, through state sponsorship, and a conscious effort to
identify with Spain and its heritage affected all parts of Dominican life.
At the height of the *Trujillato,* color considerations were so pronounced
that even a pro-regime sociologist could lament that "since Dominicans

are not predominantly of pure race, we have a complex about ethnicity, we are constantly noticing the different skin colors, hair textures and degree of white blood. Three drives are noticeable: those who do not have white blood want to acquire it; those who have some, improve it; those who are white want to preserve this gift *(don).*"[31]

There exists no better account of the behavioral results of a regime that tried to level the social class stratification system without disrupting the stratification system emphasizing color than in the memoirs of Joaquín Balaguer, who served the dictator throughout his stay in power and who is presently in his fifth term as democratically elected president.[32] To Balaguer, one of Trujillo's greatest accomplishments was to have "swept away everywhere the claims to aristocracy *('los pergaminos sociales').*" Yet Balaguer relates how the color-conscious dictator would pass his hands over a child's hair and say, "But how surprising, he's got good hair." The element of surprise indicates the dictator's concern was not over biological race (genotype) but over racial appearance (phenotype), and the latter had to do with perceptions of acceptable demeanor. According to Balaguer, it was concern over demeanor, and the impact it might have on deference, that led Trujillo to dismiss his most effective collaborator because his "rough" Negroid features were an embarrassment during a sojourn among Spain's aristocracy. The much less competent Roberto Depradel, on the other hand, was always retained; he was white, with blue eyes and easy speech. "Men of good looks and good appearance," writes Balaguer, "were always especially pleasing to the Dominican dictator."[33]

Dominicans' capacity to adjust to difficult circumstances—to be accommodating even with their most intrinsic racial identities—is evident in Balaguer himself. From the explicitly racist *La Realidad Dominicana* (1947), in which he argues Haitians' racial inferiority, to his more recent *La Isla al revés: Haiti y el destino Dominicano* (1990), in which he merely argues Haiti's cultural inferiority, Balaguer has made anti-Haitianism the linchpin of his concept of Dominican nationality. And yet, in 1990 he ends with a plea for a confederation between his country and Haiti: "By forgetting the past we can have a rebirth, two countries forcibly joined as neighbors by geography and history can create a new union, a more honorable and lasting indivisibility: that of the awareness which men on both sides have of their economic and cultural links as well as common destiny."[34]

It would be illusory to believe this 86–year-old political veteran has given up his basic identity—his private prejudices—as a Hispanic Dominican. But the politician who in 1937 could hardly conceal his approval of the slaughter of 10,000–15,000 Haitian squatters, faces in 1991 quite a different demographic and economic reality. In 1937 Dominicans estimated that some 52,000 Haitians were living in the Dominican Republic; in 1991 they calculate the number to be 1 million. Economically, Dominican agriculture depends on Haitians, as does much of the private construction industry and significant sections of the ever expanding informal economy.

Though certainly not an armed invasion, it is an invasion nevertheless. Clearly Dominicans perceive it as such. In this sense elements of comparison exist with the problem Dominicans faced in the first half of the nineteenth century: how to deal strategically with an overwhelming foreign presence. Evidently, it will not do to attack Haitians on racial grounds; too many Dominicans are classified as "negro." Fewer and fewer are able to trace their dark skins to some Indian past, the traditional concession to an expected demeanor. Today, as then, the attack is made on ethnic and national grounds: the distinctiveness of the Spanish language, and history, especially the links with Spain and the struggle to retain their identity against all invaders, Haitian and North American. The inclusive power of culture and history is not to be minimized. It was used successfully in the nineteenth century, and present performances in the political arena indicate that Dominicans have not lost their skills of strategic ethnicity.

Continuity in using nationality in the Dominican Republic reveals the strategic subordination of race and color distinctions, which are otherwise evident in private. Black politicians' rise to political prominence reflects a relaxation of public attitudes toward racial and color attributes in their leaders. The distinction between color and nationality, however, is still important in the island's politics, as the case of José Francisco Peña Gómez illustrates. His alleged Haitian origin plays an important part in public perceptions of his not being "presidenciable." On the other hand, the equally black Johnny Ventura, apolitical protégé of Peña Gómez, suffers no such handicap. He is one of the leading proponents of the island's music, the merengue, generally regarded as a major unifier of Dominicans' sense of nationality. The fear of the Haitian in Peña Gómez is clearly being accentuated by opposing elites, who no longer find the racial or color issue strategically advantageous.

Race and Social Change in Martinique, Curaçao, and Trinidad

The capacity of Haitian and Dominican elites to emphasize or mute racial and color distinctions as circumstances seem to mandate needs explanation. This is especially so for parts of the region known as the non-Hispanic Caribbean—to reflect their British, French, or Dutch colonial heritage. In these areas the capacity to maneuver strategically around pitfalls presented by entrenched and persistent concerns over race, color, and culture is even more evident. Does such a capacity indicate that despite race and color differences, non-Hispanic Caribbean peoples have forged and operate within a relatively homogeneous political culture? This was, in fact, the central question of one of the area's important theoretical debates, the argument over possible cultural homogenization in the Caribbean. On one side were those who argued there was a trend toward "creolization"—that is, cultural homogenization—and on the other were those who saw the cultural persistence of various ethnic groups resisting any such trend. The former believed that pluralism, in so far as it existed, was a result of social class stratification, not cultural or institutional divergences.[35]

Quite a different interpretation was given by the group that argued the area is characterized by social and cultural pluralism based on institutional divergences—that is, that groups of differing race and religion look inward for their strengths and orientations, reinforcing ingroup feelings at the expense of the whole. This occurs even while the groups live in close economic and demographic interdependence. In such societies order and stability is regulated by forces other than those presumed to be operating in societies integrated through a consensus on norms. They thus deny that there is a significant trend toward cultural homogenization or "creolization" in these island societies, much less in the area as a whole.[36] This same theoretical school continued to emphasize cultural differences even as they added a "structural" dimension so popular among Caribbean social scientists in the 1970s and 1980s.[37]

The complexity of Caribbean societies makes any definitive answer well nigh impossible. To be sure, throughout the area social hierarchies exist in which whites hold the upper positions. M. G. Smith's description of Jamaica applies to other small islands: the societies are divided into white, brown, and black as the order of "their current and historical dominance, and the exact reverse of their relative numerical strength."[38] As distinct from Haiti, white elites did survive in the non-Hispanic Caribbean. But as distinct from the Cuban and Dominican cases, they survived in very small numbers. With the exception of extremely small islands such as Saba and St. Barthélemy, nowhere in the non-Hispanic Caribbean do whites compose more than 3 percent of any island's population. Additionally, large immigrations of East Indians in the nineteenth century, plus economically significant numbers of Jews, Chinese, Portuguese, and Syrian-Lebanese, all make these islands socially different from the larger Hispanic ones. Trinidad, Martinique, and Curaçao are interesting cases revealing continuities in social stratification.

Among the area's earliest non-Hispanic settlers were the Dutch, in Curaçao. Here the Protestant white elite trace their roots back to the midseventeenth century.[39] Similarly, Trinidad's stratification system, with whites at the top and blacks on the bottom, was established by the conquering Spanish in the sixteenth century, promoted by the French, who arrived in large numbers after 1783, and continued by the English, who conquered the island in 1797.[40] The amount of change in the stratification system over the years was found to be minimal, even as the political and economic situation changed.

On the island of Martinique, a researcher found a white creole elite composed of 150 patronymic names, the so-called *bekés,* who could trace their roots as follows: 28 families (39 percent), arrived before 1713; 37 (22 percent) arrived between 1713 and 1784; another 35 percent arrived in the nineteenth century; while only 4 percent were first- or second-generation Martinicans.[41]

To the *bekés,* race, class, and ideology (shaped by a sense of their historical role on the island) formed the pillars of their ethnocentrism. Each *beké* child was first socialized into "the cult of the family name" and then into the "sacred duty" of maintaining the *beké* group's social characteristics. The mechanism of this group's hierarchical stability has always been endogamy; any marriage outside the group's strict norms was regarded as a "stain."

Nowhere in the Caribbean did the emancipation of slaves fundamentally change the racial stratification system. If anything, it was reinforced by two quite powerful forces: the racism of most of metropolitan ideologues, and the specter of another Haiti, which scared metropolitan and white settler alike.

Local whites used metropolitan whites, who held ultimate power over the fates of these minute colonies, as reference groups. Colonial ideologies everywhere were racist. The majority of English scholars, for instance, steadfastly held on to two fundamental tenets: first, that Teutonic, and especially Anglo-Saxon, races were superior in all regards; and second, that other races' inferiority could only be ameliorated through tutelage by the former.

The "white man's burden," thus, combined racism with paternalism.[42] The latter was essential to avoiding another Haiti. As Thomas Carlyle warned after observing emancipation's result in the midnineteenth century, "Let him, by his ugliness, idleness, rebellion, banish all white men from the West Indies, and make it all one Haiti . . . a tropical dog-kennel and pestiferous jungle. . . ."[43] Similarly, Oxford historian James Anthony Froude, having toured the Caribbean's British colonies in the mid-1880s, was convinced the white population was gradually disappearing everywhere in the region. Emancipation had finally ruined an already weak planter class, and black majority rule was in the future. "Were it worthwhile," wrote Froude, "one might draw a picture of the position of an English governor, with a black parliament and a black ministry. . . . No Englishman, not even a bankrupt peer, would consent to occupy such a position."[44] Indeed, he wrote a friend in 1887, the islands were already "becoming nigger warrens and were in danger of lapsing into barbarism of turning into Haitis."[45]

The fact is that black-dominated parliaments did emerge everywhere in the non-Hispanic Caribbean after World War II, and the small white elites remained. They survived the decolonization process, though the exact nature of their influence and status varies from island to island. It was not supposed to be this way. To Frantz Fanon, the decolonization process necessarily meant a complete change of the social structure, driven by the "impetuous and compelling" nature of the consciousness of the colonized. It was always "a violent phenomenon."[46]

How, then, to explain the persistence of white social elites, even as political, and often economic, power shifted toward new black sectors? Certainly one explanation is that "history," as important as it is in certain areas, has not dominated Caribbean politics. Derek Walcott's call for a Caribbean without "a literature of revenge written by the descendants of slaves or a literature of remorse written by the descendants of masters" has indeed been the case.[47]

As is evident in the not-so-fictional novels of a Jacques Roumain (founder of Haiti's Communist party), an Alejo Carpentier in Cuba, a Vidia Naipaul or Samuel Selvon in Trinidad, or a George Lamming in Barbados, the theme invariably is the pursuit of social and political justice, not revenge or the creation of racial hegemony. Where such hegemony was sought, as with Jamaican Marcus Garvey's Universal Negroes Improvement Association (UNIA), it was to be exercised in Africa, not in the Caribbean. In fact, Garvey did not even seek integration into North American or Jamaican society. Only *mulattos*—whom he once called "time serving, boot licking agents of subserviency to the whites"—talked of social equality. "We do not seek social equality," Garvey said. "We do not seek intermarriage. We want the right to have a country of our own where we can foster and re-establish a culture and a civilization exclusively ours."[48]

The operational complexities, in the political sense, of pursuing an identity outside the Caribbean is evident in Martinique. By 1946 a powerful nationalist and antiwhite movement was led by Aimé Césaire. He became one of the founders of the *négritude* movement, in Martinique, France, and francophone Africa. In a racially and socially bitter campaign, Césaire was elected mayor of Fort-de-France and deputy to the French Assembly on the Communist party's ticket. Despite the expressed hatred of the white world in Césaire's *négritude,* the enmity always appeared ameliorated by its mystification into something other than direct class conflict.[49] Gabriel Coulthard finds that in the literature of *négritude* generally, redemption seems to come more from an attack on reason and eulogy of primitivism than from secular social revolution.[50]

In the final analysis the tension between a Communist secular ideology and a black Caribbean experience resulted in pursuing an identity—a black identity—rather than struggling for social change.[51]

Césaire resigned from the French Communist party in 1956. As he wrote the French Communist party's secretary-general, Maurice Thorez, an alternative path existed to the "fleshless universalism" of European

Communism: "Black Africa, the dam of our civilization and source of our culture." Only through race, culture, and the richness of ethnic particulars, he continued, could Caribbean people avoid alienation. "What I wish," he wrote, "is that Marxism and Communism be utilized to benefit the man of color, not the man of color to benefit Marxism and Communism."[52]

Césaire has been re-elected in every election up to this writing. Despite his appeal to race, his political goals and policies have always been the general improvement of democracy and welfare on the island; his targets: metropolitan policies as they affect the French Antilles, not the *bekés* whom he has displaced politically, though not socially.

This capacity to use race and color strategically and situationally has also been evident in the various racial conflicts that have shaken Caribbean societies in the past three decades. The mix of Black Power and some variant of Marxism have been evident in each.

It might be, as Ivar Oxaal notes, that in the West Indies " 'Black Power' demands are, in the nature of the case, socialist demands, and should therefore be clearly labelled as such . . ."[53] Tim Hector, Antigua's leading Marxist, as he reminisced about his relationships with slain Grenadian leader Maurice Bishop and Enzi Kawayna, co-leader of Guyana's Marxist Workers and Peoples Alliance, said that there was "an unique and unbreakable bond" between them that was "forged in the Black Power movement; socialism was nothing more than a logical extension of that." The question, of course, is whose "logical extension," for nowhere in the Caribbean has socialism followed Black Power. The two movements respond to different instincts and needs, and in democratic societies the pursuit of both tends to have a mutually neutralizing effect. The cases of Curaçao and Trinidad will illustrate.

To observe pictures of the leadership of Curaçao's Frente Obrero i Liberashion in 1969 in their Castro-style fatigues and caps, and to read the rhetoric that combined Black Power, Curaçao linguistic and cultural nationalism, and Marxism, is to realize the powerful mix of ideas behind the Curaçao movement. It is no wonder the movement's ideological leader, a white Curaçaoleño named Stanley Brown, in between his anticapitalist rhetoric, repeatedly reminded his black followers that his grandmother was black.[54]

To be sure, a major difference existed between Curaçao and the rest of the Caribbean, especially the West Indies. Curaçao's official Commission of Inquiry, which looked into the May 30, 1969, troubles, noted that Curaçao and Aruba were exceptions to the rule prevailing in the rest of the Caribbean, where black elites governed. Curaçao was governed by a party led by the old, white, Protestant elite. What all the islands that had experienced racial unrest did have in common was a powerful influence from students abroad, most of them using the U.S. racial situation as their guide. The movement had begun in Jamaica in 1968 when students rioted to protest the banning of their indisputable leader, the Guyanese Dr. Walter Rodney. The commission noted, however, that despite such hemisphere-wide influences, the local movement was quite specific in its targets: it did not attack *all* white groups.[55] In fact, the true economic elite, the Sephardic Jewish banking and commercial sector, was not a direct target. Anger was aimed at the political elites, composed of native Protestant whites, a traditional group that, as Curaçaoan sociologist René Romer pointed out, had lost its economic position over the years and now ranked well below the Sephardi and expatriate whites on the economic and even the social scale.[56]

The movement's singling out of this Protestant white elite as also being the "economic establishment" (always used in English in the radical journal *Vito*) was empirically incorrect but politically useful. From a strict Marxist perspective, however, it was hardly revolutionary. All this led the Commission of Inquiry to note with irony that in the movement toward autonomy in the early 1950s, it was the White Protestant Group that took a nationalist, anti-Dutch stance. They were now accused of being "foreigners."[57]

What was involved was a classic case of rebellion against blocking the process of ethnic group succession. With the top economic slots taken by the Sephardi and other more recently arrived immigrant groups, such as Indians and Lebanese, the only area open to both local Protestant whites and newly emerging and highly educated black and colored elites were government jobs. Decolonization had unleashed a competition between these two groups, and the whites won politically in the early 1950s by advancing a more progressive and nationalist program. By the late 1960s, however, they were overtaken by the very political evolution they had engineered and became the targets of what was essentially a competition for power. This was not to be confused—as it indeed was in much of the literature—with social revolution; it was conflictive social change.

Trinidad's Black Power movement in 1970 showed a similar ambiguity in its mix of radical Black Power and socialist ideologies. It was much easier, however, to see what it was against than what it was for. If black had to do with Africa, were Indians—now 43 percent of the population—black? If the movement was socialist, what to do with the Indians' rising economic—that is capitalist—power and the large black bourgeoisie, which had held the reins of state power since 1956? Finally, were the movement's main targets—local whites—really the economy's controllers, as the movement proclaimed?

The evidence appears to be that the local whites had long been retired from any significant political involvement,[58] and had lost any control over the local economy, largely contenting themselves with running family-owned firms and holding second-level jobs in foreign-owned banks,[59] and were now a minority in prestigious professions.[60] Even their notorious country club was officially investigated and found not to discriminate on "ethnic origin, racial descent or colour," as certain

Indian and Chinese clubs were found to do.[61] What, then, did Black Power mean in such a society, other than a strategically calculated grab for power by certain groups?

Two fundamental aspects of the complex dynamics of race and politics emerge from this period. First, while the Black Power movements in Curaçao and Trinidad did not change political institutional arrangements, they did circulate elites. Second, and most important in the case of Trinidad, the Black Power movement impelled the state into an overwhelmingly dominant position in the economy. The fundamental undercurrent of social change during this period, therefore, was the push for economic empowerment of the already politically empowered black middle classes. Portraying local white dominance served the political agenda well. Since black economic control was quite limited, however, this meant new social demands could be satisfied only by creating new sources of wealth. This was to be done through state initiative. A 1972 Trinidad White Paper made it quite clear that the public sector would be the economy's prime mover and job creator. The government emphasized that, "a complex of financial and non-financial corporate bodies under public control is being progressively developed, each with terms of reference which give it greater opportunity and facility for participation in the equity of private enterprise in order to stimulate new activity."[62]

Indeed, given its oil resources and the jump in revenues from the "OPEC shock" of the 1970s, Trinidad had the wherewithal to enter into a state-led development program. Other Caribbean societies had no such source of wealth, but expectations of jobs and "localized" development were equally strong. This was the impetus behind calls for a "mixed economy," which were particularly well articulated by Michael Manley and the PNP in Jamaica. In the 1970s Black Power had helped push Caribbean governments into more centrally directed economic development. Two decades later, these democratic societies were in full swing back to private-sector-driven development.

In Trinidad it would not be an easy path. After two and a half decades of state-led policies, Indians perceived that Africans had gained the most. Africans perceived just the opposite. No group thought that whites had secured any advantages during the period. The center of gravity of the island's racial tensions had shifted to the African-Indian confrontation, two groups of more or less similar numbers.[63] And yet, when an explosive response came to the stringent measures of the economic restructuring, it had little to do with the society's racial tensions—the old black-white or new African-Indian.

In late August 1990 a group of Black Muslims attempted a coup d'état, promising a more humane regime. They had completely misinterpreted the nature of the island's political culture. While 60 percent of the people believed the rebels' cause was just, 75 percent (across all racial groups) rejected violence as the way to correct unpopular policies.[64] Democracy had indeed sunk deep roots on the island. In the final analysis, this is the best indicator that despite tensions and group prejudices in the multiracial society, accepting the rules of the democratic game provided a safeguard against institutionalized racism and discrimination.

Conclusion

If in the post–Cold War era communal conflict is quickly replacing social revolution as the dominant form of strife, what, if anything, can we learn from the Caribbean?

One lesson is that political leadership matters. Eric Williams or Aimé Césaire may have used racial identifications to boost their political careers; they never used them to oppress others. Race and ethnicity held strategic, not inherent or absolute, value. To be otherwise would be to replicate the white racism they so abhorred and combated.

Second, open, pluralistic political systems might well generate heightened racial or ethnic sentiments, but they also channel conflict into realistic directions, forcing negotiations and cross-cutting alliances. One consequence of such political pluralism is the intellectual pluralism evident in the brio and vivacity of studies in Caribbean race relations. Compare this, for instance, to the Cuban case, where the study of race relations is what Jorge Domínguez calls "a classic 'non topic.' "[65] How to evaluate Carlos Moore's assertion that the severe treatment of Cuban blacks owes as much to the severe nature of Cuban authoritarianism generally as to traditional white Cuban racism?[66] Only serious and open research can answer such a question, and this in turn requires an open political system.

If such individual and institutional factors are important, perhaps the framework for studying such societies needs changing, away from the determinism of the historical-materialist thesis and quasi determinism of the plantation society model. The individual as a rational actor, pursuing self-interest and maximizing his or her opportunities, has to be reintroduced.

Certainly this framework had prevailed in classic economic and democratic political theory.[67] It might well benefit the study of multiracial and divided societies. As Rebecca Scott demonstrated, even as a slave the black individual in the Caribbean was maneuvering to improve his desperate lot. Throughout colonialism African Caribbean peoples battled against enormous odds, at home and internationally. They still have a lot of maneuvering to do, but it is quite apparent in most of the Caribbean that they have chosen the path of pluralist politics and become skilled tacticians in the democratic game of competitive bargaining. Race is used strategically to advance their general causes, from consolidating identity to organizing for the rough-and-tumble of pluralist, party politics.

And what about small white minorities? What about that "terrifying consciousness" that Frantz Fanon spoke of and which supposedly has been part of their existence since slavery and especially since the Haitian Revolution? Is there anything to the literary critic's thesis that analyzing plots and styles of novels written by white West Indians reveals a "natural stance" among them, a "terrified consciousness"?[68] The response involves an obvious question: would anyone expect a group so terrified to remain in the islands, especially in an area where migration has been a traditional and frequently used vehicle to escape oppression or seek improvements? The fact is that they have remained. No evidence exists that these white groups have migrated in larger numbers proportionately than any other group. The Caribbean seems to offer them something not offered elsewhere, and this speaks well for the black elites who have governed since the 1950s. There certainly are inherent racial and color ethnic identities and prejudices in the Caribbean. What there is not is any iron-clad assurance that they either will always cause or, indeed, serve as rationalizations of social conflict. The history of Haitian, Dominican, Martinican, Curaçaoan, and Trinidadian use of race and color indicates their importance, but history also demonstrates the elites' ability to use race and color strategically. This strategic usage in no way indicates that these same elites abandoned their private personal and group prejudices.[69]

It is critical, therefore, to make a conceptual distinction between Caribbean elites' shared values and beliefs—the cultural biases—and their public, social relations. Certainly both compose the way of life of any society, but the operational question is how they interact. What are the particular incentives and constraints that engender or inhibit not the existence but the expression of race and color biases as overt discrimination?

In this regard, it is crucial that the observer understand the role of latent consequences in history. This in turn requires a more historical, less presentist, perspective. Two examples illustrate the importance of latent effects and serve to conclude this chapter on a positive note.

Most consensual unions in plantation societies involved a dominant white male and a subordinate black or colored female. The relationship was one of power; had the male been black, the relationship was probably one of love, however defined. This subordination had two distinct consequences: one manifest—the continued subordination of the non-white woman and her progeny; the other, latent—the affirmation of the colored woman's beauty, increasingly portrayed as the symbol of what is most vital in Caribbean life. As the Puerto Rican poet Luis Pales Matos intoned, "Now you are, mulatto girl, / the whole sea and land of my island."

This representation of the *mulatto* woman has moved from the hidden world of the powerful's frowned-on liaisons with the subordinate to an increasing phenotypical acceptability. H. Hoetink calls it the "mulattoization" of Caribbean societies, a fundamental change in social aesthetics.[70]

Even as a bit of overstatement, Hoetink's perspective deserves analysis, especially since the data on marriages in the Dominican Republic reflect a strong tendency for whites, *mulattos,* and blacks to marry *mulatas.* Pérez Cabral found of 10,813 marriages in 1960, 10,162 involved one or more *mulatto* partners, 561 joined two white partners, and 86 two black.[71]

The other example comes from the gradual transformation and democratization of Caribbean popular culture. In the nineteenth century, Spanish-Cuban elites described Afro-Cuban music as "vulgar noise."[72] In Trinidad English white elites spent the nineteenth century referring to carnival as a "diabolical festival," a "licensed exhibition of wild excesses."[73] In the Dominican Republic, a declaration that the merengue had African origins elicited the following response from an important band leader: "That outlandish statement is unpatriotic."[74] Today, Afro-Cuban music, carnival, and merengue are symbols of their islands' national identity, with male and female performers honored celebrities in all three islands.

This history is worth analyzing for the benefit of white groups, in South Africa and elsewhere, who are truly terrified of black majority rule. That the Caribbean experience provides a worthy lesson is admitted by as harsh a critic of Caribbean racism as Gordon Lewis. He ends a whole treatise on the subject by predicting that "if racial democracy is to survive anywhere in the twentieth century, then, it probably stands its best chance in the Caribbean."[75]

Notes

1. Cited in Gordon K. Lewis, *Main Currents in Caribbean Thought* (Baltimore: Johns Hopkins Univ. Press, 1983), 7.

2. Eric Williams, *Capitalism and Slavery* (Chapel Hill: Univ. of North Carolina Press, 1944).

3. Frank Tannenbaum, *Slave and Citizen: The Negro in the Americas* (New York: Knopf, 1946).

4. The debate took place in Puerto Rico in 1956 and the record of it is published in Vera Rubin (ed.), *Caribbean Studies: A Symposium* (Seattle: Univ. of Washington Press, 1960), 54–66.

5. Franklin Knight, *Slave Society in Cuba During the Nineteenth Century* (Madison: Univ. of Wisconsin Press, 1970).

6. Ibid., 194.

7. A splendid introduction to the nature of plantation societies is Sidney W. Mintz, *Caribbean Transformations* (New York: Columbia Univ. Press, 1989).

8. Rebecca Scott, *Slave Emancipation in Cuba: The Transition to Free Labor, 1860–1899* (Princeton: Princeton Univ. Press, 1985).

9. Juan Beneyto, *Historia social de España y de hispanoamerica* (Madrid: Aguilar, 1961).

10. The Spanish historian Salvador de Madariaga dates the changed attitude of the Spanish people toward the Jews and Moors at the end of the eleventh century. See *Spain: A Modern History* (New York: Praeger, 1958), 17–18.

11. J. H. Parry, *The Age of Reconnaissance* (New York: Mentor, 1964), 45.

12. Jean Descola, *Daily Life in Colonial Peru, 1710–1820*, trans. Michael Heron (London: Allen and Unwin, 1962), 26.

13. Knight, *Slave Society in Cuba*, 98.

14. Descola, *Daily Life in Colonial Peru*, 105.

15. François Chevalier, " 'Caudillos' et 'caciques' en Amerique," *Bulletin Hispanique*, 64 (1962), 34.

16. Jorge Juan and Antonio Ulloa, *A Voyage to South America*, trans. John Adams, abridged (New York: Knopf, 1964).

17. Ibid., 27.

18. Ibid.

19. Documents cited by Laureano Vallenilla Lanz, *Césarismo Democrático.* (1919; reprint, Caracas: Tipografíca Garrido, 1961), 41ff. This controversial work presents on the best interpretations of the role of race in the development of Latin American political culture generally and *caudillismo* specifically. Objections to the more even justice dealt out to the castes by Spanish officials was a major part of white creole society's anti-Spanish feelings. Cf. José Gil Fortoul, *Historia constitucional de Venezuela*, 2d. ed. (Caracas: Parra León Hermanos, 1930), 72.

20. Knight, *Slave Society in Cuba*, xix.

21. Verena Martínez-Alier, *Marriage, Class and Colour in Nineteenth-Century Cuba* (Cambridge: Cambridge Univ. Press, 1974), 15.

22. Ibid., 63.

23. This letter and other documents pertinent to the *criollo*-peninsular conflict in Latin America are found in R. A. Humphreys and John Lynch (eds.), *The Origins of the Latin American Revolutions, 1808–1826* (New York: Knopf, 1966), 243–68.

24. David Nicholls, From *Dessalines to Duvalier: Race, Colour and National Independence in Haiti* (Cambridge: Cambridge Univ. Press, 1979).

25. Ibid, 1.

26. The fundamental book for an understanding of this color competition is still James Leyburn, *The Haitian People* (New Haven: Yale Univ. Press, 1941).

27. Micheline Labelle, *Idéologie de couleur et classes sociales en Haiti* (Montreal: Les Presses de l'Université de Montréal, 1987).

28. For the conflict between Colombian whites and Venezuelan black and *mulatto* officers, see A. P. Maingot, "Social Structure, Social Status, and Civil-Military Conflict in Urban Colombia, 1810–1858," in Stephen Thernstrom and Richard Sennett (eds.), *Nineteenth-Century Cities: Essays in the New Urban History* (New Haven: Yale Univ. Press, 1969), 297–356.

29. Cf. Anthony P. Maingot, "Haiti and Aristide: The Legacy of History," *Current History* (Feb. 1992), 65–69.

30. H. Hoetink, *El Pueblo Dominicano, 1850–1900* (Santiago, R.D.: Universidad Catolica Madre y Maestra, 1971).

31. Marcio A. Mejía Ricart, *Las clases sociales en Santo Domingo* (Ciudad Trujillo: Librería Dominicana, 1953), 27–28.

32. Joaquín Balaguer, *Memorias de un cortesano de la "era de Trujillo"* (Santo Domingo: Impresora Sierra, 1988).

33. Ibid., 219–22.

34. Joaquín Balaguer, *La Isla al revés. Haiti y el destino Dominicano*. 6th ed. (Santo Domingo: Editora Corripio, 1990), 230–31.

35. Major exponents of this interpretation in one form or another are R. T. Smith, *British Guiana* (New York: Oxford Univ. Press, 1962); Daniel Crowley, "Cultural Assimilation in a Multicultural Society," and Lloyd Braithwaite, "Social Stratification and Cultural Pluralism," both in Vera Rubin, ed., "Social and Cultural Pluralism in the Caribbean" [special issue] *Annals of the New York Academy of Sciences*, 83 (1960).

36. Clearly the most significant theoretician of this school is M. G. Smith, whose many writings on the subject are available under one cover: *The Plural Society in the British West Indies* (Los Angeles: Univ. of California Press, 1965).

37. Note the similarity to the new North American stress on theories of conflict in M. G. Smith's refinement of his initial "cultural pluralism" approach. Smith recommends that the study of pluralism take into account the relationship between three levels of pluralism: structural, social, and cultural. See his "Analytic Framework of Pluralism," in Leo Kuper and M. G. Smith, (eds.), *Pluralism in Africa* (Berkeley: Univ. of California Press, 1969), 415–58.

38. M. G. Smith, *The Plural Society*, 35.

39. Cf. H. Hoetink, "Curaçao como sociedad segmentada," *Revista de Ciencias Sociales* 4:1 (March 1960), 179–92.

40. Lloyd Braithwaite, "Social Stratification in Trinidad," *Social and Economic Studies*, 2: 2–3, (Oct. 1953), 38–60.

41. Edith Kovats-Beaudoux, "A Dominant Minority: The White Creoles of Martinique," in Lambros Comitas and David Lowenthal (eds.), *Slaves, Free Men, Citizens. West Indian Perspectives* (Garden City, N.Y.: Anchor Press/Doubleday, 1973), 241–75.

42. Cf. Eric Williams, *British Historians and the West Indies* (Port of Spain: PNM Printing, 1964).

43. Ibid, 58.

44. James Anthony Froude, *The English in the West Indies* (New York: Scribner's, 1897), 285.

45. Cited in Donald Wood, "Biographical Note," in J. J. Thomas, *Froudacity* (1889; reprint, London: New Beacon Books, 1969), 19.

46. Frantz Fanon, *The Wretched of the Earth*, trans. Constance Farrington (New York: Grove Press, 1968), 29.

47. Derek Walcott, "The Muse of History: An Essay," in Orde Coombs (ed.), *Is Massa Day Dead?* (New York: Anchor/Doubleday, 1974).

48. Quoted in E. David Cronon, *Black Moses* (Madison: Univ. of Wisconsin Press, 1955), 191–92.

49. The word *négritude* appeared for the first time in print in Aimé Césaire's poem *Cahier d'un retour au pays natal* (Paris: Éditions Présence Africaine, 1947).

50. Gabriel Coulthard, *Race and Colour in Caribbean Literature* (London: Oxford Univ. Press, 1962), 59.

51. See this line of analysis in Patrick Taylor, *The Narrative of Liberation* (Ithaca: Cornell Univ. Press, 1989), 152.

52. Aimé Césaire, "Letter to Maurice Thorez" (Paris, Oct. 24, 1956), translated and published by Éditions Présence Africaine, Paris, 1957.

53. Ivan Oxaal, *Race and Revolutionary Consciousness* (Cambridge, Mass.: Schenkman, 1971), 40.

54. The best collection of photographs of this Curaçao uprising is contained in Edward A. de Jongh, *30 di mei, 1969, e día di mas histórico* (Curaçao: VAD, 1970).

55. The Official Commission of Inquiry report was published under the title *De Meidagen van Curacao* (Willemstad: Algemeen Culturele Maanblad, 1970).

56. René Antonio Romer, Un pueblo na Kaminda. (doctoral diss., Department of Sociology, Univ. of Leiden, June 1977), 179–80.

57. The Official Commission of Inquiry, *De Meidagen,* 187.

58. Cf. Acton Camejo, "Racial Discrimination in Employment in the Private Sector in Trinidad and Tobago: A Study of the Business Elite and the Social Structure," *Social and Economic Studies* (Sept. 1971), 294–318.

59. Government of Trinidad and Tobago, *Interim Report of the Commission of Enquiry into Racial and Colour Discrimination in the Private Sector* (Port of Spain, Trinidad: Government Printing Office, Oct. 1970), 5.

60. Cf. Jack Harewood, "Racial Discrimination in Employment in Trinidad and Tobago," *Social and Economic Studies* (Sept. 1971), 273–80.

61. Government of Trinidad and Tobago Report . . . to Investigate Allegations of Discriminatory Practices by the Management of the Trinidad Country Club (Port of Spain, Trinidad: Government Printing Office, Aug. 29, 1969), 28.

62. *White Paper on Public Participation in Industrial and Commercial Activities* (Port of Spain, Trinidad: Government Printing Office, 1972), 7–8.

63. Cf. Selwyn Ryan (ed.), *Social and Occupational Stratification in Contemporary Trinidad and Tobago* (St. Augustine, Trinidad: Institute of Social and Economic Research, 1991), 77.

64. Cf. Selwyn Ryan, *The Muslimeen Grab for Power. Race, Religion and Revolution in Trinidad and Tobago* (Port of Spain: Inprint, 1991).

65. Cf. Jorge I. Domínguez, Foreword, in Carlos Moore, *Castro, the Blacks and Africa* (Los Angeles: Center for Afro-American Studies, 1988), ix.

66. Moore, *Castro, the Blacks and Africa,* passim.

67. This author takes his cue from James S. Coleman, *Foundations of Social Theory* (Cambridge: Harvard Univ. Press, Belknap Press, 1990).

68. Kenneth Ramchand, *The West Indian Novel and Its Background* (London: Faber and Faber, 1972), 223–36.

69. Caribbean groups carry this capacity for strategic behavior even as they migrate. Cf. A. P. Maingot, "Relative Power and Strategic Ethnicity in Miami," in Ronald J. Samuda and Sandra L. Woods (eds.), *Perspectives in Immigrant Education* (New York: Univ. Press of America, 1983).

70. Cf. H. Hoetink, *The Two Variants of Caribbean Race Relations* (New York: Oxford Univ. Press, 1967).

71. Pedro Andrés Pérez Cabral, *La Comunidad mulata,* (Caracas: Gráfica Americana, 1967), 115.

72. Cf. Fernando Ortiz, *Africanía de la música folklórica de Cuba* (Havana: Artes Gráficos, 1965), 98.

73. Cf. Noel Norton, *Twenty Years of Trinidad Carnival* (Port of Spain: Trinidad and Tobago Insurance Co., 1990), 24.

74. Cf. Deborah Pacini Hernandez, "Merengue from Race to Gender," *Hemisphere* 3 (Summer 1991), 32–33.

75. Lewis, *Main Currents of Caribbean Thought,* 10.

11

Continent on the Move: Immigrants and Refugees in the Americas

M. PATRICIA FERNÁNDEZ KELLY AND
ALEJANDRO PORTES

Introduction

Our purpose in this essay is to summarize salient approaches to migration and relate them to circumstances in which millions of Latin Americans move within their own countries and across international borders. People in movement are a leading force shaping Latin American development; they are also the point at which the structural forces of economic development converge with personal experience.

A phenomenon with major consequences for the continent, migration has been overshadowed in the United States by preoccupations about a possible influx of Latin American people entering the country illegally. Yet the majority of international migrants from Latin America—about 5.3 million every year—move across Latin American borders. In addition, many others move from rural to urban areas in their own countries. Only a small number (300,000–450,000) end up in the United States.

We begin with a summary of perspectives explaining the factors prompting migration. Approaches emphasizing migrants' individual decisions are contrasted with more recent interpretations emphasizing structural factors. The following section reviews the relationships among migration, development, and recent transformations in Latin American cities caused by economic internationalization. The third, fourth, and fifth sections review various types of migration throughout the continent. Special attention is given to labor migration, refugee flows, and the conditions surrounding women migrants. We conclude with a brief account of theoretical and research findings.

The Causes of Migration

Margarito Ramos was only six years old and living with his parents in Santo Domingo Huehuetocan[1] when he realized that someday he would travel to Mexico City. Many of the men in his family had undertaken the journey, returning to Santo Domingo for the yearly festivities honoring the town's patron saint. During those celebrations—filled with the smell of *aguardiente,* the sound of bells, and the varied colors of festooned bulls in cavalcade—Margarito first heard about the reasons that led men away from Santo Domingo. Some had odd explanations, such as the uncle who had been chased out of town by an outraged wife, or the sacristan who had been accused of stealing the temple's relics. But the majority had ordinary stories, and all agreed on one thing: there was no future in Santo Domingo.

If not a future, Santo Domingo certainly had a past. It was a small town located in Oaxaca, a state known for the richness of its pre-Hispanic legacy. In addition to Spanish, nearly 20 indigenous languages were spoken in the region; one of them, Zapotec, was the tongue Margarito had learned in infancy.

Santo Domingo's historical profile is typical of Mexico and much of Latin America. Shaped during the colonial era as part of a rural expanse where subsistence plots coexisted with lavish *haciendas,* the region experienced neglect during the nineteenth century, a period of modernity, urbanization, and industrial growth. The Mexican Revolution of 1910 brought about some changes but not enough to push Santo Domingo out of its torpor. In the 1960s, during the same period that Mexico City grew to become a world-class metropolis as a result of accelerated investment, a few bumpy roads were built in Santo Domingo. As late as 1973, the big news in town concerned the new highway that would, sometime in the future, connect Santo Domingo with the capital city of Oaxaca, enabling *campesinos* to transport their staples with a modicum of efficiency.

Long before that, in 1968, a 20–year-old Margarito began his journey. Twenty hours and three rickety buses later he arrived in Mexico City, where a cousin awaited him with a bag of clothes. Margarito's first act upon arriving was to shed his indigenous dress and don borrowed trousers, shirt, and shoes. The gesture was meant to spare him embarrassment in a country where being an *indio* still carries the burden of stigma. He ended up taking a servant's job in a three-story house built in the middle of a rose garden.

For more than six years, Margarito worked to save money needed to sponsor the yearly festivities in Santo Domingo. But he never returned to live permanently in his hometown. Eventually he married and had several children, built his own modest home in the suburbs of Mexico City, and endured many of the triumphs and tribulations of immigrants in large metropolitan areas. He even became an entrepreneur in his own squatter neighborhood by opening a small *puesto* where he sold meals prepared by his wife, carbonated beverages, and hard-boiled eggs.

With some variations, Margarito's story has been enacted numerous times throughout Latin America. Research on domestic and international migration is a continuing attempt at explaining the causes and consequences of the experience. What then are the factors shaping migration?

For more than three decades, starting in the 1950s, the pivotal contention regarding that question centered on the importance assigned to structure versus human agency. Some scholars tended to view migration as a matter of personal choice. In this view, migrants such as Margarito moved away from their hometowns as a rational course of action based on cost-benefit assessments.[2] This perspective tended to portray migrants in the image of *Homo economicus,* a convenient ideological distortion that did not take into consideration alternative rationalities or contextual factors that diminish the attractiveness of economic gain.[3] There is little doubt that Margarito Ramos hoped for a better life. However, his paramount aspiration in moving to Mexico City was not to succeed in the receiving environment, or to adopt cosmopolitan ways of life, but to muster the cash that would enable him to sponsor a religious festivity in his own town. Achieving that goal, many years later, meant that all his painstakingly accumulated savings were spent in a single week. *Homo economicus* would have been shocked, but to Margarito and his friends and relatives, his newly achieved status had been worth the expense.

Structural approaches recognize that individuals make decisions within varying rational parameters, but they further stress individual action as severely constrained by economic, political, and cultural forces impervious to personal control.[4] In turn, structural approach critics have deplored the tendency to reify social forces and portray individuals as puppets of material imperatives.

At the heart of the debate over structure and agency lay issues of emphasis, balance, and method. The stress on individual choice tended to transform the story of migration into a morality tale in support of "Western values." On the other hand, the reduction of immigrants to an embodiment of structural dynamics tended to flatten variations of interest to science. The most recent analyses attempt to reconcile the "what" represented by personal experience in migration with the "where" of structural context underlying the experience. This too represents an effort to close the gap between microlevel research and large-scale generalization.

The methodological and substantive debate over migration began years ago with modernization theory, which continues to influence migration research even in the last decade of the twentieth century. Modernization approaches emphasize push-pull factors in the large-scale movements of people from mostly rural to urban areas and across international borders. This perspective stresses economic, social, and political factors believed to force individuals to leave their native towns or countries, and a complementary cluster of features attracting them to particular areas.

Push-pull explanations of migration are the natural heirs of orthodox economic theories that define labor as a commodity responding to the laws of supply and demand. For this reason, they emphasize wage differentials between sending and receiving regions. The perception that unlimited supplies of labor will respond in a predictable manner to higher wages in receiving areas implies that migration will occur only as a result of demand. This perception underestimates push factors. However, other explanations do exactly the opposite by overstressing expulsion determinants, including impoverishment, unemployment, underemployment, and even political persecutions that lead individuals to flee their home environments. According to these accounts, migrants are ejected, not attracted, and gravitate even to areas where wages and living conditions are below average by the standards of the host society.

Push-pull explanations have a commonsense appeal that may explain their popularity in scholarly and popular settings. Nevertheless, these accounts of the causes of migration present theoretical and empirical problems. For example, lists of push and pull factors can be drawn up almost invariably after the fact to explain existing flows—in ways similar to those favored by the kind of pop psychologists who can always attribute the problems of adult patients to ad hoc observations about their childhood. In Margarito's case, sketched above, the presence of relatives and other Huehuetocans in Mexico City may have been a more powerful reason for migration than higher wages. His family was poor by urban standards, but it lacked none of the basic resources to meet modest needs. Even poorer villages in Mexico do not eject migrants. And in Margarito's recollection, the aspiration to become a *mayordomo*— that is, a sponsor of the yearly religious festivities in his own hometown—was a major incentive that made tolerable the petty humiliations and low wages gained from employment as a servant in a citified environment.

Thus, neither push nor pull factors can explain why certain individuals, countries, or regions experience certain migratory outcomes while others in similar or even worse conditions do not. In a similar vein, history is filled with examples in which the pull of higher wages has failed to attract immigrants from less-developed regions. Costa Rica and Uruguay are modern examples. In addition, situations abound in which ruling classes have had to resort to conquest and invasion to coerce labor from masses of people unwilling to migrate voluntarily.

The inability of push-pull explanations to provide satisfactory accounts of migration led some authors to propose an alternative interpretation based on deliberate labor recruitment.[5] According to this approach, differential advantages between sending and receiving areas determine only the *potential* for migration. Actual flows start with recruitment on the part of employers seeking workers with certain characteristics and willing to provide stimuli for relocation. Original waves of immigrants thus become the substratum upon which new generations of immigrants build social networks, thus perpetuating flows to particular areas and not to others.

Although recruitment has been a factor shaping migration, not all migrant flows have been the result of recruitment through economic incentives. Many labor migrations, especially those involving undocumented workers, have been initiated without apparent recruitment. The central problem with push-pull and labor recruitment explanations is not that they fail to identify important forces in the process of migration, but that they do not consider the changing historical and economic conditions in which the movement of people takes place.

Another problem with these explanations is their inability to provide an integrated approach to migrating flows that incorporates ethnic, class, and gender diversity issues. For example, wage differentials and monetary incentives can be relatively unimportant in determining the migration of exiles and refugees to areas where they are not welcome or able to integrate into the labor force. The Guatemalans in Mexico illustrate the case. Expelled from their own country by internal strife, the Guatemalans sought sanctuary abroad, only to be confined to camps or isolated from employment because they were both foreign and indigenous. Another example is that of Haitians in the Dominican Republic, who were recruited to work in sugar cane fields but who have difficulty finding more remunerative employment for a variety of reasons, including discrimination based on color and national background. Push-pull approaches obliterate the complexity of these two experiences.

Similar things may be said of migrating women, who historically have constituted the majority of Latin American immigrants. The conditions leading wives and mothers to migrate, with or without children and husbands, are intricate and often only indirectly related to higher wages and other benefits. Emphasizing wages and economic incentives assumed to be advantageous to individual workers obscures migration's collective nature and the migrant's actual costs of relocation and settlement. The monetary benefits derived from higher wages cannot be seen in isolation from the cost of living—labor reproduction—to migrants in receiving areas. Variations in marital status and household organization must be considered. Single women and female heads of households are often impelled by economic needs similar to those felt by men. But the migration of wives who assume key household responsibilities, many of whom join the labor force in receiving areas, can be explained more effectively by focusing on the labor reproducing requirements of domestic units, rather than on higher wages.

A review of the limitations of modernization approaches to migration highlights a broader theoretical issue. Underlying the notions of push and pull factors is the premise that migrants move from relatively bounded spaces—rural areas characterized by poverty and lack of opportunity—to relatively bounded spaces—urban areas or richer countries distinguished by precisely the opposite traits. From the push-pull perspective, migration occurs between independent socioeconomic units: one that supplies labor and one that receives it. The possibility that such flows may actually be part of a broader system to which both units belong is not usually considered.

Our view is that migration in general, and that in Latin America in particular, takes place not *between* independent economic systems but *within* systems whose various sectors have experienced differing types and levels of private and public investment. Historically, these sectors have been related through unequal economic exchanges, between households and labor markets, rural and urban sectors, and underdeveloped and advanced industrialized countries. If independent economic systems existed in the world—a proposition increasingly denied by global interdependence—migration would tend *not* to occur between them, given the absence of mechanisms promoting unequal exchanges. Conversely, migration within the components of the same economic system is shaped by unequal exchange. Thus, migrants walk across the invisible bridges created by particular capital flows and political linkages.

An implication of this proposition is that the abandonment of towns such as Santo Domingo Huehuetocan is part of a larger reorganization that has enabled cities such as Mexico to grow and prosper at the expense of the countryside. Concentrating political and economic power in urban areas has been predicated on subordinating the rural sector. Migration is, therefore, a nonrandom outcome determined by the logic of the productive system. The economy's increasing globalization since the 1970s has sharpened the profile of this process. Intensive capitalist penetration in the Latin American countryside has produced or accentuated social and economic imbalances, which, in turn, have resulted in outward migration. Outward migration occurs more frequently in areas affected by capital-intensive investment in agricultural or mining production.

One example will suffice to illustrate this point. Research on the characteristics of the labor force employed in export-processing plants, or *maquiladoras,* in Ciudad Juárez, Chihuahua, revealed a large number of immigrant women from San Francisco del Oro, a mining and agricultural town in the southern portion of the same state. Throughout the twentieth century, North American companies such as John Deere invested heavily in this area. Mechanization, the virtual elimination of subsistence cultivation, and the rise of commercial crops displaced large numbers of agricultural workers. As a result, many San Franciscan families migrated to Ciudad Juárez during the 1950s and 1960s. Their hope was to situate themselves in a city allowing men easy access to the United States. But it was the daughters of those potential undocumented aliens who ended up working in the *maquiladoras* when these processing plants began booming in the early 1970s.

This case and other examples suggest that, from the immigrant's view, the pull from advanced economies is not based primarily on invidious comparisons of advantage with the outside world. The answer lies more in seeing migration as a partial solution to historically created and otherwise insoluble problems within the sending regions.

The changing character of push and pull factors, the obsolescence of labor recruitment, and the "spontaneous" character of recent migration flows are all consequences of an international economy and the shifting ways that countries incorporate into it. Two flows must thus be recognized as part of an integrated circuit of global production: the first is formed by currents of capital investment flowing from central economies to less-developed areas in search of less costly and more flexible production conditions; the second flow is formed by labor moving from less-developed countries to areas initiating capital investments.[6] The complementary nature of labor and capital flows underscores the significance of the social, political, and economic arrangements over which individuals have no direct control—the larger structural constraints—in Latin American development trends. In the next section we summarize recent changes in these trends, particularly as they refer to urbanization, labor markets, and the informal economy.

Migrants, Development, and the Changing Latin American City

Urbanization patterns in Latin America and the Caribbean have followed the course of development and migration. The quickening departure of people from rural areas has accelerated the growth of cities. As a result, rates of urban expansion have exceeded those of the total population in every country. For the most part, the continent is now one of urban dwellers. Between 1960 and 1970, the proportion of Latin American and Caribbean people living in cities increased from 32.5 percent to 40 percent; 76 percent of the urban population lived in cities of 100,000 or more.[7] With some fluctuations, migration continued during the 1980s, although its direction changed. Smaller cities, characterized by the growth of export-processing platforms, became new destinations for migrants in search of employment.

Migration is often portrayed as a problem. As squatters and street vendors, migrants are said to debase working conditions and create onerous demands on crowded cities. Moreover, migration is said to create vacuums in the countryside and to deplete rural economies. Despite this negative view, migration's real or imagined advantages are shared by several social groups, one of which is the migrants themselves. Within the limitations of underdeveloped economies, where opportunities for paid rural employment are few, migration to the city emerges as a reasonable, and sometimes the only, alternative. Migrants go to large cities seeking economic opportunities, if not in the formal economy, at least in the expanding informal sector.

In addition, private manufacturing and service firms benefit from migration in several ways. First, migrants expand, albeit in a limited manner, the demand for products such as staples, inexpensive clothing, and cheap entertainment. Second, sustained migration provides an ample supply of labor, which maintains low wages. Third, and perhaps most important, migrants involved in the informal sector often initiate small businesses. As subcontracted shopkeepers, industrial home workers, and service providers, they further reduce the cost of production for established companies.

Rural-urban migration also benefits landowners by providing a safety valve that relieves pressure on the land and deflates political mobilization and conflict. Moreover, urban masses of migrants have been vitally important to governments and political parties, which have used them to activate social movements and further their own political aims.

Finally, considerable evidence suggests that sending areas don't always lose population or suffer permanent economic stagnation as a result of migration. The occupational skills and savings accumulated by city migrants are often invested in places of origin, giving new life to local economies and attracting populations from other areas. While rural stagnation is one factor leading to migration, it need not be accentuated by population outflows.

Latin American migrants have followed paths similar to those in U.S. cities. The poor rent quarters in the decaying fringes surrounding urban centers. This type of housing—variously called *vecindades, conventillos, solares, ciudades perdidas,* or *cités*—has proved insufficient to accommodate new migrants. In turn, the scarcity of affordable housing has led to violations in zoning and land ownership structure. The result has been the emergence of squatter settlements and illegal invasions by migrants. In urban squatter settlements, migrants often construct their own homes, thus claiming urban spaces and relieving governments of the need to provide subsidized housing. In this respect, the informal economy encompasses not only activities in manufacturing and services but also construction work that addresses immigrants' reproductive necessities.[8]

Most migrants don't flow directly into impoverished squatter settlements. Rather, they tend first to seek shelter in established low-rent neighborhoods. However, the effect of rural-urban migration has been to drive up working-class rents, putting pressure both on migrants and on the city-born. At the same time, even modest housing for sale has become financially beyond the reach of these groups. Over time, even more established workers are unable to move out of rental housing into their own, legally purchased homes. The proliferation of illegal settlements has thus different causes: they are created by the poorest groups, migrant and city-born, seeking minimal shelter in the city, as well as by more established workers in search of some form of home ownership.

Contrary to the views promulgated by the media, Latin American squatter settlements are not necessarily hotbeds of unemployment. Between the 1960s and 1980 the proportion of unemployed in squatter settlements was consistently low and generally no higher than that of the total urban labor force. Unemployment is a luxury few can afford. Moreover, peripheral settlements are not inhabited only by the poorest of the poor. Rather, they are characterized by a variety of occupations and classes.

For example, a 1983 survey of Caracas "marginal" settlements found unemployment to be 9.1 percent, lower than for the city as a whole. Self-employment, a typical feature of the informal sector, accounted for 13.6 percent of total employment. The majority of those employed, 56.3 percent, were workers in manufacturing, services, and transportation. Even more surprising was that white-collar employees represented 27 percent of the working population surveyed. Of these, 16.2 percent worked in private firms and 10.8 percent in government.[9]

Another representative study of four peripheral *poblaciónes* in Santiago, Chile in the early 1970s found that 13 percent of family heads had white-collar jobs in government or private enterprises. An additional 45 percent were employed as skilled and semiskilled workers in established firms. Declared unemployment was only 6 percent, not very different from that of the Santiago labor force at the time.

These two cases suggest that squatter settlements with large numbers of immigrants need not be characterized by economic stagnation. Rather, what characterizes these neighborhoods is *poverty in employment:* wages paid to immigrant workers were often below those required to meet basic consumption needs, including minimal shelter.

In general, the depiction of squatter settlements as breeders of unemployment did not correspond to the reality of Latin American cities in the 1960s and 1970s. However, the situation changed dramatically in the following decade. The 1980s brought to Latin America its worst economic crisis since the Great Depression. The per capita regional GNP declined for the first time in 40 years.[10]

Latin American cities had varying responses to the crisis. However, three similarities are noteworthy. First, class-based spatial polarization was accentuated in some cases and underwent sudden reversals in others. In Santiago, Chile, for example, the Pinochet regime's monetarist economic policies and iron-fist measures led to a clear division of the urban space, with the impoverished, many of them immigrants, living on the periphery. The cases of Bogotá and Montevideo were different. There, under less authoritarian regimes, working-class groups hard hit by rising levels of unemployment sought proximity to affluent neighborhoods at the same time that equally hard-hit members of the middle class scrambled to find low-cost housing in working-class and immigrant neighborhoods.[11]

Second, there was a decline in the mid-1980s in urban primacy—a secular tendency in Latin America consisting of the accelerated growth of a few cities resulting from early investments in import-substitution industrialization. The decline was not primarily due to fertility drops. Instead, new investments in export-oriented manufacturing transformed smaller Latin American cities into destinations for new waves of migrants. In some cases, the 1980s economic crisis led to a reversal of migratory flows, from large cities to smaller urban centers and townships. In others it led to new waves of rural-urban migrants flowing to midsize cities characterized by export-oriented industrialization. For example, Ciudad Juárez, long known as the cradle of the *maquiladora* industry, witnessed the accelerated arrival of new immigrants from rural areas devastated by economic strife. These immigrants, the majority of whom were men, rushed to fill vacancies in the *maquiladoras* created by apparent shortages of female labor. That, as well as diversification in production, led to a partial gender recomposition of the labor force. While young urban women—the preferred *maquiladora* workers—coped with economic crisis by seeking higher wages as domestics in U.S. border cities, the vacuum created by their departure was filled by recently arrived male immigrants.

Third, the growth of declared unemployment resulting from economic crisis altered the relationship between the cities' formal and informal sectors. It is commonly believed that illegal economic activities expand in the absence of growth and employment opportunities in the formal sector. In fact, the informal sector tends to expand in Latin America at times of accelerated economic growth. Such was the case during the 1960s and 1970s when industrial output throughout the continent expanded rapidly at the same time that self-employment and unregulated economic activities also grew.

Part of the explanation for the two sectors' parallel expansion lies in the links created by subcontracting. As formal companies augment their activities, they seek ways to lower production costs and avoid government regulation. Subcontracting to informal shops allows investors to diffuse the economic and political risks of production. Immigrants tend to be heavily represented in informal operations linked by subcontracting to the formal sector. The latest recession modified the informal economy's profile, reducing its symbiotic relationship to the formal sector and increasing its raw survival features. The economic crisis also forced many immigrant and working-class households to expand, as men and women sought to reduce rent expenditures by doubling up, and as women incorporated relatives to care for their children while they pursued informal employment.[12]

The tendencies observed in the last decade point to the importance of studying migration in relation to larger economic and political changes. During the first half of the twentieth century, the absence of economic opportunities in the countryside and import-substitution industrialization drove millions of rural families into a few major cities—a phenomenon known as primate urbanization. Industries were unable to absorb all the city-born and immigrant workers. Likewise, the regulated housing market was unable to meet the shelter needs of the rapidly growing population, which led to the self-construction of shelter by the urban poor in unregulated settlements. In the 1980s, debt crises, the movement toward export-processing manufacturing, and the deregulation of national economies altered the profile of migration, as well as the relationship between immigrant workers and the formal economic sector.

Types of Latin American Migration

At least two kinds of flows must be distinguished in the study of Latin American migration. The first is formed by population streams from rural areas and towns into urban centers within the same country. This is primarily a migration of working men and women seeking opportunities at the lower levels of the occupational structure and in the informal sector.

The second type of flow encompasses people from rural areas and/ or cities who move to foreign locations within Latin America. A variant of this type is formed by the expanding masses of refugees seeking asylum. Diversity is the most prominent characteristic of population flows throughout the region. In recent years sizable migrations have included (a) refugees escaping political upheavals in their home countries, (b) highly skilled professionals in search of better opportunities abroad, and (c) manual workers—legal and undocumented—filling labor shortages in the country of destination. Even within these categories, the specific characteristics of migrant flows and their complexity defy generalization. Without being exhaustive, a summary of international currents from Latin America and the Caribbean in the last two decades would include:

1. Labor migrations from Chile, Bolivia, Paraguay, and Uruguay to Argentina, each having different origins, destination and purposes
2. Professional migration from Chile to Mexico
3. Professional and technical migration from Argentina, Colombia, the Dominican Republic, and the English-speaking Caribbean to the United States, Europe, and the rest of Latin America

4. Political refugee flows from Cuba to the United States and Puerto Rico, and from Guatemala, Argentina, Chile, and Uruguay to Mexico, the United States, and Europe
5. Rural contract labor from Haiti to the Dominican Republic and from Mexico to the United States and Canada
6. Undocumented labor flows, both rural- and urban-bound from Colombia to Venezuela and Ecuador, from El Salvador to Honduras, and from Mexico, the Dominican Republic, Haiti, Colombia, and Central America to the United States

Other finer distinctions also merit mention. The specific reasons leading workers to migrate may or may not be different from those explaining refugees' expulsion or professionals' departure. Finally, the conditions surrounding women migrants, both domestically and internationally, differ from those of male migrants. Below we examine the circumstances surrounding three groups of migrants, each reflecting a particular form of population outflow in relation to national and international economic and political realities. Our focus is on labor migration, refugees, and women migrants.

Labor in Migration: The Case of Colombians in Venezuela

The most prevalent form of population outflow throughout Latin America (and the world) is that of workers seeking better jobs. But for most of its history, Colombia did not eject migrants. Instead, highly selective governmental policies were aimed to attract foreigners. Arrivals, principally from Europe and the United States, were encouraged since the late nineteenth century as a way to diversify the country's cultural and racial composition, while at the same time consolidating new classes of professionals and skilled technicians. By the early 1950s, Colombia, as well as other less developed countries, was concerned about demographic growth resulting from its own internal expansion. The government curtailed the open immigration policies promoted in the past.

This shift in perspective coincided with the advent of industrialization and modernization. As in other Latin American countries, mechanization in agricultural production fostered labor displacement, which, in turn, took the form of rural-urban migration. As the situation grew critical in the late 1960s, more Colombians sought alternatives in other countries.

The migratory relationship between Colombia and Venezuela is noteworthy because it demonstrates international flows changing direction following a specific date, as a result of changing economic conditions. Before 1945, Colombia's relatively high development levels attracted a significant number of Venezuelan migrants. However, economic growth in Venezuela after the Second World War, as well as Colombia's economic deterioration, led to a reversal in migration currents between the two countries.

As important as the factors generating the supply of workers were the conditions creating labor demand. After the 1930s, the importance of coffee and cacao agriculture diminished in Venezuela. Oil gradually became the focus of economic activity. By 1926 oil accounted for about 53 percent of all Venezuelan exports. Ten years later oil production had trebled to make up 92 percent of all export revenues.[13]

Since the 1950s, the Venezuelan government directed a good part of the profits generated by oil exports toward highly lucrative but speculative finance, construction, and commercial transactions. For the most part, a vast infrastructure created to provide services and luxury commodities benefited affluent groups. Industry and agriculture were neglected. The boom in oil production enabled the continued importation of capital and consumer goods including raw materials and food. By 1958 half the internal demand for agricultural products was met through imports.

The imbalances resulting from this state of affairs propelled migration and urban growth. More than 67 percent of Venezuela's total population lived in cities by 1961. The rate of urban growth reached 28.6 percent between 1950 and 1960, surpassing urban growth rates throughout Latin America.

During the 1960s, new public and private investments in agriculture, particularly in sugar cane production, generated demand for unskilled, mobile, and highly replaceable seasonal labor. Colombian migrants, many of them illegal, became a vital source of this type of labor. In other words, the vacuum in the countryside—created by internal migrants seeking city employment resulting from oil-related activity—was filled by Colombians. In addition, Colombian migrants mingled with Venezuelans in cities where, as sweatshop assemblers, service providers, and domestic servants, they contributed to the expansion of the informal economy.

The counterpart of this process had taken place in Colombia during the first half of the twentieth century. Modernization had started in that country during the mid-1920s, stirred to a large extent by the occupation of the Panama Canal. Later, industrialization resulted in massive construction of highways and railroad tracks, and in the concentration of economic resources in a few major cities. Combined with stagnation in the agricultural sector, this process laid the foundation for patterns of sustained rural-urban migration. However, industrial growth failed to absorb most displaced labor. Progressive mechanization in the countryside enriched large landowners but resulted in major dislocations among agricultural workers. To give one example, only 3,821 tractors were being used in agricultural production in 1938. By 1956 there were 16,493 in use. This process of mechanization freed up a mass of individuals seeking employment alternatives in factories and service establishments near cities.

Urban growth followed. In 1938 only 27 cities in Colombia had between 10,000 and 50,000 inhabitants. Urbanites composed 30.9 percent of the total population in Colombia. By 1951 the figure had grown to 38.7 percent; in 1964 it was 52.1 percent, and it had grown to 63.6 percent in 1973. In the mid-1980s more than 36 percent of the total population in Colombia was concentrated in cities of more than 100,000 inhabitants.[14]

In addition to accelerated modernization, industrialization, and urbanization, major political factors stirred population flows. Toward the mid-1940s and throughout the 1950s, sectarianism and intransigence led to *La Violencia,* a period of violent internal struggle that threatened to paralyze productive activity and resulted in the deaths of more than 100,000 people. Displaced rural workers sought refuge in Colombian cities or abroad.

Since the 1940s, Colombian migration has been directed to a few neighboring and distant countries. Venezuela, the United States, Ecuador, and Panama have the largest concentrations of Colombian migrants, a sizable proportion of whom are illegal or undocumented. As a result, only estimates of the total number of Colombians in each of the four countries are available. In the early 1980s approximately 350,000 Colombians were living in the United States, perhaps up to 65,000 in Ecuador, and, in the case of greatest interest to us here, between 200,000 and 500,000 in Venezuela. By the beginning of the 1990s, Colombians living in the United States numbered approximately 500,000. The number of Colombians in Ecuador and Venezuela experienced a less spectacular growth, to 80,000 and 650,000 respectively.

The sustained character of migration from Colombia to Venezuela resulted in bilateral legislation to regulate the phenomenon. Colombian authorities have generally taken a passive approach, with tension between the two countries rising intermittently. Since 1965 Venezuela has been deporting increasing numbers of Colombians to their places of origin.

Surveys conducted among deported Colombian workers apprehended in Venezuela during the late 1970s and early 1980s found this type of migration to be highly selective. As with similar examples from other countries, those who migrate looking for work do not belong to the unemployed or poorest sectors. Rather, most undocumented Colombian migrants tend to have had jobs at the time of their departure. The majority are young and eager to work long, hard hours.

Colombian migrants in Venezuela are predominantly male; women account for less than 17 percent. Almost 66 percent are between 20 and 29 years of age, while approximately 89 percent are younger than

30. Two-thirds are single, and about 61 percent are childless. Although the majority (73.5 percent) have six or fewer years of schooling, a sizable proportion (25.8 percent) have completed at least eight years of schooling or more; only 5 percent have technical or professional expertise. More than a third of these migrants (35.9 percent) came from the rural sector after being self-employed (32.4 percent) or wage agricultural laborers; 27.2 percent worked as operatives in factories or services, while 17.6 percent were involved in craft production, sales, or white-collar jobs. The important point is that, by and large, Colombian immigrants tended to be employed before leaving their country, although in less than satisfactory jobs.[15]

These migrants illustrate the relationship between earnings and normative standards of consumption as a central factor leading to migration. Fifty-three percent of those interviewed credited low earnings and the difficulty of reaching a minimum level of comfort—not unemployment—as the reason for moving to Venezuela. Other reasons, particularly among immigrant women, included the desire to travel and the need to join spouses or relatives who had previously migrated.

Although most immigrants make independent decisions to move, they rely on generally accurate information provided by tightly woven networks to pattern their immediate future. This is evidenced by the ease and rapidity with which they get jobs after arriving in the receiving areas; about 30.2 percent of those leaving Colombia in the early 1980s had reliable information about where they could find employment in Venezuela. Sixty-seven percent found a job in that country within a week of their arrival, and less than 3 percent needed more than three weeks to find a job.

Like other international sojourners, Colombian migrants flow to receiving countries in response to the needs and demands of those areas. However, they face contradictory reactions: on the one hand, they are preferred as a labor pool by employers wishing to lower production costs and maintain a flexible work force; on the other hand, immigrants bear the stigma of their undocumented status. They are seen as purveyors of decay, and as unfair competitors with native-born workers.

The stigma attached to this type of migration stands in apparent contrast to the facility with which undocumented workers find jobs in the receiving countries. Yet, most authors agree, their legal vulnerability largely explains their attractiveness in certain niches of the labor market. Fearful of deportation, incapable of claiming citizen rights in a foreign country, and willing to work long and hard shifts for modest wages, these workers provide an extremely advantageous form of labor; the contradiction between stigma and employability is only apparent.

Refugees in Migration: The Case of Central Americans in Mexico

The previous examples illustrate paradoxes faced by groups of workers whose decision to cross international borders can be explained by economic imbalances nationally and internationally. The experience of refugees seeking asylum in foreign countries differs in significant ways from other forms of migration. At the same time, it illustrates the close relationship between political and economic factors leading to population movements. Many refugees are impelled by political factors such as war and repression. For many others, political vulnerability is combined with desperate poverty.

Violence in Central America during the 1980s displaced an unprecedented number of people. Most displaced individuals remain within their own countries. However, hundreds of thousands have fled to neighboring nations and to the United States. To cite one figure, by 1985 approximately 250,000 Central Americans were seeking protection from the pervasive turmoil of their homelands by migrating to Mexico.

Contrary to widespread perceptions, Central America's strife and economic dislocation is not the result of a history of economic and political atrophy. Obsolete institutional arrangements and antiquated production systems existed for many decades without perceptible popular mobilization, repression, or population outflows.

Economic growth and diversification characterized Central America in the years following the Second World War. Six nations (Guatemala, El Salvador, Honduras, Nicaragua, Costa Rica, and Panama) averaged an annual growth rate of 5.3 percent between 1950 and 1978, and real per capita income doubled. Economic vitality was enhanced by foreign aid. Between 1962 and 1980 the United States alone provided more than $2 billion in aid to Central America.[16]

But economic growth did not bring about improvements in the standard of living for most Central Americans. Instead, wealth was increasingly concentrated in the hands of a few. El Salvador represents an extreme case of class intransigence. For several centuries, a minority has controlled vital resources amid impoverished peasants. By the 1970s, 2 percent of the population owned 60 percent of the land. This figure alone goes a long way to explain popular mobilization and guerrilla warfare. Growing disparities in income distribution accompanied distorted processes of urbanization. Modernization led to serious imbalances and to population movements away from rural areas. Throughout the early 1980s Central America's poorest 20 percent received only 3.7 percent of total income, or about $90 per capita per year. The wealthiest 20 percent received seven times that amount.

In addition to economic disparities, the region experienced considerable population growth, with the total number of people living in the region tripling between 1950 and 1985, from 9.1 to 26.4 million. During the period of economic growth, the number of jobs increased in accordance with the number of people entering the labor force each year. However, a dramatic change took place during the mid-1970s with the onset of the global recession, and unemployment and underemployment escalated in the cities and countryside. Acute land concentration, combined with mechanization and the emergence of a modern, mechanized agricultural sector, further accentuated social and economic inequalities. These in turn caused a reduction in food produced for local consumption and led to a need to use scarce foreign exchange for imported basic resources.

In a nutshell, the crisis characterizing Central America during the 1980s was the result of the emergence of new groups, whose rising expectations were in radical conflict with archaic institutions. The capitalization of agriculture and urban industrial growth led to the formation of new workers' organizations. At first, these movements sought reform through peaceful means in Nicaragua, El Salvador, and Guatemala in the early 1970s. However, these efforts were blocked by powerful groups aided by military forces, sending many popular leaders and activists into exile. Fueled by the world recession, unrest escalated at the same time the cost of living rose and jobs became scarce. Violence became the daily fare in Central America, prompting thousands of displaced individuals to seek sanctuary in neighboring countries. Most feared poverty as well as possible death.

The extreme conditions faced by many of these refugees in their home countries have not ensured a welcome reception in their destination areas. Central Americans have become the object of a vigorous debate about the distinction between "political" and "economic" migrants. In the United States dissidents from Communist nations were steadily welcomed for many decades, but there has been reluctance to accept émigrés from allied, non-Communist regimes, even when they confront evident dangers after deportation. Similar contradictions are apparent in Latin America, as evidenced by the tense reception of Central Americans in Mexico.

The paradox may be understood by distinguishing two types of refugees. When refugee movements are formed by elites, their presence in a receiving country poses no problem, provided political relations between sending and receiving nations are amiable. Problems arise when working-class and indigenous peoples move en masse across international borders, presenting imaginary and real challenges to the receiving society. Economies burdened by their own internal limitations can hardly absorb new entrants into the labor force; social service networks are likewise burdened by the demands of the new arrivals. Refugee status is thus a privilege based on class membership. So-called economic refugees are trapped in situations where the political and economic factors that foster migration are difficult to separate.

In the case of Central Americans, employment opportunities and international wage differentials surely play a role in determining the directionality of migration. At the same time, it is misleading to single out economic motivation as the only or even predominant cause for Central Americans' flight from their homelands since the late 1970s. As Leonel Gómez, an observer of the Salvadoran situation, explains: "When places of work close as a result of strikes, when roads and bridges are bombed and crops are burned, when thousands of people are forced to leave their homes in terror, the consequences may be economic, but the final cause is political." [17]

Although they share some features, refugee movements are different from other forms of population outflow in four respects: (1) the decision to leave is imposed by conditions totally out of the control of the individual, family, or group; (2) relocation is thus perceived as temporary and reversible; (3) relocation is not directly related to personal or collective aspirations for better income, employment, or education; and (4) this kind of migration always involves the search for protection and movement to a different country.

An example of the blurring distinction between economic and political factors leading to migration is that of Guatemalan and Salvadoran refugees in Mexico. Mexico has historically followed a liberal asylum policy. After the fall of Salvador Allende in 1973, the Luis Echeverría government repeatedly approved the use of air vessels to transport Chilean exiles from Mexico City. Many of these exiles later gained acceptance as professors in higher education institutions. However, during the 1980s, when more than 250,000 Salvadorans and Guatemalans fled to Mexico as a result of turmoil in their own countries, the Mexican government followed an ambivalent policy that sought to maintain an image of hospitality while simultaneously trying to prevent the dispersion of the new arrivals throughout the country.

Guatemalan migratory flows fall into several categories. Two types deserve special attention here: laborers who have relocated to the Soconusco area in Chiapas (southern Mexico), and indigenous peasants who since 1980 have been clustered in refugee camps. Traditional economic migration to the Soconusco coffee plantations has regularly brought between 50,000 and 65,000 Guatemalans to southern Mexico to perform seasonal labor. Under normal circumstances, these workers return to their villages at the end of the harvest. In the 1980s, the mass of migrants living in the Soconusco by far surpassed the traditional numbers, and, unlike previous flows, they included women and children. While some of these migrants may have initially arrived looking for work, they have postponed their return indefinitely due to disruptions in their own towns. Others there are trying to escape persecution.

The majority have relatives or friends who have already been killed by rebels or government forces. None of these groups have been recognized as refugees, nor do they receive international assistance. They live as part of the local population in fear of being returned to Guatemala by Mexican authorities, since they are residing illegally in Mexico.

In 1985 there were upwards of 100,000 Guatemalans living in the Soconusco. Another 50,000 lived in border camps in Chiapas. This population, which originated in the western Guatemalan highlands, is now distributed in more than 80 camps located in distant and often inaccessible areas where assistance is difficult. Only religious organizations, particularly the Catholic Church, have been successful in providing vital help. According to the United Nations high commissioner for refugees, Guatemalans in southern Mexican camps are by and large peasants, a high percentage of whom are women "who arrived in poor conditions and are living in a state of extreme deprivation."[18] The majority are indigenous, illiterate, and speak native languages; only a few speak Spanish.

Refugees living in camps depend almost completely on the Mexican government (and some religious organizations) for food, housing, and services. Camp conditions have exposed the Mexican government to criticism from domestic and foreign sources. Moreover, the camps are a constant source of tension between Mexico and Guatemala. During the mid-1980s several violent confrontations erupted along the border, and Mexicans as well as refugees were killed by Guatemalan security forces chasing presumed guerrillas crossing the border into Mexico.

Refugees living in camps are less skilled than the average worker in Guatemala. A survey conducted in 1987 in six small camps sheltering more than 1,000 Guatemalans found that 51 percent were women and 54.4 percent were under 15 years of age. Of the adult men, 87 percent worked in agriculture and the rest were skilled in a trade. All had arrived from border villages since 1983. Another survey in a different camp in Chiapas where almost 3,500 refugees lived in 1987 showed that more than half were children under 10 years of age. The predominance of women and children in southern Mexican refugee camps shows that they are not primarily labor migrants. Their characteristics differ markedly from those prevalent among most working-class Latin American immigrants. In addition, the majority of those living in camps do not hold jobs, although many have tried to get some form of employment.

More than a third of Guatemalans in camps do not have any formal education, and the rest have fewer than six years of schooling. Perhaps more revealing is the fact that more than 77 percent of all Guatemalan refugees in camps studied to date are married couples. This means that the Guatemalan exodus has involved whole-family migration for political rather than purely economic reasons.

In addition to Guatemalan refugees waiting uncertainly on the Mexican border, others can be found in Mexico City, Guadalajara, Monterrey, and other urban centers. This group may number as many as 125,000 people. Like the Guatemalans in border camps, they are not recognized as refugees either. However, this is a very different population from that in the camps. Guatemalans living in Mexican cities are generally older, predominantly male, and better educated than average.

Another large group of refugees seeking shelter in Mexico are Salvadorans. Although the Mexican government reports 120,000 living in the country, this estimate has not changed since 1982. Other sources offer much higher numbers. For example, the Salvadoran embassy in Mexico calculates that there were approximately 500,000 Salvadorans in Mexico in 1985. Forty percent were in transit to the United States and Canada. Salvadorans concentrate mostly in Mexico City, Guadalajara, Monterrey, and other large cities. About 4,000 Salvadorans have been granted asylum. The rest are considered economic migrants who face difficulties in finding employment and possible deportation.[19]

In general, Salvadorans in Mexico tend to be males from urban and semiurban areas. Many have experience as union organizers, agricultural workers, teachers, and activists. The majority are young, as shown by a survey conducted by the Mexican Friends Services Committee of 495 Salvadorans living in Mexico City in 1985. Of 317 men interviewed, 77 percent were between the ages of 16 and 30; of 158 women interviewed, 62 percent belonged to the same age group. The same study showed 72 percent were unemployed; 34 percent had some elementary education; 30 percent had had secondary education; only 19 percent had finished high school; and 6 percent held university degrees.[20]

Other studies have confirmed the general profile outlined above and added a finding in contrast to the profile of Guatemalan refugees confined in camps: nearly half of Salvadorans living in Mexican cities are single. Not surprisingly, then, 96 percent of them come from urban areas. About 44 percent have skills in carpentry, mechanics, electrical work, nursing, and other similar trades; another 21 percent have worked in agriculture. As with other refugees living in Mexico, Salvadorans experience high rates of unemployment; fewer than 10 percent report having a job. Those who were employed in 1984 reported earning wages below 15 dollars a week. More than a third had not worked in Mexico at all since their arrival.

Guatemalans and Salvadorans represent two examples of the fusion between the economic and political determinants of international migration. The flight from terror in their own homelands, and the less than enthusiastic reception that awaits them in receiving areas, invests the experience of Central American refugees with a specially troubling dimension.

Women in Migration

Most migration studies have focused on male workers, the assumption being that large population outflows are composed predominantly of men seeking improved employment conditions in different cities or countries. As far as women are concerned, it is assumed that they remain in sending areas, caring for subsistence plots, homes, and children. A variant of this interpretation has portrayed women only as wives and mothers who eventually follow their male spouses or relatives in migration.

A surge of scholarship focusing on women over the last decade and a half has revised this simplistic profile of women on the move. It has become apparent that the massive increase in the global female labor force is to a large extent the result of female migration. Structural changes in major economies and the shift from manufacturing to services have further enhanced the demand for female labor, leading many women to migrate, both domestically and internationally.

Despite the global economy's major changes, which have created conditions for an increase in female migration, women migrants are not a new phenomenon. England's Industrial Revolution was based largely on employing migrants who had moved to cities seeking work after being displaced from the countryside. Many of these immigrants were women seeking jobs in new industries or as domestics in the homes of the wealthy. In a similar vein, Irish women outnumbered Irish men in the historical stream that brought them to the United States. According to Seller: "Women came . . . to escape the economic, political, and religious oppression that all immigrants faced in their native lands, but many also came to escape forms of oppression unique to them as women. . . . Some fled sexual harassment, others unequal wages and conditions that were more difficult than those endured by their male counterparts."[21] Thus, in addition to factors generally prompting migration, women have had special reasons, unique to their sex, for moving away from their homes and communities.[22]

In ways similar to those that precipitated nineteenth-century migration, a large rural-urban stream of people is now moving throughout developing countries. In some places it is mostly men who move to cities looking for work. However, in Latin America women have outnumbered men in the search for city jobs. The majority have found employment as domestic servants.

Women also make up a large proportion of international migrants, as part of families or on their own. Earlier we pointed out that most Guatemalan refugees on Mexico's southern border are women. Similarly, more women than men migrate from the Caribbean to the United States and Canada. For many migrant women, life in the city represents a clear improvement over conditions they left behind; for the majority, however, life in the receiving areas is fraught with contradictions, ranging from cultural shock to job discrimination. Migrant women are often found among the poorest of the poor, triply burdened by race/ethnicity, class, and sexual inequality.

What are the conditions surrounding women's migration? Although reliable figures on magnitude and configuration are scarce, several distinct cases of Latin American women migrants can be pinpointed. In addition to the migration of professional women—about which virtually nothing is known—two other groups deserve special attention: one formed by family members accompanying or following relatives, and another consisting of women migrating alone or with dependent children.

There is an abundance of aggregate and descriptive data, but a paucity of qualitative research about women who move as part of families and who have not initiated migration. The few sources that provide in-depth profiles suggest circumstances belying the image of women as mere followers. Patricia Pessar, for example, has documented differences between male and female Dominican immigrants in New York. In this case, women who have experienced social and economic gains as a result of their migration may in fact wish to remain abroad, while their husbands are strongly motivated to return to their native countries.[23]

Other authors have pointed to the influence women wield as advocates of family reunification policies and movements. Still others have emphasized the transformation of sex roles or women's labor force participation that may accompany relocation from less developed to more advanced industrial nations such as the United States. Foner notes, for example, that Jamaican women value the greater family orientation their husbands acquire in immigrant contexts.[24]

A striking example of changes in female labor force participation resulting from migration is represented by Cuban exiles in southern Florida. Prior to Fidel Castro's revolution, Cuban women had one of the continent's lowest rates of labor force participation. Nevertheless, once in the United States, Cuban women rapidly reached a higher rate of participation than any other ethnic group, including native-born Caucasian women. The incorporation of Cuban exile women into the labor force was an important factor leading to the formation of a prosperous economic enclave in southern Florida.[25]

Women who move as part of families still predominate in international migratory streams from Latin America. However, the majority of internal migrants in the continent move alone, often with small children. Sometimes the woman leaves first, either to establish a beachhead for other family members, or to search for a better life for herself and her children, if she has lost a male partner, or is young and single and wants to help her family left behind. The Salvadorans in Washington, D.C., illustrate female-led migration. Since the early 1970s, representatives of international organizations and embassies in Washington began recruiting Salvadoran women for domestic employment. Many of these women were later joined by children and husbands. As a result of internal conflict during the 1980s, a new wave, formed primarily by Salvadoran men, flowed to Washington, D.C., and became employed in the booming construction industry. Immigrant networks thus have allowed the numbers of Salvadoran immigrants in the U.S. capital to expand. More than 300,000 Central Americans, most of them Salvadorans and many of them undocumented, now live in Washington, D.C.[26]

The migration of daughters seeking wage employment in Latin American cities demonstrates the extent to which households must stretch to meet subsistence demands and maximize meager resources in a rural environment. This type of migration works in two different and often complementary ways. The movement of a young woman away from home lifts an economic burden from parents and other relatives, especially in areas where women have been displaced from subsistence agriculture and other income-generating activities. Once in the city, daughters may send remittances, which are often decisive for the survival of those left behind.

In a study of three Mexican cities affected by recent economic changes generated by national indebtedness and austerity policies, Sylvia Chant documents the ways in which migration relates to survival. Economic crisis led to the addition of new members to working-class households. As more members per family—especially wives—entered both formal and informal sectors of the economy seeking additional income, women resorted to asking younger female relatives to move to the city to provide child care services in exchange for room and board. The household, always a fluid entity, thus adjusts to meet the requirements of subsistence. However, these adjustments cannot be understood apart from the sexual division of labor, and specifically the contradictions women face as they try to reconcile the demands of reproductive work, particularly child care, and wage employment.[27]

The main reason women outnumber men as migrants in Latin America is that it is easier for women to find work as servants in urban environments. Several studies show that whether one is talking about Colombians moving to Caracas, Bolivians to Argentina, Sierra people to Lima, or Central Americans migrating to Washington, D.C., women can always find jobs as domestics or as part of the informal economy.

Whether accompanied or not, a female migrant will most likely work in paid employment on her arrival or soon afterward. Employment data show that migrant women consistently work outside the home to a larger extent than women in places of destination. Studies of employed migrant women also show that their labor force participation is not strongly correlated to their education level, training, or work experience. Instead, marital status determines women's entrance into the labor force.

Single, separated, or widowed women with dependents show extremely high levels of labor force participation.

In addition to the need to earn money, women newly arrived in cities must rebuild networks that will bridge the gap between mere survival and prospering. A man can go to and from his place of employment, but because of their domestic responsibilities, women must become acquainted with schools, churches, medical and health-delivery facilities, markets, neighborhood associations, and public transportation in order to cope with a new environment. Moreover, they may have to do all this while still learning a new language and fighting discrimination, if they and their children are ethnically different.

In their study of domestic servants and street and market vendors in Lima, Peru, Bunster and Chaney profile the most common type of migrant women. According to them, women arriving in the city tend to find jobs as domestics in middle- and upper-class homes. When they become pregnant, as often happens in large cities, the domestics are generally dismissed by employers unwilling to board a newborn child or see the services of their employee diminished by mothering responsibilities.[28]

As a result, many young mothers end up, along with their newborns, seeking jobs in the lowest levels of the labor market or as part of the informal economy, as street vendors, for example, or, if they are lucky, in large markets. Although it may seem undesirable to more affluent groups, street peddling entails distinct advantages for mothers: a child can be brought to a street corner or market stall, and the mother can tend to the child's immediate needs and at the same time earn a modest living. The same is not true in more established places of employment, which are by and large inimical to children's presence.

Conclusions

Latin America is marked by sharp contrasts. An abundance of natural resources has long coexisted with large income distribution gaps and other forms of inequality. Sometimes portrayed as an exotic continent characterized by tradition, it is instead a region where large numbers of people move, propelled by the forces of modernization. Our purpose here has been to emphasize the magnitude and diversity of Latin American migration as part and parcel of this process.

Several points discussed earlier deserve mention in this concluding section. Whether moving from the countryside to major cities or from small towns and large cities to other countries, most Latin American migrants move within the same continent and not to the United States.

Second, individual choice is not the only factor precipitating migration in general and Latin American migration in particular. The directionality of migration is additionally determined by such factors as type and destination of capital flows, and the already existing presence of immigrant networks in receiving areas. Immigrants tend to move across invisible bridges formed by unequal economic exchanges between rural and urban sectors, and between less developed and advanced industrial countries. Migrants seldom, if ever, integrate evenly into receiving economies. Rather, they tend to concentrate in specific residential and geographical areas, and in particular niches of the formal and informal labor markets. Despite the uniqueness of personal stories, there is nothing random about the process of migration.

In addition, it is generally not true that immigrants belong to the poorest of the poor. There is little empirical evidence to support the perception that people leave their places of origin pushed by the fear of starvation and abject destitution. In fact, moving away from one's place of birth requires a minimum base of material and human resources, as well as information. Therefore, it is people with some education, some money, and some knowledge about employment prospects who are most likely to migrate.

One indication of the selectivity of migration is that most international migrants hold jobs in their own countries at the time of their departure. These jobs, however, tend to yield less than satisfactory wages and benefits. Thus, it is not absolute poverty but "poverty in employment" that eventually forces people to move.

Migration is also not explained by assuming the superiority of lifestyles and earnings in receiving areas. Rather, migration is almost always prompted by a gap between earnings and consumption standards in the place of origin. This point is central to understanding population movements, because it clarifies the connection among mores often disseminated from abroad, a greater number of attractive goods, and the absence of the means necessary to acquire them. As an explanation for migration, this points to a picture more complex and "layered" than one claiming invidious comparisons between advanced and less-developed countries.

Mass migration is not an anomaly in the modernization process. Rather, it is a logical consequence of the distortions and peculiarities of socioeconomic development throughout Latin America. By emphasizing economic growth, agricultural mechanization that sacrificed subsistence cultivation for cash crops, and, later, export-oriented industrialization, this trajectory has yielded enormous benefits to groups in power. However, it has also created labor displacements, the chaotic expansion of cities, and large income inequalities. In other words, uneven development in Latin America has shaped suitable conditions for mass migration.

What is more, refugees represent a special case in the study of migration. At least two groups of refugees should be distinguished on the basis of class. In general, elites gain a hospitable reception in foreign countries. Working-class people and ethnic minorities, in contrast, often find themselves trapped in the contradictions created by economic and political definitions.

In addition, although general conditions affect all types of population movements, unique factors are associated with female migration. In this respect migration cannot be separated from the sexual division of labor and the reproductive needs of immigrants in originating and receiving environments.

Finally, one of this essay's salient implications is that migration, especially labor migration, cannot be regulated solely through legislative means. Rather, socioeconomic changes enabling more equitable distributions of wealth and resources are necessary to reduce people's need to move away from their own towns, cities, and countries.

Notes

1. With the exception of Mexico City and Oaxaca, all other names of individuals and places in this account have been altered to protect privacy.

2. W. R. Bohning, "Toward a System of Recompense for International Labor Migration," *International Migration for Employment Research Working Paper* (Geneva: International Labor Office, 1982).

3. Aristide R. Zolberg, "The Origins of the Modern World-System: A Missing Link," *World Politics* 33 (1981), 253–81. Also, Aristide R. Zolberg, "The Next Waves: Migration Theory for a Changing World," paper presented at the Conference on International Migration, Villa Serbelloni, Bellagio, 1982.

4. Alejandro Portes, "Urbanization, Migration and Models of Development in Latin America," in John Walton (ed.), *Capital and Labour in the Urbanized World* (London: SAGE Studies in International Sociology 31, 1985).

5. Barry R. Chiswick, "An Analysis of the Economic Progress and Impact of Immigrants," final report to the U.S. Department of Labor, Employment, and Training Administration (mimeo, Chicago Circle: Department of Economics, Univ. of Illinois, 1980).

6. Saskia Sassen, *The Mobility of Capital and Labor: A Study in International Investment and Labor Flow* (New York: Cambridge Univ. Press, 1988).

7. Alejandro Portes, "Latin American Urbanization During the Years of the Crisis," *Latin American Research Review* 24:3 (1989), 7–44.

8. Manuel Castells, "The Social Basis of Urban Populism: Squatters and the State in Latin America," in Manuel Castells (ed.), *The City and the Grassroots* (Berkeley: Univ. of California Press, 1983).

9. Portes, "Urbanization."

10. Carlos Alzamora and Enrique Iglesias, "Bases for a Latin American Response to the International Economic Crisis," *CEPAL Review,* 20 (Aug. 1983), 17–46.

11. Portes, "Latin American Urbanization."

12. Sylvia Chant, *Women and Survival in Mexican Cities: Perspectives on Gender, Labour Markets, and Low-Income Households* (New York: Manchester Univ. Press, 1991).

13. Ramiro Cardona Gutiérrez et al., *Migración de Colombianos a Venezuela* (Bogotá: Corporación Centro Regional de Población, 1983), 133–44.

14. *Ibid.*, 20. See also Gabriel Murillo, *La Migración de trabajadores Colombianos a Venezuela* (Bogotá: Ministerio de Trabajo, y Seguridad Social, 1979).

15. Cardona Gutiérrez et al., *Migración*, 37–66.

16. Edelberto Torres-Rivas, *Report on the Condition of Central American Refugees and Migrants* (San José, Costa Rica: Facultad Latinoamericana de Ciencias Sociales and Georgetown University Center for Immigration Policy and Refugee Assistance, 1985), 3.

17. Leonel Gómez, "Feet People," in Robert S. Leiken (ed.), *Central America: Anatomy of a Conflict* (New York: Pergamon Press, 1984), 225.

18. United Nations High Commissioner for Refugees, *Fact Sheets: Central America and Mexico*, 1985.

19. Torres-Rivas, *Central American Refugees*.

20. *Ibid.*

21. Maxine Schwartz Seller (ed.), *Immigrant Women* (Philadelphia: Temple Univ. Press, 1981), 31.

22. Nancy Foner, "Jamaican Women in New York and London," in R. Simon and C. Brettell (eds.), *International Migration: The Female Experience* (Totowa, N. J.: Rowman and Allanheld, 1986). See also Sylvia Pedraza, "Women and Migration: The Social Consequences of Gender," *Annual Review of Sociology* 17 (1991), 303–25, Sherri Grasmuck and Patricia Pessar, *Between Two Islands* (Berkeley: Univ. of California Press, 1991).

23. Patricia Pessar, "The Role of Gender in Dominican Settlement in the United States," in June Nash and Helen Safa (eds.) *Women and Change in Latin America* (South Hadley, Mass.: Bergin and Garvey, 1988). See also Rita Jane Simon and Caroline B. Brettel, *International Migration: The Female Experience* (Totowa, N. J.: Rowman and Allanheld, 1986).

24. Nancy Foner, "Jamaican Journey: Race and Ethnicity Among Jamaican Migrants in New York City," paper presented at the Conference on Immigration and the Changing Black Population in the United States, Univ. of Michigan, 1983.

25. M. Patricia Fernández-Kelly and Anna M. Garcia, "Power Surrendered, Power Restored: The Politics of Home and Work Among Hispanic Women in Southern California and Southern Florida," in Louis Tilly and Patricia Guerin (eds.), *Women and Politics in America* (New York: Russell Sage Foundation, 1990). See also Lisandro Pérez, "Immigrant Economic Adjustment and Family Organization: The Cuban Success Story Reexamined," *International Migration Review* 20:1 (1986), 4–20.

26. Terry Repak, "Labor Recruitment and the Lure of the Capital: The Central American Migration to Washington, D.C." (mimeo, Atlanta: Emory Univ. Program in Liberal Arts, 1990).

27. Chant, *Women and Survival*.

28. Ximena Bunster and Elsa M. Chaney, *Sellers and Servants: Working Women in Lima, Peru* (New York: Praeger, 1985).

12

The Americans: Latin American and Caribbean Peoples in the United States

RUBÉN G. RUMBAUT

The development of caste and class relationships stratified by racial and ethnic status has been a central theme of U.S. history, shaped over many generations by the European conquest of indigenous peoples and by massive waves of both coerced and uncoerced immigration from all over the world. Indeed, immigration, annexation, and conquest—by hook or by crook—have been the originating processes by which American ethnic groups have been formed and through which, over time, the United States itself has been transformed into arguably the world's most ethnically diverse society. The familiar Anglocentric story of the origins of the nation typically begins with the founding of the first permanent English settlement in America at Jamestown, Virginia, in 1607, and the arrival of the Pilgrims at Plymouth, Massachusetts, in 1620. Until very recently the "Hispanic" presence in what is now the United States was little noted (the term itself was not used by the Census Bureau until 1970), although that presence antedates by a century the creation of an English colony in North America and has left an indelible if ignored Spanish imprint throughout Florida and the Southwest.[1] Today the Hispanic presence has emerged, seemingly suddenly, as a pervasive fact of American life. History is filled with unintended consequences, and one of the ironies (a "latent destiny"?) of the history of a nation that expanded its influence and "manifest destiny" into Latin America and the Caribbean is that, in significant numbers, their diverse peoples have come to the United States and themselves become "Americans."

U.S. Expansion, Immigration, and the Formation of Ethnic Minorities

In 1790, the first census ever taken in the newly established United States of America counted a population of 3.9 million people, including 757,000 African Americans (more than 90 percent of whom were slaves). Excluded from those census figures were some 600,000 Native Americans, their numbers already decimated since the Europeans' arrival. Three-fourths of the nonslave population was of British origin, either immigrants or descendants of immigrants from the colonial center. Germans were the largest non-English-speaking immigrant group, concentrated in Pennsylvania, where their presence was occasionally viewed with alarm. Indeed, as early as 1751 the redoubtable Benjamin Franklin had put the matter this way: "Why should *Pennsylvania*, founded by the *English*, become a Colony of *Aliens*, who will shortly be so numerous as to Germanize us, instead of our Anglifying them?"

Much has changed since then; much has not. Today's public alarm has focused on Hispanics and their presumed lack of Anglo-conformity, as argued by former Colorado governor Richard Lamm in his book *The Immigration Time Bomb: The Fragmenting of America*, and by nativist organizations, such as U.S. English. In late 1991, in the middle of a prolonged recession, California governor Pete Wilson singled out the cost of providing public services to immigrants as a major cause of the state's budget deficit; and columnist Pat Buchanan announced his candidacy for the Republican presidential nomination on an "America First" platform that singled out immigration as a key political issue, arguing that ease of assimilation, based on language, culture, and background, should be the criterion for immigrant admissions: "I think God made all people good. But if we had to take a million in, say Zulus next year or Englishmen, and put them in Virginia, what group would be easier to assimilate and would cause less problems for the people of Virginia?"[2]

In 1790, the original 13 colonies, on the periphery of a world system dominated by European powers, covered 891,000 square miles. During the nineteenth century, the territory of the fledgling nation soon doubled with the Louisiana Purchase (1803) and the acquisition of Florida (1819). It doubled again by midcentury with the annexation of Texas (1845) and the entire Southwest (roughly half the territory of Mexico) at the end of the U.S.-Mexico War (1848), and with the acquisition of the Oregon Territory (1846) and Alaska (1867). By the end of the century the United States had acquired Puerto Rico, the Philippines, and Guam in the aftermath of the Spanish-American War (1898), and had annexed Hawaii and American Samoa. The peoples of these regions came with the territory. (Territorial expansion in the twentieth century has been limited to the purchase of the Virgin Islands from Denmark in 1917, and the acquisition after World War II of the Palau and Northern Mariana islands in the western Pacific.)

Today, the territory of the 50 states exceeds 3.7 million square miles, and, after two world wars and the end of the Cold War, the United States is the unrivaled hegemon—politically, militarily, culturally, and to a declining extent economically—at the center of the world system. Concomitantly, following the passage in the 1920s of restrictive national-origins immigration quotas, the Great Depression, and World War II, the United States has again become a nation of immigrants. By the 1980s it had attracted two-thirds of all immigrants worldwide, primarily from the developing countries of Asia and Latin America, who are transforming anew its ethnic mosaic.

In 1990 the U.S. census officially counted a population of 249 million (follow-up surveys suggested that 5 million may have been missed by census takers). About three-fourths were of European origin, most descendants of the largest transoceanic immigration in world history, which brought some 40 million Europeans to the United States in the century from the 1820s to the 1920s. Twenty-nine million African Americans accounted for another 12 percent of the total (in sub-Saharan Africa, only Nigeria and Ethiopia have larger African populations). Together with the 1.9 million American Indians and Alaska Natives, who compose less than 1 percent of the U.S. population, they actually formed the country's oldest resident ethnic groups. The census also counted more than 7 million Asian Americans and Pacific Islanders—who doubled their numbers since 1980. Among them were some of the newest ethnic groups in the country, whose large-scale immigration dates to the 1965 abolition of the national-origins laws that had barred Asians from entry, and to the largest refugee resettlement program in U.S. history, which has brought over 1 million refugees from Vietnam, Laos, and Cambodia since the end of the Indochina War.

More significantly, the census counted 22.4 million Hispanics, or 9 percent of the total U.S. population, up 53 percent from 14.6 million in 1980 and nearly six times the estimated 1950 estimate of 4 million. (This official total is not adjusted for an estimated undercount of 1 million Hispanics, and excludes the 3.5 million Spanish-speakers living in Puerto Rico, as well as all non-Hispanic nationalities from Latin America and the Caribbean.) This sharp increase has been largely due to recent immigration from Latin America and the Caribbean; these migrants now form the largest non-English-speaking immigrant group. Indeed, only Mexico, Argentina, and Colombia have larger Spanish-origin populations. If current trends continue, Hispanics as a whole may well exceed African Americans in population size sometime in the next decade.

About 60 percent—13.5 million—of all U.S. Hispanics are of Mexican origin; 12 percent are Puerto Ricans (2.7 million on the mainland,

not including the more than 3 million in Puerto Rico)[3]—making them
the nation's largest ethnic minorities after African Americans. Only four
other groups had populations above 1 million in 1990: American Indians; the Chinese (the nation's oldest and most diversified Asian-origin
minority, originally recruited as laborers to California in the midnineteenth century); Filipinos (colonized by the United States in the first
half of this century and also recruited to work in Hawaiian and Californian plantations until the 1930s); and Cubans (who acount for 5
percent of all Hispanics and whose immigration is also tied closely to
the history of U.S.-Cuba relations). The original incorporation of these
sizable groups, except the oldest, American Indians, and the newest,
Cubans, was characterized by processes of labor importation. While the
histories of each took complex and diverse forms, the country's four
largest ethnic minorities—African Americans, Mexican Americans, Puerto
Ricans, and American Indians—are peoples whose incorporation originated involuntarily through conquest, occupation, and exploitation
(followed, in the case of Mexicans and Puerto Ricans, by mass immigration during the twentieth century, much of it initiated by active labor
recruitment by U.S. companies), setting the foundation for subsequent
patterns of social and economic inequality. The next three largest
groups—the Chinese, Filipinos, and Cubans—today are largely composed of immigrants who have come to the United States since the
1960s but have built on structural linkages established much earlier.[4]

Indeed, while today's immigrants come from more than 100 different countries, the majority come from two handfuls of developing
countries located either in the Caribbean basin or Asia, all variously
characterized by significant historical ties to the United States. The former include Mexico—still by far the largest source of both legal and
illegal immigration—Cuba, the Dominican Republic, Jamaica, and Haiti,
with El Salvador emerging prominently as a source country for the first
time during the 1980s. Asia contributes immigrants primarily from the
Philippines, South Korea, Vietnam, China (including Taiwan), and India.[5] Each country's historical relationship with the United States has
given rise to particular social networks that serve as bridges of passage
to the United States, linking places of origin and destination, opening
"chain migration" channels, and giving the immigration process its cumulative and seemingly spontaneous character.[6] Regarding Mexico and
Puerto Rico, Alejandro Portes has argued cogently in this vein that

> "[T]he countries that supplied the major Spanish-origin groups in the
> United States today were, each in its time, targets of [an] expansionist
> pattern [of] U.S. intervention. . . . In a sense, the sending populations
> were Americanized before their members actually became immigrants to
> the United States. . . . The rise of Spanish-speaking working-class com-
> munities in the Southwest and Northeast may thus be seen as a dialectical

consequence of past expansion of the United States into its immediate periphery. . . . Contemporary migration patterns tend to reflect precisely the character of past hegemonic actions by regional and global powers.[7]

The Mexican-American writer and filmmaker Luis Valdés put it plainly, if pithily: "We did not, in fact, come to the United States at all. The United States came to us."

Many factors—economic, political, cultural, demographic—help explain contemporary immigration to the United States, but none can adequately do so outside its concrete historical context. Consider geographical proximity as an impetus to immigration. For example, half of all recent legal immigration and most of all illegal immigration originates in nearby Caribbean basin countries, with Mexico accounting for the greatest share. But five of the top 10 sending countries are in Asia, half a world away (the Philippines has ranked second only to Mexico over the past 30 years). Next-door neighbor Canada is not among the top sending countries. Cheap airplane travel has greatly reduced distances, but Europeans are no longer coming by the millions, as they did a century ago when ocean travel was far more difficult. More undocumented immigrants come from Mexico than any other country, but at least 100,000 Irish immigrants settled illegally (by overstaying their visas) in Boston and New York during the 1980s. Shorter distance does not explain why Salvadorans and Colombians are arriving and Costa Ricans and Venezuelans are not; nor why until fairly recently Jamaicans went to Great Britain and Surinamese to the Netherlands instead of to the United States (when Suriname achieved independence from the Netherlands in 1975, the new government could not halt the emigration of skilled Surinamese, most of them Hindus, to the Dutch metropole).

Economic inequality—especially wage differentials—between sending and receiving countries is also a factor. Since midcentury, less-developed countries (LDCs) have dominated international immigration flows, reflecting the nature of unequal exchanges in a global economy (labor flows from LDCs to more-developed countries [MDCs], capital from MDCs to LDCs). Thus Europeans and Canadians, who had composed the majority of immigrants to the United States until the early 1960s, now account for just over 10 percent of the total. The 2,000–mile U.S.-Mexico border, by contrast, is the biggest point of North-South contact in the world, and a Mexican worker can earn more in a day in the United States than in a week in Mexico. But if wage differentials alone determined migration patterns, we would expect far greater numbers of Mexican immigrants than the relatively tiny fraction of the potential pool who actually cross the border. We would also expect sizable flows to the United States from the world's poorest countries, yet none are significantly represented (except for Vietnamese, Laotians, and Cambodians, who were admitted under special legal provisions as Cold War refugees).

Population size is another factor. Certainly China and India, with more than 20 percent of the world's population, have a huge pool of potential immigrants. Yet very few immigrants come to the United States from other very large countries, such as Brazil and Indonesia, while some very small countries, including the Dominican Republic, Jamaica, Haiti, and Guyana, now send a large proportion of their populations. Demographic pressures must be considered: immigration serves as an escape valve to reduce overpopulation, but many countries with severe population growth and density problems are not main sources of U.S. immigration. Political instability in countries of origin must also be taken into account, but war and violence alone do not explain immigration to the United States. In fact, more than 90 percent of the world's refugees are people who have fled from one Third World country to another.

State immigration policies regulating exit and entry influence but do not determine the size, composition, and direction of immigrant flows. The very existence of substantial numbers of illegal immigrants underscores the limits and defeasibility of legal rules. Certainly the 1965 Immigration Act eliminated racist quotas barring Asians and others from entry to the United States and opened the door to immigrants from all countries on an equal basis (within specific numerical and other criteria, emphasizing primarily family reunification, but occupational skills as well). Yet less than a dozen countries account for the majority of today's newcomers. At the time when legislation was passed, it was widely expected that Southern Europeans would be favored over Asians and Africans, since they had few family members in the United States who could take advantage of the law's preference system. Yet what happened was precisely the opposite of what was intended by the lawmakers. The fact that Cubans have faced exit restrictions at home has not impeded their exodus. Incredibly, a 17-year-old successfully crossed the shark-infested Florida Straits riding a windsurfer in 1990, and in 1991 some 2,000 persons made the crossing on inner tubes and makeshift rafts. The fact that persons in most MDCs (excluding Japan) face no exit restrictions has not fueled their immigration.

Still, state policies have important effects. For example, Jamaican and other West Indian immigrants "switched" destinations from the United Kingdom to the United States and Canada in the 1960s, with the passage of the 1962 Commonwealth Immigration Act, which "slammed the door" on black immigration to the United Kingdom, and the passage in 1965 of the Hart-Celler Act in the United States, which benefited them because of their nations' new status as independent countries.[8] The U.S. Immigration Act of 1990, which increases authorized immigration by 40 percent annually, nearly triples—from 54,000 to

140,000—the number of visas each year for immigrant professionals, executives, and other skilled persons of exceptional ability. It also provides another 10,000 visas per year to immigrant entrepreneurs who invest a minimum of $1 million in a new U.S. commercial enterprise employing at least 10 full-time workers. While leaving family-sponsored immigration basically unchanged, the intent of the new law is to compete in a global immigration market in which skilled people have become commodities. But its effects cannot be fully anticipated. For instance, in seeking to lure the best and the brightest, the new law will further limit the legal entry of low-wage, unskilled workers (nannies, maids, restaurant workers) to 10,000 annual visas, and will increase the waiting period to more than 10 years (in 1990 the waiting list had 126,442 applicants for such "sixth preference" visas). The new law will thus unwittingly increase pressures for illegal immigration among the less skilled and will deepen class inequalities among newcomer groups.[9]

While these and other factors have consequences that are not always intended, large-scale immigration flows to the United States are not simply a function of state policies or of individual costs and benefits calculations. Nor can immigration be reduced to simple push-pull or supply-demand theories. It must be understood in the macrocontext of historical patterns of U.S. expansion and intervention, and in the microcontext of social networks created and consolidated in the process, which help sustain continued immigration and ethnic group formation. This process is illustrated by some of the largest contemporary Asian immigrant groups, including Filipinos (following 48 years of U.S. colonial rule, the pervasive Americanization of Filipino culture, development of a U.S.-style educational system, adoption of English as an official language, heavy dependence on U.S. trade and foreign investment, direct recruitment of Filipinos into the U.S. Navy, and establishment after World War II of the largest U.S. military bases in the Pacific), Koreans (following the Korean War), and Vietnamese (following the Vietnam War).

The countries of the Caribbean basin—particularly Mexico, Puerto Rico, and Cuba—perhaps have felt most strongly the weight and lure of the U.S. hegemonic presence. Since the days of Benjamin Franklin (who in 1761 suggested Mexico and Cuba as goals of American expansion) and Thomas Jefferson, the Caribbean countries were viewed as belonging, as if by some "laws of political gravitation" (as John Quincy Adams said in 1823), to the "manifest destiny" of the United States. The Caribbean, then, was viewed as "the American Mediterranean," as Alexander Hamilton called it in *The Federalist* in 1787.[10] Ironically, it is precisely the people from these countries who are visibly emerging as a significant component of American society. They are not, however, a homogeneous lot; rather, they reflect different histories, settlement patterns, immigrant types, and modes of incorporation into the United States.

Hispanics in the United States: Histories and Patterns of Settlement

Mexicans, Puerto Ricans, and Cubans trace their main historical ties to the United States to the nineteenth century, with Mexicans by far the largest and oldest of Hispanic ethnic groups. Overwhelmingly, Mexicans became incorporated into the the U.S. economy as manual laborers. When the Treaty of Guadalupe-Hidalgo ceded the Southwest territories to the United States in 1848, perhaps 80,000 inhabitants of Mexican and Spanish origin were residing in that territory—nearly three-fourths of them lived in New Mexico, with smaller numbers of *Tejanos* and *Californios*. Toward the end of the century, with the rapid expansion of railroads, agriculture, and mining in the Southwest and of the U.S. economy generally, and the exclusion in 1882 of Chinese workers and later the Japanese, Mexicans became the preferred source of cheap and mobile migrant labor. This occurred at about the same time that capitalist development in Mexico under the government of Porfirio Díaz was creating a landless peasantry. By the early 1900s railroad lines—which expedited deliberate labor recruitment by U.S. companies—had linked the Mexican interior with other states, particularly Texas, which became the major center of Mexican settlement, though under harsh, castelike conditions.[11] In other parts of the United States, from the copper and coal mines of Arizona and Colorado to the steel mills and slaughterhouses of Chicago, to Detroit and Pittsburgh, large numbers of Mexicans were working as manual laborers.

Not all these *braceros* returned to Mexico, and settler communities formed and grew. As many as 1 million Mexicans—up to one-tenth of the Mexican population—crossed the U.S. border at some point during the violent decade of the Mexican Revolution of 1910. Demand for their labor in the United States increased during World War I and the 1920s. The 1910 U.S. census counted some 220,000 Mexicans; that number more than doubled by 1920, and tripled to more than 600,000 by 1930. Largely at the urging of American growers, the restrictive national-origins immigration laws passed in 1921 and 1924 placed no limits on Western Hemisphere countries, in order to allow the recruitment of Mexican workers when needed—and their deportation when not. This happened during the 1930s, when about 400,000, including many U.S. citizens, were repatriated to Mexico, and again during the even larger deportations of "Operation Wetback" in the mid-1950s.

The large increase in the Mexican-origin population in California dates to the World War II period, which saw the establishment of the Bracero Program (1942–64) of contract-labor importation. The end of the Bracero Program prompted increased flows of illegal immigration, which peaked in 1986 when the Immigration Reform and Control Act was passed, then declined briefly but increased and stabilized again in

1989. Despite the large flows of legal and illegal Mexican immigration in recent years, the 1980 census found that 74 percent of the Mexican-origin population was U.S.-born. Though the Chicano experience and consciousness has gone through distinct psychohistorical generations and differed markedly from that of recent immigrants, the formation of the nation's second-largest ethnic group still retains the stamp of its working-class origins and history of exploitation and discrimination.[12]

Puerto Rico, a rural society based on subsistence agriculture and coffee exports, was occupied by the United States in 1898 and formally acquired as part of the Treaty of Paris, which settled the Spanish-American War. The islanders' status was left ambiguous until the passage of the Jones Act in 1917, which gave Puerto Ricans U.S. citizenship and made them eligible for the military draft. These provisions essentially remained after 1947, when a new constitution defined commonwealth status for Puerto Rico. This status defines the island's relationship with the United States and distinguishes Puerto Ricans fundamentally from other Latin American and Caribbean peoples. As U.S. citizens by birth, Puerto Ricans travel freely between the island and mainland—just as one would travel from Hawaii to California—without having to pass through screenings of the Immigration and Naturalization Service or Border Patrol, as would foreign-born immigrants.

Puerto Rican migration has been viewed as an exchange of people for capital. Soon after the military occupation, U.S. capital began flowing into Puerto Rico. This was especially true of the new and rapidly growing sugar industry, which displaced subsistence peasants into the cities and combined with high population growth to create urban unemployment. The island's capital-intensive industrialization and urbanization rapidly accelerated after the introduction of "Operation Bootstrap" in 1948, but failed to solve urban unemployment and population growth problems and intensified internal economic pressures for migration to the mainland. Though it never reached the extent it did with Mexican workers, labor recruitment began in 1900 when a large group of workers went to sugar cane plantations in Hawaii, and later to farms on the mainland. Labor recruitment became widespread among industrial employers only during and after World War II—at the same time that cheap air travel was instituted between San Juan and New York (a one-way ticket cost less than $50). Mass immigration to New York reached its peak at this time and made Puerto Ricans the first "airborne" migration in U.S. history. The Puerto Rican population on the mainland grew from about 12,000 in 1920, to 53,000 in 1930, to 301,000 in 1950, and tripled to 888,000 in 1960. Net Puerto Rican migration to the mainland during the 1950s—about 470,000—was higher than the immigration totals of any country, including Mexico. Although net migration has since decreased, travel back and forth is incessant, averaging more than 3 million people annually in the 1980s. The pattern of concentration in New York City, which accounted for more than 80 percent of the total Puerto Rican population in the U.S. mainland in 1950, gradually declined to 62 percent in 1970 and to under 40 percent in 1990. About 45 percent of the more than 6 million Puerto Ricans now reside on the U.S. mainland.[13]

Unlike Mexico, the first nation in the Americas to achieve independence from Spain, and Puerto Rico, the only territory that has never become an independent state, Cuba was the last Spanish colony. It became formally independent in 1902, following three years of U.S. military occupation at the end of the second Cuban War of Independence (1895–98) and the Spanish-American War (1898).

A notable Cuban presence in the United States goes back to the early nineteenth century, when Cuban exiles began a tradition of carrying out their political work from bases in New York and Florida. Throughout the nineteenth century, Cuba was the target of repeated annexation efforts by the United States and a main focus of U.S. trade and capital investment. However, it never became a recruiting ground for agricultural workers, as did Mexico and Puerto Rico. U.S. economic penetration of the island increased sharply after the war and the military occupation at the turn of the century, expanding U.S. control over sugar production and other sectors of the Cuban economy, including transportation, mining, construction, and public utilities. By 1929 U.S. direct investment in Cuba totaled nearly $1 billion; this was more than one-fourth of all U.S. investment in Latin America as a whole, and more than that invested by U.S. capital in any Latin American country, both in absolute terms and on a per capita basis.

Moreover, Cuba became a virtual "protectorate" of the United States after 1902 under the terms of the Platt Amendment, attached by the U.S. Congress to the Cuban constitution. Not rescinded until 1934, the Platt Amendment formalized the right of the United States to intervene in Cuban internal affairs and lease the Guantánamo Bay naval base, which the United States has held ever since. These actions have bred deep resentment of U.S. domination in various sectors of the Cuban population. Nonetheless, an informed observer could write that, at least in the cities, "it is probably fair to say that by 1959, no other country in the world, with the exception of Canada, quite so resembled the United States."[14]

At that time the Cuban population in the United States was just over 70,000. The waves of exiles that began in earnest in 1960 in the context of the East-West Cold War have continued to the present in several phases: the daily flights, suspended after the 1962 missile crisis; the orderly "freedom flights" between 1965 and 1973; boat flotillas from Camarioca in 1965 and Mariel in 1980; and the increasingly desperate crossings with the deepening economic and social crisis in Cuba after 1989. Despite U.S. government efforts to resettle the exiles away from Miami, many eventually drifted back, making the city a majority-Cuban community. At over 1 million, the Cuban-American population in 1990 represents about 10 percent of the island's population. One of the many ironies of the history of U.S.-Cuba relations is that Fidel Castro, anti-Yankee par excellence, may have done more to deepen structural linkages between Cuba and the United States than anyone else in Cuban history.[15]

Table 1 presents data from the 1990 census on the Hispanic population: its size and concentration in major states and counties of settlement. From 1980 to 1990, the U.S. population grew by 9.8 percent, and that of Hispanics by 53 percent, a growth rate that was significantly exceeded in several states and metropolitan areas. While Hispanics now constitute 9 percent of the total population, their impact is much more notable due to their concentration in particular localities. Nearly three out of four Hispanics in the United States reside in just four states: California, with over a third of the total; Texas, accounting for nearly one-fifth; and New York and Florida, with one-sixth combined.

By contrast, less than one-third of the total U.S. population resides in these states. Indeed, Hispanics now account for more than 25 percent of the populations of California and Texas. Concentration patterns are even more pronounced for specific groups: three-fourths of all Mexican Americans reside in California and Texas, half the Puerto Ricans are in the New York–New Jersey area; and nearly two-thirds of the Cubans are in Florida. Significant numbers of Mexican Americans and Puerto Ricans are also in Illinois, overwhelmingly in Chicago. The category "Other Hispanic" used by the census includes both long-established groups and recent immigrants. The long-established groups trace their roots to the region prior to the Southwest annexation after the U.S.-Mexico War and live notably in New Mexico, where Hispanics still account for more than 38 percent of the state's population, despite comparatively little recent immigration. Recent immigrants come from Central and South America and the Spanish Caribbean, with a quarter in California, another quarter in New York–New Jersey, and a tenth in Florida.

These patterns of concentration are even more pronounced in metropolitan areas, and in particular communities within metropolitan areas. Moreover, different immigrant groups concentrate in different metropolitan areas and create distinct communities within them. The main reason is that immigrants, especially working-class groups and ethnic entrepreneurs, tend to concentrate in urban areas where coethnic communities have been established by past immigration. Such spatial concentrations provide newcomers with significant sources of social, cultural, and economic support unavailable to more dispersed immigrants, such as professionals, whose settlement decisions are more a function of their credentials and job offers than of pre-existing ethnic communities.

Dense ethnic enclaves also provide immigrant entrepreneurs with access to cheap labor, working capital, credit, and dependable markets.

TABLE 1. States and Counties of Principal Hispanic Settlement in the United States, 1990

State/County	Total 1990 Hispanic Population	% Hispanic Pop. Growth, 1980–1990	% Hispanic of State or County Pop.	% of U.S. Hispanic Population	Percent of Each Group's U.S. Population			
					Mexican	Puerto Rican	Cuban	Other Hispanic
U.S. TOTAL	22,354,059	53.0	9.0	100.0	60.4	12.2	4.7	22.8
STATES:								
California	7,687,938	69.2	25.8	34.4	45.3	4.6	6.9	26.9
Texas	4,339,905	45.4	25.5	19.4	28.8	1.6	1.7	7.6
New York	2,214,026	33.4	12.3	9.9	0.7	39.8	7.1	18.9
Florida	1,574,143	83.4	12.2	7.0	1.2	9.1	64.6	9.7
Illinois	904,446	42.3	7.9	4.0	4.6	5.4	1.7	2.3
New Jersey	739,861	50.4	9.6	3.3	0.2	11.7	8.2	6.0
Arizona	688,338	56.2	18.8	3.1	4.6	0.3	0.2	1.2
New Mexico	579,224	21.4	38.2	2.6	2.4	0.1	0.1	4.9
Colorado	424,302	24.9	12.9	1.9	2.1	0.3	0.2	2.6
COUNTIES:								
Los Angeles, CA	3,351,242	62.2	37.8	15.0	NA	NA	NA	NA
Dade (Miami), FL	953,407	64.1	49.2	4.3	NA	NA	NA	NA
Cook (Chicago), IL	694,194	39.0	13.6	3.1	NA	NA	NA	NA
Harris (Houston), TX	644,935	74.7	22.9	2.9	NA	NA	NA	NA
Bexar (San Antonio), TX	589,180	27.8	49.7	2.6	NA	NA	NA	NA
Orange (Santa Ana), CA	564,828	97.3	23.4	2.5	NA	NA	NA	NA
The Bronx, NY	523,111	32.0	43.5	2.3	NA	NA	NA	NA
San Diego, CA	510,781	85.6	20.4	2.3	NA	NA	NA	NA
Kings (Brooklyn), NY	462,411	17.9	20.1	2.1	NA	NA	NA	NA
El Paso, TX	411,619	38.6	69.6	1.8	NA	NA	NA	NA
New York (Manhattan), NY	386,630	15.0	26.0	1.7	NA	NA	NA	NA
Queens, NY	381,120	45.2	19.5	1.7	NA	NA	NA	NA
San Bernardino, CA	378,582	128.2	26.7	1.7	NA	NA	NA	NA

Source: U.S. Bureau of the Census, "Persons of Hispanic Origin for the United States and States: 1990," and "Hispanic Origin Population by County: 1990 and 1980," *1990 Census of Population* (1991). Data for specific ethnic groups by county not yet available.

Over time, as immigrants become naturalized citizens and voters, local strength in numbers also provides opportunities for political representation of ethnic minority group interests. Ethnic social networks thus shape not only migration but also adaptation and settlement processes in areas of final destination. Table 1 lists the 13 largest U.S. counties of Hispanic concentration (out of more than 1,200). There were 3.4 million Hispanics in Los Angeles County alone, accounting for 15 percent of the national Hispanic population and 38 percent of the total Los Angeles population. Three other counties shown in table 1—Orange, San Diego, and San Bernardino—are adjacent southern California areas that reflected the highest rates of Hispanic population growth over the decade. Combined with Los Angeles, they account for 21.5 percent of the U.S. total. Adding Riverside, Ventura, Kern, and Imperial counties, also in southern California, would increase the proportion to 25 percent.

Nearly 8 percent of the total Hispanic population resides in four boroughs of New York City: the Bronx, Kings (Brooklyn), New York (Manhattan) and Queens counties. (However, their growth rates, while high, were below the national Hispanic average.) Half the populations of Dade County (Miami) and Bexar County (San Antonio) are Hispanic—principally of Cuban and Mexican origin, respectively—as are more than two-thirds of El Paso's population (on the Mexican border) and nearly a quarter of Houston's. Indeed, Los Angeles's Mexican-origin population today is exceeded only by that of Mexico City, Guadalajara, and Monterrey; Havana is the only city in Cuba larger than Cuban Miami; San Salvador and Santo Domingo are slightly larger than Salvadoran Los Angeles and Dominican New York; and twice as many Puerto Ricans reside in New York City as in Puerto Rico's capital, San Juan.

New Immigrants from Latin America and the Caribbean: National and Class Origins

The focus on "Hispanics" as a generic category is misleading, since it conceals both substantial generational differences among groups so labeled and contemporary immigrants' enormous diversity—in national origins, racial-ethnic and class origins, legal status, reasons for migration, modes of exit, and contexts of reception.

It is true that persons from Spanish America have dominated immigrant flows, averaging about 80 percent of the Latin American/Caribbean total in recent decades (not including Puerto Ricans, who, as U.S. citizens, are not counted in official immigration statistics). But sizable flows have also come from the non-Spanish-speaking Caribbean basin. Table 2 presents 1980 census data on the U.S. foreign-born population. (Detailed 1990 census data will not be available until 1993.) At

TABLE 2.   New Neighbors: Foreign-born Persons Counted in the 1980 U.S.
Census, by Year of Arrival, and Legal Immigrants Admitted in 1981–
1990, by Region and American Countries of Birth

Region/ Country of Birth	No. of 1980 Foreign-Born in the U.S.	% of 1980 Population of Origin	Year of Immigration to the U.S.			Immigrants Admitted in 1981–90
			Pre-1960 (%)	1960–69 (%)	1970–80 (%)	
WORLDWIDE:	14,079,906	0.3	38.2	22.2	39.5	7,338,062
Europe and USSR	5,149,355	0.7	65.6	18.0	16.3	705,630
Latin America	4,372,487	1.2	16.1	30.5	53.5	3,460,683
Asia	2,539,777	0.1	12.5	18.0	69.4	2,817,426
Africa	199,723	0.04	15.7	19.2	65.1	192,212
NORTH AMERICA:						
Canada	842,859	3.5	64.7	20.2	15.2	119,204
Mexico	2,199,221	3.1	17.5	18.9	49.7	1,653,250
CARIBBEAN:	1,258,363	4.3	11.9	45.5	42.7	892,703
Cuba	607,814	6.3	12.8	60.4	26.8	159,257
Jamaica	196,811	8.8	11.6	29.7	58.6	213,805
Dominican Republic	169,147	2.9	6.1	37.2	56.8	251,803
Haiti	92,395	1.7	4.6	30.8	64.6	140,163
Trinidad and Tobago	65,907	6.2	7.4	30.8	61.8	39,533
Barbados	26,847	10.7	19.8	24.4	56.3	17,482
CENTRAL AMERICA:	353,892	1.6	13.7	25.7	60.6	458,753
El Salvador	94,447	2.0	6.1	16.8	77.2	214,574
Guatemala	63,073	0.9	6.4	24.3	69.3	87,939
Panama	60,740	3.1	29.0	31.5	39.6	29,045
Nicaragua	44,166	1.6	18.5	20.6	60.9	44,139
Honduras	39,154	1.0	15.6	32.2	52.2	49,496
Costa Rica	29,639	1.3	14.3	38.9	46.8	15,490
SOUTH AMERICA:	560,616	0.2	10.7	37.0	56.2	455,977
Colombia	143,508	0.5	7.9	37.2	55.0	124,436
Ecuador	86,128	1.1	7.6	39.1	53.2	56,026
Argentina	68,887	0.2	16.5	40.3	43.2	25,717
Peru	55,496	0.3	9.7	30.9	59.4	64,381
Guyana	48,608	6.4	7.0	20.6	72.4	95,374
Brazil	40,919	0.03	20.6	31.3	48.1	23,772
Chile	35,127	0.3	11.3	26.9	61.9	23,439
Venezuela	33,281	0.2	10.6	16.1	73.2	17,963
Bolivia	14,468	0.3	11.8	33.6	54.5	12,252

Source: U.S. Bureau of the Census, "Foreign-Born Population in the United States—Microfiche," *1980 Census,* table 1 (1985); *Statistical Abstracts of the United States, 1990*; and U.S. Immigration and Naturalization Service, *1990 Statistical Yearbook.*

14.1 million persons, it is the world's largest immigrant population, although it constitutes only 6.2 percent of the total U.S. population, much
lower than its proportion at the turn of the century. The table, supple-
mented by INS data on all immigrants legally admitted during 1981–
90, is broken down by world region, all major sending countries in
Latin America and the Caribbean, and by decade of arrival.

As of 1980, Europeans still composed the largest foreign-born population in the United States (5.1 million), but two-thirds were older persons who had immigrated well before 1960. The relatively small number of 1981–90 immigrants from Europe reflects their declining trend over the past three decades. Canadians exhibited a similar pattern. The number of Asian and African immigrants doubled during the last decade. More than two-thirds of their 1980 populations had arrived only during the 1970s, reflecting the fact that their immigration has largely taken place since the passage of the 1965 Act. Latin America accounted for 4.4 million foreign-born persons in 1980, more than half coming just in the previous decade. The enormous number of immigrants admitted during 1981–90 (3.5 million)[16] meant that *by 1990, for the first time in U.S. history, Latin American and Caribbean peoples composed the largest immigrant population in the country.*

Mexico's 1980 immigrant population in the United States was 2.2 million, of whom about 900,000 were estimated by the Census Bureau to be undocumented. Mexican immigrants accounted for half the total from Latin America and the Caribbean. Another 1.7 million were legally admitted during the 1980s, again, accounting for half the total number of Latin American and Caribbean immigrants admitted during the decade. The Cuban-born population in 1980—608,000—was by far the next largest immigrant group, and the only one that arrived preponderantly during the 1960s. All other Latin American and Caribbean immigrants as of 1980 had arrived primarily during the 1970s.

However, the number of Cubans admitted during the 1980s—including most of the 125,000 who came in the 1980 Mariel boatlift, which occurred shortly after the 1980 census was taken—was surpassed by that of Dominicans, Salvadorans, and Jamaicans, with Haitians not far behind. The INS totals for Dominicans and especially Salvadorans and Guatemalans for the 1980s surely undercount their actual numbers: the majority of Salvadorans and Guatemalans entered illegally during the decade, most after the 1981 date required to qualify for the Immigration Reform and Control Act's amnesty provisions.

From South America the largest flow has continued to be from Colombia, although significant numbers of Ecuadorans and Peruvians came during the 1980s. The biggest increase was registered by the Guyanese, making them, surprisingly, the second-largest immigrant group from South America. Indeed, as table 2 shows, the Guyanese share a common pattern with other English-speaking groups in the Commonwealth Caribbean, principally Jamaica, Trinidad, and Barbados: the percentage of immigrants from these countries relative to their 1980 homeland populations was very high, ranging from 6.2 to 10.7 percent. The proportions grew significantly from 1981 to 1990 for Jamaicans, who more than doubled their 1980 total, and the Guyanese, who tripled it by 1990. Similarly, although not shown in table 2, the 14,436 English-speaking immigrants from Belize in the United States in 1980 constituted 10 percent of Belize's population. During the 1980s over 18,000 more emigrated to the United States. Only Cuba had sent a similarly high proportion—6.3 percent, or 7.6 percent if the 1980 Mariel "entrants" were added to the totals.

By contrast, the percentage for next-door neighbors Canada and Mexico was just over 3 percent, with Dominicans and Salvadorans just under. The proportions from Argentina, Peru, Chile, Venezuela, and Bolivia were minuscule, and that from Brazil was by far the lowest of all in Latin America (0.03 percent), lower even than that from Asia and Africa. Also minuscule were the 1980 proportions for Uruguay—0.4 percent, based on 13,278 immigrants in the United States[17]—and Paraguay—0.08 percent, based on 2,858 immigrants, the lowest total by far from any sizable Latin American country.

Table 3 extends this general picture with detailed 1980 census information on social and economic characteristics of all these immigrant groups, ranked in order of proportion of college graduates, which may serve as a proxy for social class origins. These data, compared against the norms for mainland Puerto Ricans and total U.S. population, reveal immigrants' extraordinary socioeconomic diversity in general, and those from the Americas in particular.

One point that stands out is the extremely high degree of educational attainment among immigrants from Asia and Africa: about 40 percent are college graduates, compared with 16 percent for the total U.S. population, and they are well above the norm in proportion of professionals. For some countries such as India (not shown in the table), the proportions are much higher than the continental averages. For example, more than 90 percent of Indian immigrants to the United States in the late 1960s and early 1970s had professional and managerial occupations in India prior to immigration, as did four-fifths in the late 1970s and two-thirds during the 1980s. This was true despite the fact that over time most of these immigrants were admitted under family reunification preferences. By the mid-1970s there were more Filipino and Indian medical graduates in the United States than there were American black physicians. By the mid-1980s one-fifth of all engineering doctorates awarded by U.S. universities went to foreign-born students from Taiwan, India, and South Korea alone. It has been estimated that since the early 1950s, fewer than 10 percent of the tens of thousands of students from China, Taiwan, Hong Kong, and South Korea who came to the United States for training on nonimmigrant visas ever returned home. Rather, many adjusted their status and gained U.S. citizenship through occupational connections with American industry and business, thus becoming eligible to send for family members later.

These data document a classic pattern of "brain drain" immigration. Indeed, although they come from developing countries, these immigrants as a group are perhaps the most skilled ever to arrive in the United States. This helps explain the class origins of the recent popularization of Asians as a "model minority," as well as to debunk nativist calls for restricting immigrants to those perceived to be more "assimilable" on the basis of language and culture.[18] Canadians and Europeans, though they are much older resident groups—as reflected in their low labor force participation rates and high naturalization rates—show levels of education slightly below the U.S. average, an occupational profile slightly above it, but much lower poverty rates. By contrast, Latin Americans as a whole have well-below-average levels of educational attainment, the highest rates of labor force participation, with high concentrations in lower blue-collar employment, and higher poverty rates.

However, a different picture emerges when the data are broken down by national origin, underscoring that these populations cannot sensibly be subsumed under the supranational rubric of "Hispanic" or "Latino," except as a catchall category. Among Latin Americans, the highest socioeconomic status (SES) is reflected by Venezuelans, Bolivians, and Chileans, also the smallest of the immigrant groups, and by Argentineans, who have the highest proportion of professionals among all immigrants from the Americas. This suggests that these groups consist substantially of highly skilled persons who have entered under the occupational preferences of U.S. immigration law. Peruvians and Cubans reflected levels of educational attainment slightly above the U.S. norm, and their occupational and income characteristics put them at about the national average. Occupying an intermediate position were groups from the English-speaking Caribbean—Jamaica, Trinidad, Barbados, Guyana—with SES patterns quite similar to each other and slightly below U.S. norms. The lowest SES is found among Mexicans, Dominicans, and Salvadorans, who were also the largest groups of immigrants entering both legally and illegally in the 1980s. Their characteristics approximate those of mainland Puerto Ricans, except the poverty rate for Puerto Ricans is much higher than that of any other Latin American or Caribbean immigrant group. Guatemalans, Ecuadorans, Hondurans, Nicaraguans, Haitians, and Colombians also reflected a much higher ratio of lower blue-collar to upper white-collar employment.

The Venezuelan case is puzzling and bimodal, because it shows extraordinarily low rates of labor force participation and the highest level of college graduates, but also high poverty rates. Brazilians too show below-average participation in the labor force but, by contrast, have lower-than-average levels of poverty. The reasons for the patterns of these two groups are unclear and cannot be accounted for by available demographic data.[19]

The last column of table 3 provides data on the percentage of each group naturalized as U.S. citizens as of 1980. As would be expected, immigrant groups that had resided longer in the United States—Europeans and Canadians, most of whom came before the 1960s—had a higher proportion of naturalized citizens. Recent arrivals—Asians, Africans, and Latin Americans, most of whom had come only in the 1970s

TABLE 3. Social and Economic Characteristics of the U.S. Foreign-born Population, 1980, in Rank Order of College Graduates, by Region and American Countries of Birth, Compared to Total U.S. Population

Region/ Country of Birth	Education[1]	Labor Force[2]	Occupation[3]		Income	Citizenship
	% College Graduates	Participation Rate %	% Upper White-Collar	% Lower Blue-Collar	% Families in Poverty	% U.S. Naturalized
REGION OF ORIGIN:						
Africa	38.7	60.8	36.1	12.9	13.0	38.0
Asia	37.9	62.6	31.1	15.3	11.2	34.8
Canada	14.3	50.2	29.7	12.2	4.6	61.0
Europe	12.1	47.4	23.9	18.4	5.2	72.1
Latin America	8.9	66.0	11.2	31.3	18.3	29.0
LATIN AMERICA AND CARIBBEAN:						
Venezuela	31.4	34.4	27.4	11.7	22.7	17.3
Bolivia	30.7	68.3	27.7	11.9	8.5	32.4
Chile	24.4	70.3	25.4	16.4	7.8	27.7
Argentina	24.2	69.1	28.5	15.4	8.3	38.8
Peru	20.3	70.5	21.1	22.1	10.7	28.8
Cuba	17.1	66.9	19.3	23.9	10.9	45.1
Panama	16.0	68.6	22.3	13.3	11.9	55.1
Guyana	15.0	71.0	19.6	15.9	14.4	31.2
Colombia	14.6	69.7	15.1	29.8	12.5	24.9
Haiti	13.4	72.0	12.1	28.6	19.5	26.1
Costa Rica	12.9	64.1	14.4	22.6	14.0	29.9
Trinidad and Tobago	12.4	71.7	16.3	13.1	14.3	29.3
Nicaragua	12.2	63.5	13.3	28.9	18.6	24.3
Jamaica	11.0	72.8	15.7	14.7	12.4	36.3
Brazil	10.8	58.3	24.9	17.6	8.2	35.3
Honduras	9.6	66.7	10.6	27.3	14.9	35.0
Ecuador	9.3	68.5	11.5	36.9	15.7	24.7
Barbados	8.5	70.0	14.8	14.7	10.9	42.4

Guatemala	6.9	72.2	7.5	32.4	17.5	17.9
El Salvador	6.5	72.9	5.8	32.6	18.8	14.3
Dominican Republic	4.3	62.1	6.9	33.5	31.0	25.5
Mexico	3.0	64.2	5.4	33.1	22.1	23.6
Puerto Ricans in U.S.	5.6	54.9	12.2	30.9	34.9	NA
Total U.S. Population:	16.2	62.0	22.7	18.3	9.6	NA

[1] Persons 25 years or older.

[2] Persons 16 years or older.

[3] Occupation of employed persons 16 years or older; "Upper white-collar": professionals, executives, and managers; "Lower blue-collar": operators, fabricators, and laborers.

Source: U.S. Bureau of the Census, "Foreign-Born Population in the U.S.—Microfiche," *1980 Census*, tables 2, 4, 7, 10–11 (1985).

293

and who are just beginning to make their way in the United States—were much less likely to have initiated the citizenship acquisition process. However, Latin American immigrants as a whole had the lowest proportion of naturalized citizens (29 percent), despite the fact that Asians and Africans were the most recently arrived groups (as shown earlier in table 2).

Clearly, time spent in the United States does not alone explain why different groups become U.S. citizens at different rates. But this is an important question, since, along with higher numbers and greater concentration, citizenship acquisition and effective political participation go to the heart of ethnic politics and the ability of these groups to make themselves heard in the larger society. Among legal immigrants, the research literature has shown that the motivation and propensity to naturalize is higher among upwardly mobile younger persons with higher educational levels, occupational status, English proficiency, income, and property, and whose spouses or children are U.S. citizens. A study of all immigrant cohorts arriving in the United States between 1970 and 1979—thus controlling for length of residence in the country—found that higher-SES Asian immigrants had the highest rates of naturalization, as did political refugees, such as Vietnamese and Cubans, whose return options were blocked. The lowest propensities were found among Mexicans and Canadians, economic (not political) immigrants for whom return is relatively simple and inexpensive. In fact, the combination of three variables alone—educational levels, geographical proximity, and political origin of migration—largely explained differences in citizenship acquisition among immigrant groups.[20]

Finally, table 4 presents 1980 census data on the U.S. foreign-born population's level of English-language proficiency, broken down by region and for all the largest Latin American and Caribbean immigrant groups. As a whole, Latin American and Caribbean immigrants exhibit a much lower degree of English proficiency than do Asians, Africans, and Europeans, reflecting previously noted differences in socioeconomic status and time spent in the United States. But again, even among "Hispanic" groups, as much diversity exists in their patterns of language competency as in their socioeconomic characteristics. Quite obviously, nearly all immigrants from the Commonwealth Caribbean are English monolinguals (a much higher proportion than Canadians, in fact). Among all other Latins, Panamanians—the oldest resident Latin American immigrant group, nearly a third of whom had arrived in the United States prior to 1960—were the most English proficient. In fact, about a third were already English monolinguals. Immigrants from Bolivia, Argentina, Venezuela, and Chile, the highest-SES groups from Latin America, followed in English proficiency. The least proficient, with approximately half reporting an inability to speak English well or at all, were immigrants from the Dominican Republic, Mexico, and El Salvador. As seen earlier, these were also the largest immigrant cohorts

TABLE 4. English Proficiency of the U.S. Foreign-born Population, 1980, in Rank Order, by Region and American Countries of Birth[1]

Region/Country of Birth	% Speak English Only	% Speak Very Well	% Speak Well	% Speak Not Well	% Speak Not at All
REGION OF ORIGIN:					
Canada	79.5	13.7	5.3	1.4	0.1
Africa	27.2	45.2	20.4	5.9	1.3
Europe	40.0	30.0	19.3	8.6	2.2
Asia	11.6	36.5	30.2	16.6	5.1
Latin America	13.1	24.2	23.0	23.3	16.4
LATIN AMERICA AND CARIBBEAN:					
Barbados	96.8	2.4	0.6	0.1	0.0
Trinidad and Tobago	93.2	5.0	1.5	0.3	0.0
Jamaica	94.0	4.0	1.5	0.4	0.1
Guyana	93.3	4.6	1.5	0.5	0.2
Panama	33.5	44.0	16.5	4.8	1.2
Brazil	16.3	41.5	29.3	10.8	2.1
Bolivia	7.9	45.4	29.9	13.6	3.2
Argentina	9.1	44.3	29.0	13.6	4.0
Venezuela	9.3	39.5	32.0	14.8	4.4
Chile	8.7	38.9	31.7	15.9	4.9
Costa Rica	10.0	41.7	27.6	15.5	5.2
Peru	7.6	37.5	31.3	18.2	5.5
Haiti	4.6	35.1	36.8	18.5	5.0
Honduras	14.6	33.5	26.1	18.6	7.1
Colombia	6.2	30.8	30.5	8.4	10.0
Ecuador	3.9	29.2	29.5	25.5	11.9
Nicaragua	5.1	30.1	27.3	23.6	13.9
Cuba	3.1	34.1	23.1	21.4	18.3
Guatemala	4.3	25.7	29.5	27.8	12.7
El Salvador	2.7	20.9	27.0	32.2	17.3
Mexico	2.4	21.3	24.6	29.5	22.1
Dominican Republic	2.3	21.1	23.9	29.2	23.5

[1] Persons five years of age and older.

Source: U.S. Bureau of the Census, "Foreign-Born Population in the United States—Microfiche," *1980 Census,* table 12 (1985).

entering in the 1980s, as well as the lowest-SES groups from Latin America.

In addition to education and time in the United States, age and residence within dense ethnic enclaves were also factors in the development of English proficiency. Cuban refugees, whose median age is the oldest of any immigrant group, are the best example: nearly 40 percent reported speaking English not well or at all. On closer inspection, they reveal themselves to be older or elderly persons residing in areas of high ethnic concentration, such as Miami. Still, the data in table 4 are remarkable in showing that even among the most recently arrived groups, large proportions already report being able to speak English well or very well, and indeed, that significant proportions of the foreign-born speak English *only*. This fact notwithstanding, English-language competency—particularly among Hispanic immigrants in the United States who allegedly harbor a Spanish "retentiveness" and "unwillingness" to assimilate—has become a highly charged sociopolitical issue, with nativist organizations warning about cultural "balkanization" and Quebec-like linguistic separatism in regions of high Hispanic concentration. This issue will be addressed further below.

Hispanics in the United States Today:
A Socioeconomic Portrait

The preceding section focused attention on the diversity of *immigrant* groups from Latin America and the Caribbean, given the importance of the contemporary, and rapidly increasing, immigration to the United States. The 1980 census data presented above are the most recent and, for that matter, the only available national data set that breaks down such information by country of origin. But those data are limited to the foreign-born, which by definition excludes all Puerto Ricans, as well as nearly three-fourths of Mexican Americans and almost one-fourth of Cuban Americans, who are U.S.-born.

No similarly detailed data by ancestry or national origin are available for native-born populations. For such coverage, we must rely on the U.S. Census Bureau's ethnic classification of "Hispanic-origin" groups, which is limited to five categories—persons of Mexican, Puerto Rican, Cuban, "Central/South American," and "other Hispanic" origin—and excludes all non-Spanish-speaking nationalities from Latin America and the Caribbean, such as Jamaicans, Haitians, Guyanese, and Brazilians. The category "Central/South Americans" thus lumps together groups as diverse as Dominicans, Guatemalans, Colombians, Peruvians, and Argentineans. Analyses of these data thus cannot be meaningfully interpreted. The category "other Hispanic" includes persons who trace their origins in the United States over many generations; mixed-ethnicity and residual cases that could not be clearly coded into one of the other categories; and a relatively small number of immigrants from Spain. Despite these limitations, the data do cover all members of the three largest U.S. Hispanic ethnic groups, including both immigrants and native-born, thus permitting a fuller comparative assessment of their social and economic situation. As noted previously, detailed information from the 1990 census will not become available until 1993, but equivalent current population survey data collected in March 1990 from a national sample are instructive. These are summarized in table 5 for all five Hispanic-origin groups and are compared to descriptive statistics for the total U.S. population.

As table 5 shows, significant differences exist in the socioeconomic position of Hispanic-origin ethnic minorities. Compared with the me-

TABLE 5.   Social and Economic Characteristics of Hispanic Ethnic Groups in the United States, Compared to the Total U.S. Population, 1990

Characteristic	Total U.S. Population	Mexican Origin	Puerto Rican Origin	Cuban Origin	Central/South American	Other Hispanic*
Age						
Median age	32.8	24.1	27.0	39.1	28.0	31.1
% 55 years and over	20.6	8.7	12.8	28.5	8.0	19.4
Education[1]						
% College graduates	21.3	5.4	9.7	20.2	15.6	15.2
% < 5 years of school	2.4	15.5	9.7	5.8	8.8	3.9
Labor Force Status[2]						
Men (% in labor force)	74.6	81.2	69.2	74.9	83.7	75.3
Men (% unemployed)	5.9	8.6	8.2	6.3	6.9	6.2
Women (% in labor force)	57.2	52.9	41.4	57.8	61.0	57.0
Women (% unemployed)	5.1	9.8	9.1	5.1	6.3	5.9
Occupation (men):[3]						
% Upper white-collar	26.0	8.3	11.2	25.9	12.2	16.6
% Lower white-collar	20.5	12.6	19.4	20.2	17.1	18.6
% Upper blue-collar	19.4	21.2	22.0	20.9	17.0	21.1
% Lower blue-collar	20.3	31.7	24.5	20.9	31.3	23.3
% Service occupations	9.8	15.1	20.6	11.3	19.8	17.7
% Farming, fishing	4.0	11.2	2.6	1.1	2.6	2.8
Occupation (women):[3]						
% Upper white-collar	26.4	14.2	23.1	22.1	14.1	20.3
% Lower white-collar	44.9	38.1	43.5	47.5	31.4	42.3
% Upper blue-collar	2.2	3.2	1.9	1.3	1.9	2.6
% Lower blue-collar	8.1	18.8	12.0	10.4	17.4	10.5
% Service occupations	17.4	23.9	18.8	18.3	35.0	23.6
% Farming, fishing	1.0	1.8	0.3	0.4	—	0.3
Economic Status						
Mean family income ($)	41,506	27,488	26,682	38,497	32,158	33,388
% Families in poverty	10.3	25.7	30.4	12.5	16.8	15.8
% Female-headed families	16.5	19.6	38.9	18.9	25.0	24.5
% Own–buying home	64.1	44.9	28.4	46.7	24.4	54.4

*See text for definition of "Other Hispanic."

[1] Persons 25 years or older.

[2] Persons 16 years or older.

[3] "Upper white-collar": professionals, executives, managers; "Lower white-collar": technical, sales, and administrative support; "Upper blue-collar": precision production, craft, and repair; "Lower blue-collar": operators, fabricators, and laborers.

Source: U.S. Bureau of the Census, *The Hispanic Population of the United States: March 1990* (Current Population Reports, 1991).

dian age of 32.8 years for the total U.S. population in 1990, Cubans are notably older—39.1 years—and Mexicans, younger—24.1 years. This in part reflects below-average and above-average fertility, respectively. About 20 percent of adult Americans are college graduates—the same proportion as Cubans—but only 5 percent of Mexican Americans[21] and almost 10 percent of Puerto Ricans are college graduates. Indeed, on every measure of socioeconomic performance listed in table 5—labor force participation rates, occupations of men and women, family income and poverty rates, and the percent of female-headed families—Cubans were the only Hispanic ethnic group that had essentially reached parity with norms for the U.S. population as a whole. Only with respect to home ownership are Cuban Americans still lagging behind the national norm (47 percent to 64 percent).

Other Hispanic groups exhibit patterns of socioeconomic attainment generally below that of the U.S. average. Among them Puerto Ricans are in the worst socioeconomic situation, though they are all U.S. citizens and more highly educated than Mexican Americans. Puerto Rican men and especially women have much lower rates of labor force participation—69 and 41 percent, respectively, compared with 75 and 57 percent for the total U.S. population. This is partly a reflection of the fact that 39 percent of Puerto Rican families are female-headed, compared with the U.S. average of 16.5 percent, and have higher poverty rates, lower mean family incomes, and fewer home owners.

Mexican men, and Central/South American men and women, exhibit the highest rates of labor force participation, although Mexican men and women also have the highest unemployment rates. Mexicans and Central/South Americans are disproportionately concentrated in lower blue-collar occupations (operators, fabricators, laborers), as are Mexican men in agricultural work, and Mexican and particularly Central/South American women in the low-wage service sector. Despite their high poverty rate (25.7 percent), 45 percent of Mexican families in the United States own their homes and only about 19 percent are female-headed. Both these figures compare proportionately to the Cubans, and the latter percentage is close to the national average. Since Mexicans compose 60 percent of the national Hispanic population, their characteristics tend to dominate aggregate figures when presented for the Hispanic population as a whole (which, as the data in table 5 clearly show, should not be taken as a homogenous unit). An issue posed by these data, then, is how to explain the significant socioeconomic differences among the various groups.

Cubans' general socioeconomic advantage relative to other Hispanic groups can be accounted for by the upper- and middle-class origins of the first waves of exiles, who left after the 1959 revolution. But their upper- and middle-class origins do not account for research findings showing Cubans maintaining above-average occupations and family incomes, even after controlling for their educational levels and other "human capital." Similarly, Mexicans' and Puerto Ricans' general socioeconomic disadvantage relative to Cubans and others can be accounted for by their particular histories of discrimination and exploitation. But the histories do not account for the significant differences between Mexicans and Puerto Ricans in their present circumstances.

With regard to the Cuban advantage, the Cubans' mode of incorporation was assisted by the favorable governmental reception given them as political exiles fleeing a Communist revolution (although other Cold War refugees in the United States, notably the Indochinese, have received much greater levels of public assistance without comparable socioeconomic gains).[22] The consolidation of an ethnic enclave economy by south Florida's Cuban entrepreneurs has been more significant. This helps explain how successive cohorts of Cuban immigrants have been able to exceed expected levels of socioeconomic attainment. In Miami, Cuban-owned enterprises increased from about 900 to 25,000 between the late 1960s and the late 1980s. By 1985 Hispanic-owned firms in Dade County reported $2.2 billion in sales, pushing the area to first place in gross receipts among all Hispanic firms nationwide. A longitudinal survey of Cuban refugees who arrived in Miami in 1973 showed, that by 1979, 21.2 percent were self-employed and another 36.3 percent were employed in businesses owned by Cubans. These figures were quadruple and double, respectively, the proportionate figures in a parallel sample of Mexican immigrants who arrived in the United States at the same time. A subsequent survey of Mariel Cubans who arrived in Miami in 1980 found that 28.2 percent were self-employed by 1986, and another 44.9 percent were employed by co-nationals.[23]

Regarding the Mexican and Puerto Rican situations, available analyses point to different modes of incorporation in different labor markets and ethnic hiring queues. Briefly stated, these analyses suggest that Mexican low-wage workers in the Southwest and Midwest have been employers' preferred sources of pliable labor, not least because many are immigrants and a substantial proportion are undocumented. In contrast, Puerto Ricans, who are U.S. citizens by birth and not subject to deportation, often entered the Northeast's highly unionized labor markets, but massive industrial restructuring over the past two decades has resulted in the rapid decline or elimination of jobs in which they were disproportionately concentrated. The Puerto Ricans appear to have been displaced, as employers shift to other immigrant groups—especially Dominicans, Colombians, and other undocumented immigrants—willing to work in low-wage jobs and under poor working conditions. During this period many have migrated back to Puerto Rico, and those remaining in the Northeast have experienced unemployment levels, withdrawal from the labor force, and disrupted family structures characteristic of the inner-city "underclass."

Significantly, a study by Marta Tienda found that Cuban workers in the New York–New Jersey area during the same restructuring period did not have similar experiences, despite their disproportionate representation in some of the same labor markets as Puerto Ricans. This suggests that Cubans may have been ranked higher in employment queues or were more successful in finding alternative employment by moving to Miami. In any case, this scholarship underscores the import of structural factors and historical contexts of reception and incorporation in shaping socioeconomic outcomes among different ethnic groups.

It also debunks an undue "culture of poverty" emphasis on inner-city residents' individual attributes or Hispanics' supposed lack of "assimilability."[24]

Language and the Politics of Linguistic Assimilation

In the context of a recent and broader public debate over "multiculturalism" in American life, much attention has been focused on concerns raised by nativist organizations, including U.S. English, the Federation for American Immigration Reform (FAIR), and others. They are worried about the "fragmenting of America" by new immigrants, primarily Spanish-speakers from Latin America, and what they see as the impending demise of the English language in areas of immigrant concentration. By planting concern that today's immigrants, unlike yesterday's, do not want to assimilate, these groups have focused the discussion on the survival of English as the nation's only language and as its cultural centerpoint. As reflected by the passage of "English Only" measures in several states, pressures against bilingualism in America are rooted in more fundamental social and political concerns that date back to the origins of the nation (as reflected by Benjamin Franklin's comments cited at the beginning of this essay). The point was underscored by Theodore Roosevelt during the peak immigration years at the turn of the century: "We have room but for one language here, and that is the English language; for we intend to see that the crucible turns our people out as Americans, and not as dwellers in a polyglot boardinghouse."

The paradox is that, while the United States has probably incorporated more bilingual people than any other nation in the world since Franklin's time, American history is notable for its near mass-extinction of non-English languages. A generational pattern of progressive anglicization is clear: first-generation immigrants learn survival English but speak their mother tongue to their children at home; the second generation in turn speaks accentless English at school and work, where its use is required and its social advantages are unmistakable. Meanwhile, the use of the mother tongue atrophies (for example, Spanish quickly becomes "Spanglish" and Vietnamese, "Vietglish"); with very few exceptions the third generation grows up as English monolinguals. This process explains why the United States has been called a "language graveyard."

For all the alarm about Quebec-like linguistic separatism in the United States today, the last census suggests that this generational pattern remains as strong as in the past. In 1980 well over 200 million Americans spoke English only, including substantial proportions of foreign-born (as shown in table 4). Among new immigrants who had arrived in the

TABLE 6.   Monolingualism and Bilingualism among Hispanic Adults and
             Children in the United States, 1976

Current Language Spoken (%)	Mexican Origin	Puerto Rican Origin	Cuban Origin	Central/South American	Other Hispanic
Adults (18 years and older):					
Spanish Only	20	21	33	25	10
Spanish Usually (also English)	23	36	40	29	18
English Usually (also Spanish)	35	32	25	30	24
English Only	21	10	1	15	48
Children (5–17 years old):					
Spanish Only	3	5	1	7	1
Spanish Usually (also English)	19	17	26	19	12
English Usually (also Spanish)	38	52	62	34	27
English Only	40	25	11	40	60

Source: David E. López, *Language Maintenance and Shift in the United States Today,* vol. 1 (Los Alamitos, Calif.: National Center for Bilingual Research, 1982), tables II-D and II-E. Data from the 1976 Survey of Income and Education.

United States between 1970 and 1980, 84 percent spoke a language other than English at home, but over half, adults as well as children, reported being able to speak English well. Among pre-1970 immigrants, 62 percent still spoke a language other than English at home, and the overwhelming majority of them—77 percent of the adults, and 95 percent of the children—spoke English well. Among native-born, less than 7 percent spoke a language other than English at home, and more than 90 percent of them, both adults and children, spoke English well.

More detailed studies have confirmed that in all American ethnic groups, without exception, children consistently prefer English to their mother tongue. With any ethnic group, the use of English increases in direct ratio to the proportion of U.S.-born. Table 6 presents related findings from a unique 1976 data set on patterns of monolingualism and bilingualism among all adults and children for the main Hispanic ethnic groups (including both the native-born and foreign-born). Among Mexican Americans, the largest Hispanic group, 20 percent of adults spoke Spanish only, 21 percent spoke English only, and the remaining three-fifths spoke both languages, although a majority usually spoke English. Among the children, 40 percent were already English monolinguals, and a minuscule 3 percent, mainly preschoolers, spoke Spanish only. Tiny percentages of Spanish monolinguals also characterized the children of all other Hispanic groups. Cuban adults in this 1976 sample, overwhelmingly recent immigrants, were the least likely Hispanic group to have shifted to English, yet they were also the most successful among Hispanic ethnic groups in socioeconomic terms. At the same time, three-fourths of Cuban children aged 5 to 17 already spoke English only or usually—a proportion similar to that seen for Mexican, Puerto Rican, and Central and South American children (the proportion for "other Hispanic" was nearly nine-tenths).

As pointed out earlier, immigrant groups vary significantly in their rates of English-language ability, reflecting differences in educational and occupational levels. But even among Spanish speakers, who are considered the most resistant to language shift, the trend toward anglicization is present. Language loyalty among them, especially Mexicans, is due largely to the effect of continuing high immigration to the United States. For example, a recent study of a large representative sample of Mexican-origin couples in Los Angeles found that among first-generation women, 84 percent used Spanish only at home, 14 percent used both languages, and 2 percent used English only. By the third generation there was a complete reversal, with 4 percent speaking Spanish only at home, 12 percent using both, and 84 percent shifting to English only. Among the men, the pattern was similar, except their shift to English was even more marked by the second generation.[25] Indeed, in U.S. immigrant families, grandparents and grandchildren often cannot communicate with one another except through bilingual relatives, usually the parents.[26]

English proficiency has always been a key to immigrants' socioeconomic mobility and full participation in their adoptive society. It is worth noting that in 1986, with the passage of Proposition 63, the initiative declaring English California's official language, more than 40,000 immigrants were turned away from ESL classes in the Los Angeles Unified School District alone: the supply of services could not meet the vigorous demand for English training. The efforts of linguistic nativists to compel immigrants to shed their foreign languages contrast sharply and ironically with the efforts of elite native youth to acquire a halting command of often the same foreign languages in U.S. universities.

English-language dominance is not threatened in the United States today—or for that matter in the world, where it has become already firmly established as the premier international language of commerce, diplomacy, education, journalism, aviation, technology, and mass culture. What is threatened is a more scarce resource: the survival of languages brought by immigrants themselves, which, in the absence of social structural supports, are destined to disappear. Given the immense pressure for linguistic conformity put on immigrant children by peers, schools, and the media—and later through exogamous marriages and integration into the mainstream economy and society—the preservation of fluent bilingualism beyond the first generation is an exceptional outcome. It is dependent on parents' intellectual and economic resources, their efforts to transmit the mother tongue to their children, *and* on the presence of institutionally complete ethnic communities where literacy in a second language is taught in schools and is valued in business and the labor market (such as that found in large entrepreneurial enclaves). The combination of these factors is rare: Miami may provide the closest approximation in the United States today, but even there the rapid and progressive anglicization of the Cuban second generation is evident.

Where such supports for bilingualism are lacking, the outcome is not only rapid English acquisition but the equally rapid loss of the home language. Such enforced linguistic homogeneity is an undesirable goal at a time when the United States finds itself enmeshed in global economic competition—including competition for skilled talent in a global immigration market, as reflected in the new Immigration Act of 1990. The need for Americans who fluently speak foreign languages becomes increasingly compelling, and the second generation now growing up in many American cities could fulfill such a need. In any event, far from posing a social or cultural threat, the existence of areas where foreign languages are fluently spoken enriches American culture, in the full sense of the phrase, and the lives of natives and immigrants alike.

The Europeans who founded and in large part dominated the United States have finally stopped coming, except in relatively small trickles. Latin Americans, and increasingly Asian Americans, are now beginning to remake it. While the immediate future augurs an acceleration of present trends, they too, like the Europeans, will at some point cease coming. All such passages contain their own internal contradictions, albeit in forms that defy safe or sage predictions. Europeans who came to the United States in the peak period of immigration in the nineteenth and early twentieth centuries helped transform the country, but not in their own image. They were transformed by American society more than the other way around. The peoples of Latin America and the Caribbean, and of Asia, who are now coming to the United States in this new peak immigration period that will most probably continue into the twenty-first century, are also helping transform America. But, as in the past, they will not do so in their own image.

Notes

1. See, for example, Rubén G. Rumbaut, "The Hispanic Prologue," in David Cardús (ed.), *A Hispanic Look at the Bicentennial* (Houston: Institute of Hispanic Culture, 1978), 5–22; Carlos M. Fernández-Shaw, *Presencia Española en los Estados Unidos* (Madrid: Ediciónes Cultura Hispánica, 1972); and Joseph P. Sánchez, "Hispanic American Heritage," in Herman J. Viola and Carolyn Margolis (eds.), *Seeds of Change: A Quincentennial Commemoration* (Washington, D.C.: Smithsonian Institution Press, 1991), 173–85. Indeed, half a dozen states bear Spanish names, and several of the largest U.S. cities and most of the cities of its most populous state are named in Spanish after Catholic saints and symbols. The presence of hundreds of "Indian" tribes comprising perhaps 5 million people in the territory of what is now the United States at the time of the arrival of the European colonists has also been largely ignored, and it has prob-

ably never occurred to most Americans that the names of 26 of the 50 states—from Alabama and Alaska to Texas, Wisconsin, and Wyoming—have indigenous names; and one, Indiana, reflects also the fact that Columbus's mistake has not yet been corrected after 500 years.

2. Richard D. Lamm and Gary Imhoff, *The Immigration Time Bomb: The Fragmenting of America* (New York: Dutton, 1985). On Wilson's views, see Robert Reinhold, "In California, New Discussion on Whether to Bar the Door," *New York Times,* Dec. 3, 1991, A-1. For Buchanan's remarks, see the *San Diego Union,* Dec. 9, 1991, A-11; and Cathleen Decker, "Buchanan Uses Whatever It Takes in Long-Shot Bid," *Los Angeles Times,* Jan. 14, 1992, A-1.

3. Although Puerto Ricans are U.S. citizens by birth, the U.S. Census only includes Puerto Ricans living on the mainland in reporting U.S. population totals. A separate count is kept for Puerto Rico, as well as Guam and other territories.

4. In the case of Cuba, consider this extraordinary excerpt from President William McKinley's State of the Union message on December 5, 1899: "The new Cuba yet to arise from the ashes of the past must needs be bound to us by ties of singular intimacy and strength if its enduring welfare is to be assured. Whether those ties shall be organic or conventional, the destinies of Cuba are in some rightful form and manner irrevocably linked with our own, but how and how far is for the future to determine in the ripeness of events." Cited in Louis A. Pérez, Jr., *Cuba and the United States: Ties of Singular Intimacy* (Athens: Univ. of Georgia Press, 1990), ix.

5. For an analysis of contemporary (including Asian) immigration to the United States, see Alejandro Portes and Rubén G. Rumbaut, *Immigrant America: A Portrait* (Berkeley: Univ. of California Press, 1990); David M. Reimers, *Still the Golden Door: The Third World Comes to America* (New York: Columbia Univ. Press, 1985); and Rubén G. Rumbaut, "Passages to America: Perspectives on the New Immigration," in Alan Wolfe (ed.), *America at Century's End* (Berkeley: Univ. of California Press, 1991), 208–44. It is beyond the scope of this essay to provide a comprehensive listing of the voluminous literature that has accumulated on contemporary immigration to the United States; the reader is referred to the extensive references cited in the above.

6. On social networks in the immigration of Mexicans and Dominicans to the United States, see Douglas Massey, Rafael Alarcón, Jorge Durand, and Humberto González, *Return to Aztlán: The Social Process of International Migration from Western Mexico* (Berkeley: Univ. of California Press, 1987); Sherri Grasmuck and Patricia Pessar, *Between Two Islands: Dominican International Immigration* (Berkeley: Univ. of California Press, 1991). See also Guillermina Jasso and Mark R. Rosenzweig, *The New Chosen People: Immigrants in the United States* (New York: Russell Sage Foundation, 1990).

7. Alejandro Portes, "From South of the Border: Hispanic Minorities in the United States," in Virginia Yans-McLaughlin (ed.), *Immigration Reconsidered: History, Sociology, and Politics* (New York: Oxford Univ. Press, 1990), 160–94. For a critical historical assessment of two centuries of U.S. expansion and intervention in Latin America, see Frank Niess, *A Hemisphere to Itself: A History of US-Latin American Relations* (London: Zed, 1990).

8. See Dawn Marshall, "A History of West Indian Migrations: Overseas Opportunities and 'Safety-Valve' Policies," in Barry B. Levine (ed.), *The Caribbean Exodus* (New York: Praeger, 1987), 15–31. See also Ransford W. Palmer (ed.),

In Search of a Better Life: Perspectives on Migration from the Caribbean (New York: Praeger, 1990); Franklin W. Knight and Colin A. Palmer (eds.), *The Modern Caribbean* (Chapel Hill: Univ. of North Carolina Press, 1989); and Robert A. Pastor (ed.), *Migration and Development in the Caribbean: The Unexplored Connection* (Boulder, Colo.: Westview Press, 1985).

9. For a discussion of the 1990 Act, see Francesco Isgro, "The New Employment-Based Immigration Selection System," *Migration World* 19: 5 (1991), 34–37.

10. See Niess, *A Hemisphere to Itself;* Eric Williams, *From Columbus to Castro: The History of the Caribbean* (New York: Random House, 1984); Franklin W. Knight, *The Caribbean: The Genesis of a Fragmented Nationalism,* 2d ed. (New York: Oxford Univ. Press, 1990).

11. See David Montejano, *Anglos and Mexicans in the Making of Texas, 1836– 1986* (Austin: Univ. of Texas Press, 1987); David J. Weber, *The Mexican Frontier, 1821–1846: The American Southwest Under Mexico* (Albuquerque: Univ. of New Mexico Press, 1982); Sarah Deutsch, *No Separate Refuge: Culture, Class, and Gender on an Anglo-Hispanic Frontier in the American Southwest, 1880–1940* (New York: Oxford Univ. Press, 1987). For a comparative historical study of Mexican Americans in San Antonio, Santa Fe, Tucson, and Los Angeles, see Richard Griswold del Castillo, *La Familia: Chicano Families in the Urban Southwest, 1846 to the Present* (Notre Dame, Ind.: Univ. of Notre Dame Press, 1984).

12. See Lawrence A. Cardoso, *Mexican Immigration to the United States, 1897– 1931* (Tucson: Univ. of Arizona Press, 1980); Mario Barrera, *Race and Class in the Southwest* (Notre Dame, Ind.: Univ. of Notre Dame Press, 1979); Rodolfo Alvarez, "The Psycho-Historical and Socio-economic Development of the Chicano Community in the United States," in Carol A. Hernández, Marsha J. Haug, and Nathaniel N. Wagner (eds.), *Chicanos: Social and Psychological Perspectives* (St. Louis: Mosby, 1976), 38–51; Mario T. García, *Mexican Americans: Leadership, Ideology, and Identity, 1930–1960* (New Haven: Yale Univ. Press, 1989); Juan Gómez Quiñones, *Chicano Politics: Reality and Promise, 1940–1990* (Albuquerque: Univ. of New Mexico Press, 1990).

13. See Portes, "From South of the Border"; Joan Moore and Harry Pachón, *Hispanics in the United States* (Englewood Cliffs, N.J.: Prentice-Hall, 1985); Virginia E. Sánchez Korrol, *From Colonia to Community: The History of Puerto Ricans in New York City, 1917–1948* (Westport, Conn.: Greenwood Press, 1983); Frank Bonilla and Ricardo Campos, "A Wealth of Poor: Puerto Ricans in the New Economic Order," *Daedalus* 110 (1981), 133–76; Joseph P. Fitzpatrick, *Puerto Rican Americans: The Meaning of Migration to the Mainland,* 2d ed. (Englewood Cliffs, N.J.: Prentice-Hall, 1987).

14. Wayne S. Smith, *Portrait of Cuba* (Atlanta: Turner Publishing, 1991), 63. See also Pérez, *Cuba and the United States;* Niess, *A Hemisphere to Itself;* Hugh Thomas, *Cuba: The Pursuit of Freedom* (New York: Harper & Row, 1971).

15. For a provocative essay on the subject, see Carlos Alberto Montaner, *Cuba: Claves para una Conciencia en Crisis* (Madrid: Editorial Playor, 1983); see also Carlos Alberto Montaner, "The Roots of Anti-Americanism in Cuba: Sovereignty in an Age of World Cultural Homogeneity," *Caribbean Review* 13 (1984), 13–46. Cf. Portes and Rumbaut, *Immigrant America,* and Portes, "From South of the Border."

16. As noted, the figure of 3,460,683 immigrants from Latin America and the Caribbean refers only to persons *legally* admitted as permanent residents

during 1981–90 and does not include an estimate of illegal immigration. However, the figure does include 1,359,186 formerly illegal immigrants (of whom 71 percent were Mexican nationals) who qualified for legalization of their status in 1989 and 1990 under the amnesty provisions of the Immigration Reform and Control Act (IRCA). INS immigration data for 1991 and 1992 will add to the regular immigration totals another 1.7 million persons who qualified for legalization under IRCA as they complete the bureaucratic process of obtaining a "green card," the majority of them being from Mexico and other Latin American countries. A total of 3.1 million undocumented immigrants were found eligible for legalization under IRCA; most of them had resided in the United States since 1981 or earlier (the remainder were Special Agricultural Workers who could demonstrate that they had worked in the United States during 1985–86). See Rumbaut, "Passages to America"; cf. Leo R. Chávez, *Shadowed Lives: Undocumented Immigrants in American Society* (Fort Worth: Harcourt Brace Jovanovich, 1991).

17. This does not mean that Uruguayans do not emigrate. On the contrary, according to recent reports, the Uruguayan "brain drain" may be the largest in Latin America; there are nearly 1 million Uruguayans living outside their country, about a fourth of the population (another 3 million reside in Uruguay). They have gone not to the United States but to Mexico and elsewhere. See Isgro, "The New Employment-Based Immigration Selection System," 37; and the essay in this volume by M. Patricia Fernández Kelly and Alejandro Portes.

18. See Rumbaut, "Passages to America," for a comparative analysis of the class origins of contemporary Asian and Latin American immigrant nationalities in the United States. For a contemporary local assessment, cf. David Rieff, *Los Angeles: Capital of the Third World* (New York: Simon & Schuster, 1991).

19. For a related detailed analysis based on public use samples of the 1960, 1970, and 1980 censuses, see Frank D. Bean and Marta Tienda, *The Hispanic Population of the United States* (New York: Russell Sage Foundation, 1987). With respect to the Venezuelan case, Bean and Tienda "suspect that a large share of this group consists of individuals who are independently wealthy individuals and not compelled to work" (294). A similar explanation may apply in part to the Brazilians (who, as non-Hispanics, were not included in their study).

20. For a comparative-historical analysis of generational patterns of ethnic identity, citizenship acquisition, and political participation among immigrant and ethnic groups, with a focus on the diverse experiences of Mexicans, Cubans, Dominicans, Colombians, and other groups from Latin America—and the unlikely prospects for a nationwide "Hispanic" politics, at least in the short term, based on efforts to mobilize groups of different national and class origins under a common generic label—see Portes and Rumbaut, *Immigrant America*, chap. 4. Like African Americans, Mexican Americans reflect a reactive political history marked by institutionalized discrimination and disenfranchisement, but differ in their proximity to and strong identification with the country of origin—factors that have presented added obstacles to effective political organization and participation in the United States, despite the watershed of the Chicano movement of the late 1960s and early 1970s. Cf. García, *Mexican Americans;* and Gómez Quiñones, *Chicano Politics.*

21. An earlier study found that as of the early 1970s out of 24 million African Americans there were 2,200 who had earned Ph.D.'s, while among the 8 million Mexican Americans only 60 individuals had earned a Ph.D., when a

similar level of disadvantage would have yielded about 730. This may be taken as an indicator of the level of available technical expertise (that is, one can infer the number of doctors, lawyers, and master's and bachelor's degrees from it), and it underscores the fact that "Mexican Americans were almost entirely lacking in certification for middle-class status" until very recently. See Alvarez, "Psycho-Historical and Socio-economic Development."

22. On the import of government aid to the Cuban exiles, see Silvia Pedraza-Bailey, *Political and Economic Migrants in America: Cubans and Mexicans* (Austin: Univ. of Texas Press, 1985). On the case of the Indochinese, see Rubén G. Rumbaut, "The Structure of Refuge: Southeast Asian Refugees in the United States, 1975–1985," *International Review of Comparative Public Policy* 1 (1989), 97–129.

23. See Alejandro Portes and Robert L. Bach, *Latin Journey: Cuban and Mexican Immigrants in the United States* (Berkeley: Univ. of California Press, 1985); Alejandro Portes and Leif Jensen, "The Enclave and the Entrants: Patterns of Ethnic Enterprise in Miami Before and After Mariel," *American Sociological Review* 54 (Dec. 1989), 929–49; Alejandro Portes, "The Social Origins of the Cuban Enclave Economy of Miami," *Sociological Perspectives* 30 (Oct. 1987), 340–72.

24. Marta Tienda, "Puerto Ricans and the Underclass Debate," *The Annals* 501 (Jan. 1989), 105–19. See also the articles collected in Edwin Meléndez and Clara Rodríguez (eds.), "Puerto Rican Poverty and Labor Markets," *Hispanic Journal of Behavioral Sciences* (special issue) 14 (Feb. 1992); Portes, "From South of the Border"; Nicholas Lemann, "The Other Underclass," *The Atlantic*, Dec. 1991, 96–110.

25. David E. López, "Chicano Language Loyalty in an Urban Setting," *Sociology and Social Research* 62 (1978), 267–78. See also Portes and Rumbaut, *Immigrant America*, chap. 6; Calvin Veltman, *Language Shift in the United States* (Berlin: Mouton, 1983), Melvyn C. Resnick, "Beyond the Ethnic Community: Spanish Language Roles and Maintenance in Miami," *International Journal of the Sociology of Language* 69 (1988), 89–104; Ray Hutchison, "The Hispanic Community in Chicago: A Study of Population Growth and Acculturation," *Research in Race and Ethnic Relations* 5 (1988), 193–229. The appearance of widespread Spanish-language loyalty is not typically presented in the popular media as a function of high levels of contemporary immigration and tends to leave the impression that English is being gradually supplanted; cf. Claudia Puig, "The Explosion of *Radio en Español:* Why Southern California's Spanish-Language Stations Are Zooming Off the Charts," *Los Angeles Times*, April 7, 1991, Calendar-9.

26. See Michael Quintanilla, "The Language Gap: Third-Generation Minorities Learn There's Sometimes a Price to Be Paid for 'English Only,'" *Los Angeles Times*, June 9, 1991, E-1.

Contributors

Alfred Stepan is Burgess Professor of Political Science at Columbia University, where for eight years he was also Dean of the School of International and Public Affairs. He began his career in Latin America as a special foreign correspondent for *The Economist* and subsequently directed the Council on Latin American Studies at Yale University for nearly a decade. He is the author of *The Military in Politics: Changing Patterns in Brazil* and *Rethinking Military Politics: Brazil and the Southern Cone,* both of which were best-sellers in Brazil. His other books include *The State and Society: Peru in Comparative Perspective* and, with Juan J. Linz, *Problems of Democratic Transition and Consolidation: Eastern Europe, Southern Europe and South America* (forthcoming). He is editor of *Democratizing Brazil* and, with Juan J. Linz, *The Breakdown of Democratic Regimes.* Alfred Stepan is a Fellow of the American Academy of Arts and Sciences.

Margaret E. Crahan received her Ph.D. in history from Columbia University and has taught at the City University of New York, the School of Advanced International Studies of Johns Hopkins University, and Occidental College, where she is currently the Henry R. Luce Professor of Religion, Power, and Political Process. She has written about Latin America from the sixteenth through the twentieth centuries. Her publications include *Africa and the Caribbean: The Legacies of a Link* and *Human Rights and Basic Needs in the Americas.* Forthcoming are *Religion, Churches and Change in Contemporary Latin America* and *Debora: Portrait of a Political Prisoner.*

M. Patricia Fernández Kelly is a Research Scientist and Associate Professor of Sociology at the Johns Hopkins University Institute for Policy Studies. A social anthropologist specializing in international development, she has conducted research on export-processing zones, Hispanic women in the garment and electronics industries in southern California and southern Florida, and international migration. She is the author of *For We Are Sold, I and My People: Women and Industry in Mex-*

ico's Frontier. With June Nash she coedited *Women, Men, and the International Division of Labor*. With filmmaker Lorraine Gray she coproduced the Emmy Award–winning documentary *The Global Assembly Line*, which focuses on the effects of economic restructuring on women and their families in the Philippines, the United States, and along the U.S.-Mexican border. She is currently studying changes under way in the *maquiladora* labor force in Ciudad Juárez, Mexico, and the potential effects of the proposed North American Free Trade Agreement on labor mobility in Mexico and the United States.

Albert Fishlow is Class of 1959 Professor of Economics and Dean of International and Area Studies at the University of California at Berkeley. He served as Deputy Assistant Secretary of State for Inter-American Affairs from 1975 to 1976 and has been a member of many public task forces related to Latin American affairs. He is currently co-editor of the *Journal of Development Economics*. His most recent work (joint with Eliana Cardoso) is *Macroeconomics of the Brazilian External Debt*. His articles on income distribution, economic policy, the role of the state in development, American railroads, and Brazilian development have appeared in journals such as *The American Economic Review, Journal of Development Planning, The Journal of Economic History, Journal of Economic Perspectives, International Organization,* and *Foreign Affairs*.

Cornelia Butler Flora is Professor of Sociology and head of the Department of Sociology at Virginia Polytechnic Institute and State University. She has worked with the Ford Foundation in the Andean region and in the Southern Cone of Latin America. She is the author of *Pentecostalism in Colombia: Baptism by Fire and Spirit* and is coeditor of *Rural Policy for the 1990s* and *Sustainable Agriculture in Temperate Zones*. She has published extensively on religion in Latin America, women and rural development, and gender and mass culture in Latin America in such journals as *Agriculture and Human Values, Rural Sociology, Journal of Church and State, Journal of Popular Culture,* and *Studies in Latin American Popular Culture*. She is past president of the Rural Sociological Society and the Midwest Association of Latin American Studies and has served on the Executive Council of the Latin American Studies Association.

Jean Franco is Professor of Comparative Literature at Columbia University and has taught at Stanford University. She recently authored *Plotting Women and Gender Representation in Mexico* and has written extensively on Latin American literature, film, art, and culture. Dr. Franco is past president of the Latin American Studies Association, as well as former director of the Institute of Latin American and Iberian Studies at Columbia University.

Franklin W. Knight is Leonard and Helen R. Stulman Professor of History and Director of the Latin American Studies program at the Johns Hopkins University. Between 1975 and 1986, he edited the Caribbean section of the *Handbook of Latin American Studies,* published by the Hispanic Division of the Library of Congress. His major publications include *Slave Society in Cuba during the Nineteenth Century; The African Dimension of Latin American Societies; The Caribbean: The Genesis of a Fragmented Nationalism; Africa and the Caribbean: Legacies of a Link,* coedited with Margaret E. Crahan; *The Modern Caribbean,* coedited with Colin A. Palmer; and *Atlantic Port Cities: Economy, Culture and Society in the Atlantic World, 1650–1850,* coedited with Peggy K. Liss.

Anthony P. Maingot is Professor of Sociology and editor of *Hemisphere,* a magazine of Latin American and Caribbean studies, at Florida International University. He is a member of the Board of Contributors of the *Miami Herald;* Board of Directors, *Caribbean Affairs;* Senior Vice President of the Caribbean Resources Development Foundation (CARDEV); and contributing editor, Caribbean Politics, in *The Handbook of Latin American Studies.* Professor Maingot has held positions at Yale University, the University of the West Indies, Trinidad, and, since 1974, at Florida International University. He has been a visiting professor at the Institute of Developing Economies, Tokyo, the Institute d'Études Politiques, Aix-en-Provence, and the Rand Corporation. He is coauthor of *A Short History of the West Indies,* now in its fourth edition. His most recent book is *Small Country Development and International Labor Flows: Experience in the Caribbean.*

Marysa Navarro-Aranguren is the Charles Collis Professor of History at Dartmouth College and is currently a visiting professor at the University of California, Santa Cruz. She has written on the Right in Argentina, Eva Perón, and the Mothers of Plaza de Mayo, and she is at present working on a book about Argentine women during the 1976–83 military dictatorship. She has also written about Latin American feminism and attended the five *Encuentros* of Latin American and Caribbean feminists.

Alejandro Portes is John Dewey Professor of Sociology and International Relations at the Johns Hopkins University. He has written extensively on Latin American urbanization, international migration, the informal economy, and the growth of ethnic economic enclaves. He coauthored *Labor, Class, and the International System, Latin Journey: Cuban and Mexican Immigrants in the United States,* and *Immigrant America: A Portrait.* He is currently heading an extensive study of the children of immigrants in the United States, and a research project on urbanization in Central America and the Caribbean. During 1992–93 he will be a visiting scholar at the Russell Sage Foundation in New York.

Rubén G. Rumbaut is Professor of Sociology at San Diego State University. He previously taught at the University of California, San Diego, where he is Senior Research Fellow at the Center for U.S.-Mexican Studies. He is coauthor, with Alejandro Portes, of *Immigrant America: A Portrait*. He is finishing a book, with Kenji Ima, called *Between Two Worlds: Southeast Asian Youth in America*, and is coediting a volume of essays, with Silvia Pedraza, titled *Immigration, Race and Ethnicity in America: Historical and Sociological Perspectives*. He has published a wide range of articles on the adaptation of immigrants in the United States, focusing on refugees from Vietnam, Laos, and Cambodia, and is conducting a comparative study of Asian, Latin American, and Caribbean second-generation immigrant youth in the Miami and San Diego metropolitan areas.

Helen I. Safa is the author of *The Urban Poor in Puerto Rico* and coauthor of *In the Shadows of the Sun: Caribbean Development Alternatives and U.S. Policy*, as well as several other books and articles on migration, urbanization, ethnicity, and development. She has edited *Women and Change in Latin America* and numerous other publications on women and development, particularly in Latin America, and she has been a consultant to the United Nations and other international bodies on issues of women and development. Professor Safa is currently Professor of Anthropology and Latin American Studies at the University of Florida, where she was Director of the Center for Latin American Studies; she received her Ph.D. from Columbia University, has taught at Syracuse and Rutgers universities, and is past president of the Latin American Studies Association.

Peter H. Smith is Professor of Political Science, Simón Bolívar Professor of Latin American Studies, and Director of the Center for Iberian and Latin American Studies at the University of California, San Diego. A specialist on long-term patterns of political change, he is author of *Politics and Beef in Argentina: Patterns of Conflict and Change, Argentina and the Failure of Democracy: Conflict among Political Elites,* and *Labyrinths of Power: Political Recruitment in Twentieth-Century Mexico.* With Thomas Skidmore, he coauthored *Modern Latin America,* now in its third edition; he also edited *Drug Policy in the Americas.* Professor Smith has held faculty positions at Dartmouth College, the University of Wisconsin, and the Massachusetts Institute of Technology. He is past president of the Latin American Studies Association and has been Executive Director of the Bilateral Commission on the Future of United States–Mexican Relations.

Kay B. Warren is Professor of Anthropology at Princeton University, where she earned her Ph.D. Her recent edited collection *The Violence Within: Cultural and Political Opposition in Divided Nations* places her Latin

American research in comparative perspective. Warren's studies of racism and religion in Guatemala during the 1970s were published in *The Symbolism of Subordination: Indian Identity in a Guatemalan Town*. Her collaborative project with Susan C. Bourque on gender, class, and community in Peru appeared as *Women of the Andes: Patriarchy and Social Change in Rural Peru*. Currently she is finishing *Meanings of Ethnic Resurgence: Race and Representation in the Americas,* which is based on her return to Guatemala after two decades to examine culture, conflict, and ethnic renewal.

Index